Divine Kosher Cuisine
catering to family & friends

MW00995296

Risé Routenberg and Barbara Wasser
Co-authors and Recipe Editors

Arlene Mendelson
Recipe Coordinator

Annette Keen
Text Author and Editor

Harvey Mendelson
Photographer

A Congregational Project to Benefit Educational Programs at
Congregation Agudat Achim, **Niskayuna, New York.**

"If there is no flour, there is no Torah"
Pirkei Avot, Ethics of Our Fathers, 3:21

~ Rabbi Elazar ben Azariah

V'samachta b'chagecha
"Thou Shalt Rejoice in Thy Festivals"

Our Needlepoint Tapestry is the handiwork of 50 congregants.

This cookbook reflects the dedicated teamwork of many members of *Congregation Agudat Achim*. It is the product of many hands and many hearts striving together, very much like the needlepoint tapestry pictured on the cover of this cookbook. Titled *V'samachta b'chagecha*, "Thou Shalt Rejoice in Thy Festivals" (Deuteronomy 16:14), the tapestry hangs in the foyer just outside our synagogue sanctuary. Dedicated in 1981, the tapestry took over six years to complete. It is the creative stitchery of 50 members of the synagogue community. Measuring 10½ feet by 5½ feet, the tapestry weaves together 36 individual, 12-inch needlepoint squares. In a field of gently modulating blue hues, it depicts ceremonial objects and festival symbols circling an open *Torah* scroll that embraces the Biblical Tree of Life and Tree of Knowledge.

ISBN: 09770172-0-6
LCCN: 2005929758
1st Printing   March 2006   6,000 copies
2nd Printing   July 2006   6,000 copies

Printed by:

WIMMER
COOKBOOKS

A CONSOLIDATED GRAPHICS COMPANY

800.548.2537 wimmerco.com

How to Order *Divine Kosher Cuisine*
• Mail in the order form in the back
• Go online to www.divinekosher.com
• Telephone (518) 344-1190

Contents
Page

The **yad** is an ornately fashioned word pointer **Torah** readers use to keep their place while chanting. When not in use, the **yad** hangs from a chain over the dressed **Torah**.

The Cookbook Project
Never Too Many Cooks

"*Too* many cooks spoil the broth" does not sound like a piece of rabbinic wisdom. Our tradition favors a variety of approaches to every question. Membership in the ancient religious authority, the Sanhedrin, was based on the ability to produce 70 different solutions to a single problem. We rabbis thrive on multiple opinions on an issue. The effort to arrive at a consensus, the spirited exchange of ideas, the attention to small detail and the looking at the big picture all come together in the end. The "broth" is far richer for having had so many cooks, because they blended their ideas. This cookbook was conceived as a synagogue community effort. It was created in collaboration to benefit educational

Stained glass from old (Agudat Achim) enshrined in new building, 1971.

programs at *Congregation Agudat Achim*. There were never too many cooks. Each additional set of hands involved in the project enriched the process of community building. The final product even sounds like a community tending to the varying needs of its constituents. Each recipe comes with alternatives so that different people can adjust and adapt it to their personal tastes. Coming together in such large numbers to produce this cookbook has fortified the bonds of congregational community. We can all take pride in the success of our joint venture. *Mazel Tov.*

Rabbi Robert Kasman
Congregation Agudat Achim
Cookbook Kashrut Authority

Steering to Success

*O*ur mission was to steer to success one of the most ambitious collaborative congregational efforts of our synagogue's 113-year history. We would finance, produce and market worldwide a premier kosher cookbook, whose proceeds would benefit our education projects. The cookbook would draw on treasured recipes of congregants and the culinary expertise of our internationally acclaimed, in-house catering service. When we came together to map out the Cookbook Project in summer of 2004, we created a three-prong structure to actuate our goal: fundraising, production and marketing. These committees quickly developed their strategies, brought together talented staffers, organized an army of volunteers, and everyone rolled up their sleeves and went to work. Our mission was launched. Even for a congregation like ours, with a long history of good works and volunteerism, the exuberant coming together of hundreds of volunteers, working arduously for uncountable hours to produce this beautiful cookbook has been a marvel that rivals the pride we now take in the finished product. Therefore, it is with sincere pleasure, enormous gratitude and heartfelt appreciation that we dedicate *Divine Kosher Cuisine* to our devoted congregants who have given so much of themselves to this project. You made it happen.

The Steering Committee
Risé Routenberg, Chairperson

Paul Fraster	*Jane Israel*	*Este Sylvetsky*
Barrie Handelman	*Marvin Israel*	*Barbara Wasser*
Eileen Handelman	*Sharon Kasman*	*Ann Zonderman*

For Every Season and Every Reason

By Annette Keen
Text Author and Editor

Divine Kosher Cuisine contains a wealth of information about kosher cooking. It addresses every season and every reason that calls for kosher food, lovingly prepared. Easy to read and expertly illustrated with Harvey Mendelson's gorgeous color photographs, *Divine Kosher Cuisine* facilitates happy, hassle-free meal preparation, whether you are cooking for a few or a crowd, observing a Jewish holiday or celebrating a family milestone. It takes the mystery and worry out of hosting larger gatherings with simple grids that scale recipes and calculate how much food to prepare. *Divine Kosher Cuisine* deftly blends traditional dishes, made from classic ingredients, with contemporary variations for lighter or limited palates, which require trimmed-down, vegetarian or nondairy versions. For the kids and grandkids, it features kid-friendly recipes that children love to prepare as much as to eat. *Divine Kosher Cuisine* is the product of a splendid collaborative effort at *Congregation Agudat Achim* in Niskayuna, New York, which brought together a rich tapestry of talent. The cookbook includes recipes graciously

Congregation Agudat Achim in Niskayuna, New York

shared by congregants from their treasured family collections — some going back generations — along with favorite and signature recipes — some never before revealed — from our all-volunteer, in-house *As You Like It Kosher Catering* service. This is no typical congregational caterer. Built on more than 30 years of experience, enriched by generations of congregants, *As You Like It* has been a busy profit center for the synagogue. As a sophisticated, premier kosher catering service, it has brought home an international prize for excellence, the 2003 Gold Solomon Schechter Award. *As You Like It* has dazzled guests at congregational dinners, brunches and lunches, *b'nai mitzvah,* anniversary and wedding receptions. It has worked side-by-side with top area chefs, catering at the New York State Governor's Mansion and the New York State Legislature in Albany. Gifted chefs Risé Routenberg and Barbara Wasser envisioned this cookbook, drawing on their considerable personal cooking experience and their many years as co-chairpersons of *As You Like It*. Their culinary expertise informs every page of this collection, whose production they coordinated, along with Arlene Mendelson, who coordinated the recipes. From this storehouse of superb recipes and shared culinary wisdom comes *Divine Kosher Cuisine*. More than a collection of recipes, it is a gift of love from our congregational family. May it fill your kitchen with marvelous aromas, grace your dining table with wonderful food and fill your life, and the lives of all those you love, with kosher cooking that is truly divine.

Creating Food Memories

*F*or me, Jewish cooking is about more than preparing food. It is a multigenerational family affair, laden with rich memories, to which each generation adds its own special imprint, before passing it on to the next. The power of a food memory is enormous. The aroma of baking rolls still springs me back 45 years to my Russian grandmother's kitchen in Upper Peninsula Michigan, where as one of triplet sisters, I waited impatiently for her bulky golden rolls to cool. Grandma Fanny was an innately talented cook from the old school. In the early 1910s, she settled in the then non-Jewish area, and kept kosher, preparing her foods from scratch, without measuring spoons and cups, or even recipes. As Grandma gingerly mixed a half juice glass of water, a coffee cup of locally farmed eggs, a few handfuls of nuts and several soup spoons of flour, my mother Diane recorded the recipes, which she personalized and passed on to me. A spectacular cook and baker herself, Mom placed twice as a finalist in the Pillsbury Bake-Off. I too have a passion for kosher cooking, as do my daughters Melissa and Robin and my son Evan. As much as I owe to Grandma and Mom, I am also indebted to my husband Larry and my children, for their unwavering help and support. Over the years, they have served at *As You Like It Kosher Catering* events as waiters, soda pourers, bartenders and kitchen sous chefs. My mother-in-law Annette was a regular kitchen volunteer, and when my mother visited from Wisconsin, she too was dragged into service. How well I remember years ago preparing a dinner for 100 guests as three month-old Robin slept peacefully in her infant seat on the counter in the synagogue's commercial kitchen. My culinary life has been a wonderful adventure and a sacred connector, not only between generations, but also among friends. Working together with chefs and helpers for countless hours has forged friendships of a lifetime. *Divine Kosher Cuisine* contains much of what my synagogue family of volunteer chefs, helpers and I have learned along the way. *Divine Kosher Cuisine* fulfills my personal dream to compile a cookbook that includes the treasured personal recipes contributed by our superb congregational chefs, along with many of the recipes developed and perfected by *As You Like It Kosher Catering*. By publishing, we are finally fulfilling the requests of our fans from around the country to make public our much sought after recipes.

Risé Routenberg

Risé

A Rite of Passage

Barbara Wasser

I began cooking when I was 11 years old, starting dinner as my mother Sadye hurried home from work. Helping out this way taught me about Jewish family values, the importance of tradition and the place of food in a kosher home. I cherish the memory of Grandma Annie feeding her goose in her Pittsburgh backyard to make sure that the bird would be kosher for Passover. My mother, a good cook and an excellent baker, crystallized for me the notion of food as legacy when she informed me that before I could leave home for college, I must master making *blintzes*! It was my rite of passage, the symbol of tradition passing to a new generation. I have come a long way since my first dinner party, when as a young wife I attempted my first cheesecake. As the cake baked in the oven, I suddenly noticed three eggs sitting on the counter and realized that I forgot to beat them into the batter. I served the eggless cheesecake anyway and, although my husband Steve still raves that the cake tasted great, I did reinstate the eggs to the recipe. However, I did not lose a willingness to try new ideas that is so important to creative cooking. Nor did I fail to pass on my mother's lesson of cooking as a family affair. Not only are my children David, Amy and Scott each excellent cooks and bakers, but wherever we gather, we prepare meals together. During a family vacation in Italy, three generations of Wassers baked *challah* together to celebrate *Shabbat*, including our grandchildren, who kneaded the dough. *As You Like It Kosher Catering* has been a huge part of my life. Everyone in my family has worked in some phase of it. I thank my husband Steve for his patience and his humor, which always lightened the load. He often joked that we were married to *Catering* and offered to set up cots for us in the synagogue kitchen. Working with a large group of dedicated volunteers for *As You Like It* and helping to build a first-class catering business has been a wonderful experience. This collection is the culmination of my long love affair with kosher cooking. I am pleased to share beloved home recipes from our congregation and popular recipes from *As You Like It Kosher Catering*, which we specially tailored for your at-home cooking and dining pleasure.

Barbara

7

How to Use This Cookbook

For flawless cooking, keep in mind these explanations and recommendations about menus, recipes, ingredients, terminology and keys that appear repeatedly in the collection.

About the Menus

Our menus suggest dishes that go well together at meals. These range from small luncheons and dinners to variously sized and accurately scaled larger gatherings, which include holidays, festivals and significant occasions. These menus are meant as planning guides, which may be used as suggestions, or as springboards to your own creative combinations.

What the Keys Indicate

 An *As You Like It Kosher Catering* recipe.

 A Kid-Friendly recipe.

 A Suitable-for-Passover recipe.

 A Wine suggestion.

 "Non-G" indicates a recipe that is *non-g'brocht* (see Cooking for Passover).

"Signature" in the name indicates a most sought after *As You Like It* recipe.

In the Index
Bold face recipe name indicates an accompanying photograph.
Bold face recipe number indicates an accompanying diagram.

About the Recipes

- When a capitalized recipe name appears as part of a different recipe or in a menu selection, it refers the reader to the index for page location.

- Recipes are designated as dairy, *pareve* or meat. The *pareve* designation indicates that a recipe may be used with meat, poultry or dairy meals.

- Some *pareve* recipes substitute nondairy ingredients and may be served at a meat meal.

- Some *Kashrut* authorities do not permit Worcestershire sauce that contains fish (anchovies) to be used in meat dishes. We recommend using a nonfish variety for meat dishes, so check the product label.

- The recipes in this collection comply with the common laws of *Kashrut*. For more insight, address questions to your local *Kashrut* authority.

- Before using meat, poultry or fish, rinse and pat dry with paper towels.

About the Ingredients

The Item:	**Unless otherwise specified:**
Sugar	Use white granulated sugar.
Chocolate	Use semisweet, dairy or *pareve*, as required.
Flour	Use all-purpose variety.
Butter	Use unsalted variety.
Margarine	Use unsalted *pareve* variety.
Veggie Schmaltz	Use this flavor enhancer (see index) instead of margarine, butter or oil, except in baking.
Olive oil	May replace margarine or butter, except in baking.
Salt	Use coarse kosher salt.
Pepper	Use black pepper. Freshly ground gives extra flavor.
Herbs	Use fresh herbs. Dried herbs may be substituted by halving amount: 1 teaspoon fresh equals ½ teaspoon dried.
Pan Grease	We prefer convenient and healthier vegetable cooking spray. You may also use butter, margarine or solid vegetable shortening to grease pan or line pan with parchment paper.
Citrus	For extra flavor, use fresh orange, lemon or lime juice.
Soy Sauce	Use lower sodium variety.
Dairy	**Nondairy Substitutes**
Milk	Use *pareve* soy or rice milk.
Heavy cream	Use liquid nondairy whipped topping.
Sour cream	Use tofu-based sour cream.
Cream cheese	Use tofu-based cream cheese.
Ice cream	Use tofu-based ice cream.

About Kosher-for-Passover Recipes

- Kosher-for-Passover recipes appear in the Cooking for Passover feature, however, in select recipes throughout the collection, a *matzoh* symbol indicates that it is also suitable for Passover.

- When Passover recipes call for ingredients that have been altered to make them suitable for Passover, these ingredients carry the symbol K-P.

- Use only Kosher-for-Passover foods and ingredients when preparing the recipes recommended for Passover.

Cooking Kosher for the Contemporary Palate

Divine Kosher Cuisine brings kosher home cooking into the 21st Century. It responds to a growing trend that indicates strong commitment to maintaining kosher homes. We believe that keeping a kosher home offsets the fast-spinning, work-a-day world with a personal, home-based ritual that raises the kitchen and the dining table to altars, where how we prepare food and what we eat become sacramental. Every meal creates an uplifting spiritual oasis where the Jewish family can enjoy good food and each other's company, in the warm embrace of an enduring tradition. We laud and encourage following the Jewish dietary laws, as we acknowledge and respond to the pull of contemporary food trends and the evolving needs of specific health diets. Like many cuisines with a long history, classic kosher fare can contain recipes too rich for modern diets. Consequently, in addition to the many wonderful recipes made from traditional ingredients, *Divine Kosher Cuisine* also pays special attention to *pareve* cooking, and cooking for restricted diets and lighter palates. Special, for your special-diet guests, *Divine Kosher Cuisine* offers many vegetarian and nondairy recipes, as well as some trimmed-down versions of traditional appetizers, entrées, side dishes and desserts. Our goal in creating these special recipes has been to make them contemporary, not counterfeit. Taste is everything! Neutral ingredients like Veggie Schmaltz and nondairy substitutes enable you to create foods that you can serve at meat and poultry meals. Prepare amazingly tasteful recipes, perfectly kosher, so that yes, you can crown that beautiful beefy brisket meal with our I Can't Believe It's Not Cheese, Cheesecake!

Common Laws of Kashrut

- Pork or shellfish, or fish without scales and fins are prohibited.
- All meat and poultry should be purchased from an approved kosher butcher.
- Dairy products may not be mixed with poultry or meat in cooking or eating.
- Separate sets of dairy and meat tableware and utensils should be maintained.
- *Pareve* foods may be eaten with meat, poultry or dairy meals. *Pareve* foods include fruits, vegetables, eggs, nuts, grains, sugar, coffee, tea and vegetable fats and oils. Fish is *pareve*, but has other serving restrictions. For more insight, consult your local *Kashrut* authority.
- Some Worcestershire Sauce contains anchovies. In meat recipes, use the nonfish containing variety.
- The recipes in this collection comply with the common laws of *Kashrut*. For more insight, address questions to a local *Kashrut* authority.

The Jewish Holiday Table

Gorgeous presentation and intoxicating aromas stir our taste buds long before we lift a fork. Beyond stimulating the senses, eating can trigger all kinds of connections, seasoning our enjoyment of food with memories of other times and other places. It can get us thinking of who we are and from where we came. Recalling an ancient heritage, the holidays and festivals that dot the Jewish calendar reflect Biblical times and historic events that forged the Jewish People. Special festival and holiday meals, peppered with symbolic foods, bring history and heritage to the dinner table. They transmit the ancient yet modern yearning for peace, reconciliation, abundance — all life's blessings — to our own times. For these special family meals, *Divine Kosher Cuisine* suggests a variety of holiday and festival foods and menus. Choose from traditional, international and contemporary versions, or create your own holiday menu and start a new family tradition.

> ## Seudot Mitzvah: Religiously Required Meals In Joy and In Sorrow
>
> **Bridal Week:** For seven days following the wedding, the couple is honored with meals at which the *Shevah Brachot*, the seven blessings, are repeated over wine. Any menu is suitable.
>
> **Shivah Meals:** Meals are provided to the grieving family during the seven-day *Shivah* mourning period. See menu that appears in the Catering Section.

> • *All recipes suggested in The Jewish Holiday Table section appear in the index.*
> • *All menus include vegetarian options.*

Shabbat

Shabbat is a happy celebration that crowns every week with a day to rest from the pace and tension of the work-a-day world. Traditional *Shabbat* dishes include chicken soup, *gefilte* fish and either a chicken or a meat main course. Made in advance dishes like Cabbage Borscht with Beef and Festival Carrot Tzimmes are *Shabbat* staples.

Dinner table dressed for Shabbat.

Traditional Menu
Bean, Barley and Mushroom Soup
Fig-Walnut Chopped Chicken Liver
Signature Mixed Green Salad
Signature Roasted Chicken
Savory Vegetable Strudel
Egg Barley with Vegetables
Layered Sweet Potatoes and Apples
Chocolate-Orange Cake
Thumbprint Cookies

Shabbat (continued on next page)

Updated Traditional Menu

Purée of Parsnip Soup
Signature Whitefish Salad on mesclun
Garlic-Dijon Encrusted London Broil
Tofu Chili
Kasha Varnishkes
Irresistible Mushrooms
Green Beans with Tahini and Garlic
Iced Carrot Cake
Brownie in a Cup

Asian Menu

Carrot-Mango Soup
Pineapple Cole Slaw on iceberg wedges
Indonesian Chicken
Indonesian Tofu
Vegetable Stir-Fry
Coconut Basmati Rice
Signature Almond Horns
Lime Tart

Italian Menu

Olive Baguette with Roasted Garlic Bulb
Artichoke-Potato Soup
Mango Salad with
Red Onion and Lime
Chicken Cacciatore
Baked Eggplant Stack
Sautéed Spinach with Garlic
Crusty Roasted Potatoes, Italian Style
Double Almond Biscotti
Poached Pears with
Raspberry Coulis
Espresso

Mediterranean Menu

Eggplant Soup
with Red Pepper Garnish
Chickpea Salad on greens
Mideastern Chicken
Garlicky Portobello Mushrooms
Moroccan Carrot Salad
Fresh Garden Couscous
Baklava Tartlets
Eggless Chocolate Cake

Holiday Table Blessings

Blessings over lighted candles, ceremonial wine and loaves of *challah* — *matzoh* at Passover — usher in most of our holidays. On *Shabbat*, the blessing is recited traditionally over two braided *challahs*.

Dairy Menu

Apple Brie Soup
White Bean and Rosemary Spread
Caesar Salad
Sesame Salmon with
Spinach-Watercress Sauce
Garbanzo Bean Burgers
Cornbread-Stuffed Zucchini Boats
Polenta Wedges
Sour Cream Chocolate Cake
Thumbprint Cookies

The High Holy Days

*T*hese most important days of the Jewish calendar bring together family and friends to share special meals. Families sit down to festive dinners that usher in the Jewish New Year, *Rosh Hashanah*. Another special dinner precedes the beginning of the redemptive *Yom Kippur* fast. After a long day of fasting, break-the-fast meals, usually served buffet-style, conclude the Day of Atonement. For the Holy Days, plain and raisin *challahs* are baked round to symbolize the perfect wholeness wished for in the New Year. These might also have ladders and wings baked on top to signify ascending prayers. To invoke a sweet year, honey is liberally used, both

as a dip for *challah* and apple slices, and as a basic recipe ingredient, as in Spiked Honey Cake and Apple-Honey Dessert Pizza. For *Rosh Hashanah* and *Erev Yom Kippur* meals, choose from the following suggested menus, or any *Shabbat* dinner menu. For lighter palates, choose any combination of vegetarian or dairy dishes. For ending the fast, we offer a traditional dairy menu and one offering an array of Mediterranean foods.

The ancient shofar rings in the New Year.

Traditional Rosh Hashanah Menu

Caramelized Onion Chopped
Liver on red leaf lettuce
Signature Vegetarian Chopped
Liver on red leaf lettuce
Signature Chicken Soup with
No-Fail Matzoh Balls
Chickenless Chicken Soup with
No-Fail Matzoh Balls
Signature Mixed Green Salad
with Meringue Baked Pecans
Bulgarian Chicken
Signature Brisket
Black Bean-Stuffed Cabbage
Carrot Festival Tzimmes
Pecan-Lemon Green Beans
Fruit Platter with Ginger Syrup
Streusel-Topped Apple Pie
Spiked Honey Cake

Updated Traditional Rosh Hashanah Menu

White Bean and Rosemary Spread
Fragrant Carrot Soup with Indian Spices
Sweet and Savory Salad
Salmon with Maple Syrup and
Toasted Almonds
Garlicky Portobello Mushrooms
Fruited Rice Combo
Roasted Broccoli with Red Peppers
Oven-Roasted Tomatoes
Meringue-Topped Apples
Chocolate-Cherry-Almond Mandelbrot
Apple-Honey Dessert Pizza

Holiday Wines and Spirits

In addition to serving ceremonial wine and grape juice for the *Kiddush* blessing, you may want to offer dinner wines and after dinner dessert wines, liqueurs and brandy.

The High Holy Days (continued on next page)

Erev Yom Kippur Menu

Apple-Rutabaga Soup
Mesclun Salad with Roasted Asparagus
Italian Roasted Chicken
Vegetarian Stuffed Peppers
Signature Potato Kugel
Brussels Sprouts in Lemon Mustard
Glazed Parsnips with Apricots
Marinated Fruit Salad
Spiked Honey Cake
Chocolate-Filled Lace Sandwich Cookies

Harvest centerpiece

Break-the-Fast Buffets

Dairy Menu

Dress Up Your Bagel
Nova Smoked Salmon Display
Herring Antipasto
Signature Whitefish Salad
Carrot-Asparagus Salad
Strata with Fresh Herbs
Sliced tomatoes, onions and cucumbers
Signature Cheese Blintz Soufflé
Signature Sesame Noodles
Chunky Apple Cake
Mix and Match Rugelach
Cream Cheese-Topped Brownies

Mediterranean Menu

Greek Pasta Salad
Spinach Quajada
Moroccan Carrot Salad
Falafel Bar
Roasted Red Pepper Hummus
with pita
Zesty Eggplant Slices
Baklava
Simple Fruit Sorbet
Citrus and Grapes in
Muscat Wine

At the end of a long day of fasting, self-serve, made-in-advance buffets make the after-fast meal an ease and delight for hosts and guests.

Sukkot, Shemini Atzeret and Simchat Torah

Late autumn harvests launch a season of rejoicing that runs from *Sukkot* to *Shemini Atzeret*, ending with *Simchat Torah*, which marks the annual completion of *Torah* readings in the synagogue. *Sukkot-Shemini Atzeret* celebrate the fruits of the field. Colorful vegetables, fruits, gourds and pumpkins hang decoratively in *sukkahs* built for the seven-day festival. They also make up centerpieces on the holiday dinner table. Foods symbolic of harvest yields are served, including stuffed vines and cabbage leaves, strudel and other stuffed pastries, and fruit and nut desserts. Choose from among our many recipes that fall within this category.

Whimsically dressed Torahs

Chanukah

A welcome midwinter break, *Chanukah*, our Festival of Lights, brightens Jewish homes with happy preparations, merrymaking and gift giving. To commemorate the faithful generation that rededicated the Temple, families light successive candles on the *Chanukah menorah* during the eight-day festival and feast on traditional potato latkes. It is a special joy for children, who look forward to receiving among their gifts, gold-foiled chocolate *gelt*. Kids love to help prepare and bake cookie cutter cookies shaped into *dreidels*, coins, Stars of David, *Torahs* and *menorahs*. Confections made from sesame seeds, chopped nuts and honey are also favorites.

Chanukah symbols

Dairy Buffet Menu

Baked Brie in Bread Bowl
Moroccan Chickpea Soup
Salad Niçoise
Spanakopita
Lots o' Latkes, applesauce and sour cream
Floating Sandwich Cookie Cake
Apple Fritters

Chanukah Parties

At home or in the synagogue, buffet-style parties are very popular. Choose from our contemporary menus or mix and match with the more traditional fare.

Meat Buffet Menu

Caponata
Tarragon Pea Soup
Signature Mixed Green Salad with Meringue Baked Pecans
Brisket with Burgundy-Orange Sauce
Vegetarian Stuffed Cabbage
Lots o' Latkes, applesauce and nondairy sour cream
Curried Apple Squash Rings
Signature Almond Horns
I Can't Believe It's Not Cheese, Cheesecake

Tu b'Shevat

*T*u b'Shevat, the New Year of the Trees, originated in ancient Palestine, at the first signs of spring. In Israel, it is celebrated with the planting of trees, and many Jews living elsewhere in the world arrange for trees to be planted in Israel on this Arbor Day. In the home, *Tu b'Shevat* is commemorated with festive meals that feature such Holy Land fruits as dates, nuts, figs, raisins, almonds and honey.

Tu b'Shevat table with fruit, nuts and wine

Purim

*P*urim commemorates deliverance from the great villain *Haman,* who plotted to destroy the Jewish People in ancient Persia. Yet for all its gravity, it is a light-hearted frolic, from beginning to end, as family and friends exchange food gifts, *mishloach manot,* and eat three-cornered cakes named *hamantaschen,* which are traditionally stuffed with prune or poppy fillings. A happy carnival atmosphere dominates at home and in the synagogue. Self-serve buffets that quickly accommodate larger gatherings, whether at home or at synagogue receptions, enable people to attend the *Purim* synagogue reading of the Scroll of Esther, the *Megillah.* Try our suggested menu or choose from among the traditional favorites.

Purim Centerpiece

Meat, Pareve or Dairy Menu

- Giant Stuffed Hamburger for meat
- Marinated Grilled Salmon for *pareve*
- Eggplant Manicotti for dairy
- Black Bean-Stuffed Cabbage for vegetarian

Fresh Vegetables with Curry Dip

Quick and Delicious Vegetable Soup

Apple-Apricot Kugel

Pecan-Lemon Green Beans

Cookie Dough Hamantaschen

Grapes and Clementine oranges

Coffee, tea and apple juice

Traditional Favorites
Refer to each recipe for pareve, meat or dairy versions

• Cookie Dough and Sour Cream-Yeast Dough Hamantashen with assorted fillings • Festival Apple Strudel • Carrot Strudel • Oodles of Strudels with cheese and mixed fruit fillings • Won Tons a.k.a. Kreplach, with potato-cheese or potato-cauliflower fillings • Vegetarian Kishke • Vegetarian-Stuffed Cabbage or Peppers • Meat Cabbage Rolls and Stuffed Peppers • Stuffed Portobello Mushrooms • Signature Potato Kugel • Potato-Cheese Kugel • Signature Noodle Kugel

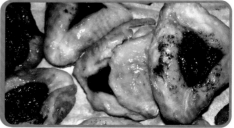

Hamantaschen

Passover Seder Menus

These menus suggest recipes for your *Seders* and for various meals throughout the festival week. They refer to recipes that are located in our special "Cooking for Passover" section (see index). Additionally, you will find suitable-for-Passover recipes throughout our collection, as indicated by a .

The Seder Plate Symbol Foods

Z'Roa: a roasted bone for the "mighty arm" of God.

Baytzah: a roasted egg for the festival Temple sacrifice.*

Maror: (horseradish) bitter herbs for the bitter lot of slavery.

Charoset: fruit-nut mixture for brick mortar the slaves made.

Karpas: parsley, potato or other vegetable for fruit of the earth.

Chazeret: a vegetable that tends to bitterness like lettuce.

Matzoh: three whole *matzohs*.

* To brown an egg for the seder plate, wrap hard-boiled egg, shell on, in onion skins and foil. Bake 1 hour.

Seder I Menu

Hard-boiled eggs and salt water
Popovers with Roasted Garlic Bulb
Zesty Eggplant Slices
Signature Chicken Soup with Kugelach
Chickenless Chicken Soup with Kugelach
Cornish Hens in Wine Sauce
Meatballs in Sauerkraut
Fruited Quinoa Primavera
Baked russet and sweet potatoes
Pineapple Pudding
Roasted Asparagus
Marinated Cucumbers with Dill
Apricot and Linzer Tarts
Fruit-Filled Jelly Roll
Fruit-Nut Passover Mandelbrot
Chocolate-Chocolate Chip Macaroons

Passover Seder Table

Seder II Menu

Hard-boiled eggs and salt water
Popovers with Herb Spread
Spring Vegetable Soup with
No-Fail Matzoh Balls
Chicken in Orange Sauce
Veal and Peppers
Potato-Vegetable Patties
Roasted Broccoli with Red Peppers
European Fruit Pudding
Signature Potato Kugel
Fudgy Passover Brownies
Passover Chocolate Chip Cookies
Passover Lemon Bars
Meringue Drops

Lag b'Omer

Lag b'Omer, the 33rd counted day after Passover, is variously linked to scholars, martyrdom, military victories and deliverance from enemies. Arriving after Passover and before *Shavuot,* it is celebrated with barbecuing and picnicking, as family and friends gather outdoors to enjoy games and sports, and singing and dancing. Israelis celebrate with parades and giant bonfires. For your *Lag b'Omer* celebration, choose from the following food suggestions.

Hot Off The Grill

Picnic Menu

Mango Salsa with tortilla chips
Garden Gazpacho
Chilled Cherry Soup
Hot Off the Grill at Carrot Festival
Garlicky Portobello Mushrooms
Grilled Vegetable Stacks
Red Potato Salad
Black Bean and Corn Salad
Pineapple Cole Slaw
Marinated Cucumbers with Dill
Sliced tomatoes and red onions
on romaine
Chocolate Chip-Oatmeal Cookies
Banana-Chocolate Chip Carrot Loaf
Brownie in a Cup
Double Almond Biscotti
Coconut-Walnut Squares
Marinated Fresh Fruit Salad
Spiced Iced Tea Punch
Wine and beer

Baklava

Shavuot

Shavuot commemorates the Giving of the *Torah.* In Biblical times, it also coincided with early crops and first fruits, so to its deeply serious core, it took on a harvest festival aspect, which has endured. Fresh and cooked fruits and vegetables grace the table. Dairy dishes and honey concoctions are served to symbolize that *Torah* is as nutritious as milk and as sweet as honey.

Milk and Honey

Traditional dishes include cheese-filled *blintzes, kreplach,* noodle *kugels,* cooked fruits, vegetables and honey concoctions.

Contemporary Menu

Garden Gazpacho
Feta-Pear Layered Salad
Asparagus-Smoked Salmon Strudel
Savory Cheese Scones
Asian Style Tilapia
Eggplant Manicotti
Cheesy Cauliflower
Confetti Hash Brown Potatoes
Variations on a Cheesecake
Southern Lemon Pound Cake
Sandwich Cookie Truffles

Starters

Goat Cheese Terrine

Veggie Schmaltz   Non-G

PAREVE · YIELD: 4 CUPS

Veggie Schmaltz is a flavor enhancer, par excellence! It is much more than a vegetarian substitute for oil, margarine and butter. It imparts all the savory flavor and rich texture of animal fat schmaltz in every recipe that uses it. Its fans and devotees are legion and many of our recipes call for it. We would like to thank our dear Israeli friend who introduced us to this fabulous recipe.

2 cups vegetable oil	2 large carrots, chopped
1 pound margarine	16 garlic cloves, chopped
2 large onions, chopped	

1. Melt margarine and oil in saucepan. Add remaining ingredients and bring to boil. Reduce heat and simmer, stirring occasionally.

2. Cook until mixture turns golden brown. Remove from heat.

3. Strain vegetables. Chill schmaltz. May be frozen.

Use leftover strained vegetables for recipes like mashed potatoes and vegetable fillings.

Roasted Red Peppers with Garlic   Non-G

PAREVE · YIELD: 8 SERVINGS

Liven up an antipasto platter with roasted red peppers. Garlic lovers will adore the whole roasted garlic cloves. These peppers freeze well.

2 large red peppers, seeded and cut into strips	8 garlic cloves, whole
	2 tablespoons olive oil

1. Preheat oven to 400°F. Prepare ungreased 9 x 13-inch pan.

2. Combine ingredients in pan and roast until edges of peppers are blackened, but not burnt and garlic is tender. Stir occasionally to prevent scorching.

Asparagus-Smoked Salmon Strudel

DAIRY   YIELD: 40 PIECES

The filling may be prepared the day before and strudel may be rolled 4 to 6 hours ahead of time. Cover loosely with plastic wrap and chill or freeze. Additional time is necessary if baking them frozen.

16 spears asparagus, trimmed
1   cup ricotta cheese
⅓ cup grated Parmesan cheese
¼ cup packed fresh basil, chopped
2   ounces Nova smoked salmon, chopped
1½ tablespoons chopped fresh chives
1½ tablespoons chopped fresh parsley
1   large egg yolk, beaten

1   teaspoon butter
1   large green onion, chopped
1   garlic clove, minced
⅛ teaspoon salt to taste
¼ teaspoon pepper
½ pound phyllo dough, thawed
10 tablespoons butter, melted for brushing phyllo

1. Preheat oven to 400°F. Grease cookie sheet or line with parchment.
2. Steam asparagus until crisp-tender, about 2 minutes. Drain and pat dry.
3. Combine cheeses, basil, Nova, chives and parsley. Mix in yolk.
4. Melt 1 teaspoon butter in small skillet and sauté onions and garlic until soft. Stir into cheese mixture. Add salt and pepper.
5. Place 1 phyllo sheet on work surface. Keep remaining phyllo covered with plastic wrap and lightly dampened cloth to prevent drying.
6. Brush phyllo lightly with melted butter. Top with second sheet and brush with more butter. Continue until 4 sheets are stacked one on top of the other.
7. Divide filling into 4 equal amounts, about ½ cup for each. Shape filling into log and place across long end of phyllo stack, ¼-inch from edge.

8. Arrange 4 asparagus spears on top of filling and roll up like jelly roll. Place seam side down on sheet and brush with more melted butter. Score through the phyllo, diagonally, for easier cutting. Repeat with remaining ingredients.
9. Bake strudel until golden brown, 15 minutes. Cool 10 minutes. Slice with serrated knife.

It's a Wrap

DAIRY, PAREVE OR MEAT

YIELD: 24 HORS D'OEUVRES
OR 4 ENTRÉE PORTIONS

Wraps are easy to make, look pretty, taste wonderful and appeal to people of all ages. Basically, a wrap is a flour tortilla filled with any combination of ingredients. Prepare the vegetables, spreads and dressings ahead of time. To serve, stack wraps pyramid style on a serving tray or display in a decorative basket.

Grilled Vegetable Wraps

DAIRY OR PAREVE

Olive oil for drizzling
1 small eggplant, cut into ½-inch slices
1 medium zucchini, cut into ½-inch slices
2 red peppers, cut into thin strips

4 flour tortillas
¼ cup Chipotle Spread or ⅓ cup Hummus
8 ounces thinly sliced Cheddar cheese for dairy

1. Preheat oven to 400°F or preheat grill. Grease cookie sheet or grill pan.
2. Drizzle vegetables with oil and grill or roast until tender.
3. Spread tortillas with Chipotle Spread or Hummus leaving 1-inch border. Top with vegetables and cheese.
4. Fold in both sides and roll up tightly. Cover with plastic wrap and chill 1 hour.
5. Slice in half diagonally and secure with toothpick or slice each into 6 bite-size portions.

Chipotle Spread

PAREVE

2 teaspoons chili powder
2 teaspoons minced Chipotle chilies
5 garlic cloves, minced

5 tablespoons lemon juice
3 tablespoons mayonnaise
2 tablespoons honey

1. Purée all ingredients.

Garlic-Infused Olive Oil

PAREVE

½ cup olive oil

4 garlic cloves, minced

• Mix oil with garlic in saucepan and heat 3 minutes over medium heat or microwave 1 minute. Cool.

Olive Tapenade Wrap

DAIRY OR PAREVE

4	flour tortillas
1	cup Olive Tapenade
4	ounces thinly sliced cheese for dairy

⅓	cup artichoke hearts packed in oil, drained
2	ounces sun-dried tomatoes, diced
1	cup shredded salad greens

1. Spread tapenade on tortillas, leaving 1-inch border.
2. Top with cheese, artichoke hearts, sun-dried tomatoes and greens.
3. Fold in both sides and roll up tightly. Cover with plastic wrap and chill 1 hour.
4. Slice in half diagonally and secure with toothpick or slice into 6 bite-size portions.

Smoked Turkey Wrap

MEAT

4	flour tortillas
½	cup Hummus
8	slices smoked turkey breast
1	cup roasted red pepper strips

1	cup shredded salad greens
2	tablespoons prepared onion salad dressing

1. Spread Hummus on tortillas, leaving 1-inch border, followed by 2 slices turkey, peppers and greens. Drizzle with salad dressing.
2. Fold in both sides and roll up tightly. Cover with plastic wrap and chill 1 hour.
3. Slice in half diagonally and secure with toothpick or slice into 6 bite-size portions.

Salad Wraps

• Use our Tuna with a Twist or Signature Egg Salad to build your wrap. Place lettuce in center of each flour tortilla or lavash bread and spread with tuna or egg salad. Roll up and cut in half crosswise.

Savory Vegetable Strudel

DAIRY OR PAREVE   YIELD: 10 TO 12 STARTER SERVINGS

These crispy brown filled strudels are an ever-impressive dish, sliced and served with sour cream or nondairy sour cream for a pareve meal. Or try them with our dairy or pareve version of Caliente Sour Cream. Also, a perfect hors d'oeuvre, just make smaller portions.

Filling

2	tablespoons olive oil	2	tablespoons flour
1	cup minced onions	2	tablespoons Sherry wine
1	large carrot, peeled and diced	1	large egg, slightly beaten
1	cup chopped broccoli	¼	cup minced parsley
½	pound mushrooms	¼	cup unseasoned breadcrumbs
4	garlic cloves, minced		Salt and pepper to taste
1	teaspoon dried dill		

1. Heat oil in large skillet and sauté onions until soft. Add carrot, broccoli, mushrooms, garlic and dill and continue to cook until vegetables are bright and just tender.
2. Add flour and Sherry and cook 5 minutes more. Cool to room temperature.
3. Mix in egg, parsley and breadcrumbs.

Strudel

½	pound phyllo dough, 10 sheets	½	cup ground walnuts or hazelnuts, divided
¾	cup butter for dairy, melted (use margarine for pareve)		

1. Preheat oven to 400°F. Grease cookie sheet.
2. Divide filling in half and use 5 sheets of phyllo for each strudel roll.
3. Lay 1 sheet of phyllo on surface and brush with melted butter or margarine and sprinkle with 1 tablespoon of nuts. Repeat with 4 more sheets but omit nuts on 5th sheet.
4. Place a log of filling along one long edge of dough and roll up like jelly roll.
5. Place roll on sheet, seam down, and brush top with butter or margarine. Make second roll. Score rolls through top layer of phyllo into ½-inch portions using sharp knife.
6. Bake 20 to 25 minutes or until dough is crisp and browned.
7. Cut and serve immediately or cool and cut into portions and freeze. Reheat in 375°F oven until filling is hot.

Chicken-Pastrami Roll

MEAT   YIELD: 18 SERVINGS

This rolled starter combines the tang of Dijon mustard with an aromatic garlic crust to create mouth-watering chicken tidbits.

6   chicken breast halves, boned and skinned
4   teaspoons Dijon mustard
12   pastrami slices
1½   cups seasoned breadcrumbs
½   teaspoon salt
1½   teaspoons garlic powder
1½   teaspoons paprika
½   teaspoon pepper
2   large eggs, beaten
     Mustard Vinaigrette Dressing

1. Preheat oven to 375°F. Grease 9 x 13-inch baking pan and cookie sheet.

2. Butterfly chicken breasts and pound thin.

3. Spread breasts with mustard and cover with 2 pastrami slices. Roll up, enclosing pastrami. Secure with wooden toothpicks.

4. Mix breadcrumbs with seasonings. Dip rolls into egg and coat with breadcrumbs.

Chicken-Pastrami Roll with Polenta Wedges

5. Place seam side down in pan and bake 20 to 25 minutes or until golden brown.

6. Chill until firm and cut diagonally into 1-inch slices. Reheat on sheet at 325°F until hot. Serve with Mustard Vinaigrette Dressing.

How to Butterfly Chicken Breast

1. Split chicken breast open by slicing three quarters of the way through breast, holding it firmly with your palm, so long straight edge of breast forms a hinge.

2. Open split breast like a book and place between 2 sheets of plastic wrap. Pound lightly.

Pastry-Wrapped Hot Dog Medallions

MEAT OR PAREVE   YIELD: 30 PIECES

5	beef hot dogs for meat, cut into 1-inch medallions (use tofu hot dogs for pareve)
1	sheet puff pastry dough
1	large egg, slightly beaten
¼	cup Dijon or deli mustard

1. Preheat oven to 400°F. Grease cookie sheet.

2. Cut pastry into thirty ½-inch strips long enough to wrap around hot dog medallion.

3. Wrap pastry around each medallion and pull slightly to overlap ends. Dab with beaten egg to seal. Bake on cookie sheet until pastry is golden brown, about 10 minutes. Dot mustard in center of each appetizer to serve.

Zesty Eggplant Slices Non-G

PAREVE   YIELD: 10 SERVINGS

This eggplant dish may be served as an appetizer or a side dish. A good choice for a pot luck dinner or picnic.

1	pound eggplant
2	teaspoons salt
3	garlic cloves, minced
2	tablespoons red wine vinegar
¼	cup olive oil
	Salt and pepper to taste
2	tablespoons chopped fresh cilantro

1. Preheat oven to 375°F. Prepare ungreased cookie sheet.

2. Zebra stripe eggplant (see How to Zebra Stripe) and cut into ½-inch slices.

3. Place eggplant in colander, toss with salt, cover with plate and weight down with cans for 30 minutes. Rinse eggplant and pat dry.

4. Combine garlic and vinegar and set aside.

5. Brush eggplant with oil and bake on sheet, turning occasionally until tender and golden. Cool.

6. Arrange eggplant in layers in serving dish and sprinkle each layer with vinegar-garlic mixture, salt and pepper and cilantro. Cover and chill at least 2 hours.

Marinated Vegetables

PAREVE   YIELD: 6 TO 8 SERVINGS

Marinades tenderize raw fresh vegetables as they infuse their aromatic flavors. Any of the vegetables can be dressed with marinade of your choice. Vary the marinades for a balance of flavors.

Tangy Vegetable Marinade

1	tablespoon lemon juice	2	tablespoons finely chopped fresh parsley
2	tablespoons red wine vinegar		
½	cup extra virgin olive oil	1	teaspoon salt
1½	teaspoons Worcestershire sauce	1½	teaspoons sugar to taste
3	tablespoons finely chopped onions	⅛	teaspoon pepper to taste
3	garlic cloves, minced	1½	teaspoons dried tarragon
2	tablespoons chopped pimento or fresh red pepper		

1. Combine all liquid ingredients. Add chopped vegetables, herbs and seasonings.

Italian Vegetable Marinade

¼	cup olive oil	2	garlic cloves, minced
1	tablespoon lemon juice	⅛	teaspoon salt
1	tablespoon balsamic vinegar	⅛	teaspoon black pepper
1	teaspoon dried oregano		

1. Combine all ingredients.

Vegetables – Choose One

½	pound kalamata olives, rinsed and drained	½	pound broccoli florets, blanched
½	pound fresh green beans, trimmed and blanched	½	pound carrots, peeled, cut into sticks and blanched
½	pound water packed artichoke hearts, drained	½	pound mushrooms
½	pound cauliflower florets, blanched	½	pound asparagus, trimmed and blanched

1. Pour choice of marinade over vegetables. Cover and chill overnight.

Antipasto Platter

• Create a colorful antipasto platter by choosing from the following: Roasted Red Peppers with Garlic, Zesty Eggplant Slices and Marinated Vegetables.

• Select 3 items for 10 guests or 5 items for 20 guests.

• Mix and match a variety of colors and textures.

Wontons a.k.a. Kreplach

DAIRY OR PAREVE   YIELD: 50 WONTONS

These filled dough pockets defy cultural profiling. Serve Potato-Cheese-Filled pockets with melted butter, sour cream, chives or Parmesan cheese as a dairy dish. Serve Potatoes and Cauliflower, Indian style pockets with Raita or the non-dairy version of Caliente Sour Cream as a pareve dish.

Potato-Cheese Filling

3   tablespoons butter, divided
½   cup finely chopped onion
1   garlic clove, minced
1   baking potato, boiled
2   tablespoons ricotta
¼   cup shredded Cheddar or
       Muenster cheese
       Salt and pepper to taste

1. Heat 2 tablespoons butter in large skillet and sauté onions and garlic until soft.
2. Mash potato with remaining butter. Mix with cheeses, salt and pepper. Fold into onion mixture.

Assembly

50   prepared wonton wrappers
1   recipe Potato-Cheese Filling for dairy **or**

½   recipe finely chopped Potatoes and Cauliflower, Indian Style for pareve
       Vegetable oil for frying, optional

1. Grease cookie sheets.
2. Center teaspoon of filling on each wrapper and brush edges with water. Fold dough over to form triangle, pinch edges together and seal tightly.
3. Place in single layer on cookie sheets. Do not stack. Wontons may be frozen at this point. When frozen, store in plastic bags. Thaw 30 minutes and cook.
4. Cook by either boiling in salted water 7 to 8 minutes or until they float to top, or deep frying until golden brown. Drain on paper towels.

Reheat fried wontons in a 325°F oven.

English Muffin-Spinach Tarts

DAIRY   YIELD: 6 SERVINGS

*G*et your kids into the kitchen to help make this crowd pleaser. They will invite their friends for dinner.

2 tablespoons butter	⅓ cup shredded Swiss cheese
6 English muffins, split	1 large onion, finely chopped
Garlic powder	10 ounces frozen chopped spinach,
⅓ cup shredded mozzarella cheese	thawed and drained
⅓ cup shredded Cheddar cheese	½ cup mayonnaise

1. Preheat oven to 375°F ten minutes before baking. Grease cookie sheet.
2. Butter muffins and sprinkle with garlic powder.
3. Combine cheeses with onions, spinach and mayonnaise. Spread mixture on muffin halves. Sprinkle with more garlic powder and freeze 1 hour. Cut into quarters and bake 15 minutes.

Top a baked potato with the cheese-spinach mixture.

Mozzarella Sticks

DAIRY   YIELD: 10 SERVINGS

*P*repare these wonderful, gooey sticks for all the kids in your family. Make extra because everyone will snap them up.

1 pound mozzarella cheese	Vegetable oil for frying
½ cup flour	Marinara sauce or Raspberry
2 large eggs, beaten	Coulis for dipping sauce
1¼ cups seasoned breadcrumbs	

1. Preheat oven to 375°F ten minutes before cooking. Grease cookie sheets.
2. Cut cheese into 2½ x ½-inch wide sticks.

3. Coat by dipping into flour, beaten egg and then seasoned breadcrumbs. Freeze on sheet 1 hour.
4. Fry sticks in hot oil until golden brown, 1 to 2 minutes per side. Drain on paper towels. Serve with dipping sauce.

Sticks may be reheated in 275°F oven until just heated through. Do not overheat.

Stuffed Grape Leaves

PAREVE   YIELD: 48 ROLLS

6   tablespoons dried currants
3   tablespoons white wine
¾   cup olive oil, divided
1½ cups finely diced onions
¾   teaspoon salt
½   teaspoon pepper
1½ cups rice
2¼ cups water
9   tablespoons lemon juice, divided
6   tablespoons minced fresh parsley

¼   cup pine nuts, lightly toasted
1½ tablespoons finely chopped fresh mint
2¼ teaspoons finely chopped fresh oregano
½   teaspoon ground allspice
½   teaspoon ground cinnamon
1   16-ounce jar grape leaves
3   cups vegetable broth

1. Soak currants in wine 1 hour. Remove currants with slotted spoon, reserving currants and wine.

2. Heat 6 tablespoons oil in large skillet and sauté onions until soft. Sprinkle with salt and pepper.

3. Add rice, water, 3 tablespoons juice and reserved wine. Cover, bring to boil, reduce heat and simmer 10 minutes. Uncover skillet and cook until all remaining moisture evaporates.

4. Add currants, parsley, pine nuts, mint, oregano, allspice and cinnamon for filling.

5. Unfold grape leaves. Rinse in cold and then hot water and drain.

6. Spread leaves shiny side down and cut off tough stems.

7. Spoon 2 teaspoons of filling on each leaf and roll like Meat Cabbage Rolls.

8. Heat remaining oil at low temperature in extra large skillet. Arrange rolls in skillet in concentric circles.

9. Mix broth with remaining juice and pour over rolls. Cover with plate and weight down with heavy cans. Bring to boil, reduce heat and simmer 20 minutes or until leaves are tender.

Signature Sesame Noodles

PAREVE

YIELD: 3 TO 4 MAIN COURSE OR
12 TO 16 BUFFET SERVINGS

These sesame noodles have become so popular that when As You Like It *prepares them for an event, we factor in overages to accommodate a sesame noodle call-list! Congregants are notified when they are available in take-home batches.*

2	tablespoons tahini	¼	cup sesame oil
¼	cup chunky peanut butter	¼	teaspoon cayenne pepper to taste
4	garlic cloves, minced	2	tablespoons red wine vinegar
¼	cup brewed tea	1	pound linguine
1	tablespoon sugar to taste	4	green onions, finely chopped
6	tablespoons soy sauce	1	red pepper, thinly sliced

1. Purée tahini, peanut butter and garlic.
2. Add tea, sugar, soy sauce, sesame oil, cayenne and vinegar and process until relatively smooth. There may be some peanut chunks visible.

3. Cook linguine al dente. Drain, rinse under cold water and drain again.
4. Combine with sauce. Toss with onions and peppers just before serving.
5. Serve warmed or at room temperature.

Porcini-Stuffed Mushrooms Non-G

DAIRY   YIELD: 26 MUSHROOMS

Mushroom Caps

26 button mushrooms, remove   2 tablespoons olive oil
    stems and reserve   Salt and pepper to taste

1. Preheat oven to 400°F. Grease cookie sheet.
2. Brush mushrooms with oil and sprinkle with salt and pepper.
3. Place mushrooms, cap side up, on sheet and roast until golden, 6 to 7 minutes. Drain on paper towels.

Stuffing

1 tablespoon butter   2 tablespoons white wine
   Reserved mushroom stems, finely   Salt and pepper to taste
    chopped   2 tablespoons Parmesan cheese
2 garlic cloves, minced   2 tablespoons crumbled feta cheese
1 shallot, chopped   1 tablespoon chopped fresh basil
¼ pound porcini mushrooms, finely
    chopped

1. Heat butter in large skillet and sauté reserved stems with garlic and shallots.
2. Add porcini mushrooms and cook 2 minutes more. Add wine and cook until it evaporates.
3. Season with salt and pepper and cool.
4. Combine mushroom mixture with Parmesan, feta and basil and set aside.

Topping

2 tablespoons crumbled feta cheese   1 tablespoon chopped fresh basil

1. Combine ingredients and set aside.

Assembly

1. Mound stuffing mixture into mushroom caps.
2. Broil 2 to 3 minutes. Sprinkle with topping.

Artichoke Jack Tartlets

DAIRY

YIELD: 48 MINITARTS

These clever tarts, filled with a creamy artichoke dip, are mouth-watering morsels. Hard to resist, they go like peanuts!

Crust

6	ounces cream cheese, room temperature
1	cup butter, room temperature
2	cups flour
½	teaspoon salt

1. Preheat oven to 350°F. Grease minimuffin tins and prepare ungreased cookie sheet.
2. Mix cream cheese and butter at medium speed with electric mixer. Add flour and salt to form ball. Cover with plastic wrap and chill 1 hour.
3. Roll dough into 48 walnut-size balls. With lightly floured spoon, press dough to cover bottom and three-fourths up sides of each tin.
4. Bake 12 to 15 minutes or until golden brown. Cool and remove from tins and place on cookie sheet.

Filling

⅓	cup mayonnaise
8	ounces cream cheese, room temperature
2	garlic cloves, minced
⅛	teaspoon hot pepper sauce to taste
2	cups shredded Monterey Jack cheese
14	ounces artichoke hearts, drained and chopped
1	medium tomato, seeded and chopped
2	green onions, finely sliced

1. Combine mayonnaise, cream cheese, garlic and hot sauce at medium speed with electric mixer until smooth.
2. Fold in Monterey Jack cheese, artichoke hearts, tomatoes and onions.
3. Fill each crust with mixture and bake until filling is hot and lightly browned, about 5 to 10 minutes.

Vegetarian Sushi

PAREVE   YIELD: 32 PIECES

Sushi rolls are deceptively easy to roll. You will need nori sheets (dried seaweed) and a bamboo mat (available in any Asian market) on which you will construct and layer and then roll your sushi. Go for it! You'll be an expert before you know it.

Sushi Rice

1	cup rice, sticky or short grain	1	tablespoon sugar
1⅔	cups water	1	teaspoon salt
2	tablespoons rice wine or white vinegar		

1. Mix vinegar, sugar, and salt in small saucepan and heat until sugar dissolves. Chill.
2. Wash and drain rice.
3. Boil water in medium pot, add rice, reduce heat and cook 2 minutes, stirring constantly. Cover and simmer 15 minutes or until water is absorbed.
4. Remove from heat, lift off cover and place towel over top of pot, then recover with lid. Allow rice to steam 15 minutes.
5. Transfer rice to glass or plastic bowl and toss with vinegar-sugar mixture. Using a nonmetal spatula, fold and fan rice to cool. Use immediately.

Filling and Assembly

Use at least three of the following filling items in each sushi roll, varying them for color and texture.

1	egg	⅛	teaspoon salt
1	teaspoon water	1	carrot, peeled, julienned and blanched
	Salt and pepper		
½	avocado, peeled and sliced	1	green onion, julienned
1	teaspoon lemon juice		Sesame seeds, toasted
¼	cucumber, peeled, seeded and julienned	4	nori sheets

1. Cover bamboo mat with plastic wrap for easy cleanup.
2. Beat egg with water, add salt and pepper and cook omelet style. Allow to cool and julienne.
3. Toss avocado strips with juice in non-reactive bowl immediately after cutting. Pat dry before using.
4. Sprinkle cucumber with salt. Cut green onion just before using.

5. Lay mat on surface with its bamboo strips horizontally aligned. Cover with sheet of nori, shiny side down.

6. Wet hands and clap to shake off excess water. Spread 5 tablespoons rice on three-fourths of nori, leaving 1-inch border all around.

7. Place strips of filling ingredients lengthwise in center of rice mixture. Roll up tightly in mat, slightly squeezing entire roll and form a sushi cylinder. Remove roll from mat and repeat with remaining nori. Roll in plastic wrap and chill if using later. Roll should be tight with ingredients directly in center.

8. Cut roll in half and cut each piece in half again, making 8 pieces of sushi. Repeat with remaining nori, varying the fillings. Serve with Oriental Dipping Sauce and Wasabi Sauce.

For inside out roll, place nori on mat and completely cover with rice. Flip nori over and place filling directly on nori. Follow step 7 for rolling and press rice into sesame seeds. Finish with step 8.

Smoked Salmon Nigirizushi

PAREVE   YIELD: 20 PIECES

East meets west in this very popular smoked salmon sushi tidbit. Make in bulk — they disappear fast. You can make the Pickled Ginger well in advance as it keeps in the refrigerator for a month.

Sushi Rice

3   tablespoons rice wine vinegar or white vinegar
2   tablespoons sugar

¼   teaspoon salt
¾   cup sticky or short grain rice
1   cup water

1. Heat vinegar, sugar and salt in small saucepan until sugar dissolves. Chill.
2. Wash and drain rice.
3. Boil water, add rice, reduce heat and cook 2 minutes, stirring constantly. Cover and simmer 15 minutes or until water is absorbed.
4. Turn heat off, remove cover and place towel over top of pot and re-cover with lid. Allow rice to steam another 15 minutes.
5. Transfer rice to glass or plastic bowl and toss with vinegar-sugar mixture. Using a nonmetal spatula, fold and fan rice to cool. Use immediately.

Nigirizushi

1   recipe Sushi Rice
4   ounces sliced Nova smoked salmon

Quick Wasabi Sauce,
   Pickled Ginger,
   Oriental Dipping Sauce

1. Form 20 small ovals of rice in palm of hand using 1½ tablespoons for each piece. Cover and set aside.
2. Cut Nova into 1½ x ¾-inch pieces, place dab of wasabi on Nova and press wasabi side onto rice oval.

3. Serve with additional Quick Wasabi Sauce, Pickled Ginger and Oriental Dipping Sauce.

Quick Wasabi Sauce

PAREVE

2 tablespoons wasabi powder

2 tablespoons water

• Mix ingredients to form a paste.
• For less heat, dilute with equal parts of soy sauce and rice wine vinegar.

Pickled Ginger

10 inches fresh gingerroot	¾ teaspoon white wine
1½ tablespoons rice wine vinegar	½ teaspoon sugar
1½ teaspoons sweet red wine	

1. Scrub gingerroot under cold running water. Blanch in boiling water 1 minute. Drain and thinly slice.
2. Heat vinegar, wines and sugar in small saucepan until sugar dissolves. Cool and pour over ginger. Cover and chill 3 or 4 days before using.

Oriental Dipping Sauce

½ cup soy sauce	1½ teaspoons finely chopped fresh gingerroot
3 green onions, thinly sliced	
2 tablespoons chopped fresh cilantro	1½ teaspoons hot chili oil or hot sauce

1. Combine all ingredients. Make 1 day ahead.

Sun-Dried Tomato and Black Olive Bruschetta

PAREVE OR DAIRY   YIELD: 12 SERVINGS

*T*he perfect complement to a crusty Italian bread, this colorful melange of savory tomatoes and olives should chill overnight for full flavor. Serve with toasted bread slices brushed with Garlic-Infused Oil.

1½ ounces sun-dried tomatoes, diced	1 shallot, minced
5 large plum tomatoes, peeled and chopped	2 garlic cloves, blanched and julienned
½ cup chopped kalamata olives	1½ tablespoons chopped fresh basil
2 tablespoons extra virgin olive oil	Salt and pepper to taste
1 teaspoon lime juice	1 large Italian bread, sliced
1 teaspoon red wine vinegar	1 recipe Garlic-Infused Oil
1 teaspoon chopped fresh parsley	⅔ cup crumbled feta cheese for dairy

1. Steep sun-dried tomatoes in boiling water 15 minutes. Drain.
2. Combine all ingredients, except bread and Garlic-Infused Oil. Chill overnight to meld flavors.
3. Brush bread slices with Garlic-Infused Oil and lightly toast.
4. Mix cheese with tomato-olive mixture and spread on bread.

Steeping Liquid

• Instead of discarding drained steeping liquids, add them to soups and salad dressings as flavor enhancers.

Vegetarian Chopped Liver

PAREVE   YIELD: 12 SERVINGS

For those who avoid real liver but long for that Old World taste, one bite of this vegetarian version will hook you.

½	cup Veggie Schmaltz or olive oil, divided	2	15-ounce cans baby peas, drained
3	large onions, chopped	6	large hard-boiled eggs
6	garlic cloves, minced	1	cup chopped walnuts
1	pound mushrooms, chopped		Salt and pepper to taste
		½	cup onions, minced to taste

1. Heat ¼ cup schmaltz or oil in large skillet and sauté chopped onions until caramelized. Add garlic and sauté until soft. Remove.
2. Sauté mushrooms in same skillet. Add onion mixture and peas and stir until hot. Cool.
3. Purée mixture with eggs, nuts, salt and pepper. Fold in minced onions.

Fig-Walnut Chopped Chicken Liver Non-G

MEAT   YIELD: 12 SERVINGS

Pack liver mixture into a fancy mold and turn out on a platter for a dramatic presentation. Garnish with figs and walnuts, a clue to the unusual flavors.

1	cup sweet red wine	1	cup Veggie Schmaltz or margarine
¾	cup dried figs	1	tablespoon cognac (use K-P brandy for Passover)
1	pound chicken livers, kashered (see How to Kasher Liver)		Salt to taste
1	cup chicken broth	½	cup chopped toasted walnuts
1	small onion, thinly sliced		Dried figs and walnuts for garnish

1. Bring wine to boil and remove from heat. Add figs and let stand 15 minutes to soften. Drain, discard wine and chop figs. You may prepare figs a day ahead and chill.
2. Combine livers, broth and onions in saucepan and boil, reduce heat, cover and simmer until onions are soft, 10 minutes.
3. Purée liver mixture with schmaltz or margarine, cognac and salt until smooth. Add figs and walnuts and pulse until blended. Chill.

Caramelized Onion Chopped Liver  Non-G

MEAT   YIELD: ABOUT 2 CUPS

The versatile Jewish classic, here glorified with golden caramelized onions. Serve as an appetizer/salad, garnished with additional chopped egg and onions. Spread on crackers, party breads for hors d'oeuvres. Makes a mouth-watering sandwich, topped with lettuce, tomato and sliced onions.

1	pound chicken livers, kashered	2	garlic cloves, minced
½	teaspoon garlic powder	1	tablespoon brandy, optional
½	teaspoon paprika	2	large hard-boiled eggs
½	teaspoon pepper	½	teaspoon salt
1	cup chopped onions	¼	cup minced onion to taste
¼	cup Veggie Schmaltz, divided		

1. Season liver with garlic powder, paprika and pepper. Set aside.

2. Caramelize onions in 2 tablespoons schmaltz until browned, about 30 minutes. Add garlic and sauté until soft.

3. Add liver to onion mixture and continue to sauté until onions are browned. Add brandy and cook 2 minutes more. Cool.

4. Grind liver, onions and eggs, adding raw onion and 2 tablespoons schmaltz as needed to moisten. Chill 4 hours or overnight.

How to Kasher Liver

1. Preheat broiler. Prepare 2 disposable pans.

2. Punch holes through one pan and rest it in the other pan. This provides a grate for juices to drip through.

3. Wash and trim livers, drain and pat dry. Lightly salt liver.

4. Broil, turning once, until no longer bloody, but still soft, about 10 minutes per side. Check to make sure livers are cooked completely.

Perfect Hard-Boiled Eggs Every Time

1. Place eggs in saucepan and cover with water.

2. Bring to boil, turn off heat and cover. Let stand on burner 10 minutes.

3. Drain, rinse under cold water and peel.

A Sundry of Salsas

PAREVE
YIELD: 8 TO 12 SERVINGS

Mild or spicy, these fruit and vegetable salsas make flavorful dipping appetizers, served with chips or veggies. Try them as a sauce over your favorite grilled chicken, fish or Portobello mushrooms. The Caribbean Pineapple Salsa and Tropical Salsa are low-fat choices.

Black Bean Salsa

1	15-ounce can black beans, drained and rinsed
2	tomatoes, diced
1	green pepper, diced
1	red pepper, diced
1	jalapeño pepper, minced
1½	cups corn

½	cup diced onions
⅓	cup chopped fresh cilantro
⅓	cup olive oil
½	teaspoon salt
⅓	cup lime juice
½	teaspoon ground cumin
	Cayenne pepper to taste

1. Combine all ingredients and chill 4 hours.

Mango Salsa

2	mangoes, peeled, seeded and diced
1	papaya, peeled, seeded and diced
1	red pepper, diced
2	jalapeño peppers, minced
1	large red onion, diced

	Salt and pepper to taste
3	tablespoons chopped fresh cilantro, optional
¼	cup extra virgin olive oil
¼	cup red wine vinegar

1. Combine fruits and vegetables. Add salt, pepper and cilantro.
2. Toss with oil and vinegar. Chill 4 hours.

Cantaloupe is a good substitute for papaya.

How to Handle Hot Peppers

- Use rubber gloves or wash hands immediately after handling. Do not touch eyes.
- Remove white veins, which hold the most heat and seeds.
- Soak hot peppers in salt water for 1 hour to decrease heat.
- Skewer pepper with toothpick to aid in retrieval.

Low Fat Caribbean Pineapple Salsa

1 teaspoon brown sugar, firmly packed	1 pineapple, peeled, cored and diced
2 tablespoons apple cider vinegar	2 small jalapeño peppers, minced
2 medium tomatoes, peeled, seeded and diced	3 green onions, thinly sliced
	1 cup chopped fresh cilantro or parsley
	½ teaspoon salt

1. Combine sugar and vinegar until dissolved. Mix in remaining ingredients and chill 4 hours.

Low Fat Tropical Salsa

1 cup peeled and chopped fresh pineapple	½ cup chopped fresh cilantro
1 cup diced mango	1 jalapeño pepper, minced
½ cup chopped red onion	Salt and pepper to taste

1. Combine all ingredients and chill 4 hours.

Watermelon or cantaloupe may be substituted for pineapple.

White Bean and Rosemary Spread

PAREVE   YIELD: 8 SERVINGS

Use as a dip with vegetables or spread it on hearty bread.

6 garlic cloves

2 tablespoons extra virgin olive oil, divided

1 15-ounce can cannelloni beans, drained and rinsed

1 tablespoon fresh rosemary leaves

Salt and pepper to taste

1. Preheat oven to 375°F.
2. Place garlic cloves in foil, drizzle with 1 tablespoon oil, seal and roast 20 minutes or until soft.
3. Purée beans, rosemary and garlic. Add remaining oil and blend until smooth.
4. Season with salt and pepper. Thin with additional oil to spreading consistency.

Fruited Salsa with Avocado

PAREVE

The light, slightly nutty flavor of avocados makes them a perfect addition to any of the fruited salsas.

1 salsa recipe with fruit

1 avocado, diced

• Prepare salsa according to directions and fold in avocado.

Hummus with Parsley Drizzle

PAREVE   YIELD: ABOUT 2¼ CUPS

Hummus

1	15-ounce can chickpeas, drained, liquid reserved	½	teaspoon ground coriander
¼	cup tahini	¼	teaspoon ground cumin
¼	cup lemon juice	¼	teaspoon paprika
4	garlic cloves, roasted	⅛	teaspoon cayenne pepper
			Black olives and paprika

1. Purée chickpeas, tahini, juice and garlic. Use reserved liquid to thin if necessary. Mix in spices.
2. Decorate with black olives, paprika and Parsley Drizzle.

Parsley Drizzle

2   tablespoons extra virgin olive oil
1   tablespoon lemon juice
1   cup packed fresh parsley

1. Purée all ingredients and drizzle over hummus.

Roasted Red Pepper Hummus

1 recipe Hummus with Parsley Drizzle

4 ounces roasted red peppers, drained and puréed

• Prepare Hummus and stir in peppers. Decorate with Parsley Drizzle.

Glazed Pastrami Roll-Ups

MEAT   YIELD: 24 PIECES

½	pound pastrami, thinly sliced	½	cup Sweet and Sour Glazed Corned Beef sauce or teriyaki sauce
24	canned pineapple chunks, drained		
24	water chestnuts, drained	¼	cup Dijon or deli mustard

1. Preheat oven to 400°F. Grease cookie sheet.
2. Stack water chestnut on each pineapple chunk and wrap with slice of pastrami. Secure with wooden toothpick and brush with sauce.
3. Bake 10 minutes or until pastrami is crisp. Serve with mustard.

Baked Brie in Bread Bowl

DAIRY   YIELD: 8 TO 12 SERVINGS

2	tablespoons butter	2	teaspoons lemon juice
1	large onion, chopped	2	teaspoons brown sugar, firmly packed
6	garlic cloves, minced	1	teaspoon Worcestershire sauce
8	ounces Brie, rind removed		Salt and pepper to taste
8	ounces cream cheese, cut into 1-inch pieces	1	round sourdough bread
¾	cup sour cream	3	tablespoons paprika

1. Preheat oven to 400°F. Prepare ungreased cookie sheet.
2. Melt butter in large skillet and sauté onions and garlic until golden brown, 10 minutes.
3. Melt Brie and cream cheese in microwave.
4. Whisk in onion mixture, sour cream, juice, sugar, Worcestershire, salt and pepper.
5. Cut off top of bread. Scoop out bread center and reserve, leaving ¾-inch shell.

6. Spoon cheese mixture into bread bowl. Top with bread lid, wrap in foil and place on sheet. Bake until cheese bubbles, 1 hour.
7. Unwrap, remove bread lid and sprinkle with paprika. Serve with reserved bread chunks and/or cut fresh vegetables.

Olive Tapenade

PAREVE   YIELD: ABOUT 2 CUPS

1	pound kalamata olives, pitted	6	garlic cloves
10	ounces roasted red peppers	4	teaspoons extra virgin olive oil
¼	cup capers, rinsed		

1. Finely chop all ingredients in processor.
2. Serve with crackers, party-size breads or cut fresh vegetables.

Palmiers

MEAT, PAREVE OR DAIRY   YIELD: 18 HORS D'OEUVRES

These elegant French puff pastry creations are well worth the fuss. The rolling is easier than you might think.

Smoked Turkey Palmiers

MEAT

1 puff pastry sheet	10 ounces smoked turkey breast,
¼ cup Dijon mustard, divided	thinly sliced and divided

1. Preheat oven to 400°F. Grease cookie sheets.
2. Cut pastry in half lengthwise and roll 1 piece at a time on lightly floured surface into rectangle, ⅛-inch thick.
3. Brush surface with mustard and top with half the turkey.
4. Fold long sides of rectangle towards center until edges meet. Repeat folds in same direction. Fold in half in same direction, ending with 9 x 3-inch rectangle. Cover with plastic wrap and chill 1 hour. Repeat with second pastry sheet.
5. Cut into ½-inch slices and place on sheets cut side down. Bake 10 to 12 minutes until pastry is browned and crisp.

Assemble ahead of time and freeze unbaked. Bake just before serving.

Asparagus Pesto Palmiers

PAREVE OR DAIRY

½ pound asparagus	½ cup extra virgin olive oil
½ cup fresh basil	½ cup finely chopped sun-dried
¼ cup fresh parsley	tomatoes
1 tablespoon pine nuts, toasted	1 frozen puff pastry sheet, thawed
8 garlic cloves	½ cup Parmesan cheese for dairy
½ teaspoon salt	
½ teaspoon pepper	

1. Preheat oven to 400°F. Grease cookie sheets.
2. Break off woody ends from asparagus, cut each stalk into thirds and blanch until crisp-tender, about 2 minutes.

3. Purée asparagus, basil, parsley, nuts, garlic, salt and pepper.
4. Slowly add oil with processor running until mixture resembles texture of mayonnaise. Fold in tomatoes.

5. Follow rolling procedures for Turkey Palmiers, substituting asparagus filling for mustard and turkey and sprinkling with Parmesan cheese if desired.

Sweet and Sour Meatballs

MEAT   YIELD: 24 MINIMEATBALLS

*S*erve these tangy meatballs as buffet **hors d'oeuvres** *from a chafing dish, over a bed of rice or orzo, or as a starter course.*

Meatballs

1½	tablespoons ketchup	½	teaspoon salt
1½	tablespoons water	⅓	teaspoon pepper to taste
½	teaspoon garlic powder	1	pound ground beef
½	teaspoon onion powder		

1. Preheat oven to 375°F. Cover rimmed cookie sheet with parchment paper.
2. Mix ketchup with water and seasonings and combine with beef.
3. Shape meat into ½-inch balls and place on sheet.
4. Bake 10 to 12 minutes until lightly browned. Drain.

Sauce

¾	cup chili sauce	1	tablespoon lemon juice to taste
½	cup sweet red wine	1	bay leaf
¾	cup jellied cranberry sauce		

1. Combine all ingredients. Bring sauce to boil in saucepan, reduce heat and simmer 20 minutes.
2. Add meatballs and continue to simmer 20 to 30 minutes. Remove bay leaf.
3. Meatballs and sauce may be chilled at this point. Skim fat before reheating.

Chicken Satay with Spicy Dipping Sauce

MEAT   YIELD: 30 SKEWERS

*S*atay *dishes — marinated, skewered and broiled cubes of meat or chicken — are a staple throughout Indonesia, Malaysia and Singapore. The use of peanut butter tags our recipe to enchanting Bali, whose cuisine abounds in peanuts.*

Spicy Dipping Sauce

2	teaspoons vegetable oil	2½	tablespoons peanut butter
¼	cup minced red onion	¼	teaspoon ground coriander
3	garlic cloves, minced	1½	tablespoons ketchup
½	teaspoon minced fresh gingerroot	1½	tablespoons lime or lemon juice
1½	teaspoons red wine vinegar	¼	teaspoon pepper
1½	teaspoons brown sugar, firmly packed	⅛	teaspoon hot pepper sauce
		¼	cup hot water
1	teaspoon sesame oil	¼	teaspoon turmeric

1. Heat vegetable oil in large skillet and sauté onions, garlic and ginger until soft.

2. Add vinegar and sugar and continue cooking until sugar dissolves.

3. Remove from heat and stir in remaining ingredients. Purée until smooth.

Chicken

¾	pound chicken breast halves, boned and skinned	1	garlic clove, minced
1¼	tablespoons sesame oil	1	teaspoon minced fresh gingerroot
1¼	tablespoons vegetable oil	⅛	teaspoon salt
2½	tablespoons dry Sherry wine	⅛	teaspoon pepper
2½	tablespoons soy sauce	⅛	teaspoon hot sauce
1¼	tablespoons lemon juice	30	6-inch skewers, soaked in water

1. Preheat grill 10 minutes before cooking.

2. Cut chicken into strips ½ inch by 3 inches.

3. Combine remaining ingredients except skewers and pour over chicken. Chill 1 hour.

4. Skewer chicken, discarding marinade and grill 5 to 10 minutes or until tender. Serve with Spicy Dipping Sauce.

Pastrami Appetizer Cups

MEAT   YIELD: 24 APPETIZERS

As pastrami cooks, it forms luscious holders for the savory bread filling. Minicups make bite-size starters. Full-size muffin cups make larger portions to be served as a side dish.

24 slices pastrami, thinly sliced
2   cups cubed challah, toasted
1   cup hot broth or water
1   tablespoon olive oil
2   tablespoons finely chopped
      onions

2   garlic cloves, minced
¼   cup finely chopped green pepper
¼   cup finely chopped red pepper
¼   teaspoon ground sage
¼   teaspoon pepper
    Salt to taste

1. Preheat oven to 350°F. Grease 24 minimuffin tins.
2. Place 1 slice pastrami into each minimuffin tin. Allow edges of pastrami to ruffle.
3. Cover challah with broth or water and coarsely mash.
4. Heat oil in large skillet and sauté onions, garlic and peppers until soft and blend with spices and challah mixture. Fill each cup to the top.
5. Bake 15 minutes or until pastrami cups hold their shape.

Two cups prepared stuffing mix may be substituted for the challah cubes.

Layered Taco Salad

Serve this lovely layered salad immediately after assembly.

Refried Beans

3	tablespoons olive oil	½	teaspoon pepper
1	medium onion, minced	¾	teaspoon ground cumin
3	garlic cloves, minced	¼	teaspoon turmeric
1	15-ounce can kidney beans, drained and rinsed	⅛	teaspoon cayenne pepper to taste
¾	teaspoon dried oregano	½	teaspoon chili powder to taste
		¼	teaspoon salt

1. Heat oil in large skillet and sauté onions and garlic until soft.
2. Purée beans with onion mixture. Add remaining ingredients. Thin with additional olive oil if needed to reach spreading consistency.

Assembly

1	large avocado, peeled and mashed	1	cup sliced black olives
2	teaspoons lime juice	6	green onions, sliced
1	head iceberg lettuce, shredded	¾	cup shredded Monterey Jack cheese
1⅓	cups Refried Beans	2	tablespoons chopped fresh cilantro for garnish
1½	cups Fresh Tomato Salsa or prepared salsa		Lime wedges for garnish
1	recipe Caliente Sour Cream		Tortilla chips
2	medium tomatoes, diced		

1. Mix avocado with juice.
2. Place lettuce on serving plate and layer ingredients as follows: Refried Beans, avocado mixture, salsa, Caliente Sour Cream, tomatoes, olives, green onions and cheese.
3. Garnish and serve with tortilla chips.

Caliente Sour Cream

DAIRY OR PAREVE

1 cup sour cream for dairy (use nondairy sour cream for pareve)

½ teaspoon garlic powder

½ teaspoon chili powder

¼ teaspoon ground cumin

¼ teaspoon salt to taste

¼ teaspoon white pepper to taste

• Combine all ingredients.

Herring Antipasto

PAREVE   YIELD: 16 SERVINGS

A perfect integration of savory flavors with ingredients that defy identification makes this herring antipasto an intriguing opener at your holiday gathering. Serve with party-size rye or pumpernickel bread or crackers. Will keep in refrigerator for two weeks.

1 15-ounce can black olives, drained	⅓ cup marinated artichoke hearts, drained and diced
12 ounces herring in wine sauce, drained, liquid reserved	½ cup finely chopped parsley, divided
1 green or red pepper, diced	12 ounces chili sauce
½ red onion, diced	

1. Reserve 10 olives for garnish and chop remaining olives. Cut herring into small pieces.

2. Combine olives, herring, peppers, onions, artichoke hearts and ¼ cup parsley with chili sauce. Add 2 to 3 tablespoons reserved herring liquid for flavor.

3. Place in bowl, cover and chill 24 hours to blend flavors.

4. Serve garnished with remaining parsley and reserved black olives.

Curry Dip

PAREVE   YIELD: 2 CUPS

The fragrance of curry powder permeates this spicy dip, sweetened with honey. A lively partner to serve with fresh vegetables.

2 cups mayonnaise	1½ teaspoons curry powder
1 tablespoon ketchup	⅛ teaspoon salt
1 tablespoon honey	⅛ teaspoon hot pepper sauce to taste
1 tablespoon grated onion	

1. Combine all ingredients and chill 2 hours.

Things to Do with Pesto Sauce ♔

DAIRY OR PAREVE

Pesto sauce is convenient to have on hand in the refrigerator as it has a two week shelf life. It freezes very well. It mixes well with any pasta, including cheese ravioli or tortellini for a dairy meal. Try it smeared on a vegetable wrap with Roasted Savory Tomatoes.

Traditional Pesto Sauce

DAIRY OR PAREVE   YIELD: ABOUT 2 CUPS

2	cups packed fresh basil	½ cup extra virgin olive oil
2	tablespoons pine nuts, toasted	½ cup Parmesan cheese for dairy
3	garlic cloves, minced	Salt and pepper to taste

1. Wash basil and strip leaves from stems. Pat dry.
2. Purée basil, pine nuts, garlic and oil until smooth. Add cheese, salt and pepper.

This recipe makes enough pesto to coat 1½ pounds of pasta.

Pesto may be frozen in small plastic cups, plastic bags or ice cube trays.

Cilantro Pesto

DAIRY   YIELD: ABOUT 2 CUPS

Cilantro pesto also perks up salad greens.

2	cups packed cilantro leaves	1 tablespoon lime juice
½	cup extra virgin olive oil	½ cup grated Parmesan cheese
¼	cup pine nuts, toasted	Salt and pepper to taste
6	garlic cloves	

1. Purée all ingredients until smooth.

Pesto Cheese Torte

DAIRY   YIELD: 16 TO 20 SERVINGS

2	cups butter, room temperature	2 cups pesto sauce, your choice
1	pound cream cheese, room temperature	Basil leaves and cherry tomatoes

1. Beat butter and cream cheese at medium speed with electric mixer until smooth.

2. Line bowl or mold with plastic wrap.

3. Spoon one-third cheese mixture into bottom of bowl. Cover with one-half pesto and top with one-third cheese, then remaining pesto and cheese.

4. Cover bowl with plastic wrap and chill overnight.

5. Turn upside down to unmold on serving plate while still cold. Serve at room temperature. Garnish top with basil and cherry tomatoes. Serve with crackers or party breads.

Caponata

PAREVE

YIELD: 12 TO 14 BUFFET OR
6 TO 8 STARTER SERVINGS

This succulent medley of simmered vegetables is frequently mounded on a buffet platter and served at room temperature with crackers or cocktail bread. Also makes a nice first course served on a bed of lettuce, garnished with black olives. May be made up to two days in advance and freezes well.

¼ cup olive oil	¼ cup capers, drained
1 large eggplant, unpeeled and cut into ½-inch dice	3 tablespoons pine nuts, toasted
1 large onion, chopped	½ cup tomato paste
½ cup chopped mushrooms	⅓ cup water
⅓ cup chopped green pepper	2 tablespoons red wine vinegar
4 garlic cloves, minced	1½ teaspoons sugar
½ cup chopped stuffed green olives	1 teaspoon salt
¼ cup chopped black olives	½ teaspoon pepper
	½ teaspoon dried oregano

1. Heat oil in stock pot and sauté eggplant, onions, mushrooms, green pepper and garlic until onions are soft.

2. Mix in remaining ingredients. Cover and simmer 25 minutes, stirring occasionally. Eggplant should be tender, but not overly soft. Chill overnight. Serve at room temperature.

Caponata-Stuffed Tomato

• Stuff Caponata into scooped out medium-size tomatoes and serve as a cold side dish.

Goat Cheese Terrine

DAIRY

YIELD: 8 TO 12 SERVINGS

This eye-catching stunner is one of the most elegant and colorful recipes in our collection. It is deceptively easy to prepare. As the centerpiece on a cocktail buffet, guests will flock to it.

4 ounces goat cheese, room temperature	½ cup prepared Traditional Pesto Sauce
¼ cup butter, room temperature	¾ cup pine nuts, toasted
6 ounces cream cheese, room temperature	⅓ cup sun-dried tomatoes, diced
12 slices Provolone cheese, thinly sliced	Basil leaves

1. Line 9 x 5 x 3-inch loaf pan with plastic wrap.
2. Combine goat cheese, butter and cream cheese and microwave 30 seconds or until melted.
3. Place 4 or 5 slices Provolone cheese on bottom and sides of pan.
4. Layer with half of each: cheese mixture, pesto, pine nuts and tomatoes.
5. Place 4 slices of Provolone on top of mixture and spread with remainder of cheese mixture, pesto, pine nuts, and tomatoes. Top with remaining Provolone.
6. Cover with plastic wrap. Place cans on top of loaf to compress terrine. Chill overnight.
7. Unmold by inverting on serving plate. Decorate with basil leaves. Serve with crackers and party-size rye or pumpernickel breads.

Spinach Dip

DAIRY OR PAREVE   YIELD: 12 SERVINGS

5   ounces frozen chopped spinach,
     thawed
¼   cup sour cream for dairy (use
     nondairy sour cream for pareve)
¼   cup mayonnaise
1   green onion, sliced
1½ teaspoons chopped fresh dill

¼   cup chopped fresh parsley
⅛   teaspoon hot pepper sauce to
     taste
¼   teaspoon salt to taste
⅛   teaspoon pepper
¼   cup finely diced red pepper,
     divided

1. Squeeze water from spinach.
2. Purée all ingredients, except red pepper. Fold in red pepper, reserving
    1 tablespoon for garnish. Chill. Serve sprinkled with reserved red
    pepper.

*To vary taste, add one or more of the following to the dip to taste: horseradish,
chopped roasted garlic, finely diced yellow and/or green peppers, sliced water
chestnuts.*

Meringue Baked Pecans Non-G

DAIRY OR PAREVE   YIELD: 2¼ CUPS

*These glazed pecans are a delicious crunchy topping for leafy green vegetable or
fruit salads. Pack in an attractive container for gift giving.*

2   large egg whites
½   teaspoon ground cinnamon
½   teaspoon salt
⅔   cup sugar

½   cup butter for dairy, melted
     (use margarine for pareve)
1   pound pecan halves

1. Preheat oven to 325°F. Grease cookie
    sheet.
2. Beat whites until stiff. Combine
    cinnamon, salt and sugar and add to
    whites.
3. Fold in melted butter or margarine
    and pecans. Spread mixture on sheet
    and bake 15 minutes.
4. Turn nuts over and toast on other
    side, about 15 minutes. Watch
    carefully to avoid burning.

*Any leftover glazed pecans may be frozen in
a plastic bag.*

Pita Crisps

DAIRY OR PAREVE   YIELD: 36 CRISPS

A great tasting appetizer, easy to fix. Kids love to help make these to enjoy with their friends.

3   large pitas
½   cup melted butter for dairy
       (use olive oil for pareve)
1   tablespoon dried parsley
1   teaspoon dried oregano
⅛   teaspoon garlic powder
⅛   teaspoon onion powder
¼   cup grated Parmesan cheese for
       dairy

1. Preheat oven to 350°F. Grease cookie sheets.
2. Split pitas in half, exposing rough interior.
3. Combine butter or oil and spices, and brush pitas. Sprinkle with cheese.
4. Cut each pita half into 6 wedges and arrange in single layer on sheet. Bake 12 to 15 minutes until browned.

Parmesan Pumpernickel Toast

DAIRY   YIELD: 8 TO 10 SERVINGS

A versatile sidekick for dips, soups and salad.

1   frozen pumpernickel bread   ½   cup butter, melted
2   garlic cloves, minced   ½   cup grated Parmesan cheese

1. Preheat oven to 275°F. Prepare ungreased cookie sheet.
2. Cut bread into paper-thin slices.
3. Combine remaining ingredients and brush mixture on one side of each bread slice.
4. Arrange slices on sheets and bake 20 minutes or until edges curl.

Perfect Party Punches

> ### Decorative Ice Mold
> #### PAREVE
>
> 1. Place any combination of thinly sliced lemon, orange, strawberries or other berries and edible flowers in ring mold and fill with cold water or fruit juice.
>
> 2. Freeze until solid. Unmold in punch bowl just before serving.

Champagne Punch

PAREVE   YIELD: 40 (4-OUNCE) SERVINGS

Keep these party punches frosty by adding a fruited ice mold to the punch bowl.

2 cups vodka, chilled	2 lemons, sliced
1 liter apricot brandy, chilled	4 oranges, sliced
3 liters ginger ale, chilled	Decorative Ice Mold, optional
3⅛ cups (750 ml) Champagne, chilled	

1. Combine all liquids in large punch bowl.
2. Add fruit slices and stir gently.

Piña Colada Punch

PAREVE   YIELD: 20 (4-OUNCE) SERVINGS

1 15-ounce can cream of coconut	3 cups ginger ale or rum, chilled
46 ounces pineapple juice, chilled	Decorative Ice Mold, optional

1. Combine cream of coconut and pineapple juice in punch bowl.
2. Add ginger ale or rum just before serving, stirring gently.

To reduce sweetness, substitute club soda for half of the quantity of ginger ale.

Perfect Party Punches (continued on next page)

Pink Lemonade Punch

DAIRY OR PAREVE   YIELD: 32 (4-OUNCE) SERVINGS

For nonalcoholic punch, substitute 64 ounces cranberry juice for wine.

24 ounces frozen pink lemonade, thawed	8½ cups (2 liters) lemon/lime, grapefruit or half-and-half soda
16 ounces frozen strawberries or raspberries, unsweetened	½ gallon fruit sherbet for dairy (use nondairy sorbet for pareve)
6¼ cups (1500 ml) White Zinfandel wine	Decorative Ice Mold, optional

1. Combine all ingredients except sherbet or sorbet in large punch bowl.
2. Drop sherbet or sorbet by heaping tablespoons into punch.

Spiced Iced Tea Punch Non-G

PAREVE   YIELD: ABOUT 16 CUPS

For easier removal, wrap cloves and cinnamon in cheesecloth or place in a closeable tea strainer.

Sugar to taste	10 cups cold water
1 teaspoon whole cloves	1½ cups orange juice
1 cinnamon stick	¼ cup lemon juice
8 tea bags	Decorative Ice Mold, optional
4 cups boiling water	

1. Combine sugar, cloves, cinnamon and tea bags in pitcher.
2. Pour boiling water over mixture and steep 10 minutes.
3. Remove tea bags, cloves and cinnamon. Stir in remaining ingredients and chill.

Soups

Fragrant Carrot Soup with
Indian Spices and Tarragon Pea Soup

Apple Brie Soup Non-G

DAIRY   YIELD: 6 TO 8 SERVINGS

2	tablespoons butter	1	medium potato, peeled and grated
1	cup coarsely chopped onion	½	pound Brie cheese, rind removed and cut into small chunks
¼	cup sliced leeks, white part only		
3	Granny Smith apples, peeled and sliced	1½	cups heavy cream, warmed
2	cups vegetable broth	½	teaspoon dried rosemary
1	bay leaf	⅛	teaspoon salt
½	teaspoon dried thyme	⅛	teaspoon white pepper

1. Melt butter in soup pot, add onions, leeks and apples and sauté until soft.
2. Add broth, bay leaf and thyme. Bring to boil, reduce heat and simmer 2 minutes. Add potato and simmer until thickened.
3. Remove bay leaf and purée mixture. Add Brie and remaining ingredients and continue to purée until smooth. Return to pot and warm.

• *For those who prefer a thinner soup, add up to ¼ cup additional broth.*

• *For a different taste, substitute beer (not suitable for* Passover) *for half of the broth.*

Apple-Rutabaga Soup

PAREVE OR DAIRY   YIELD: 8 TO 10 SERVINGS

This versatile soup blends unexpected ingredients together for a unique taste treat.

½	cup olive oil	1	cup peeled and chopped Granny Smith apple
1	cup chopped onion		
1	cup peeled and chopped rutabaga	4	cups vegetable broth
1	cup peeled, seeded and chopped butternut squash	2	cups liquid nondairy whipped topping for pareve (use heavy cream for dairy)
1	cup peeled and chopped carrots	¼	cup maple syrup
1	cup peeled and chopped sweet potato		Salt, pepper and cayenne pepper to taste

1. Heat oil in soup pot and sauté vegetables and apples until onions are soft.
2. Add broth and bring to boil. Reduce heat and simmer 20 minutes. Purée.
3. Return to pot. Add nondairy whipped topping or heavy cream and maple syrup. Heat on low and add salt, pepper and cayenne.

For a lower fat dairy version, substitute nonfat evaporated milk for heavy cream.

Immersible Blender Tips

• Make quick work of puréeing soups, sauces and gravies right in the cooking pot or bowl.

• Emulsify dip and dressing ingredients.

• Foam warm milk for specialty coffees.

Carrot-Mango Soup

PAREVE   YIELD: 8 SERVINGS

The sweet tangy flavors of mango, coconut, chili and ginger add an exotic Asian or sunny Caribbean savor to this interesting soup.

3 tablespoons vegetable oil	1 large mango, peeled and chopped
1¼ pounds carrots, peeled and chopped	1 bunch green onions, thinly sliced
2 medium onions, chopped	1 red chili pepper, finely chopped
1 tablespoon peeled and grated fresh gingerroot	1 tablespoon lime juice or more to taste
3 cups vegetable broth	Salt and pepper to taste
1 15-ounce can cream of coconut	1 tablespoon snipped fresh chives for garnish

1. Heat oil in soup pot and sauté carrots 5 minutes. Stir in onions and ginger and continue to sauté until onions are soft. Do not brown.

2. Add broth and simmer 8 to 10 minutes. Purée half the vegetables and return to broth.

3. Add cream of coconut, mango, onions and chili and heat. Add juice, salt and pepper. Garnish.

For a less sweet soup, add additional lime juice 1 teaspoon at a time to taste.

Snipped Fresh Chives

- Hold chives tightly in your hand and using scissors, snip short strands — much easier than chopping. Snipped herbs look fresher and greener than chopped.

Bean, Barley and Mushroom Soup

MEAT OR PAREVE   YIELD: 6 SERVINGS

For vegetarian option, omit meat and add basil, thyme or dill for more flavor.

1	cup navy beans, rinsed	¾	cup peeled and diced carrots
1	pound beef short ribs or chuck for meat	½	cup diced celery
2	pounds soup bones for meat	¾	cup sliced mushrooms
10	cups vegetable broth	8	garlic cloves, minced
1	tablespoon salt to taste	¼	cup chopped fresh parsley
½	cup barley	½	tablespoon pepper to taste
¾	cup diced onion	½	tablespoon paprika

1. Cover beans with water and soak overnight, adding more water if needed. Drain and rinse.
2. Place meat and bones in soup pot and cover with broth. Add salt and bring to boil. Skim foam.
3. Add remaining ingredients, partially cover pot and cook slowly until thickened and meat is tender.

Quick and Delicious Vegetable Soup

PAREVE   YIELD: 10 SERVINGS

10	ounces frozen cut green beans	1	tablespoon dried minced onion
10	ounces frozen peas and carrots	1	bay leaf
10	ounces frozen lima beans	½	teaspoon dried thyme
10	ounces frozen chopped spinach	1½	teaspoons dried basil
10	ounces frozen corn	¼	teaspoon garlic powder
1	28-ounce can tomatoes		Salt and pepper to taste
1	15-ounce can kidney beans, drained	5	cups water
8	ounces tomato sauce	2½	cups cooked orzo, minipasta or rice

1. Combine all ingredients except orzo, pasta or rice in soup pot. Bring to boil, stirring occasionally.
2. Break up large clumps of frozen vegetables and tomatoes.
3. Cover and simmer 30 minutes. Discard bay leaf.
4. Ladle soup into bowls that contain ¼ cup cooked orzo, minipasta or rice.

A Tip for Skimming Soup

• A fine mesh strainer works great for skimming foam from soup.

Black Bean and Salsa Soup

PAREVE OR DAIRY   YIELD: 10 SERVINGS

T̲his is one of the quickest recipes to prepare in this collection. Add two tablespoons chopped fresh cilantro to enhance this soup's flavor.

5   15-ounce cans black beans, drained and rinsed, divided
3   cups vegetable broth
2   cups chunky prepared salsa
2   teaspoons ground cumin
3   garlic cloves

½   cup nondairy sour cream for pareve (use sour cream for dairy)
¼   cup thinly sliced green onions
2   tablespoons chopped fresh cilantro

1. Reserve 1 can of beans and process remaining beans, broth, salsa, cumin and garlic until smooth.
2. Add whole beans to puréed mixture and heat.
3. Top with a dollop of sour cream or nondairy sour cream, onions and cilantro.

Escarole and White Bean Soup

PAREVE OR DAIRY   YIELD: 10 SERVINGS

1   bunch escarole, chopped
8   cups vegetable broth
1   15-ounce can Northern white beans, drained and rinsed
3   garlic cloves, minced
¼   teaspoon red pepper flakes to taste

1   teaspoon dried basil
    Pepper to taste
1   cup small-size pasta
½   cup grated Parmesan cheese for dairy

1. Soak escarole in cold water 5 minutes. Rinse thoroughly and drain.
2. Bring broth to boil in covered soup pot. Reduce heat and simmer.
3. Mash 1 cup beans and add to broth with remaining beans, escarole and seasonings. Cover and simmer 30 minutes.
4. Add pasta and continue to simmer until pasta is al dente. Serve with Parmesan cheese.

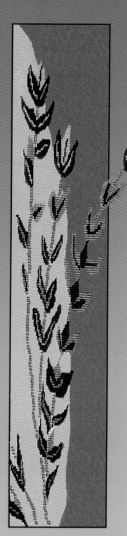

Purée of Parsnip Soup

PAREVE OR DAIRY   YIELD: 6 TO 8 SERVINGS

Puréeing gives this earthy vegetable soup an elegant velvety texture. It makes a soul-satisfying addition to any fall or winter menu.

2 tablespoons margarine for pareve (use butter for dairy)	6 cups vegetable broth
1½ pounds parsnips, peeled and chopped	1 bay leaf
1 carrot, peeled and chopped	2 cups liquid nondairy whipped topping for pareve (use heavy cream for dairy)
½ onion, chopped	
1 celery stalk, chopped	Salt, white pepper and freshly grated nutmeg to taste

1. Melt margarine or butter in soup pot, add vegetables and sauté until onions are soft.

2. Add broth and bay leaf and bring to boil. Simmer 20 to 25 minutes, or until vegetables are tender. Remove bay leaf and purée.

3. Return to pot and add liquid whipped topping or heavy cream, salt, pepper and nutmeg. Serve hot.

Artichoke-Potato Soup Non-G

PAREVE   YIELD: 8 SERVINGS

1 tablespoon extra virgin olive oil	3 cups peeled, chopped potatoes
4 cups artichoke hearts (fresh, frozen or canned in water), quartered	1 bay leaf
	½ teaspoon dried thyme
	1 teaspoon dried oregano
1 cup diced onion	4 cups vegetable broth
1 cup chopped celery	¼ teaspoon salt
2 garlic cloves, minced	¼ teaspoon pepper

1. Heat oil in soup pot and sauté artichokes, onions and celery until onions are soft. Add garlic and cook 1 minute.

2. Stir in potatoes, bay leaf, thyme and oregano. Add broth and bring to boil.

3. Reduce heat and simmer until potatoes are tender, 20 to 25 minutes. Add salt and pepper.

4. Remove bay leaf and purée until smooth, return to pot and warm. Add additional broth if too thick.

Steamed Artichokes

Non-G

PAREVE

4 fresh artichokes
1 bay leaf
1 lemon, sliced
6 peppercorns

1. Remove stems, tough outer leaves and thorny leaf tips.

2. Place 1-inch of water in large pot, add all ingredients and simmer until artichoke bottoms are fork-tender, 30 to 45 minutes. Serve with Garlic-Infused Olive Oil.

Moroccan Chickpea Soup

PAREVE

YIELD: 6 MAIN COURSE OR
12 STARTER SERVINGS

3 tablespoons olive oil
1 large onion, finely chopped
1 celery stalk including leaves, finely chopped
1 teaspoon turmeric
1 teaspoon pepper
½ teaspoon ground cinnamon
1 28-ounce can whole tomatoes, chopped
⅔ cup chopped fresh cilantro, divided

1 15-ounce can chickpeas, undrained
8 cups vegetable broth
1 cup lentils
2 ounces angel hair pasta, broken into 1-inch pieces
½ cup chopped fresh parsley
Salt to taste
6 lemon wedges for garnish

1. Heat oil in soup pot and sauté onions and celery until soft. Add turmeric, pepper and cinnamon and cook 3 minutes.
2. Add tomatoes, ⅓ cup cilantro, chickpeas, broth and lentils.
3. Bring to boil. Reduce heat and simmer covered until lentils are tender, about 35 minutes.
4. Stir in pasta and cook until tender, about 3 minutes. Add parsley, remaining cilantro and salt. Garnish.

Eggplant Soup
with Red Pepper Garnish  Non-G

PAREVE

YIELD: 6 SERVINGS

1 large eggplant, about 2 pounds
1 large red pepper
¼ cup olive oil
1 medium red onion, diced

4 garlic cloves, minced
¼ teaspoon salt
⅛ teaspoon pepper
4 cups vegetable broth

1. Preheat broiler. Grease cookie sheet.
2. Broil eggplant and red pepper, turning often until skins are blackened.
3. Set eggplant aside to cool and place pepper in covered bowl to steam.
4. Peel eggplant and chop.
5. Heat oil in soup pot and sauté eggplant, onions and garlic until vegetables are tender, 15 minutes. Add salt, pepper and broth. Purée until smooth and heat.
6. Peel, seed and purée pepper. Swirl pepper mixture into each serving bowl for garnish.

Lentil Facts
Did you know that lentils are:

• Quick-cooking
• A good protein substitute for meat
• Available in a variety of colors
• Easily stored for up to a year well-wrapped at room temperature
• Low in fat and high in fiber

Tarragon Pea Soup

PAREVE   YIELD: 6 SERVINGS

See what magic a dash of pungent cayenne and a drizzle of fragrant tarragon does to this perennial favorite.

¼ cup olive oil	1½ pounds frozen green peas
1 large onion, coarsely chopped	⅛ teaspoon cayenne pepper to taste
2 garlic cloves, minced	½ teaspoon pepper to taste
4 cups vegetable broth	2 tablespoons dried tarragon
1 large potato, peeled and quartered	

1. Heat oil in soup pot and sauté onions and garlic until soft.

2. Add broth and potatoes and bring to boil. Reduce heat and simmer until potatoes are tender.

3. Add peas, cayenne and pepper and return to boil. Remove from heat and stir in tarragon. Cool and purée soup. Serve warm.

For a dramatic presentation, swirl Tarragon Pea Soup into Fragrant Carrot Soup with Indian Spices.

Vegetable Broth Non-G

PAREVE   YIELD: 3½ QUARTS

¼ cup vegetable oil	8 garlic cloves, minced
1 large onion, coarsely chopped	16 cups cold water
1 leek, green and white parts sliced	10 sprigs parsley
1 celery stalk, chopped	½ teaspoon thyme
2 carrots, peeled and chopped	2 bay leaves
1 turnip or parsnip, chopped	1 teaspoon cracked peppercorns
2 tomatoes, chopped	Salt to taste

1. Heat oil in soup pot and sauté vegetables and garlic until soft.

2. Add water, herbs and salt and simmer 30 to 40 minutes.

3. Allow to cool 2 hours. Strain. Freezes well.

Lighter 'Tater Chips

PAREVE OR DAIRY

For dropping into soup or healthy snacking.

• Preheat oven to 375° F. Place 1 pound thinly sliced potatoes in single layer on cookie sheets. Brush lightly with oil and sprinkle with spices, seeds, and Parmesan cheese for dairy. Bake 20 minutes or until crisp.

Spring Vegetable Soup  Non-G

PAREVE   YIELD: 12 SERVINGS

This is a perfect vegetarian substitute at holiday meals.

¼	cup vegetable oil	6	garlic cloves, minced
3	carrots, peeled and diced	6	cups vegetable broth
2	cups broccoli florets	1	28-ounce can tomatoes with juice, diced
2	small zucchini, diced	¼	cup packed fresh basil, chopped
2	small yellow squash, diced	⅛	teaspoon ground cloves
1	sweet potato, peeled and diced		Salt and pepper to taste
½	pound mushrooms, quartered		
6	green onions, chopped		

1. Heat oil in large soup pot. Add all the fresh vegetables including garlic and sauté until tender, about 10 minutes.
2. Stir in broth, tomatoes with juice, basil and cloves.
3. Reduce heat and simmer until vegetables are tender, about 20 minutes. Add salt and pepper.

Chickenless Chicken Soup Non-G

PAREVE   YIELD: 10 CUPS

2	teaspoons olive oil	4	garlic cloves, minced
1	cup chopped onions	3	sprigs fresh thyme
½	cup chopped celery	2	bay leaves
½	cup peeled and diced carrots	8	cups vegetable broth
1	cup peeled and diced sweet potatoes	1	teaspoon salt
1	cup peeled and diced parsnips	1	teaspoon pepper
		½	cup minced fresh dill

1. Heat oil in soup pot and sauté vegetables and garlic until lightly browned. Add thyme, bay leaves and broth.
2. Bring to boil, reduce heat and simmer 45 minutes until vegetables are tender. Add salt, pepper and dill.
3. Cool soup and strain.

Cook soup on a low simmer to keep the broth clear.

---

*Cheesy Crouton
Soup Topper*

DAIRY
Yield: 4 slices
**A pungent topper
for vegetable soup.**

*4 slices French bread,
toasted
1 garlic clove
4 slices Muenster cheese
2 teaspoons
Parmesan cheese*

1. Preheat oven to 375°F. Prepare cookie sheet.

2. Rub toast with garlic. Top with cheese, sprinkle each with ½ teaspoon Parmesan and bake until cheese melts.

Signature Chicken Soup   Non-G

MEAT   YIELD: 10 SERVINGS

*O*ur signature version of this venerable Shabbat and festival soup incorporates a teaspoon of the yellow-orange spice turmeric to intensify flavor and color. For a sharper flavor, add a half teaspoon ground cumin and/or curry powder. You may add some of the shredded chicken to the soup. Save the remainder for our Chicken Chili.*

4 pounds chicken, cut in eighths	½ large sweet potato, peeled and halved
16 cups cold water	15 peppercorns
3 medium carrots, peeled and halved	6 sprigs fresh dill
2 celery stalks with leaves, cut in thirds	6 sprigs fresh parsley
1 extra large onion, unpeeled and quartered	5 garlic cloves
1 parsnip or turnip, peeled and halved	2 teaspoons salt to taste, divided
	1 tablespoon paprika
	1 teaspoon turmeric
	2 carrots, peeled, cooked and sliced

1. Place chicken in soup pot and cover with water. Cover pot and bring to boil. Skim foam.

2. Add remaining ingredients reserving 1 teaspoon salt and sliced carrots.

3. Reduce heat, partially cover pot and simmer about 2½ hours or until chicken is tender, stirring several times. Add water during cooking to keep chicken submerged. Adjust salt.

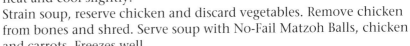

4. Remove from heat and cool. Chill overnight.

5. Skim fat and discard. Warm soup, remove from heat and cool slightly. Strain soup, reserve chicken and discard vegetables. Remove chicken from bones and shred. Serve soup with No-Fail Matzoh Balls, chicken and carrots. Freezes well.

This soup is non-g'brochts except when served with Matzoh Balls.

How to Vary Chicken Soup

• Toss 1 cup fine egg noodles into hot soup 5 minutes before serving.

• Five pounds of chicken wings and/or backs will produce a richer broth.

• Make removal of herbs easier by placing them in a closed tea strainer.

No-Fail Matzoh Balls

PAREVE   YIELD: 16 BALLS

This no fail recipe will produce light feathery matzoh balls.

½ cup Veggie Schmaltz or   ¾ cup matzoh meal
    margarine, room temperature   Salt and pepper to taste
3 large eggs

1. Combine all ingredients with fork until well blended. Allow to stand 15 minutes.
2. Form into 16 balls, drop into large pot of gently boiling salted water and cover. Balls will double in size as they cook.
3. Cook about 50 minutes or until cooked through.

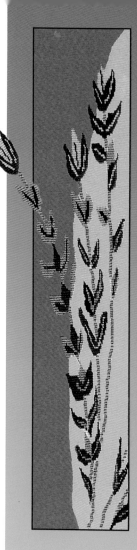

Turkey Mulligatawny Soup

MEAT   YIELD: 8 SERVINGS

Of all the wonderful things to make from leftover turkey, soup from the carcass may be one of the best.

4 garlic cloves   3 carrots, peeled and sliced
3 inch piece gingerroot, peeled   2 tablespoons curry powder
⅓ cup water   ¾ teaspoon ground cumin
¼ cup vegetable oil   1 cup coconut milk
10 cups Turkey Broth, divided   ¼ cup lime juice to taste
1 pound potatoes, peeled and   Salt and pepper to taste
    chopped   ⅓ cup finely chopped fresh cilantro
4 cups chopped onion

1. Purée garlic and ginger with water.
2. Heat oil in soup pot and sauté garlic mixture 2 minutes.
3. Add 5 cups broth, potatoes, onions, carrots, curry and cumin. Simmer until vegetables are soft, 30 minutes.
4. Cool and purée. Add remaining stock, coconut milk, juice, salt and pepper and warm. Stir in cilantro.

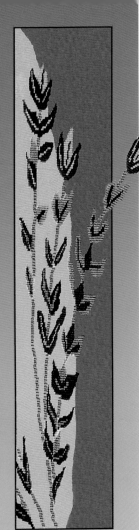

Turkey Rack Soup

MEAT   YIELD: 15 SERVINGS

This broth tastes better the longer it simmers. Watch the pot carefully so the liquid doesn't cook away. Add more water as necessary.

Turkey Broth

15 pound roast turkey carcass with some meat remaining, broken into pieces
   Defatted pan juices or leftover turkey gravy
16 cups water to completely cover carcass
2 medium onions, coarsely chopped
2 celery stalks with leaves, coarsely chopped
1 large carrot, peeled and chopped
1 large leek, chopped

1 parsnip or turnip, chopped
4 garlic cloves, minced
¾ teaspoon salt
6 sprigs fresh parsley
½ teaspoon dried thyme
1 bay leaf
2 teaspoons garlic powder
1 teaspoon dried basil
1 teaspoon dried oregano
1 teaspoon pepper
1 teaspoon dried sage

1. Combine all ingredients in large soup pot, bring to boil and simmer partially covered for 2½ hours. Cool and chill overnight.
2. Skim fat and strain broth, reserving turkey meat for soup. Broth may be frozen at this point.

Turkey Soup

2   tablespoons olive oil
1½ cups chopped onion
6   garlic cloves, minced
1½ cups peeled and diced carrots
1½ cups peeled and diced potatoes
½   cup diced celery
12 cups Turkey Broth
2   bay leaves
¾   teaspoon dried marjoram
¼   teaspoon cayenne pepper to taste

1   tablespoon garlic powder
½   teaspoon dried thyme
1   teaspoon dried basil
1   teaspoon dried sage
    Salt and pepper to taste
    Hot pepper sauce to taste, optional
1½ cups cooked barley or rice, optional
1½ cups diced cooked turkey meat, optional
3   tablespoons chopped fresh parsley

1. Heat oil in soup pot and sauté onions and garlic until soft. Add carrots, potatoes and celery and cook 5 minutes, stirring occasionally.
2. Add broth and all seasonings except parsley. Bring to boil and reduce heat. Partially cover pot and simmer until vegetables are tender, about 1 hour. Cool.
3. Remove bay leaves, purée and return to pot. Add optional items and warm. Sprinkle with parsley.

Garden Gazpacho

PAREVE   YIELD: 8 SERVINGS

Native to Spain and Latin America, this popular cold vegetable soup has many variations. Gazpacho works best with fresh peak-of-the-season tomatoes. If you have a craving for this wonderful cold soup earlier in the year, use three fresh tomatoes and two cups of canned peeled tomatoes.

Soup

2	garlic cloves	½	teaspoon salt
1	medium onion	½	teaspoon pepper
6	tomatoes, peeled	2	tablespoons wine vinegar
1	green or red pepper	2	tablespoons olive oil
1	cucumber, peeled and seeded	⅛	teaspoon hot pepper sauce

1. Purée all ingredients and chill 3 hours.

Vegetables for Topping

Choose two vegetables for topping the soup.

1	medium onion	½	medium cucumber
1	medium tomato	½	cup croutons, optional
½	red pepper		

1. Finely chop any 2 vegetables and garnish top of soup.
2   Sprinkle with croutons.

How to Peel Tomatoes

1. Boil water in saucepan. Prepare bowl of ice water.

2. Cut an "X" through skin at bottom end of tomato and place in boiling water in one layer.

3. Remove tomatoes with slotted spoon when peel separates from flesh. Place in ice water and remove when cool. Peel with paring knife.

Six-Fruit Soup

DAIRY OR PAREVE

YIELD: 12 SERVINGS

A refreshing fresh-fruit soup served in season or fix it anytime with canned or frozen fruit.

2½ cups water, divided
1 cup sugar
3 tablespoons lemon juice
2⅔ cups apricot nectar
3 tablespoons cornstarch
¼ pound black cherries, pitted

¼ pound peaches, peeled and sliced
1 pint strawberries, sliced
6 ounces Mandarin oranges
1 cup sour cream or plain yogurt for dairy (use nondairy sour cream for pareve)

1. Boil 2 cups water, sugar, juice and nectar.
2. Mix cornstarch with ½ cup water, add to soup and return to boil. Reduce heat.
3. Add fruit and simmer 5 minutes. Remove from heat and chill.
4. Top with sour cream, yogurt or nondairy sour cream and swirl with a knife or place a dollop on each serving. Serve chilled.

Chilled Cherry Soup

PAREVE

YIELD: 8 SERVINGS

4 cups cold water
1¼ cups sugar
¼ teaspoon ground cinnamon
30 ounces pitted tart cherries, undrained
30 ounces pitted black cherries, undrained

2 tablespoons lemon juice
1 cup dry red wine
¼ teaspoon dried dill
¼ teaspoon white pepper
1 tablespoon cornstarch
2 tablespoons water, room temperature

1. Combine all ingredients except cornstarch and 2 tablespoons water and bring to boil. Reduce heat, partially cover and simmer 1 hour.
2. Whisk cornstarch with water and continuously stir into soup until it boils. Reduce heat and simmer 2 minutes. Chill 1 hour.

Salads

Sweet and Savory Salad

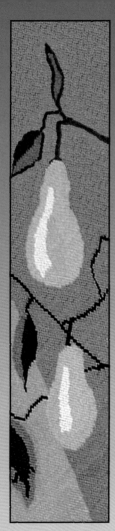

Salad Niçoise

PAREVE

Use this classic French salad originating in Nice as a show-stopper for an all-in-one luncheon entrée. Also great as an offering on a buffet table. Serve on a combination of mesclun, romaine, spinach and green or red leaf lettuce.

1	clove garlic
¼	teaspoon salt
3	tablespoons wine vinegar
2	teaspoons Dijon mustard
½	teaspoon pepper to taste
9	tablespoons extra virgin olive oil
¼	pound mixed greens
1	pound red-skin potatoes, quartered and steamed

¾	pound green beans, trimmed and blanched
1	6-ounce jar marinated artichoke hearts, quartered
3	tomatoes, quartered
3	hard-boiled eggs, halved
½	cup kalamata or black olives, pitted
6	ounces canned tuna, drained and chunked

1. Mash garlic with salt into paste and whisk in vinegar, mustard and pepper. Drizzle in oil while whisking constantly to emulsify.

2. Arrange greens on platter and decoratively top with potatoes, beans, artichoke hearts, tomatoes, eggs, olives and tuna. Drizzle with vinaigrette.

Salad Spinner

• A salad spinner makes quick work of drying delicate greens and herbs without bruising.

Roasted Potato Salad
with Chipotle-Dijon Vinaigrette

PAREVE   YIELD: 8 SERVINGS

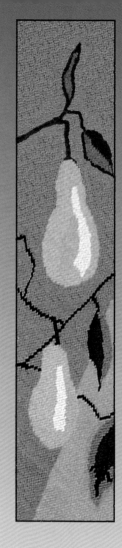

Chipotle-Dijon Vinaigrette

1	tablespoon red wine vinegar	1	garlic clove
2	tablespoons lime juice	½	teaspoon salt
½	teaspoon Dijon mustard	⅓	cup olive or vegetable oil
½	teaspoon crushed Chipotle chili peppers		

1. Process vinegar, juice, mustard, pepper, garlic and salt. Slowly add oil to emulsify.

Roasted Potato Salad

2 pounds red-skin potatoes, sliced
  Olive oil
  Salt and pepper to taste
1 medium red onion, peeled and sliced into ½-inch rings

1 yellow or red pepper, sliced into 1-inch strips
2 garlic cloves, minced and sautéed in ½ teaspoon olive oil
1 tablespoon chopped cilantro
1 cup mixed salad greens

1. Preheat oven to 400°F. Grease large roasting pan and cookie sheet.
2. Lightly coat potatoes with oil and toss in pan. Sprinkle with salt and pepper. Cover and roast until tender, 35 to 40 minutes. Cool.
3. Place onions and peppers on sheet and add salt and pepper. Roast uncovered until browned.
4. Toss potatoes with peppers and onions. Add garlic and cilantro.
5. Arrange greens on serving platter and cover with potato mixture. Drizzle with Chipotle-Dijon Vinaigrette.

Red Potato Salad

PAREVE   YIELD: 6 SERVINGS

This crunchy potato salad gets its name from three red ingredients: red potatoes, red peppers and red apple.

3 pounds red-skin potatoes, sliced ½-inch thick	1 cup mayonnaise
½ cup finely chopped onion	1 tablespoon Dijon mustard
½ cup chopped celery	1 tablespoon chopped fresh dill
2 large hard-boiled eggs, chopped	2 tablespoons chopped fresh parsley
1 large red apple, diced	Salt and pepper to taste
½ cup roasted red peppers, finely chopped	

1. Steam potatoes until tender, about 15 minutes. Drain and cool. Transfer to large bowl. Add onion, celery, egg, apple and red pepper.

2. Combine mayonnaise, mustard, dill and parsley. Fold into potato mixture. Season with salt and pepper.

Greek Pasta Salad

DAIRY   YIELD: 8 SERVINGS

Greek Vinaigrette

¾ cup olive oil	1½ teaspoons dried oregano
1 large shallot, minced	2 tablespoons dried basil
2 garlic cloves, minced	½ teaspoon pepper
¼ cup lemon juice or liquid from olives	

1. Combine all ingredients and cook over medium heat for 2 minutes or microwave 1 minute.

Salad

8 ounces ziti	½ cup packed fresh basil leaves, chopped
1 cup chopped kalamata olives	4 ounces feta cheese, crumbled
1 cup chopped red peppers	¾ cup artichoke hearts, marinated or water-packed, diced
4 green onions, sliced	
3 plum tomatoes, chopped	

1. Cook pasta al dente, drain, rinse with cold water and drain again.

2. Combine pasta with remaining ingredients and toss with Greek Vinaigrette.

Feta-Pear Layered Salad 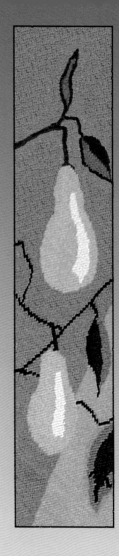 Non-G

DAIRY   YIELD: 4 TO 6 SERVINGS

This colorful and crunchy salad makes a decorative entrée salad for anytime of year. It is especially suitable for Passover. Pistachios substitute well for walnuts and bleu cheese for feta.

Creamy Balsamic Vinaigrette

½ cup olive oil
½ cup balsamic vinegar (use K-P balsamic vinegar for Passover)
1 tablespoon mayonnaise
¼ cup lemon juice

1 tablespoon honey
1 tablespoon apple juice
2 teaspoons salt to taste
Pepper to taste

1. Whisk all ingredients in bowl until smooth.

Layered Salad

2 romaine hearts, torn into bite-size pieces
1 green pepper, cut into 1-inch chunks
1 red pepper, cut into 1-inch chunks
1 large carrot, peeled and diced
1 cucumber, peeled and diced

1 large pear, peeled and diced
½ pound crumbled feta cheese
½ cup grated Parmesan cheese
1 cup halved grape tomatoes
¾ cup coarsely chopped walnuts
Pomegranate seeds, optional

1. Combine romaine, peppers, carrots, cucumbers and pears. Place half in serving bowl.

2. Mix cheeses with tomatoes for topping mixture.

3. Drizzle salad with half the dressing and sprinkle with half the topping mixture.

4. Cover with remaining romaine mixture followed by remaining topping and drizzle with remaining dressing. Top with nuts and Pomegranate seeds.

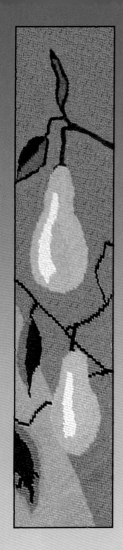

Tortellini Salad with Tarragon Vinaigrette

DAIRY

YIELD: 6 ENTRÉES OR
8 TO 10 SIDE DISH SERVINGS

This is a cool, nourishing one-dish meal, perfect for a summer dinner, or served as a side salad.

Tarragon Vinaigrette Dressing

2	shallots, minced	1	teaspoon sugar
¼	cup tarragon vinegar	2	ounces egg substitute or 1 Coddled Egg
2	teaspoons lemon juice	1	tablespoon dried tarragon
2	teaspoons Dijon mustard	1¼	cups vegetable oil
½	teaspoon salt		
½	teaspoon white pepper		

1. Process shallots, vinegar, juice, mustard, salt, pepper and sugar.
2. Add egg and tarragon and continue blending.
3. Pour in oil slowly, while processor is running, until dressing emulsifies.

Tortellini Salad

1	pound cheese tortellini	24	cherry tomatoes
2	tablespoons extra virgin olive oil	¼	cup chopped green peppers
3	cups assorted chopped vegetables (broccoli, cauliflower, carrots, snow peas or zucchini)	¼	cup chopped red peppers
		¼	cup chopped yellow peppers
		¼	cup minced fresh parsley
½	cup chopped green onions	½	cup grated Parmesan cheese

1. Cook tortellini according to package directions. Drain and toss with oil.
2. Blanch 3 cups assorted vegetables in boiling water until crisp-tender. Run cold water over vegetables and drain.
3. Add all vegetables, parsley and cheese to tortellini. Toss with Tarragon Vinaigrette Dressing. Chill.

Black Bean and Corn Salad

PAREVE   YIELD: 8 SERVINGS

Smoked Chili Vinaigrette

⅓ cup red wine vinegar or lime juice	⅔ cup extra virgin olive oil
1 teaspoon sugar	1 dried Chipotle pepper
½ teaspoon salt	2 garlic cloves, minced
½ teaspoon pepper	

1. Combine ingredients and let stand several hours at room temperature to blend flavors.
2. Remove Chipotle pepper before using.

Salad

2 15-ounce cans black beans, rinsed and drained	1 tablespoon ground cumin
2 15-ounce cans corn, drained	½ cup chopped fresh cilantro
½ cup finely chopped red onion	1 tablespoon salt to taste
½ cup finely sliced green onion	1 pound tomatoes, diced
	Cilantro sprigs for garnish

1. Combine beans, corn, onions, cumin, cilantro and salt.
2. Toss salad with Smoked Chili Vinaigrette. Add tomatoes and garnish.

Black Bean and Corn Salad with Grilled Chicken

MEAT   YIELD: 8 SERVINGS

Vary this spicy pareve *salad by adding grilled chicken.*
Place salad on bed of four cups torn romaine or mixed greens.

1 recipe Grilled Chicken Breasts   Cilantro sprigs for garnish
3 large oranges, peeled and sectioned

1. Prepare Black Bean and Corn Salad.
2. Cut grilled chicken into strips and decorate salad with chicken slices and orange sections. Garnish.

Herbed White Bean-Artichoke Salad

PAREVE   YIELD: 18 SERVINGS

Serve this salad cold or at room temperature on a buffet or as a starter with fresh vegetables.

3   cups canned cannellini beans, drained and rinsed
8   ounces artichoke hearts in water, drained and quartered
⅔   cup diced red pepper
⅓   cup sliced pitted black olives
¼   cup finely chopped red onion
¼   cup chopped fresh parsley

2   teaspoons chopped fresh mint leaves
1½ teaspoons chopped fresh basil leaves
⅓   cup extra virgin olive oil
¼   cup red wine vinegar
    Salt and pepper to taste

1. Combine beans, artichoke hearts, peppers, olives, onions, parsley, mint and basil.
2. Mix oil with vinegar and pour over bean mixture. Add salt and pepper and toss.
3. Cover salad and chill 6 hours or overnight.

Chickpea Salad

PAREVE   YIELD: 8 SERVINGS

This salad tastes best when served at room temperature.

1   15-ounce can chickpeas, drained and rinsed
½   cup finely diced red onion
2   plum tomatoes, minced
3½   tablespoons extra virgin olive oil
3   garlic cloves, crushed
¼   jalapeño pepper, minced or ¼ teaspoon cayenne pepper

1⅓ teaspoons finely chopped fresh cilantro
2½ teaspoons finely chopped fresh parsley
⅔   teaspoon dried mint leaves
⅔   teaspoon ground cumin
1⅓ teaspoons lemon juice
1⅓ teaspoons red wine vinegar
    Salt and pepper to taste

1. Combine chickpeas, onions and tomatoes.
2. Whisk oil with remaining ingredients and pour over chickpea mixture. Add salt and pepper. Let stand at least 30 minutes.

Fresh Herbs Versus Dried

• Use leaves only from fresh herbs.

• Substitute half the amount of dried herbs. When a recipe calls for 1 tablespoon fresh basil, use 1½ teaspoons dried basil. This ratio works for any herb substitution.

• Dried herbs lose their potency; they should be replaced twice a year.

Mesclun Salad with Roasted Asparagus

PAREVE   YIELD: 8 SERVINGS

Garlic Streusel

¾   cup challah crumbs   2   cloves garlic, minced
1½ teaspoons extra virgin olive oil

1. Combine breadcrumbs with oil and garlic and toast in small skillet 5 to 7 minutes. Cool and store up to 2 days.

Salad

½   pound mesclun mix   Prepared raspberry vinaigrette
16 Roasted Asparagus spears   24 fresh raspberries, rinsed and
                                              dried

1. Toss greens lightly with dressing and arrange on individual plates, top with asparagus.
2. Sprinkle Garlic Streusel over asparagus and garnish with raspberries.

Tuna Fish Salad with a Twist

PAREVE   YIELD: 6 LUNCH ENTRÉES OR
                                          12 BUFFET SERVINGS

18 ounces canned tuna fish, packed   1   tablespoon lemon juice
      in water, drained and flaked   1   teaspoon onion powder
2   celery stalks, finely chopped   ½   teaspoon garlic powder
6   tablespoons mayonnaise to taste   ¼   teaspoon white pepper

1. Combine all ingredients, adding more mayonnaise if desired.

Tuna Twist

Build on this favorite and create interesting varieties from the basic recipe.

- Add ¼ to ½ cup of any of the following: halved grapes, dried cranberries, raisins, chopped nuts, sunflower or pumpkin seeds, olives or chopped onions.

- Enhance flavor with 1 teaspoon of deli or Dijon mustard, dill, basil, cilantro or curry powder.

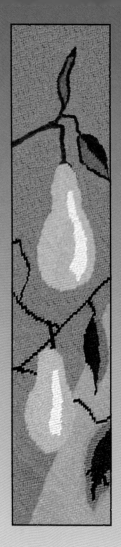

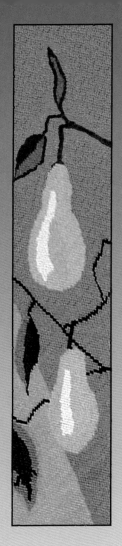

Signature
Mixed Green Salad  Non-G

PAREVE   YIELD: 8 SERVINGS

Serve this colorful salad family style from one large bowl or on individual plates. Goes well with croutons — store-bought or homemade — or try bagel chips or slices of toasted and seasoned French baguette bread.

3 cups mesclun mix	½ large red onion, thinly sliced
2 romaine lettuce hearts	¼ cup sliced almonds, toasted
1 pint cherry or grape tomatoes	Croutons
1 cucumber, scored and chunked	Dress Up Your Salad, choose 2
1 red pepper, chunked	
1 11-ounce can Mandarin oranges, drained	

1. Tear romaine into bite-size pieces.
2. Combine all ingredients except croutons.
3. Serve with dressing. Top with croutons just before serving.

How to Steam Vegetables

Cooking time will vary.

1. Steam vegetables in large skillet or pot with ½-inch water. Simmer uncovered until crisp-tender.

2. Transfer to ice water with slotted spoon to stop cooking action and set color.

Carrot-Asparagus Salad

PAREVE   YIELD: 10 TO 12 SERVINGS

The unusual shape of the enoki mushroom makes this salad unique.

2 pounds baby carrots	¼ cup prepared Italian salad dressing
2 bunches asparagus, trimmed, cut into 1½-inch pieces	1 tablespoon soy sauce
1 pound fresh enoki mushrooms	1 teaspoon sesame oil
	¼ teaspoon red pepper flakes

1. Steam carrots 2 minutes, add asparagus and cook covered 4 minutes until al dente. Drain, plunge into ice water and pat dry.
2. Toss with mushrooms and remaining ingredients adding more dressing if needed. Chill.

Tuna-Pasta Salad

DAIRY OR PAREVE   YIELD: 6 SERVINGS

*T**his tasty salad may be prepared** pareve **by eliminating the Parmesan cheese.
Boost the flavor by increasing the spices and seasoning.**

Basil-Mayonnaise Dressing

½   cup walnuts, toasted   1   cup mayonnaise
½   cup packed fresh basil leaves   1   tablespoon lemon juice
2   garlic cloves   ½   cup Parmesan cheese for dairy

1. Process walnuts, basil and garlic. Mix in remaining ingredients.

Pasta

8   ounces rotelle pasta   1   teaspoon pepper
3   cups broccoli florets   ½   cup grated Parmesan cheese for
12 ounces canned tuna fish, water-   dairy
    packed, drained and flaked   ½   cup chopped red pepper
1   cup cherry tomatoes, halved   3   green onions, sliced
¾   cup pitted black olives, sliced

1. Cook pasta according to package directions. Add broccoli for last
    2 minutes of cooking. Drain and rinse under cold water and drain
    again.
2. Combine pasta with remaining ingredients and toss with Basil-
    Mayonnaise Dressing.

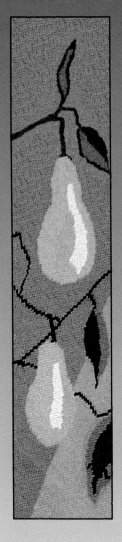

Moroccan Carrot Salad Non-G

PAREVE   YIELD: 8 SERVINGS

2   tablespoons lemon juice   1   teaspoon ground cumin
2   teaspoons paprika   1   tablespoon sugar
½   teaspoon ground cinnamon   ⅓   cup extra virgin olive oil
¼   teaspoon cayenne pepper   8   carrots, peeled and julienned

1. Whisk juice, paprika, cinnamon, cayenne, cumin and sugar.
    Gradually add oil until dressing is smooth.
2. Steam carrots until crisp-tender. Drain and toss immediately with
    dressing.

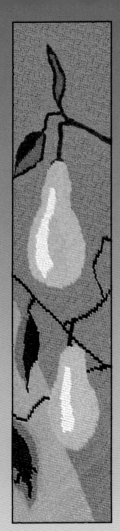

Signature Whitefish Salad   Non-G

PAREVE   YIELD: 8 SERVINGS

Sunday family brunch, Sabbath kiddush centerpiece and perennial buffet favorite, our Signature Whitefish Salad may be shaped into an oval on a serving plate and decorated with the head and tail. Follow the step-by-step photos for an elegant presentation.

¾ pound whole smoked whitefish	¼ cup mayonnaise to taste
1 large hard-boiled egg, chopped	½ teaspoon pepper to taste
1 celery stalk, finely chopped	Cucumber slices, lemon slices,
1 tablespoon grated onion	capers, fresh dill or parsley for
1 teaspoon lemon juice to taste	garnish

1. Remove head and tail and reserve for decoration. Bone fish and shred making sure all bones are removed. This step may be done a day ahead.

2. Combine fish with eggs, celery and onion. Add juice, mayonnaise and pepper. Garnish.

Step 1

Step 2

Step 3

Sweet and Savory Salad

DAIRY OR PAREVE   YIELD: 12 SERVINGS

This salad combines the sweetness of caramelized almonds and fresh fruit with a tangy salad dressing. Avocados may replace the bite-size fruit and any variety of nuts may replace the almonds.

Savory Dressing

½   cup red wine vinegar
½   cup olive oil
2   garlic cloves, minced

1   tablespoon Dijon mustard
    Salt and pepper to taste

1.   Combine all ingredients. Chill 2 hours or overnight.

Caramelized Almonds

1   tablespoon butter for dairy
    (use margarine for pareve)

3   tablespoons sugar
3   tablespoons slivered almonds

1.   Prepare ungreased cookie sheet.
2.   Melt butter or margarine in small skillet over medium heat and add sugar, stirring until golden.
3.   Add almonds, stir quickly and remove from heat. Spread on sheet to harden. Break into small pieces.

Salad

3   heads lettuce: red leaf, Boston and romaine
1   tart apple, cored, peeled and diced

1   11-ounce can Mandarin oranges, drained
1   cup fresh fruit (strawberries, pears, kiwi and/or blueberries), cut into bite-size pieces

1.   Tear greens into bite-size pieces in salad bowl. Combine with fruit and caramelized almonds and toss with Savory Dressing.

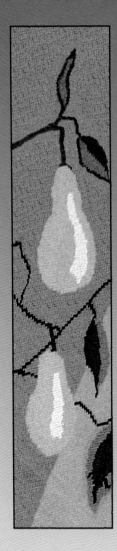

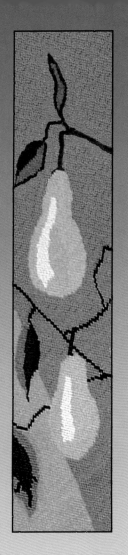

Mango Salad with Red Onion and Lime

PAREVE   YIELD: 10 TO 12 SERVINGS

1   small red onion, thinly sliced
½   small dried red chili pepper,
    minced
3   ripe mangoes, peeled and
    julienned
3   tablespoons lime juice

1   tablespoon chopped fresh cilantro
⅛   teaspoon salt to taste
⅛   teaspoon Worcestershire sauce
½   cup chopped roasted peanuts
    Cilantro sprigs

1. Combine onions
    with remaining
    ingredients except
    peanuts and
    cilantro. Cover
    and chill 1 hour.

2. Top with peanuts
    and cilantro
    sprigs.

Signature Egg Salad

PAREVE   YIELD: 10 TO 12 SERVINGS

*O*ur signature egg salad. As You Like It *has served gallons of this egg salad over the years. A popular staple at luncheon buffets.*

8   large eggs, hard-boiled and
    peeled
¼   cup mayonnaise
1   teaspoon Dijon mustard
½   teaspoon salt to taste

¼   teaspoon white pepper
¼   teaspoon garlic powder
¼   teaspoon onion powder
    Paprika for dusting

1. Chop eggs and mix in remaining ingredients.
2. Dust with paprika before serving.

Marinated Cucumbers with Dill  Non-G

PAREVE   YIELD: 6 SERVINGS

2   large cucumbers, peeled or   2   tablespoons water
    scored, thinly sliced   2   tablespoons sugar
    Salt to taste   Pepper to taste
½   cup red wine vinegar or apple   1   tablespoon chopped fresh dill
    cider vinegar   1   medium onion, thinly sliced

1. Sprinkle cucumbers lightly with salt and let stand 2 hours. Rinse off salt and drain.

2. Combine vinegar with remaining ingredients and add to cucumbers. Cover and chill 1 hour.

Bleu Cheese Dressing

DAIRY   YIELD: 6 TO 8 SERVINGS

½   cup mayonnaise   2   tablespoons dry red wine
¼   cup ketchup   4   ounces bleu cheese, crumbled
2   tablespoons sweet pickle relish

1. Combine mayonnaise, ketchup, relish and wine.
2. Fold in cheese. Allow to sit 1 hour to develop flavors.

Dress Up Your Salad

PAREVE   YIELD: 10 TO 12 SERVINGS

*H*ere are a variety of all-purpose salad dressings to enhance your favorite greens. They should be chilled before using.

American French Dressing

1	tablespoon finely grated onion	¾	teaspoon Worcestershire sauce
1	cup olive oil	¼	teaspoon paprika
¼	cup cider vinegar	⅛	teaspoon hot pepper sauce
½	cup ketchup	⅛	teaspoon white pepper
2	tablespoons sugar	1	tablespoon mayonnaise
2	cloves garlic, minced		

1. Purée all ingredients until dressing is thick.

Dill Mustard Vinaigrette

2½	tablespoons Dijon mustard	½	teaspoon pepper
½	cup red wine vinegar	1	cup extra virgin olive oil
½	teaspoon dried tarragon	2	tablespoons chopped fresh dill

1. Combine mustard, vinegar, tarragon and pepper.
2. Drizzle in oil slowly, whisking constantly until vinaigrette is thick. Stir in dill.

Basil Mayonnaise

1	cup mayonnaise	1	cup packed fresh basil, finely chopped
2	teaspoons finely chopped fresh parsley	½	cup walnuts, toasted and finely chopped

Fresh Basil Substitute

• Substitute 1 cup fresh parsley for fresh basil and add 2 teaspoons dried basil.

1. Combine mayonnaise, parsley and basil and stir in walnuts.

Thousand Island Dressing

1½	cups mayonnaise	⅓	teaspoon pepper
⅓	cup ketchup	¾	teaspoon fresh lemon juice to taste
1½	tablespoons sweet pickle relish		

1. Combine all ingredients.

Asian Salad Dressing

9   tablespoons vinegar or lemon juice

9   tablespoons soy sauce

3   tablespoons sugar

⅓   cup sesame oil

3   tablespoons fresh grated gingerroot

3   tablespoons sesame seeds, toasted

1. Combine vinegar or juice, soy sauce and sugar. Add oil slowly, whisking constantly. Add ginger and sesame seeds.

Hummus Salad Dressing

1   cup Hummus

¾   cup lemon juice

½   cup olive oil

2   teaspoons ground cumin

Cayenne pepper to taste

1   teaspoon salt

1   teaspoon pepper

1. Combine all ingredients.

Pineapple Cole Slaw  Non-G

PAREVE   YIELD: 8 SERVINGS

Diluting the mayonnaise with the juice makes the dressing go farther and decreases the caloric and fat content of the slaw.

1   pound green cabbage, shredded

¼   pound peeled and shredded carrots

8   ounces canned pineapple chunks, drained, liquid reserved

2   green onions, thinly sliced

2   celery stalks, finely diced

¼   cup mayonnaise to taste

Salt and pepper to taste

1. Combine cabbage, carrots, pineapple, onions and celery.

2. Mix mayonnaise with half the reserved juice and pour over salad. Season with salt and pepper.

Quick Pineapple Cole Slaw

8 ounces prepared cabbage slaw mix

8 ounces pineapple chunks, drained

Prepared Italian dressing

• Toss cabbage with pineapple and moisten with Italian dressing to taste.

Caesar Salad

DAIRY OR PAREVE   YIELD: 4 SERVINGS

The classic Caesar Salad is a North American creation! Food historians differ over the origin of this salad. Most say it was invented in Tijuana, Mexico, in the 1920's. Some attribute it to an Italian chef in Chicago at the turn of the century. Garlic figures large in this salad. To intensify its flavor, rub a cut garlic clove into the wooden salad bowl. For fewer calories and less fat in dressing, decrease olive oil by ¼ cup and substitute with ¼ cup water and reduce the amount of Parmesan cheese. Eliminate cheese for a pareve salad.

Caesar Dressing

DAIRY OR PAREVE   YIELD: ABOUT 1 CUP

3	garlic cloves, minced	3	tablespoons lemon juice
½	cup extra virgin olive oil	1	teaspoon Dijon or dry mustard
2	ounces egg substitute or 1 Coddled Egg	⅛	teaspoon cayenne pepper

1. Whisk garlic with oil and add egg.
2. Blend in juice, mustard and cayenne.

Salad

1   head romaine lettuce
½   cup grated Parmesan cheese for
     dairy (use 1 teaspoon
       Worcestershire sauce for pareve)
    Pepper to taste
    Croutons

1. Wash, dry and tear romaine into bite-size pieces. Place in bowl.
2. Add Worcestershire sauce to dressing for pareve. Toss greens gently, coating each piece.
3. Sprinkle with Parmesan cheese for dairy. Add pepper and toss. Top with croutons.

Coddled Egg

PAREVE

Yield: 1 egg
Substitute a fresh egg for egg product called for in a recipe.

• Coddle 1 large egg by boiling it for 1 minute or break into dish, cover and microwave 20 seconds.

Garlic-Dijon Encrusted
London Broil

89

Signature Brisket

MEAT   YIELD: 12 SERVINGS

This is As You Like It's most popular brisket recipe. The slow cooking produces a rich fragrant gravy.

3 large onions, chopped	1¼ cups ketchup
10 garlic cloves, minced	⅔ cup dry red wine
5½ pounds beef brisket	1¼ cups water
Salt, pepper and paprika to taste	2 pounds mushrooms, quartered, optional
1¼ cups French salad dressing	

1. Preheat oven to 375°F. Prepare ungreased large roasting pan.

2. Add two-thirds of the onions and garlic to pan. Rub meat with salt, pepper and paprika and place fat side up in pan. Cover with remaining onions and garlic.

3. Combine dressing, ketchup, wine and water and pour over meat. Cover.

4. Roast 2½ hours. Add mushrooms and cook 30 minutes, until meat is fork tender. Add additional water if liquid evaporates.

5. Cool, slice and return to pan. Chill overnight to skim fat from gravy.

Shiraz

Brisket with Burgundy-Orange Sauce

MEAT   YIELD: 8 SERVINGS

1 envelope onion soup mix	1½ teaspoons fresh orange zest
1½ cups Burgundy wine	2 teaspoons sugar
¼ cup water	4 garlic cloves, minced
2 tablespoons flour	½ teaspoon pepper to taste
1 tablespoon dried basil	4 pounds beef brisket
2 teaspoons dried thyme	1 pound mushrooms, quartered
⅓ cup orange marmalade	

Brisket with Burgundy-Orange Sauce (continued)

1. Preheat oven to 300°F. Prepare roasting pan large enough to hold brisket flat.

2. Combine soup mix, wine and water in pan. Stir in flour, basil, thyme, marmalade, zest, sugar, garlic and pepper. Add brisket and spoon sauce over top of meat.

3. Cover and bake 3 hours, basting every hour until meat is fork tender.

4. Place brisket on cutting surface and cut across grain in thin slices. Return brisket to pan, add mushrooms and top with sauce. Cover.

5. Increase oven temperature to 325°F and roast until mushrooms are tender.

   Chill meat and sauce separately if not serving immediately. Skim fat from sauce and reheat at 325°F. Freezes well.

 Beaujolais

Garlic-Dijon Encrusted London Broil

MEAT   YIELD: 4 SERVINGS

This easy-to-fix, versatile coating for your main holiday course — whether beef, chicken or fish — seals in the food's natural juices, creating a golden bubbly crust of roasted garlic and Dijon mustard, redolent of French Provençal cooking. Makes for an elegant presentation.

20 cloves garlic, minced
3   tablespoons olive oil
1½ tablespoons chopped fresh
      rosemary

1½ tablespoons chopped fresh thyme
3   tablespoons Dijon mustard
2½ pounds London broil
      Pepper and onion powder to taste

1. Preheat broiler or grill.
2. Combine garlic, olive oil, herbs and mustard.
3. Season beef with pepper and onion powder.
4. Broil or grill beef, turning once. Remove 10 minutes before done. Cover with mustard-garlic mixture and return to broiler or grill. Continue cooking until reaching desired degree of doneness.

 Cabernet Sauvignon

Dijon-Garlic Crust Variations

MEAT OR DAIRY

• For poultry, add tarragon, oregano or basil.

• For dairy, use dill with fish and add ¼ cup Parmesan cheese.

Marinated London Broil ♕

MEAT

This marinade insures a succulent meat dish that broiling seals in. At a London broil carving station, serve thinly sliced meat on carving board with party rye, pumpernickel or crostini. Display with bowls of mustard, pickles and green olives.

¾ cup olive oil	2 tablespoons minced garlic
3 tablespoons soy sauce	2 teaspoons dried oregano
3 tablespoons red wine vinegar	2 teaspoons dried basil
3 tablespoons lemon juice	2½ pounds London broil

1. Preheat broiler or grill 10 minutes before cooking.
2. Combine all ingredients except meat for marinade. Pour over London broil and chill 24 hours.
3. Remove meat and discard marinade. Broil or grill to desired degree of doneness. Slice on diagonal.

Cabernet Sauvignon

Boneless Rib Roast ♕

MEAT

YIELD: 6 SERVINGS

This is an expensive cut of meat but definitely worth it for special occasions.

5 pounds boneless beef rib eye, excess fat removed	6 garlic cloves, minced
¼ cup olive oil	Salt and pepper to taste
1½ cups finely chopped onion	Paprika

1. Preheat oven to 325°F ten minutes before cooking. Prepare large roasting pan.
2. Rub meat with oil, onions, garlic and seasonings. Chill uncovered to age and marinate 1 to 2 days.
3. Allow meat to come to room temperature.
4. Roast uncovered until internal temperature reaches 130°F to 140°F for rare to medium rare. It takes 20 to 25 minutes per pound to reach desired temperature. After 1 hour, check temperature every 10 minutes with meat thermometer. For medium, the thermometer should read between 150°F and 160°F, or for well done, 170°F.
5. Remove from oven and let rest 15 to 20 minutes before slicing.

Hamburgers Au Poivre

MEAT   YIELD: 4 SERVINGS

Here is a ground beef variation of the classic French steak dish. Upscale it with a flambé-at-table presentation.

2	pounds ground beef	2	teaspoons Worcestershire sauce
4	teaspoons coarsely ground pepper	1	teaspoon lemon juice
	Salt to taste	2	tablespoons brandy, warmed
2	teaspoons olive oil	1	tablespoon chopped fresh parsley
¼	teaspoon hot pepper sauce to taste	1	tablespoon chopped fresh chives

1. Shape beef into four patties. Press pepper into both sides of meat. Set aside 30 minutes.

2. Sprinkle light layer of salt over bottom of large skillet, heat on high until salt begins to brown.

3. Add patties. Cook until well browned on 1 side. Turn over and cook to desired degree of doneness. Remove.

4. Add oil, sauces and juice and scrape loose browned bits. Add brandy.

5. Return patties to skillet and cover with sauce. Top with parsley and chives.

Beef Chili with Pasta

MEAT   YIELD: 4 TO 6 SERVINGS

Our version of the Southwestern classic beef chili, this pairs nicely with a crusty loaf of bread and a fresh green salad.

2	tablespoons olive oil	4	teaspoons chili powder
½	cup chopped onion	½	teaspoon salt
4	cloves garlic, minced	½	teaspoon pepper
1½	pounds ground beef	⅛	teaspoon cayenne pepper to taste
1	15-ounce can kidney beans, rinsed and drained	12	ounces water
6	ounces tomato paste	1	cup cooked small-size pasta

1. Heat oil in large skillet and sauté onions and garlic until soft.

2. Add beef and continue to sauté, breaking meat up until cooked through.

3. Mix in beans, tomato paste, seasonings and water. Cover and simmer 1 hour, stirring occasionally. Stir in pasta before serving.

How to Flambé

Flaming a dish with brandy or liqueur must be done safely.

• Two options: warm brandy or liqueur in small skillet, ignite and pour over finished dish, or pour directly into cooking pan with food, warm and remove from heat. Ignite.

• Use long kitchen matches and stand back when igniting.

Meatballs in Sauerkraut Non-G

MEAT   YIELD: 6 SERVINGS

A hearty, full-flavored meal. Always popular.

2 pounds ground beef	½ teaspoon salt
¼ cup ketchup (use K-P ketchup for Passover)	1 32-ounce jar sauerkraut with liquid
3 tablespoons water	23 ounces tomato mushroom sauce
¾ teaspoon pepper, divided	1 tablespoon caraway seeds, optional (not for Passover)
1 teaspoon garlic powder, divided	Lemon juice or sugar to taste

1. Preheat oven to 375°F. Grease 9 x 9 x 4-inch pan.

2. Combine beef, ketchup, water, ¼ teaspoon pepper, ½ teaspoon garlic powder and salt. Roll into golf-size balls and place in pan.

3. Mix sauerkraut into sauce. Add remaining pepper, garlic powder and caraway seeds. Pour sauce over meatballs.

4. Add juice or sugar. Cover and bake 2 hours.

How to Lower the Fat

• Make day ahead and skim chilled fat from surface before warming.

• Shape smaller meatballs and prebake on parchment-lined pan 10 minutes at 375°F.

Giant Stuffed Hamburger

MEAT   YIELD: 6 SERVINGS

This is a clever, kid-friendly meal that boosts the well-loved hamburger into an appealing new form. A sure-fire winner for young family fare.

2   tablespoons margarine, melted
1¼   cups pareve cubed herb stuffing
        mix or croutons
1   large egg, beaten
½   cup chopped mushrooms
⅓   cup beef broth
¼   cup sliced green onions
¼   cup toasted chopped almonds

¼   cup packed fresh parsley,
        chopped
1   teaspoon lemon juice
2   pounds ground beef, turkey, veal
        or chicken
1   teaspoon salt
3   garlic cloves, minced

1.   Preheat grill or broiler.
2.   Combine margarine, stuffing mix or croutons, egg, mushrooms, broth, onions, almonds, parsley and juice.
3.   Mix meat with salt and garlic and form into two 8-inch patties.
4.   Spread stuffing mixture over 1 patty to within 1-inch of edge. Top with second patty and press down to seal edges. Grill or broil 10 to 12 minutes on each side until desired degree of doneness. Cut into 6 wedges.

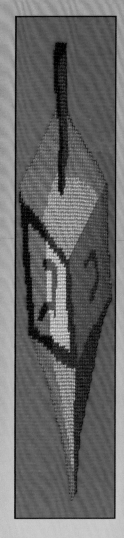

How to Make a Juicy Burger

• Choose a piece of chuck roast and have the butcher grind it. Freshly ground meat retains its moisture and produces a juicy and flavorful burger, as well as meatballs and meatloaf.

Cabbage Borscht with Beef Non-G

MEAT   YIELD: 8 SERVINGS

This hearty Russian staple has many variations. In ours, the sour salt or lemon juice joins the tartness of the apple to counter the sweetness of the raisins. Slow cooking bathes the meat in this luscious melange of flavors. Serve as a main course with salad and peasant bread for dipping.

2   pounds flanken, top rib
1   large cabbage, thinly sliced
1   28-ounce can tomato purée
1   15-ounce can beets, diced
1   cup white raisins

1   large tart apple, peeled and diced
2   medium potatoes, peeled and diced
    Salt, sugar, sour salt or lemon juice to taste

1. Place meat in soup pot with enough water to cover. Bring to boil and skim surface.

2. Add cabbage, tomato purée, beets, raisins, apples and potatoes. Reduce heat and simmer until all vegetables are soft and meat is tender.

3. Add salt, sugar, sour salt and/or juice.

Substitute chuck or stew meat for flanken.

To defat the borscht, make a day ahead, chill and skim fat.

Sweet and Sour Unstuffed Cabbage

MEAT   YIELD: 8 SERVINGS

The sweet peppery taste of ginger ale merges with the brown sugar, ketchup and lemon juice to create a perfect sweet and sour cabbage blend that permeates the meatballs. Capture the taste of stuffed cabbage without all the fuss and in much less time.

1   large cabbage, coarsely chopped
1¼ cups ketchup (use K-P ketchup for Passover)
4   cups ginger ale
½   cup brown sugar, firmly packed

¼   cup lemon juice
2   pounds chopped beef or turkey
1   large egg
¼   cup matzoh meal
    Salt and pepper

1. Combine cabbage, ketchup and ginger ale in large soup pot. Boil, reduce heat and simmer until cabbage is soft, 20 minutes. Add brown sugar and juice.

2. Combine meat, egg and matzoh meal. Add salt and pepper.

3. Form into 2-inch balls and add to cabbage mixture. Simmer 40 minutes.

Sweet and Sour Short Ribs

MEAT   YIELD: 4 SERVINGS

½ cup soy sauce	1 tablespoon finely grated fresh gingerroot
¼ cup Sherry wine	
¼ cup pineapple juice	1 small pear, cut into 1-inch chunks
2 tablespoons sugar	3 tablespoons sesame oil
Salt to taste	2 teaspoons cayenne pepper to taste
3 garlic cloves, minced	2 teaspoons pepper
¼ cup finely sliced green onions	4 pounds meaty short ribs
¼ cup chopped onion	

1. Preheat grill or broiler 10 minutes before cooking.
2. Purée all ingredients for marinade except ribs.
3. Marinate ribs in refrigerator 6 hours or chill overnight. Shake off excess marinade. Cook until tender.

Sweet and Sour Glazed Corned Beef

MEAT   YIELD: 10 ENTRÉE OR
                                        25 TO 30 BUFFET SERVINGS

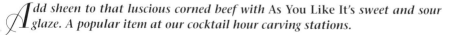

Add sheen to that luscious corned beef with As You Like It's sweet and sour glaze. A popular item at our cocktail hour carving stations.

2 tablespoons vegetable oil	1½ cups brown sugar, firmly packed
1 tablespoon dry mustard	3 pounds cooked single brisket corned beef
5 tablespoons ketchup	
3 tablespoons red wine vinegar	

1. Preheat oven to 350°F. Grease roasting pan.
2. Combine all ingredients, except corned beef, in saucepan and bring to boil. Reduce heat and simmer glaze 10 minutes.
3. Brush glaze over corned beef and roast in pan 20 minutes. Baste occasionally.

Meat Cabbage Rolls and Stuffed Peppers

MEAT   YIELD: 8 ROLLS

*M*eat-filled cabbage rolls are a great favorite in Middle European countries and a classic Jewish dish. This is As You Like It's *tried and true recipe for stuffing cabbage as well as peppers of all colors. Just stuff and bake. For* hors d'oeuvres, *use half a cabbage leaf and walnut-size meat filling.*

Meat Cabbage Rolls

1 large cabbage	¼ cup rice
3 cups tomato purée	1 large egg
¼ cup brown sugar, firmly packed	½ cup finely chopped onions
1 tablespoon apple cider vinegar	3 garlic cloves, minced
¼ cup lemon juice	½ teaspoon salt
1 pound ground beef, turkey, veal or chicken	½ teaspoon pepper

1. Preheat oven to 375°F. Grease large roasting pan.

2. Remove and discard core from cabbage and place head into boiling water 15 minutes or until leaves can be separated. Leaves should be pliable but not soft.

3. Bring tomato purée, sugar and vinegar to boil, reduce heat and simmer 15 minutes. Remove from heat and add juice.

4. Combine meat with remaining ingredients.

5. Place ¼ cup filling on bottom third of cabbage leaf, and roll. Push ends of cabbage into roll to secure filling.

6. Spoon thin layer of sauce onto bottom of pan. Arrange cabbage rolls, seam down, in single layer and top with remaining sauce. Cover and bake 1½ hours or until rolls are tender.

How to Separate Cabbage Leaves by Freezing

1. Remove cabbage core and freeze head overnight.

2. Defrost 4 hours and remove leaves.

3. Blanch leaves in boiling water or microwave if not pliable.

Meat Stuffed Peppers

MEAT   YIELD: 4 PEPPERS

4   peppers   Meat Cabbage Rolls sauce and
                                        filling

1. Preheat oven to 375°F. Prepare deep baking pan to hold peppers upright.
2. Cut off top 1 inch of peppers and reserve.
3. Loosely stuff filling into peppers and cover with reserved top. Top with sauce.
4. Cover and bake 1 to 1½ hours, until peppers are tender.

Veal with Lemon and Capers

MEAT   YIELD: 4 TO 6 SERVINGS

A take-off on a classic Roman dish with the tang of lemon and capers. You may also use boned and skinned chicken breast halves, pounded thin.

2   pounds veal scallops, pounded   Olive oil for sautéing
    thin   ¼   cup white wine
    Flour seasoned with salt, pepper, 1   cup chicken or beef broth
    garlic powder and paprika to   1   lemon, sliced
    taste   ¼   cup capers
2   large eggs, slightly beaten   ¼   cup packed fresh parsley,
    Seasoned breadcrumbs for   chopped
    coating

1. Dredge veal in flour. Dip in egg and coat with breadcrumbs. Chill 1 hour.
2. Heat oil in large skillet and sauté veal on both sides until browned. Remove from pan.
3. Add wine and broth to skillet and heat. Scrape loose browned bits from bottom of skillet.
4. Return veal to skillet and add lemon slices, capers and parsley. Cover skillet and simmer until veal is tender.

Cabernet-Merlot

Veal Meatloaf

MEAT   YIELD: 6 TO 8 SERVINGS

8   ounces tomato sauce   2   pounds ground veal
¼   cup apple cider vinegar   1   large egg
¼   cup brown sugar, firmly packed   1¼   cups unflavored breadcrumbs
1   tablespoon Dijon mustard   Salt and pepper to taste
1   medium onion, finely chopped

1.   Preheat oven to 350°F. Grease 9 x 13-inch pan.
2.   Combine sauce, vinegar, sugar, mustard and onions for sauce.
3.   Mix half the sauce with meat, egg, breadcrumbs, salt and pepper.
     Shape into loaf in pan and cover with remaining sauce.
4.   Bake covered 30 minutes. Uncover and bake 1 additional hour,
     basting frequently.

Substitute ground beef, turkey or chicken for veal.

Veal and Peppers

MEAT   YIELD: 4 SERVINGS

*S**erve this flavorful dish over rice, mashed potatoes or egg noodles to absorb all
the gravy.*

2   pounds veal, cubed   1   medium onion, chopped
     Flour for dredging, seasoned   3   garlic cloves, minced
       with salt, pepper, garlic powder 6   large green olives, chopped
       and paprika   1   tablespoon capers
3   tablespoons olive oil, divided   1   tablespoon red wine vinegar
4   green peppers, thinly sliced   ¼   cup water

1.   Dredge veal in flour.
2.   Heat 1½ tablespoons oil in large skillet, add peppers, onions and
     garlic and sauté until soft. Transfer to bowl, add olives and capers and
     cover.
3.   Heat remaining oil in skillet and brown veal on all sides. Add vinegar
     and water and scrape loose browned bits. Add pepper mixture and
     simmer covered until veal is tender. Add more water if needed.

Pinot Noir

**Don't Touch
That Meat!**

**Tip for those
who don't like to
handle meat.**

• Place all
ingredients in
sealable plastic bag
and knead until
mixed.

Stuffed Veal Roast

MEAT   YIELD: 6 TO 8 SERVINGS

This dish makes a beautiful and delicious presentation. It does take a little more preparation time but your guests will really appreciate it. Begin roasting three hours before you plan to serve.

Stuffing

2	tablespoons olive oil	10	ounces frozen chopped spinach, thawed and drained
½	cup chopped onion		
⅓	cup chopped carrot	¼	cup unseasoned breadcrumbs
1	celery stalk, diced	½	teaspoon salt
2	garlic cloves, minced	¼	teaspoon pepper
1	pound Italian veal sausage		

1. Heat oil in large skillet and sauté onions, carrots and celery until soft. Add garlic and sauté 1 minute.

2. Crumble sausage into skillet and cook 5 minutes. Fold in spinach, breadcrumbs, salt and pepper and remove from heat.

Assembly

⅓	cup olive oil	½	teaspoon fresh lemon zest
2	shallots, finely chopped	4	pounds boned veal shoulder, rolled and tied
4	cloves garlic, minced		
2	tablespoons soy sauce		Salt and pepper to taste
1	tablespoon lemon juice	1½	pounds baby carrots
¼	cup white wine	8	medium potatoes, quartered
1½	teaspoons dried thyme		

1. Preheat oven to 325°F ten minutes before roasting. Grease large roasting pan.

2. Mix oil, shallots, garlic, soy sauce, juice, wine, thyme and zest in small saucepan and cook 5 minutes.

3. Unroll veal and pound with meat mallet to ½-inch thick. Spread stuffing on veal to within 1 inch on all sides and roll again. Tie with string or use wooden toothpicks for securing roll.

4. Place roast in large plastic bag and pour sauce over meat. Chill overnight to marinate.

5. Remove meat from marinade, center in pan and roast 2½ hours, basting with marinade every ½ hour. Add carrots and potatoes to roasting pan during last hour of cooking.

6. Remove from oven and allow to rest 15 minutes before slicing.

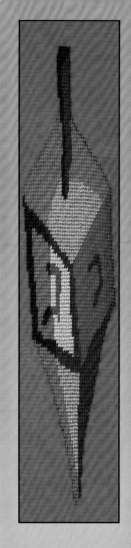

Grilled Lamb Pita Pockets

MEAT   YIELD: 6 SERVINGS

This dish, redolent of Asian and Mediterranean fare, will waft intriguing aromas across your kitchen. Substitute beef, chicken or turkey for lamb.

Grilled Lamb Filling

2 tablespoons currants	½ cup drained diced canned tomatoes
2 tablespoons red wine	¾ teaspoon ground allspice
2 tablespoons olive oil	¾ teaspoon ground cinnamon
1 large onion, chopped	¾ teaspoon salt
3 garlic cloves, minced	¾ teaspoon pepper
¾ pound ground lamb	¼ cup unsalted pistachios or pine nuts, toasted
¼ teaspoon dried thyme	
3 tablespoons chopped fresh parsley	

1. Soak currants in wine 10 minutes.
2. Heat oil in large skillet and sauté onions and garlic until soft. Add lamb and sauté until cooked.
3. Add currants and remaining ingredients except nuts. Cook 2 minutes and stir in nuts.

Tahini Sauce

½ cup tahini	¼ cup olive oil

1. Whisk tahini with olive oil until smooth.

Assembly

6 large pitas	Olive oil for brushing

1. Preheat grill, skillet or grill pan.
2. Cut pitas along the top, carefully opening to form deep pocket but leaving pitas whole.
3. Fill with equal portions of meat mixture. Drizzle with tahini sauce and press to close.
4. Brush both sides of pita with oil. Place on cooking surface to brown both sides.

Place pitas in 250°F oven on cookie sheet to keep warm until ready to serve.

Ground Lamb Lettuce Wraps

MEAT

1 recipe Grilled Lamb Filling

16 large iceberg or romaine leaves Tahini Sauce

1. Place filling in center of iceberg lettuce leaf, folding sides inward and rolling up. Romaine leaves should be served open-face and secured with toothpicks.

2. Serve with tahini sauce.

Ground Lamb in Phyllo Cups

MEAT   YIELD: 15 MINITARTS

1   recipe Grilled Lamb Filling   ¼   cup packed fresh parsley, minced
15   prepared phyllo minicups   ¼   cup finely chopped fresh tomatoes

1.   Preheat oven to 350°F. Grease 15 minimuffin tins.
2.   Place phyllo cups in tins and fill with lamb mixture. Bake until phyllo
     is golden. Garnish with parsley and tomatoes.

Baby Rib Lamb Chops

MEAT   YIELD: 12 CHOPS

*T*hese delectable baby chops make elegant hors d'oeuvres.

12   single baby rib lamb chops,   2   tablespoons minced fresh mint
     frenched (about 2½ pounds)   1   tablespoon lemon juice
¼   cup extra virgin olive oil   1   teaspoon salt
6   garlic cloves, minced   ½   teaspoon pepper
1   tablespoon fresh rosemary

1.   Preheat broiler 10 minutes before cooking. Prepare broiler pan.
2.   Place chops into plastic bag. Combine oil, garlic, rosemary, mint,
     juice, salt, and pepper and pour over chops. Turn to coat on both
     sides. Let sit at room temperature 30 minutes, or cover and chill up to
     4 hours.
3.   Place chops in single layer on pan and broil until medium-rare and
     browned 2 to 3 minutes per side. Serve immediately.

Mansion Dijon-Crusted Lamb
with Apple Mint Relish

MEAT   YIELD: 4 SERVINGS

*T*his is a signature recipe from the award-winning chefs at the Glen Sanders Mansion, who have teamed with As You Like It to cater kosher dining events, sharing and complementing their considerable culinary expertise. The Glen Sanders Mansion is a premier restaurant, caterer and inn, housed in a pre-revolutionary landmark site in the town of Scotia. This variant of the elegant French classic boosts the amount of mustard eight-fold, balancing Dijon's aromatic pungency with the sweet and sour savor of chopped Granny Smith apples, simmered in sugared cider vinegar, topped with fresh mint.

Rack of Lamb

1	cup Dijon mustard	1	tablespoon chopped fresh thyme
2	garlic cloves, minced	1	tablespoon chopped fresh parsley
1	tablespoon chopped fresh rosemary	4	pound rack of lamb
		2	cups unflavored breadcrumbs

1. Preheat oven to 400°F. Prepare large skillet and shallow roasting pan with rack.
2. Combine mustard, garlic, rosemary, thyme and parsley and rub into meat. Be careful not to get mixture on bones. Coat rack with breadcrumbs.
3. Pan sear lamb in hot skillet until browned on both sides.
4. Place lamb on rack. Roast to desired degree of doneness; 7 to 9 minutes for medium rare, add 5 to 7 minutes for medium. Serve with Apple Mint Relish.

Apple Mint Relish

1½	teaspoons vegetable oil	2	small Granny Smith apples, peeled and finely diced
¼	cup finely diced red onion	1	tablespoon finely chopped fresh mint
¼	cup cider vinegar		
¼	cup sugar		

1. Heat oil in medium skillet and sauté onions.
2. Add vinegar, sugar and apples. Simmer 10 minutes. Add mint and chill. Serve at room temperature.

Poultry

Arroz con Pollo

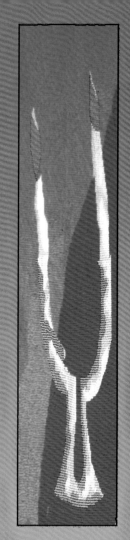

Chicken with Chickpeas, Olives and Tomatoes

MEAT   YIELD: 6 SERVINGS

The Lebanese call chickpeas hummus. The Spanish call them garbanzos. A Middle East-Spanish-Mediterranean crossover, this chicken dish makes clever use of chickpeas, green olives and tomatoes, enhanced by a hint of cinnamon.

6	chicken breast halves, boned and skinned	¾	cup green olives with pimento, sliced
	Salt and pepper to taste	2	15-ounce cans chickpeas, drained and rinsed
	Flour for dredging	1	teaspoon ground cinnamon
	Olive oil for sautéing	2	tablespoons chopped fresh thyme
1	onion, chopped	¼	cup packed fresh parsley, chopped
4	garlic cloves, minced		
4	medium tomatoes, coarsely chopped		

1. Preheat oven to 350°F. Grease 9 x 13-inch pan.

2. Season chicken with salt and pepper and dredge in flour. Heat oil in large skillet and sauté until golden brown. Remove chicken and sauté onions and garlic in same skillet.

3. Add tomatoes, olives, chickpeas, cinnamon and thyme to skillet. Simmer 10 minutes.

4. Arrange chicken in pan and top with tomato mixture. Bake uncovered 30 minutes or until chicken is tender. Sprinkle with fresh parsley.

 Gewürztraminer

Bulgarian Chicken Non-G

MEAT   YIELD: 4 TO 6 SERVINGS

Slow baking on a bed of potatoes and tomatoes in a tart, garlic sauce infused with fragrant dill and rosemary brings out the Eastern European savor of this all-in-one chicken meal.

Sauce

½	cup olive oil	3	tablespoons finely chopped fresh parsley
2	tablespoons lemon juice	1	teaspoon dried dill
3	tablespoons red wine vinegar	1	teaspoon dried rosemary
2	garlic cloves, minced		Salt and pepper to taste

Add International Flair to Chicken
Here's a way to turn ordinary chicken into French cuisine. Combine the flavors, to taste, for 3 variations.

• Thyme, red wine, broth and tomato paste
• Parsley, onion powder, tarragon, white wine and broth
• Paprika, onion powder, Marsala wine and sweet and sour sauce

Bulgarian Chicken (continued)

1. Whisk sauce ingredients.

Chicken

5	medium potatoes, peeled and coarsely chopped
5	medium tomatoes, peeled and coarsely chopped

3½ pounds chicken, cut into eighths or 6 chicken breasts, boned and skinned
1 teaspoon paprika

1. Preheat oven to 350°F. Grease 9 x 13-inch baking pan.
2. Place potatoes and tomatoes in pan, cover with chicken and brush with half the sauce. Sprinkle with paprika. Bake uncovered 20 minutes.
3. Baste with remaining sauce and bake until tender.

 Riesling

Indonesian Chicken

MEAT   YIELD: 8 SERVINGS

*I*ndonesian dishes have many influences — British, Dutch, Malaysian and Chinese — but the native cuisines found among the nearly 8,000 islands that comprise Indonesia are truly distinctive. Note the skillful infusion of exotic spices; these were brought to this tropical, equatorial area by Indian and Middle East traders.

8	chicken breast halves, boned and skinned	½	teaspoon ground coriander
	Salt and pepper	1	tablespoon peeled, minced fresh gingerroot
½	cup flour for dredging		
	Olive oil for sautéing	1	tablespoon fresh orange zest
1½	tablespoons finely chopped shallots	½	cup coconut milk
		½	teaspoon minced chili pepper
3	garlic cloves, minced	¼	teaspoon cayenne pepper
½	teaspoon ground cumin	¼	cup soy sauce
		¼	cup ketchup

1. Season chicken with salt and pepper and dredge in flour. Heat oil in extra large skillet and sauté until golden brown. Remove. Sauté shallots and garlic until soft in same skillet.
2. Add remaining ingredients to skillet, stirring constantly for 2 minutes.
3. Return chicken to skillet and cook until tender, about 20 minutes.

 *Gewürztraminer*

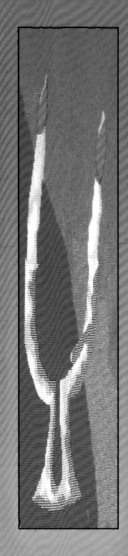

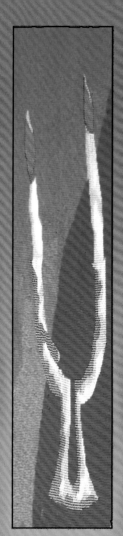

Chicken Cacciatore

MEAT   YIELD: 6 SERVINGS

*T*he use of rice in place of noodles lends a hint of Northern Italian cooking to this classic "hunters style" chicken. The nutty flavor of jasmine rice works especially well with the melange of fresh vegetables flavored with herbs and olive oil. Preparing this dish a day in advance allows the flavors of the cooked ingredients to merge and intensify.

12	chicken pieces	1	bay leaf
½	teaspoon salt	¼	teaspoon dried thyme
¼	teaspoon pepper	¼	teaspoon dried marjoram
¼	teaspoon white pepper	¼	teaspoon dried rosemary
½	cup flour for dredging	¼	teaspoon dried oregano
5	tablespoons olive oil, divided	1	tablespoon Worcestershire sauce
3	shallots, chopped	8	ounces tomato sauce
3	garlic cloves, minced	½	cup white wine
1	green pepper, cut into thin strips	1½	cups sliced mushrooms
1	red pepper, cut into thin strips	3	cups prepared aromatic rice
5	tomatoes, coarsely chopped		

1. Season chicken with salt and peppers. Dredge with flour and brown in 4 tablespoons oil in large skillet. Remove.

2. Add remaining oil and sauté shallots, garlic and pepper strips until tender.

3. Add tomatoes, bay leaf, and remaining herbs, sauces and wine. Simmer 10 minutes.

4. Return chicken to skillet and cover with sauce. Bring to boil, reduce heat, cover and simmer 30 minutes. Add mushrooms and cook uncovered 15 minutes or until chicken is tender.

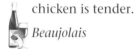 *Beaujolais*

Oven Method Chicken Cacciatore

1. Preheat oven to 350°F. Grease large roasting pan.

2. Follow Chicken Cacciatore directions through step 3. Place browned chicken in pan, top with sauce, cover and bake 45 minutes.

3. Uncover and add mushrooms. Return to oven 15 minutes or until chicken is tender.

Chicken-Asparagus Crêpes

MEAT   YIELD: 6 SERVINGS

A lavish yet easy to prepare dish, these elegant chicken-filled crêpes, similar to chicken divan, are dressed up with asparagus, sun-dried tomatoes and artichoke hearts.

Sauce

¼   cup Veggie Schmaltz or margarine   1½ cups chicken broth
½   cup flour   1   bay leaf
1½ cups nondairy milk   Salt and pepper to taste

1. Heat schmaltz or margarine with flour in saucepan. Whisk in nondairy milk and broth and bring to boil. Add bay leaf.
2. Reduce heat and simmer until thickened. Remove bay leaf, add salt and pepper and cool.

Filling

18 ounces chicken breast halves,   1   tablespoon thinly sliced green
        boned and skinned   onions
    Salt and pepper to taste   ¼   cup diced sun-dried tomatoes
½   cup white wine   1   tablespoon chopped fresh basil
1   bunch fresh asparagus, trimmed   1   teaspoon dried tarragon
        and cut into ½-inch pieces   3   tablespoons Sherry wine
¼   cup olive oil or margarine   ½   cup quartered artichoke hearts,
½   cup diced onions   drained
¼   cup diced red peppers   ¼   cup sliced water chestnuts
½   cup thinly sliced mushrooms   12   prepared 6-inch unfilled Crêpes
                                          ¼   cup snipped chives

1. Preheat oven to 350°F. Grease 9 x 13-inch pan.
2. Season chicken with salt and pepper and simmer in white wine until tender. Cool and cut into ½-inch cubes. Steam asparagus 2 minutes. Cool.
3. Heat oil or margarine in large skillet and sauté onions, peppers and mushrooms until soft. Add green onions and cook 1 minute more.
4. Add asparagus, tomatoes, basil, tarragon, Sherry, artichokes and water chestnuts. Heat until warm. Stir in chicken.
5. Coat bottom of pan with half the sauce.
6. Spoon equal amounts of chicken mixture in center of each crêpe, top with 1 tablespoon of remaining sauce. Fold 1 side of crêpe over filling, fold in opposite side and roll up to enclose filling.
7. Place filled crêpes in pan, seam side down and cover with remaining sauce. Bake uncovered 15 to 20 minutes until hot. Top with chives.

Beaujolais Blanc

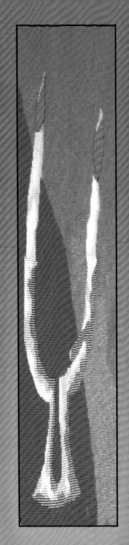

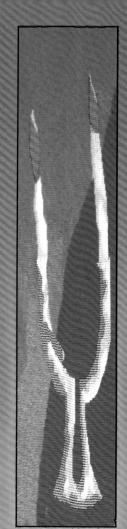

Arroz con Pollo

MEAT   YIELD: 4 SERVINGS

*C*hicken and rice dishes abound in Latin American cuisines and this Puerto Rican variant is a little moister than most. Use your most unusual serving platter to wow your guests. This recipe calls for overnight marinating.

Chicken

1 tablespoon dried oregano	2 6-ounce jars pimentos, chopped
1 tablespoon paprika	1½ cups rice
2½ teaspoons garlic powder	1 28-ounce can plum tomatoes, crushed
1½ teaspoons dried cilantro	
1½ teaspoons pepper	¾ cup chopped green olives
½ teaspoon cayenne pepper	2 cups water
2 lemons	½ teaspoon saffron or turmeric
3½ pounds chicken, cut into eighths or 3 pounds boned and skinned chicken breast halves	1½ cups white wine or beer
	2 cups chicken broth
	2 tablespoons red wine vinegar to taste
1½ tablespoons olive oil	
1¼ pounds onions, finely chopped	1 pound frozen peas
10 garlic cloves, minced	8 steamed asparagus spears
1½ green peppers, diced	1 6-ounce jar pimentos, cut in strips
2 red peppers, diced	

1. Preheat oven to 375°F ten minutes before cooking. Grease large roasting pan.

2. Combine oregano, paprika, garlic powder, cilantro, pepper and cayenne for spice mixture.

3. Juice lemons. Rub chicken with lemon rinds and spice mixture. Sprinkle chicken with juice, cover and chill overnight.

4. Broil chicken 10 minutes per side to brown. Place in pan.

5. Heat oil in large skillet and sauté onions, garlic and peppers until soft. Mix with pimentos, rice, tomatoes and olives. Transfer to roasting pan.

6. Combine water, saffron or turmeric, wine or beer, broth and vinegar and stir into chicken-rice mixture. Cover and bake 45 minutes, stirring occasionally. Add peas and bake 15 minutes more or until chicken and rice are tender. Add more water or broth as needed. Garnish with asparagus and pimentos.

 Soave

Italian Roasted Chicken Non-G

MEAT   YIELD: 8 SERVINGS

5	pound whole roasting chicken	12	cloves garlic
	Salt and pepper to taste	2	tablespoons olive oil
1	lemon, halved		Dried basil, dried oregano and
1	large onion, thickly sliced		paprika to taste

1. Preheat oven to 425°F. Prepare open roasting pan fitted with "V" rack.
2. Liberally salt and pepper inside of chicken. Stuff cavity with lemons, onions and garlic. Brush outside of chicken with oil and sprinkle with salt, pepper, basil, oregano and paprika.
3. Tie chicken legs together with string and tuck wing tips under body. Place chicken in pan, breast side down. If a "V" rack is not available, use open roasting pan.
4. Roast 20 minutes, turn breast side up and continue roasting until juices run clear when pierced with fork, about 1½ hours.
5. Transfer to carving board and loosely cover with foil. Let rest 15 minutes. Prepare gravy in same pan.

Chenin Blanc

Savory Poultry Gravy

MEAT   YIELD: 4 CUPS

	Poultry drippings	3	tablespoons flour (use 2 tablespoons
1	cup red or white wine or broth,		potato starch for Passover)
	warmed		Salt to taste
			Chicken or turkey broth

1. Pour drippings from roasting pan into bowl.
2. Place pan over low heat and deglaze pan with wine or broth. Add mixture to bowl drippings.
3. Let stand until fat rises to top. Measure 3 tablespoons fat and heat in saucepan. Whisk in flour or potato starch and salt. Stir until mixture turns golden.
4. Skim and discard fat from bowl. Measure drippings, adding additional broth if needed to equal 3½ cups.
5. Gradually whisk drippings mixture into flour or potato starch mixture and cook until gravy is smooth and thick.

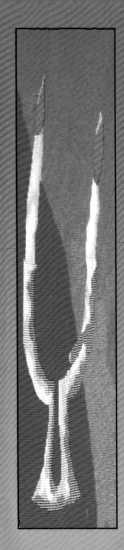

Deglaze Pan
1. Remove poultry from pan and heat pan over low heat.
2. Add red or white wine or broth and scrape up bits.

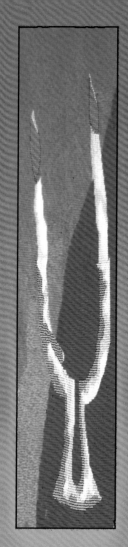

Pineapple Chicken

MEAT   YIELD: 4 SERVINGS

A perfect kid-friendly dish, easy for busy families.

1	20-ounce can pineapple chunks, drained, juice reserved	6	garlic cloves, minced
¼	cup honey	1	tablespoon orange juice
¼	cup soy sauce	1	chicken, cut into eighths
		2	teaspoons capers, optional

1. Preheat oven to 350°F. Grease 9 x 13-inch pan.
2. Combine reserved pineapple juice, honey, soy sauce, garlic and orange juice.
3. Place chicken in pan and cover with juice mixture.
4. Add pineapple and capers and bake 1 hour or until tender.

Substitute lemon juice for orange juice for a tart taste.

Sauvignon Blanc

Yakitori Chicken Skewers

MEAT   YIELD: 6 SERVINGS

This is an Asian version of a classic chicken kebab. Serve with individual bowls of white rice. Also makes a tasty appetizer. Just cut smaller pieces and use shorter skewers.

½	cup soy sauce	1½	pounds chicken, white or dark, skinned and cut in bite-size pieces
½	cup sweet or Sherry wine		Wooden skewers, 10 to 12 inches long
2	tablespoons sugar		
1	tablespoon cornstarch	6	green onions, cut in 2-inch pieces
1	cup water	2	green peppers, cut in 2-inch pieces

1. Preheat broiler or grill 10 minutes before cooking.
2. Bring soy sauce, Sherry and sugar to boil in small saucepan, stirring until sugar dissolves.
3. Combine cornstarch and water to form paste and slowly add to soy sauce mixture, cooking until slightly thickened for sauce. Cool.
4. Marinate chicken in sauce 1 hour. Soak skewers in cold water.
5. Thread chicken and vegetables alternately on skewers. Broil or grill, basting with remaining sauce. Discard unused sauce.

Gewürztraminer

Asian Chicken to Taste
Concoct these Asian Chicken versions to your taste.

• Ginger, garlic, soy sauce, sweet and sour sauce, pineapple, nuts, sesame seeds, peppers, onions and broccoli.

• Garlic, ginger, sesame oil, rice wine, peanut butter, soy sauce, peanuts, scallions, sugar snap peas.

Hot and Spicy Chicken

MEAT   YIELD: 2 SERVINGS

This flavorful chicken dish is low fat and quick to prepare.

2	chicken breast halves, boned and skinned
1½	tablespoons vegetable oil, divided
1	small chopped chili pepper to taste
1	red pepper, cut in strips

3	green onions, cut in 1-inch slices
1½	teaspoons minced fresh gingerroot
6	garlic cloves, minced
2	tablespoons Sherry wine
6	tablespoons water
¼	cup soy sauce

1. Cut chicken into strips.
2. Heat 1 tablespoon oil in large skillet and sauté peppers, onions, ginger and garlic until soft. Add remaining oil and chicken and continue sautéing, 3 minutes.
3. Stir in Sherry and water. Cover and cook 5 minutes.
4. Add soy sauce, cover and cook until chicken is tender.

 *Gewürztraminer*

Chicken in Orange Sauce

MEAT   YIELD: 6 SERVINGS

Chicken and oranges are a popular Israeli combination inspired by the country's large production of poultry and oranges. This is our version.

6	chicken breast halves, boned and skinned
	Salt and pepper to taste
½	cup flour for dredging
½	cup olive oil, divided
1	medium onion, chopped
1	pound fresh mushrooms, sliced

½	cup chicken broth
½	cup Port or Sherry wine
6	ounces frozen orange juice, undiluted
½	teaspoon dried oregano
½	teaspoon garlic powder

1. Preheat oven to 350°F. Grease 9 x 13-inch baking pan.
2. Season chicken with salt and pepper and dredge in flour. Heat ¼ cup oil in extra large skillet and brown chicken. Arrange in pan.
3. Sauté onions and mushrooms in remaining oil in same skillet. Add broth, port or Sherry and juice. Cook until sauce is smooth.
4. Pour sauce over chicken and sprinkle with oregano and garlic powder. Bake 1 hour or until tender.

Chenin Blanc

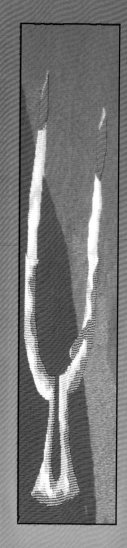

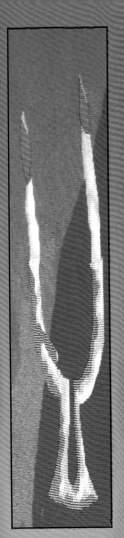

Chicken Wellington with Raspberry Sauce

MEAT   YIELD: 8 SERVINGS

A masterly creation of pure elegance that combines a luscious spinach and leek-filled chicken breast encased in golden puff pastry served with a velvety raspberry sauce.

Spinach Mixture

½   cup margarine
10 garlic cloves, minced
3   shallots, minced
½   cup peeled and grated carrots
½   cup diced onion
½   cup sliced mushrooms

⅓   cup finely sliced leeks
½   cup diced roasted red peppers
1   pound frozen chopped spinach, thawed, drained and squeezed dry
    Salt, pepper and onion powder to taste

1. Melt margarine in large skillet and sauté garlic and shallots until soft. Add carrots and onions and cook 5 minutes.
2. Stir in mushrooms, leeks and red peppers and cook 5 minutes more. Cool.
3. Add spinach to vegetables and season with salt, pepper and onion powder.

Chicken

8   chicken breast halves, boned and skinned
    Salt, pepper, garlic powder and onion powder to taste

8   4-inch puff pastry squares
    Flour for rolling
1   large egg, beaten with 1 tablespoon water

1. Preheat oven to 400°F. Grease cookie sheets.
2. Season chicken breasts with spices.
3. Form spinach mixture into 8 balls. Place ball in center of each chicken breast and fold chicken around spinach.

4. Roll out each pastry square to 6-inch square on lightly floured surface. Brush edges with egg wash. Place stuffed chicken breast, open-side up,

Chicken Wellington with Raspberry Sauce (continued)

on each pastry square. Fold 4 corners of pastry to center of breast, forming an oval. Turn over seam-side down.

5. Transfer to sheets and brush with egg wash. Chill until pastry is cold.

6. Bake 25 to 30 minutes until golden brown. Serve with warm Raspberry Sauce.

Raspberry Sauce

1	cup Concord grape wine	2	pounds seedless raspberry preserves

1. Boil wine in saucepan. Add preserves and cook until sauce is smooth, stirring occasionally.

For a dramatic presentation, Raspberry Sauce may be spooned underneath chicken as well as swirled around the serving platter.

Chardonnay

Mideastern Chicken

MEAT   YIELD: 6 SERVINGS

*T*his is an exciting **Shabbat** *chicken dinner. Like the Middle East region itself, it exhibits the influence of Moroccan cuisine. This variant is traditionally served with couscous but we recommend a bed of rice to absorb the delicious sweet and sour sauce.*

¼	cup olive oil	4	cups chicken broth
4	pounds chicken, cut into eighths	1	cup pitted prunes
1¾	pounds onions, chopped	½	cup dried apricot halves
6	garlic cloves, minced	⅓	cup lemon juice
2	tablespoons flour	¼	cup honey
1	tablespoon ground ginger	¾	cup Burgundy wine
1	tablespoon ground cinnamon		Salt and pepper to taste
1	tablespoon ground cumin	½	cup chopped fresh cilantro

1. Heat oil in large skillet and sauté chicken until browned. Remove.

2. Sauté onions and garlic in same skillet until soft. Add flour, ginger, cinnamon, and cumin, stirring 1 minute. Whisk in broth.

3. Add prunes, apricots, juice, honey and wine. Boil until sauce thickens, whisking occasionally. Add salt and pepper.

4. Reduce heat and return chicken to skillet. Cover and simmer until tender. Sprinkle with cilantro.

Pinot Grigio

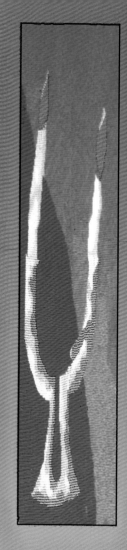

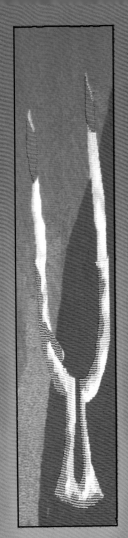

Cherry-Glazed Stuffed Chicken Breasts

MEAT   YIELD: 8 SERVINGS

*C*herry glaze parties up almost any dish. Takes a bit of preparation but the results are worth it. This chicken dish may be prepared 1 day in advance and chilled. Bring to room temperature before cooking. For a dramatic presentation, flambé cherries. Use 1½ cups drained canned cherries and ignite with 2 tablespoons liquor or liqueur and follow tips.

Stuffing

1 6-ounce package long grain and wild rice mix	½ cup slivered almonds, toasted

1. Cook rice according to package directions. Stir in almonds.

Chicken

½ cup margarine	1½ teaspoons garlic powder
8 chicken breast halves, boned and skinned	½ teaspoon salt
	½ teaspoon pepper
1½ teaspoons paprika	½ cup flour

1. Preheat oven to 350°F. Grease 9 x 13-inch pan.
2. Melt margarine in pan.
3. Place chicken breasts in plastic bag and pound to flatten. Sprinkle with paprika, garlic powder, salt and pepper.
4. Place one-eighth of rice mixture in center of each breast. Fold in sides and roll up like jelly roll, making sure filling is contained. Skewer closed with wooden toothpicks.
5. Coat breasts in flour, roll in margarine and arrange in pan. Bake covered 30 minutes. Prepare Cherry Glaze while chicken is cooking.
6. Uncover pan and baste with glaze and cook until chicken is tender. Remove toothpicks and serve.

Cherry Glaze

1 cup cherry preserves	2 teaspoons fresh orange zest
⅓ cup frozen orange juice concentrate, undiluted	

1. Combine all ingredients in saucepan and heat.

 White Zinfandel

Roasted Turkey Breast
with Mulled Cranberry Sauce

MEAT   YIELD: 6 TO 8 SERVINGS

A version of As You Like It's roasted chicken recipe created for turkey, this dish marinates overnight. Double the recipe for marinade and use for a 12 to 16-pound turkey, adjusting cooking time.

Turkey

6	pound turkey breast, bone in	1	tablespoon onion powder
1	cup olive oil	1	tablespoon paprika
¼	cup white wine or White Zinfandel	1	tablespoon pepper
2	tablespoons garlic powder	1	teaspoon salt

1. Preheat oven 375°F ten minutes before roasting. Prepare large roasting pan.

2. Place turkey breast in plastic bag. Combine all remaining ingredients and pour over turkey and rub into flesh. Chill overnight.

3. Discard marinade and move turkey to pan. Cover and roast 2 hours. Uncover and continue roasting until juices run clear when turkey is pierced or meat thermometer registers 175°F. Let rest 10 minutes before carving.

Mulled Cranberry Sauce

12	ounces fresh cranberries	1	tablespoon fresh orange zest
6¼	cups (1½ liters) Merlot wine	½	teaspoon ground cinnamon
1¼	cups brown sugar, firmly packed	½	teaspoon ground allspice
⅓	cup minced crystallized ginger	¼	teaspoon ground cloves

1. Combine all ingredients and bring to boil in saucepan, stirring until sugar dissolves. Reduce heat and simmer until thick, about 12 minutes.

 Riesling

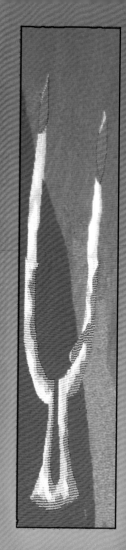

Cider-Basted Turkey with Roasted Apple Gravy

MEAT

YIELD: 10 SERVINGS

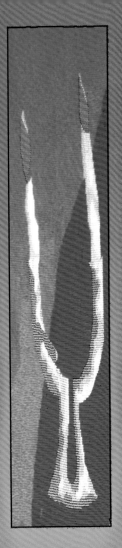

Turkey

1 cup apple cider	10 Golden Delicious apples peeled and cored, divided
¼ cup apple brandy	1 large onion, sliced
¼ cup soy sauce	6 fresh thyme sprigs
2 tablespoons apple cider vinegar	8 large sage leaves
2 teaspoons dried sage	16 pound turkey
¾ teaspoon ground cinnamon, divided	Salt and pepper to taste
	¼ cup margarine, room temperature

1. Preheat oven to 325°F. Prepare large roasting pan.

2. Combine cider, brandy, soy sauce, vinegar and dried sage in saucepan for basting liquid. Add ½ teaspoon cinnamon and bring to boil. Remove from heat.

3. Quarter 2 apples and mix with onions, fresh thyme and sage and remaining cinnamon.

4. Place turkey into pan and season cavity with salt and pepper. Spoon apple mixture into cavity. Tuck wing tips under turkey and loosely tie legs together.

5. Rub breast and legs with margarine. Pour half the basting liquid over turkey. Sprinkle with salt and pepper.

6. Roast turkey 30 minutes. Pour remaining basting liquid over turkey. Roast 2 hours, basting frequently with pan juices. Add water if juices evaporate.

7. Cut remaining apples into eighths and add to pan. Cover turkey loosely with foil to keep from browning too quickly. Continue roasting about 1½ hours until apples are tender, turkey is brown and juices run clear. Baste frequently.

8. Transfer turkey to platter, tent loosely with foil and let rest 30 minutes. Remove apples with slotted spoon and reserve.

Chardonnay

Apple Gravy

Pan juices	¼ cup apple cider
Turkey or chicken broth	2 tablespoons cornstarch
Reserved apples	Salt and pepper to taste

1. Measure pan juices and add enough broth to measure 4 cups. Simmer in saucepan 5 minutes. Add apples and simmer 2 minutes more.

2. Combine apple cider and cornstarch to form paste and whisk into pan juice mixture. Boil until gravy thickens, about 2 minutes. Season with salt and pepper.

Potato-Latke Turkey Stuffing

• Stuff turkey with Potato Latkes which have been cut into crouton-size pieces. Latkes may be prepared one day ahead.

Cornish Hens in Wine Sauce 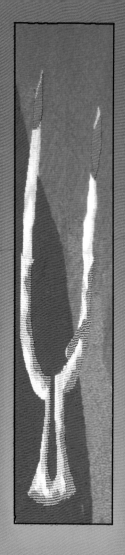 Non-G

MEAT   YIELD: 6 SERVINGS

This recipe uses two-pound Cornish game hens cut in half, but if one-pound hens are available, they may be substituted.

2 tablespoons olive oil, divided	¼ cup sweet red wine
3 Cornish game hens, 2 pounds each	1 tablespoon cornstarch (use potato starch for Passover)
Salt, pepper, garlic powder, onion powder and paprika to taste	¼ cup red wine vinegar
½ cup raspberry or apricot preserves	Salt and pepper to taste
3 tablespoons lemon juice	4 garlic cloves, minced

1. Preheat oven to 400°F. Prepare large roasting pan.
2. Rub 1 tablespoon of oil onto hens and sprinkle with seasonings. Place in pan and bake 35 minutes.
3. Heat remaining oil, preserves, juice and wine in saucepan. Dissolve cornstarch or potato starch in vinegar and whisk into pan. Add remaining ingredients and bring to boil. Reduce heat and simmer until thickened.
4. Reduce oven temperature to 350°F. Pour glaze over hens and bake 45 to 60 minutes, basting occasionally until tender. Split 2-pound hens in half for serving.

Blanc de Noir

Microwave Chicken Oriental

MEAT   YIELD: 4 SERVINGS

4 chicken breast halves, boned, skinned and cut into strips	2 tablespoons vegetable oil
1 tablespoon corn starch	¼ cup soy sauce
2 tablespoons brown sugar, firmly packed	¾ cup white wine
¼ teaspoon dried oregano	½ green pepper, thinly sliced
1 garlic clove, minced	½ red pepper, thinly sliced
	½ pound mushrooms, thinly sliced

1. Prepare 2 quart microwavable container.
2. Place chicken into container.
3. Mix remaining ingredients and pour over chicken.
4. Cover and microwave on high 11 to 13 minutes or until fully cooked.

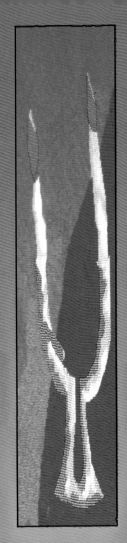

Signature Roasted Chicken Non-G

MEAT   YIELD: 6 SERVINGS

The white wine and olive oil marinade keeps the chicken pieces succulent and allows the aromatic seasoning to infuse each piece during cooking. Brown this surprisingly easy As You Like It signature dish to a golden hue for a fabulous caramelized flavor. Our most popular chicken dish for Shabbat dinner. Chicken marinates overnight.

½	cup olive oil	½	teaspoon pepper
2	tablespoons white wine	1	teaspoon salt to taste
2½	teaspoons garlic powder	2	teaspoons paprika
2	teaspoons onion powder	3½	pounds chicken, cut into eighths

1. Preheat oven to 375°F ten minutes before roasting. Prepare ungreased rimmed cookie sheet.
2. Whisk oil, wine and seasonings for marinade. Coat chicken, cover and chill overnight.
3. Discard marinade and arrange chicken on sheet and allow to come to room temperature. Roast 50 to 60 minutes, or until chicken is tender.

Sauvignon Blanc

Dijon-Tarragon Grilled Chicken

MEAT   YIELD: 6 SERVINGS

This marinade may be used to prepare chicken and beef kebabs as well as Portobello mushrooms. Just thread marinated items on skewers along with onions, peppers, mushrooms, corn on the cob quarters and tomatoes.

⅓	cup chopped fresh tarragon	1	tablespoon honey
¼	cup Dijon mustard	6	chicken breast halves, boned and skinned
¼	cup white wine		
1	tablespoon olive oil		

1. Preheat grill 10 minutes before cooking.
2. Combine all ingredients except chicken for marinade.
3. Place chicken in marinade and chill 2 hours.
4. Remove chicken and discard marinade. Grill until tender, about 15 to 20 minutes.

Sauvignon Blanc

Chicken with Lemon and Figs  Non-G

MEAT   YIELD: 8 SERVINGS

Lemon and vinegar sharpen this dish as their tartness mingles with the delicately sweet juice released by the roasting figs. Using the biblical fruit of the fig tree makes this another creative Shabbat chicken dinner.

3 tablespoons lemon juice	1 lemon, thinly sliced
¼ cup brown sugar, firmly packed	5½ pounds chicken, cut into eighths
¼ cup red wine vinegar	Salt and pepper to taste
¼ cup water	3 tablespoons chopped fresh
12 ounces dried figs, cut in half	parsley, divided

1. Preheat oven to 400°F. Grease large roasting pan.
2. Combine juice, sugar, vinegar and water.
3. Place figs and lemon slices in roasting pan and top with chicken pieces. Pour vinegar mixture over chicken and sprinkle with salt, pepper and 2 tablespoons parsley.
4. Bake 50 minutes or until chicken is tender, basting frequently. Turn figs if they begin to brown. Place chicken, figs and lemon slices on serving plate, top with sauce and garnish with remaining parsley.

Chardonnay

Chicken Chili

MEAT   YIELD: 4 SERVINGS

Gives new life to leftover soup chicken as well as leftover turkey.

1½ tablespoons olive oil	1 15-ounce can kidney beans,
⅓ cup chopped onions	rinsed and drained
3 garlic cloves, minced	1 tablespoon chili powder
½ cup tomato paste	½ teaspoon salt
1 cup water	½ teaspoon pepper
1 pound cooked soup chicken, shredded	⅛ teaspoon cayenne pepper to taste

1. Heat oil in extra large skillet and sauté onions and garlic until soft.
2. Mix tomato paste with water until smooth.
3. Add tomato mixture, chicken, beans and seasonings to skillet. Cover and simmer 1 hour.

White Zinfandel

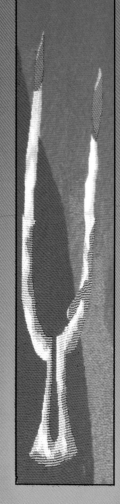

What to do with Leftover Soup Chicken

• Prepare Chicken Chili.

• Prepare chicken salad, adding curry powder to taste, nuts and Granny Smith apples.

• Add shredded chicken to blintz-potato filling.

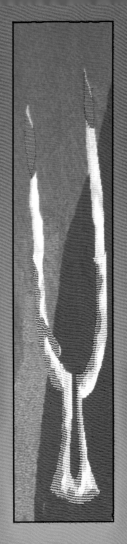

Grilled Chicken Breasts with Fresh Tomato Salsa Non-G

MEAT   YIELD: 4 SERVINGS

Vary this dish by substituting any salsa in this collection.

Fresh Tomato Salsa

YIELD: ABOUT 2 CUPS

4 ripe tomatoes, coarsely chopped	2 tablespoons minced cilantro
1 onion, coarsely chopped	2 tablespoons minced parsley
2 garlic cloves, minced	1 tablespoon olive oil
1 small chili pepper, finely chopped, optional	1 lime, juiced
	Salt and pepper to taste

1. Combine all ingredients and chill 2 hours.

Grilled Chicken Breasts

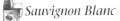

¼ cup olive oil	3 garlic cloves, minced
1 teaspoon dried oregano	4 chicken breast halves, boned and skinned
½ teaspoon pepper	
1 teaspoon ground cumin	

1. Preheat grill 10 minutes before cooking.
2. Combine all ingredients except chicken. Marinate chicken in mixture and chill 2 hours.
3. Discard marinade and grill chicken until tender. Top each breast with Fresh Tomato Salsa.

Sauvignon Blanc

Marsala Sauce

MEAT   YIELD: 6 SERVINGS

Top prepared chicken or veal with this mushroom-wine sauce for a quick International meal.

½ pound mushrooms, sliced	2 tablespoons Marsala wine
2 tablespoons olive oil	1 teaspoon lemon juice
½ cup chopped onions	½ cup beef or chicken broth
2 garlic cloves, minced	1 tablespoon flour
½ teaspoon dried thyme	Salt and pepper to taste
1 teaspoon dried tarragon	

Marsala Sauce (continued)

1. Sauté mushrooms with oil in large skillet, 3 minutes. Add onions and garlic and sauté until soft.
2. Whisk in thyme, tarragon, wine, juice, broth and flour. Simmer until sauce is smooth. Add salt and pepper.
3. Add chicken or veal and simmer until heated through.

Roast Asian Duck with Cherry Sauce

MEAT   YIELD: 4 SERVINGS

This duck preparation requires marinating the duck two days before cooking.

Roast Duck

1 cup soy sauce	4 garlic cloves, minced
2 tablespoons Sherry wine	1 tablespoon sesame oil
2 tablespoons brown sugar, firmly packed	1 teaspoon five-spice powder
	Cayenne pepper to taste
2 tablespoons honey	5 pound duck
2 tablespoons hoisin sauce	

1. Preheat oven to 400°F ten minutes before roasting. Prepare roasting pan with rack.
2. Combine all ingredients except duck to make marinade. Place duck and marinade in large plastic bag and turn to coat. Chill 2 days, turning occasionally.
3. Remove duck and discard marinade. Pat dry with paper towels. Arrange duck, breast side up, on rack in pan.
4. Roast 45 minutes. Turn duck over and roast until tender and dark brown, about 15 minutes more.
5. Tilt duck allowing juices to drain out of cavity. Transfer to platter and let rest 15 minutes before carving. Serve warm Cherry Sauce on side or pour over duck.

Cherry Sauce

¾ cup red wine	¾ cup beef broth
1½ cups cherries, canned or jarred, drained	2 teaspoons flour

1. Heat wine, cherries and broth in saucepan. Bring to boil and simmer 10 minutes to reduce by half.
2. Add enough water to flour to make thick paste. Add paste to sauce, stirring constantly until thickened.

Merlot

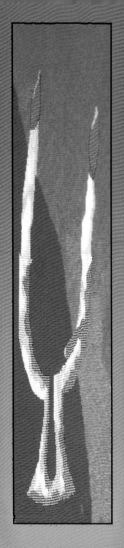

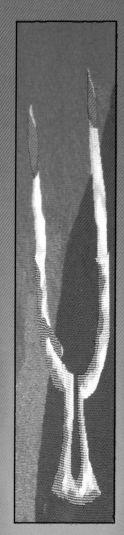

Canton Duck

MEAT   YIELD: 4 SERVINGS

*C*hinese cuisine, like French, makes creative use of the delicately adaptable taste of fresh oranges. In this recipe, orange liqueur intensifies the orange flavor without overwhelming the distinctive taste of duck.

Orange Glaze

7	ounces beef broth	1	tablespoon orange liqueur
1½	tablespoons margarine, melted	½	cup sugar
1	tablespoon Sherry wine	1	cup water
1½	tablespoons flour	10	ounces currant jelly
1	teaspoon Worcestershire sauce	1	large whole orange, pulverized

1. Combine broth, margarine, Sherry, flour, Worcestershire and liqueur in bowl.
2. Boil sugar with water in saucepan, stirring until sugar dissolves. Add jelly and orange. Stir in broth mixture, reduce heat and simmer, 10 minutes.

Pulverize the unpeeled orange by cutting into quarters, removing seeds and processing.

Duck

5	pound duck, halved	Salt and pepper to taste

1. Preheat oven to 375°F. Prepare large pan fitted with wire rack.
2. Place duck on rack, skin side up. Season with salt and pepper. Roast 1 hour and pour off fat.
3. Increase oven temperature to 400°F. Continue to roast until tender and skin is crisp, piercing skin occasionally to release fat. Quarter duck and pour off fat. Return to pan.
4. Reduce oven temperature to 350°F. Pour Orange Glaze over duck and roast. Baste occasionally until glazed, about 10 minutes.

Merlot

Fish

Marinated Grilled Salmon

Ginger Baked Halibut

DAIRY OR PAREVE   YIELD: 6 SERVINGS

An exotic melange of sweet and sour flavors spiced with garlic and ginger and cooled with peaches and pineapple.

Ginger Sauce

4	garlic cloves, minced	8	ounces Sherry wine
¼	cup peeled, chopped fresh gingerroot	2	bunches green onions, julienned
		½	cup apple cider vinegar
1½	tablespoons brown sugar, firmly packed	2	tablespoons chopped fresh sage

1. Combine all ingredients and simmer in saucepan 1 hour.

Halibut

2½	pounds halibut Flour for dredging	1	15-ounce can peach halves in juice
¼	cup butter for dairy (use olive oil for pareve)	½	fresh pineapple, chopped
		2	sliced green onions for garnish

1. Preheat oven to 400°F. Grease 9 x 13-inch pan.
2. Dredge fish in flour.
3. Melt butter or oil in large skillet and pan-sear fish until golden.
4. Place fish in baking pan, add fruit and cover with Ginger Sauce. Bake 20 minutes. Garnish.

 *Gewürztraminer*

To Coat or Not to Coat

• Thick pieces of fish do not require a coating. The outside browns nicely and develops a savory crust before the inside overcooks.

• Thin fish fillets brown better and stay moist when coated.

Salmon with Maple Syrup and Toasted Almonds

PAREVE   YIELD: 4 SERVINGS

This sweet and nutty dish, sparked with pungent Dijon mustard, is deceptively simple to prepare. If you prefer fish less sweet, use less sugar.

¼	cup brown sugar, firmly packed	¼	teaspoon pepper
¼	cup maple syrup	4	6-ounce salmon fillets
3	tablespoons Dijon mustard	¼	cup sliced almonds, toasted

1. Preheat oven to 425°F. Grease 9 x 13-inch baking pan.
2. Combine sugar, maple syrup, mustard and pepper.
3. Lay fillets in pan and top with sugar mixture. Cover pan and bake 10 minutes. Uncover, sprinkle with toasted almonds and bake 10 minutes more.

 Soave

Salmon en Croûte

PAREVE OR DAIRY   YIELD: 4 SERVINGS

1½	pounds skinless salmon fillets	5	ounces frozen chopped spinach, thawed and drained
2	puff pastry sheets		
	Flour for rolling	4	ounces Nova smoked salmon, minced
¼	teaspoon salt		
¼	teaspoon pepper	1	large egg, beaten with 1 tablespoon water for egg wash
6	ounces pareve garlic herb cream cheese, softened (use herb cream cheese for dairy)		

1. Heat oven to 400°F ten minutes before baking. Grease cookie sheet or cover with parchment paper.
2. Cut salmon into 4 equal portions. Cut each pastry sheet into 4 equal squares.
3. Roll each piece of pastry on lightly floured surface into 6-inch square. Place salmon in middle of pastry and sprinkle with salt and pepper.
4. Mix cheese with spinach and Nova. Divide into 4 portions and place in center of each fillet.
5. Brush edges of pastry with egg wash, cover with second pastry square and press to seal edges. Brush tops with egg wash. Chill 1 hour.
6. Bake 30 minutes or until golden.

 Soave

Sesame Salmon with Spinach-Watercress Sauce

DAIRY   YIELD: 6 SERVINGS

Salmon crowned with a creamy sesame-coated crust makes for a regal presentation.

Spinach-Watercress Sauce

1 cup white wine	½ cup trimmed and packed watercress
2 shallots, chopped	
1 cup heavy cream	1 tablespoon chopped fresh dill
½ cup packed baby spinach	¼ cup butter
	Salt and pepper to taste

1. Bring wine and shallots to boil in saucepan and reduce to ¼ cup, about 7 minutes.
2. Reduce heat and add cream. Simmer until reduced to ¾ cup, about 10 minutes.
3. Purée cream mixture with spinach, watercress and dill. Add butter and purée until melted and smooth. Add salt and pepper and keep warm.

Sesame Salmon

6 6-ounce skinless salmon fillets	¼ cup vegetable oil
Salt and pepper to taste	Dill sprigs for garnish
½ cup sesame seeds	

1. Sprinkle salmon with salt and pepper and coat with sesame seeds.
2. Heat oil in large skillet and sauté salmon until opaque in center, about 3 minutes each side.
3. Spoon Spinach-Watercress Sauce onto plates, top with salmon and garnish.

Chardonnay

Savory Salmon Quiche

DAIRY   YIELD: 4 TO 6 SERVINGS

9-inch deep-dish pie crust,
   unbaked
1   cup shredded Swiss cheese
¼   cup chopped sun-dried tomatoes
2   green onions, thinly sliced
½   cup broccoli florets

4   ounces Nova smoked salmon,
   chopped
3   large eggs
1   cup heavy cream
½   cup milk
½   teaspoon salt to taste
1   teaspoon pepper

1. Preheat oven to 425°F. Prepare ungreased cookie sheet.
2. Bake pie shell 10 minutes and cool 5 minutes. Sprinkle cheese over crust.
3. Top with tomatoes, onions, broccoli and Nova. Place pie pan on cookie sheet.
4. Whisk eggs, cream, milk, salt and pepper until blended. Pour over vegetable mixture.
5. Bake in center of oven 30 to 40 minutes or until filling is golden and puffed and tester inserted in center comes out clean.

Cucumber Dill Sauce

DAIRY OR PAREVE   YIELD: 2 CUPS

Pairs deliciously with salmon as a topping or served on the side.

1   cucumber, peeled and seeded
1   cup sour cream for dairy (use nondairy sour cream for pareve)
1   tablespoon minced onion

½   teaspoon Worcestershire sauce
1   tablespoon chopped fresh dill
¼   teaspoon salt

1. Grate cucumber and drain in colander. Squeeze out excess liquid.
2. Add remaining ingredients and mix well.

Salmon with Mustard-Chive Butter

DAIRY   YIELD: 8 SERVINGS

The lemony mustard-chive butter that coats the salmon during baking adds just the right piquancy to this dish.

Mustard-Chive Butter

½ cup butter, room temperature	1 teaspoon fresh lemon zest
1½ tablespoons lemon juice, divided	½ teaspoon salt
2 tablespoons snipped chives	⅛ teaspoon pepper
1 tablespoon Dijon mustard	

1. Combine all ingredients. Shape into small roll, cover with plastic wrap and chill. Cut into 11 equal portions.

Fish

8 6-ounce salmon fillets	Salt and pepper to taste
3 tablespoons lemon juice	2 tablespoons snipped chives

1. Preheat oven to 450°F. Line cookie sheet with foil and rub 3 portions mustard-chive butter over foil.

2. Place fillets, skin side down, on foil and drizzle with juice. Season with salt and pepper and top each filet with 1 portion mustard-chive butter.

3. Bake until fish is cooked to desired degree of doneness, 10 to 12 minutes. Garnish with chives.

Sauvignon Blanc

Spicy Salmon Rub

PAREVE

4 teaspoons paprika

2 teaspoons salt

1 teaspoon ground ginger

1 teaspoon ground cinnamon

½ teaspoon cayenne pepper

½ teaspoon ground allspice

1. Combine all ingredients and rub fish lightly with mixture.

2. Cook as desired.

Basil Marinated Scrod

PAREVE   YIELD: 6 SERVINGS

¼ cup olive oil	¾ cup packed fresh basil leaves, chopped
1½ teaspoons Dijon mustard	
1½ teaspoons lemon juice	2 pounds scrod
2 garlic cloves, minced	Lemon wedges and basil leaves for garnish

1. Preheat broiler or grill 10 minutes before cooking.

2. Combine all ingredients except fish for marinade. Pour over fish and marinate 30 minutes.

3. Discard marinade and broil or grill scrod. Garnish.

Marinated Grilled Salmon   Non-G

PAREVE   YIELD: 4 SERVINGS

The judicious use of full-flavored and scented herbs in the marinade makes this grilled salmon dish a delicious, easy-to-fix meal.

½	cup extra virgin olive oil	½	teaspoon pepper
1½	teaspoons dried rosemary	1½	teaspoons lemon juice
1½	teaspoons dried basil	6	garlic cloves, minced
1½	teaspoons dried oregano	4	6-ounce skinless salmon fillets

1. Preheat grill, broiler or oven to 375°F ten minutes before cooking. Prepare ungreased 9 x 13-inch pan.

2. Combine oil, herbs, pepper, juice and garlic for marinade. Place salmon in pan and marinate 20 minutes.

3. Discard marinade and cook fish until desired degree of doneness.

 Pinot Grigio

Grilled Tuna Schwarma Kebabs

PAREVE   YIELD: 8 SERVINGS

The aromatic flavors that infuse the schwarma marinade add a distinct Mideastern tang to this dish. Serve at room temperature or hot off the grill.

¼	teaspoon pepper	2½	tablespoons lemon juice
¼	teaspoon ground cinnamon	2	tablespoons olive oil
¼	teaspoon cayenne pepper	2	pounds tuna fillets, cut into 1-inch cubes
¼	tablespoon salt	8	12-inch skewers
¼	teaspoon ground allspice	2	large onions, cut into 1-inch pieces
¼	teaspoon ground cloves	2	red peppers, cut into 1-inch pieces
1	teaspoon ground cardamom		

1. Preheat grill or broiler 10 minutes before cooking.
2. Combine spices, juice and olive oil. Add tuna, cover and chill 1 hour.
3. Soak skewers in water 10 minutes.
4. Discard marinade and skewer tuna, onions and peppers, alternately.
5. Grill kebabs uncovered until tuna is desired degree of doneness, turning once.

Pinot Noir

Give Fish a Flavor Boost

• Allow fish to marinate 30 to 45 minutes to boost flavor.

Sea Bass with Roasted Tomatoes and Green Beans

PAREVE   YIELD: 4 SERVINGS

Roasting on a bed of vegetables spiced with fresh ginger and curry powder gives this dish a distinctive flavor.

1½ pounds plum tomatoes, cut into 8 wedges
1   large onion, cut into 8 wedges
2   garlic cloves, minced
1   tablespoon extra virgin olive oil
     Salt and pepper to taste

8   ounces green beans, trimmed and cut diagonally into 2-inch pieces
2   teaspoons curry powder
2   teaspoons peeled, minced fresh gingerroot
4   6-ounce sea bass fillets, about 1½ inches thick

1. Preheat oven to 400°F. Grease rimmed cookie sheet and 9 x 13-inch pan.
2. Combine tomatoes, onions and garlic, toss with oil and place on sheet. Sprinkle with salt and pepper.
3. Roast in oven until onions begin to brown, about 35 minutes, stirring occasionally. Remove pan from oven and increase temperature to 450°F.
4. Add beans, curry powder and ginger to tomato mixture and place half in pan.
5. Top with fish and remaining tomato mixture. Bake until opaque in center, about 18 to 20 minutes.

Beaujolais

Marinated Mahi-Mahi

PAREVE   YIELD: 4 SERVINGS

⅓ cup olive oil
⅓ cup balsamic vinegar (use K-P balsamic vinegar for Passover)
1 teaspoon salt
½ teaspoon pepper
¼ teaspoon dried thyme

2 garlic cloves, minced
4 6-ounce mahi-mahi fillets
1 red pepper, thinly sliced
1 yellow pepper, thinly sliced
1 green pepper, thinly sliced

1. Preheat grill 10 minutes before cooking.
2. Combine oil, vinegar, salt, pepper, thyme and garlic.
3. Pour mixture over fish and peppers and marinate 30 minutes at room temperature.
4. Discard marinade and grill until peppers are tender and fish is opaque.

Chardonnay

Seared Tuna with Wasabi Sauce

PAREVE   YIELD: 4 SERVINGS

The Wasabi Sauce pungently flavors this versatile dish with a rich medley of Asian spices. Cut tuna into thin slices and serve with sauce over a bed of julienned cucumbers and radishes. Use for a main course or as an appetizer.

Wasabi Sauce

½ cup water	1½ teaspoons sesame oil
3½ tablespoons wasabi powder or to taste	1 tablespoon Sherry wine
⅓ cup soy sauce	1½ teaspoons minced fresh gingerroot
2 tablespoons vegetable oil	4 green onions, thinly sliced

1. Whisk together water and wasabi powder to form smooth paste.
2. Mix in soy sauce, oils, sherry and ginger. Stir in onions.

Marinade

3 garlic cloves, minced	2 tablespoons vegetable oil
3 tablespoons sesame oil	2 fresh limes, juiced

1. Combine all ingredients.

Tuna

1½ pounds Ahi tuna steaks, 1-inch thick	2 cucumbers, peeled, seeded and julienned
1 tablespoon vegetable oil	½ cup julienned daikon radish

1. Marinate tuna for 20 minutes.
2. Discard marinade and sear tuna in hot oil in large skillet, 3 minutes per side. Cut into ¼-inch slices.
3. Place cucumber on serving plate, top with tuna slices, drizzle with Wasabi Sauce and top with radish.

Tuna should be served rare and may be grilled.

Gewürztraminer

Asian Style Tilapia

PAREVE   YIELD: 4 SERVINGS

Sautéing the sesame-coated filets seals in their delicate flavor, making them receptive to the gingery-garlic sauce and sautéed mushrooms that complement this dish.

Sauce

⅓ cup soy sauce	6 garlic cloves, minced
2 tablespoons Sherry wine	2 tablespoons wine vinegar
1½ teaspoons minced fresh gingerroot	1 teaspoon sugar
	Pepper to taste

1. Combine all ingredients in saucepan and simmer 5 minutes.

Adjust soy sauce to taste. If using less, dilute with water to equal ⅓ cup liquid.

Mushrooms

1 tablespoon vegetable oil	1 cup sliced mushrooms
1 tablespoon sesame oil	2 garlic cloves, minced

1. Heat oils in medium skillet and sauté mushrooms and garlic.

Use a nonstick skillet and reduce amount of oil for sautéing.

Fish

¾ cup unflavored breadcrumbs	2 large eggs, slightly beaten
2 tablespoons sesame seeds	3 tablespoons vegetable oil
1½ pounds tilapia fillets	1 tablespoon sesame oil
¾ cup cornstarch	4 garlic cloves, minced

1. Mix breadcrumbs with sesame seeds. Dip fish in cornstarch, then egg and breadcrumb mixture. Chill 30 minutes.

2. Heat oils with garlic in large skillet and sauté filets until crispy on both sides.

3. Serve mushrooms over fish with sauce on side.

Riesling

Sole Roll-Ups

DAIRY   YIELD: 6 TO 8 SERVINGS

This fish dish may be prepared for Passover by substituting matzoh farfel for stuffing mix. Flounder substitutes well for sole.

⅓   cup butter
⅓   cup lemon juice
     Salt and pepper to taste
½   teaspoon dried basil
1   tablespoon chopped fresh parsley
2   garlic cloves, minced
1   tablespoon butter for sautéing

½   cup chopped onions
1½ cups dry stuffing mix (use
     matzoh farfel for Passover)
10 ounces frozen chopped broccoli,
     thawed and drained
2   cups shredded Cheddar cheese,
     divided
8   sole fillets

1. Preheat oven to 375°F. Grease 9 x 13-inch square baking pan.

2. Melt ⅓ cup butter in saucepan and add juice, salt, pepper, basil, parsley and garlic.

3. Heat 1 tablespoon butter in small skillet and sauté onions until soft.

4. Moisten stuffing or matzoh farfel with hot water until soft and squeeze out excess liquid. Combine with broccoli, onions, half the cheese and half the butter-lemon mixture.

5. Top fillets with equal portions of stuffing mixture. Roll up and place seam side down in pan. Pour remaining butter-lemon mixture over fish and sprinkle with remaining cheese. Bake 25 minutes.

Crumb-Topped Baked Fish

DAIRY   YIELD: 4 TO 6 SERVINGS

1½ *pounds fish filets*   ½   *teaspoon pepper*
3   *tablespoons mayonnaise to taste*   ½   *cup butter, melted*
1¼ *cups crushed buttery crackers*   *Paprika*

1. Preheat oven to 400°F. Grease 9 x 13-inch pan.
2. Place fish fillets in single layer in pan and spread with mayonnaise.
3. Combine cracker crumbs with pepper and butter.
4. Sprinkle crumb mixture over fish and sprinkle with paprika.
5. Bake 10 to 15 minutes until crumbs are brown and fish flakes easily.

Hoisin Barbecue Sauce

PAREVE   YIELD: ½ CUP

Hoisin *Barbecue Sauce is delicious with salmon and chicken. Why not try it on hamburgers or steak too? It keeps forever in the refrigerator, so mix up a batch and have it ready for the grill.*

5   *tablespoons honey*   ¼   *teaspoon bottled liquid smoke,*
¼   *cup hoisin sauce*   *optional*
2   *tablespoons ketchup*   ½   *teaspoon pepper to taste*
3   *garlic cloves, minced*   ½   *teaspoon onion powder*
1   *tablespoon minced fresh gingerroot*   *Cayenne pepper to taste*
¼   *teaspoon hot pepper sauce*

1. Combine all ingredients.
2. Store in refrigerator but bring to room temperature before using.

How to Keep Fish Fresh

• Enclose freshly purchased fish in plastic bag. Place that bag into another plastic bag and immerse in bowl of ice cubes in the coldest part of the refrigerator. Replenish the ice cubes as they melt. Prepare fish within 2 days.

Vegetarian

Baked Eggplant Stack

Feta-Spinach French Bread Pizza

DAIRY   YIELD: 6 LARGE OR 24 APPETIZER SLICES

Cut into smaller portions, this recipe for feta, spinach and tomato French bread pizza doubles well as a hot appetizer.

10	ounces frozen chopped spinach, thawed and drained	½	cup crumbled feta cheese
1	plum tomato, chopped	¼	cup mayonnaise
¼	cup chopped onion	¼	cup sour cream
3	garlic cloves, minced	½	teaspoon dried dill
		1	French bread

1. Preheat oven to 375°F. Grease cookie sheet.
2. Combine spinach, tomato and onions. Add remaining ingredients.
3. Slice bread in half lengthwise and place on sheet. Spread with spinach mixture and bake 10 to 12 minutes or until topping is melted.

Tamale Pie

DAIRY   YIELD: 6 SERVINGS

¼	cup butter, divided	1	cup cornmeal
½	cup chopped onions	2	tablespoons sugar
⅓	cup chopped green pepper	½	teaspoon salt
20	ounces canned red kidney beans, rinsed and drained	½	teaspoon pepper
8	ounces canned tomato sauce	1	large egg, slightly beaten
1	tablespoon chili powder, divided	½	cup milk
½	teaspoon dried oregano	2	tablespoons butter, melted
½	teaspoon ground cumin	10	ounces corn
		¾	cup shredded Cheddar cheese

1. Preheat oven to 350°F. Grease 9-inch pie pan.
2. Heat butter in large skillet and sauté onions and peppers until soft, 10 minutes. Remove from heat and stir in beans, sauce, 2 teaspoons chili powder, oregano and cumin.
3. Combine cornmeal, sugar, salt and pepper. Stir in egg, milk, butter and corn for crust. Press into pie pan.
4. Spoon bean mixture over crust. Bake 20 minutes.
5. Mix cheese with remaining chili powder and sprinkle over filling. Bake until cheese melts. Let rest 5 minutes before cutting.

Indonesian Tofu

PAREVE   YIELD: 4 SERVINGS

*O*ur Indonesian Chicken recipe was such a hit at a taste-test, we created this vegetarian version. If time permits, press tofu for several hours to enhance marinade absorption and flavor.

1 14-ounce package firm tofu, pressed and cut into 1-inch squares	3 garlic cloves, minced
⅓ cup teriyaki sauce	½ teaspoon ground cumin
½ teaspoon pepper	½ teaspoon ground coriander
½ cup flour	1 tablespoon peeled, thinly sliced fresh gingerroot
¼ cup olive oil, divided	1 tablespoon fresh orange zest
1 red pepper, cut into strips	½ cup coconut milk
1 yellow pepper, cut into strips	½ teaspoon minced chili pepper
1 bunch green onions, cut into 2-inch pieces	¼ teaspoon cayenne pepper
1½ tablespoons finely chopped shallots	¼ cup soy sauce
	¼ cup ketchup

1. Marinate tofu in teriyaki sauce 1 hour, tossing occasionally. Remove from sauce with slotted spoon, reserving sauce. Mix pepper with flour and coat tofu.

2. Heat 2 tablespoons oil in large skillet and sauté peppers, onions and shallots until soft. Add garlic and sauté 1 minute more. Remove from pan with slotted spoon and set aside.

3. Heat remaining oil in same skillet and sauté tofu until browned on all sides. Remove and add to pepper mixture.

4. Add remaining ingredients to skillet, stirring continuously 2 minutes.

5. Add tofu-pepper mixture and reserved sauce to skillet and cook 5 minutes.

How to Press Tofu
Pressing the tofu blocks with heavy weights extracts moisture and enables the marinade to be readily absorbed, improving flavor.

1. Cut tofu block horizontally into two equal pieces.

2. Place halves side-by-side on board and cover with second board. Weight top down with heavy cans. Let rest several hours.

Coconut Milk
PAREVE

8 ounces unsweetened coconut
1½ cups boiling water

1. Blend coconut and boiling water 30 seconds. Cool mixture 15 minutes.

2. Put cheese cloth-lined sieve over bowl and ladle coconut mixture into cloth. Gather ends of cloth together and squeeze to extract milk.

3. Discard coconut. Chill milk and use within 2 days.

Wild Mushroom Tart

DAIRY   YIELD: 8 SERVINGS

*R*ustic wild mushroom flavor. Making this recipe is time consuming, so prepare filling while dough is chilling.

Pastry

1½ cups flour
½   teaspoon salt
½   cup butter, cut into small pieces

3   tablespoons ice water
    Flour for rolling

1. Preheat oven to 375°F. Grease 9-inch tart pan with removable bottom.
2. Combine flour, salt and butter in processor and add water until dough forms ball. Cover with plastic wrap and chill 1 hour.
3. Roll dough on lightly floured surface and fit into tart pan. Freeze 10 minutes.
4. Cover with foil or parchment paper and fill with pie weights. Bake 20 minutes. Remove weights and foil or parchment paper and cool.

Wild Mushroom Filling

4   sun-dried tomatoes, chopped
2   tablespoons balsamic vinegar, warmed
3   tablespoons olive oil
2   garlic cloves, minced
4   green onions, finely sliced
½   pound fresh shiitake mushrooms, stems removed and sliced

½   pound fresh cremini mushrooms, sliced
¼   cup porcini mushrooms, sliced
    Salt and pepper
¼   cup packed fresh parsley, chopped
3   large eggs, beaten
¾   cup heavy cream
½   cup shredded mozzarella cheese
½   cup grated Parmesan cheese

1. Steep sun-dried tomatoes in vinegar.
2. Heat oil in large skillet and sauté garlic, onions and mushrooms until soft.
3. Add salt and pepper and simmer uncovered 15 minutes. Remove from heat and stir in tomato-vinegar mixture and parsley.
4. Whisk eggs with cream and add cheeses. Fold into mushroom mixture and pour into tart shell. Bake 30 minutes or until set. Cool 5 minutes before cutting.

 Rosé

Spinach-Potato Pie

DAIRY OR PAREVE

*This dish goes well along side salmon, or serve as a vegetarian main dish accompanied by a large salad. For **pareve**, double the amount of dill, oregano and salt to replace flavor of omitted cheeses.*

2½ potatoes, peeled

⅓ cup melted butter for dairy, divided (use olive oil for pareve)

½ cup milk for dairy (use nondairy milk for pareve)

Salt and pepper to taste

2 large eggs, slightly beaten

1 cup grated Parmesan cheese for dairy, divided

7 garlic cloves, minced

6 green onions, thinly sliced

2 pounds frozen chopped spinach, thawed and drained

2½ teaspoons dried dill

2½ teaspoons dried oregano

½ teaspoon ground nutmeg

6 ounces feta cheese for dairy, crumbled

1. Preheat oven to 400°F. Grease 9 x 13-inch pan.

2. Cook potatoes until soft. Drain, cool and mash.

3. Beat in 3 tablespoons butter or oil, milk or nondairy milk, salt, pepper, eggs and 6 tablespoons Parmesan cheese.

4. Heat 1 tablespoon butter or oil in large skillet and sauté garlic and onions. Add spinach, reduce heat and cook covered 3 minutes.

5. Remove from heat and add dill, oregano and nutmeg. Mix in feta cheese.

6. Add 1 tablespoon butter or oil to baking pan and spoon half the potato mixture into bottom, pressing down. Layer spinach mixture and top with remaining potato mixture. Sprinkle with remaining Parmesan cheese and drizzle with remaining butter or oil.

7. Bake 50 minutes or until top is lightly browned.

Vegetable Quiches

DAIRY   YIELD: 10 SERVINGS

We present seven quiche variations for your enjoyment. Try them all! A store-bought pie crust may be used.

Basic Quiche

9-inch pie crust, unbaked	2 large eggs, beaten
1 large egg white, beaten	1 cup heavy cream or half-and-half
2 teaspoons olive oil	¼ teaspoon salt
1 small onion, finely chopped	⅛ teaspoon cayenne pepper
1 green onion, finely sliced	⅛ teaspoon ground nutmeg
2 garlic cloves, minced	1 teaspoon dried dill
1 cup shredded Swiss or Cheddar cheese	1 teaspoon chopped fresh parsley

1. Preheat oven to 425°F.
2. Brush pie shell with egg white, prick with fork and bake 5 minutes. Cool.
3. Heat oil in small skillet and sauté onions and garlic until soft. Cool slightly and add cheese. Sprinkle over crust.
4. Mix remaining ingredients and pour over vegetables.
5. Bake 10 minutes and reduce oven temperature to 325°F. Bake 20 minutes more until filling is set and golden.

Variations to Basic Quiche
Choose one of these vegetable options and add to onion mixture in step 3.

- 4 ounces chopped and drained frozen spinach
- 8 ounces sliced mushrooms, sautéed in 1 tablespoon olive oil
- 8 ounces asparagus, blanched and coarsely chopped
- 4 ounces broccoli, coarsely chopped
- 4 ounces artichoke hearts, packed in water, drained and coarsely chopped
- ⅓ cup finely chopped red pepper, sautéed in 2 teaspoons olive oil

Vegetarian Chili

PAREVE OR DAIRY

YIELD: 6 TO 8 SERVINGS

1   tablespoon olive oil
1   large onion, cut into 1-inch chunks
1   green pepper, cut into 1-inch chunks
1   red pepper, cut into 1-inch chunks
1   28-ounce can tomatoes,
       undrained and chopped
1   15-ounce can dark red kidney
       beans
1   15-ounce can light red kidney
       beans
1   15-ounce can black beans
1   15-ounce can chickpeas
1   cup corn

1   teaspoon pepper to taste
1½ teaspoons salt to taste
¼   cup sugar
⅛   teaspoon cayenne pepper
1   tablespoon chili powder
½   teaspoon ground coriander
1   tablespoon chopped fresh parsley
½   teaspoon dried oregano
½   teaspoon dried basil
1½ cups vegetable broth
½   cup grated Parmesan cheese for
       dairy
    Tortilla chips

1. Heat oil in soup pot and sauté onions and peppers until soft.

2. Rinse and drain beans and chickpeas. Add to pot.

3. Stir in remaining ingredients, reduce heat and simmer 1 hour. Serve with tortilla chips. For dairy, sprinkle with cheese.

Tofu Chili

PAREVE OR DAIRY

YIELD: 4 SERVINGS

A nonstick pan works best when browning the tofu.

¼   cup vegetable oil
1   pound firm tofu, drained and
       mashed
1   large onion, chopped
8   ounces sliced mushrooms
3   garlic cloves, minced
1   15-ounce can kidney beans,
       rinsed and drained
2   cups corn

2   teaspoons chili powder
1   teaspoon ground cumin
    Salt, pepper and hot pepper
     sauce to taste
2   cups tomato sauce
¼   cup shredded Cheddar cheese for
       dairy
    Tortilla chips

1. Heat oil in soup pot and brown tofu. Add onions and mushrooms and sauté until onions are soft. Add garlic and sauté 2 minutes more.

2. Stir in remaining ingredients. Bring to boil, reduce heat and simmer 10 minutes.

3. Top with cheese and serve with tortilla chips.

Tofu in Tomato-Sauerkraut Sauce with Mushrooms

PAREVE   YIELD: 4 SERVINGS

1	14-ounce package firm tofu
½	pound mushrooms, sliced
	Vegetable oil for frying
1	egg, slightly beaten
¼	cup flour seasoned with salt, pepper, garlic powder and paprika

1	32-ounce jar sauerkraut with liquid
23	ounces tomato mushroom sauce
	Lemon juice or sugar to taste

1. Preheat oven to 375°F. Grease 9 x 9 x 4-inch pan.
2. Press tofu and cut into 1-inch cubes. See How to Press Tofu.
3. Sauté mushrooms in oil in large skillet until soft and remove.
4. Dip tofu in egg, coat with flour and fry in same skillet in hot oil until browned.
5. Combine tofu, mushrooms, sauerkraut and sauce and pour into pan.
6. Add juice or sugar for balance of flavors. Cover and bake 1½ hours.

Garbanzo Bean Burgers

PAREVE OR DAIRY   YIELD: 6 BURGERS

Top these burgers with lettuce and tomato and serve on pita or hard rolls.

1	15-ounce can garbanzo beans, drained but not rinsed
1⅓	cups rolled oats
1	cup water
½	small onion, minced
¼	cup finely chopped mushrooms
¼	teaspoon garlic powder

¼	teaspoon ground cumin
⅛	teaspoon cayenne pepper or paprika to taste
1½	tablespoons soy sauce
	Olive oil for sautéing
6	slices Cheddar cheese for dairy

1. Mince beans in processor and add remaining ingredients. Let stand 15 minutes until water is absorbed. Shape into 6 burgers.
2. Heat oil in large skillet and sauté burgers until golden brown on both sides. Top with cheese.

Pasta with Kalamata Olives

DAIRY   YIELD: 6 TO 8 SERVINGS

*C*ontrol the "heat" by adjusting how much dried red pepper you add, but don't
eliminate it altogether because this dish begs for a fiery punch.

6 tablespoons olive oil	1 pound penne or linguine pasta
1½ cups chopped onions	2½ cups shredded Havarti cheese
2 garlic cloves, minced	⅓ cup grated or shaved Parmesan cheese
3 28-ounce cans whole tomatoes, drained and crushed	⅓ cup kalamata olives, pitted and sliced
2 teaspoons dried basil	¼ cup packed fresh basil leaves, chopped
1½ teaspoons dried red pepper flakes	
2 cups vegetable broth or water	

1. Preheat oven to 425°F ten minutes before baking. Grease 9 x 13-inch pan.

2. Heat oil in large saucepan and sauté onions and garlic until soft.

3. Mix in tomatoes, dried basil, pepper flakes and broth or water. Reduce heat, cover and simmer 1½ hours, stirring occasionally.

4. Cook pasta al dente and drain. Mix pasta with warm sauce and cheese. Pour into pan and sprinkle top with Parmesan, olives and fresh basil. Bake 30 minutes.

Presto Pasta Sauce Non-G

PAREVE   YIELD: 2¼ CUPS

*T*his quick-to-prepare chunky pareve sauce is excellent for any Italian style
dish. Use it with chicken cacciatore, lasagna, stuffed peppers or pasta. Freezes
well.

¼ cup olive oil	1 28-ounce can tomatoes, crushed
6 garlic cloves, minced	½ cup dry red wine
1 medium carrot, peeled and chopped	1 teaspoon dried basil
1 celery stalk, chopped	1 teaspoon dried oregano

1. Heat oil in soup pot and sauté garlic and remaining vegetables until lightly browned. Add wine and herbs. Simmer 1 hour, partially covered.

Meat or Mushroom Pasta Sauce

Non-G

MEAT OR PAREVE

• For meat, heat 1 tablespoon olive oil in large skillet and sauté ½ pound ground beef, turkey or chicken and add to Presto Pasta Sauce.

• For pareve, heat 2 tablespoons olive oil in large skillet and sauté ¾ pound mushrooms until soft and add to Presto Pasta Sauce.

Cheese Ravioli in Mushroom Sauce

DAIRY   YIELD: 6 SERVINGS

Our spin on the homey classic Italian dish infuses a sophisticated taste with the clever use of specialty mushrooms in a luscious lemony yogurt sauce served over prepared cheese ravioli.

1 pound onions, sliced	¼ teaspoon cayenne pepper to taste
3 garlic cloves, minced	1¼ teaspoons fresh lemon zest
1 cup vegetable broth, divided	½ teaspoon salt
¾ pound cremini mushrooms, sliced	¼ teaspoon pepper to taste
¾ pound shiitake mushrooms, sliced	⅔ cup plain yogurt
	2½ tablespoons chopped fresh dill
2½ tablespoons dry Sherry	2½ tablespoons chopped fresh parsley
1 tablespoon paprika	1 pound prepared cheese ravioli

1. Simmer onions and garlic in ½ cup broth until soft. Add mushrooms and simmer 5 minutes. Add Sherry and cook 2 minutes more.

2. Stir in paprika, cayenne, zest and remaining broth. Simmer uncovered until liquid is reduced by one-third. Add salt and pepper. Remove from heat, cool 5 minutes and stir in yogurt, dill and parsley. Keep warm.

3. Cook ravioli according to package directions. Drain, reserving ⅓ cup cooking water to thin sauce if needed. Combine ravioli with sauce.

Rasp Tips

• Rasps have come out of the workshop to revolutionize food grating. Their sharpness slides easily through firm hard cheese like Parmesan and zests citrus and ginger.

Vegetarian Lasagna

DAIRY   YIELD: 12 SERVINGS

1 pound lasagna noodles	2¼ cups sliced mushrooms
1 cup olive oil	6 cups ricotta cheese
2 shallots, minced	8 cups pasta sauce
12 garlic cloves, minced	1½ pounds mozzarella cheese, shredded
1½ tablespoons dried basil	Parmesan cheese
1½ tablespoons dried oregano	Salt and pepper to taste
20 ounces frozen spinach, thawed and drained	

1. Preheat oven to 350°F. Grease 9 x 13-inch pan.

2. Cook noodles according to package directions. Rinse and drain.

3. Heat oil in large skillet and sauté shallots, garlic, basil and oregano until soft.

4. Add spinach and mushrooms and cook until tender. Cool slightly and add ricotta.

5. Place one-third of the sauce into pan and cover with layer of noodles, half the spinach mixture and one-third mozzarella. Cover with one-third more sauce and repeat with layer of noodles, remaining spinach mixture and one-third mozzarella. Top with remaining noodles, mozzarella and sauce. Sprinkle with Parmesan.

6. Bake 45 minutes. Let rest 10 minutes before cutting. Freezes well.

Spinach Quajada

DAIRY   YIELD: 12 TO 16 SERVINGS

This rich attractive spinach-cheese combo makes an interesting brunch dish or side to a fish entrée. Lower fat cheese also works well with this recipe.

¼ cup olive oil	8 large eggs, beaten
1 large onion, chopped	1 cup packed fresh parsley, chopped
4 garlic cloves, minced	1 28-ounce can plum tomatoes, drained and chopped
20 ounces frozen chopped spinach, thawed and drained	1 teaspoon salt to taste
8 ounces feta cheese, crumbled	1 teaspoon pepper to taste
1 cup shredded Cheddar cheese	1 tablespoon dried dill
2 cups grated Parmesan cheese	8 slices white bread, cubed

1. Preheat oven to 375°F. Grease 9 x 13-inch baking pan.

2. Heat oil in large skillet and sauté onions and garlic until soft. Add spinach and cool.

3. Combine cheeses, eggs and parsley in large bowl. Add spinach mixture, tomatoes, seasonings and bread. Pour into pan and bake 40 to 45 minutes or until set.

4. Remove from oven and let rest 5 minutes before cutting into squares.

Perk Up Pasta Sauce

• A spoonful of fresh orange zest adds pungency to pasta sauce.

Black Bean Stuffed Cabbage

PAREVE   YIELD: 8 SERVINGS

Try this spicy version of stuffed cabbage. All our recipe testers loved this one — vegetarians and carnivores.

Filling and Cabbage

2 tablespoons olive oil	3 cups corn
2 celery stalks, finely chopped	2 teaspoons ground cumin
1 medium onion, finely chopped	Salt to taste
½ cup finely chopped green pepper	½ teaspoon pepper
5 garlic cloves, minced	¼ teaspoon cayenne pepper
1 15-ounce can black beans, drained and rinsed	½ cup rice
2 cups salsa	1 large egg, beaten
2 tablespoons chopped fresh cilantro	1 large cabbage

1. Heat oil in large skillet and sauté celery, onions, green pepper and garlic until soft.
2. Mix in beans, salsa, cilantro, corn, cumin, salt, pepper and cayenne.
3. Simmer until liquid is absorbed and remove from heat. Mix in rice and egg.
4. Prepare cabbage leaves as directed in Meat Cabbage Rolls.

Sauce

3 tablespoons olive oil	2 teaspoons ground cumin
2 cups finely chopped red onions	1 teaspoon salt
5 garlic cloves, minced	½ teaspoon pepper
1 28-ounce can tomatoes	2 tablespoons chopped fresh cilantro
1 tablespoon lemon or lime juice	2 teaspoons dried oregano
1 cup vegetable broth	¼ teaspoon red pepper flakes to taste

1. Heat oil in soup pot and sauté onions and garlic until soft.
2. Add remaining ingredients and simmer 15 minutes.

Assembly

1. Preheat oven to 375°F. Grease large baking pan.
2. Place filling on lower third of each cabbage leaf. Roll up, securing ends by pushing them inside roll.
3. Pour thin layer of sauce into pan, arrange rolls and cover with remaining sauce. Cover and bake 1½ hours or until rolls are tender.

Vegetarian Stuffed Cabbage or Peppers

PAREVE   YIELD: 8 SERVINGS

This is a hearty vegetable filling for cabbage roll-ups as well as peppers. For an appetizer, prepare smaller morsels from half-size cabbage leaves. Vary the filling by adding pine nuts or currants. Bake stuffed green, yellow or red peppers for an autumn festive look.

Sauce

3 cups tomato purée	Salt and pepper to taste
¼ cup brown sugar, firmly packed	¼ cup lemon juice to taste
1 tablespoon apple cider vinegar	

1. Place all ingredients, except juice, in soup pot and boil. Reduce heat and simmer 15 minutes.
2. Remove from heat and add juice.

Filling and Cabbage

1 large cabbage	¼ cup chopped plum tomatoes
¼ cup basmati rice	3 garlic cloves, minced
½ cup water	¼ cup chopped frozen spinach, thawed and drained
¼ teaspoon salt	¼ cup chopped pitted black olives
3 tablespoons olive oil	1 tablespoon chopped fresh parsley
10 ounces mushrooms, chopped	⅛ teaspoon dried thyme
1 large onion, finely chopped	1 large egg, beaten
1 medium carrot, peeled and grated	Salt and pepper to taste

1. Preheat oven to 375°F. Grease 9 x 13-inch baking pan.
2. Prepare cabbage leaves as directed in Meat Cabbage Rolls.
3. Cook basmati rice in water with salt until al dente. Drain and cool.
4. Heat oil in large skillet and sauté mushrooms and onions until soft and caramelized. Combine with rice and remaining ingredients.
5. Cover bottom of pan with thin layer of sauce. Place ¼ cup filling on bottom third of cabbage leaf, roll up, pushing ends of cabbage inside roll to secure filling. Arrange rolls in pan and top with remaining sauce. Cover and bake 1½ hours or until tender.

Stuffed Portobello Mushrooms

DAIRY   YIELD: 4 SERVINGS

Mushrooms

4   Portobello mushrooms, stems   2   tablespoons olive oil
    removed

1. Preheat oven to 350°F. Grease cookie sheet.
2. Place mushrooms, cavity side up, on sheet and drizzle with oil.
3. Stuff each cavity with filling choice. Bake 30 minutes or until mushrooms are tender.

Tex-Mex Filling

1   recipe Black Bean-Stuffed   1   cup shredded Cheddar cheese
    Cabbage filling

1. Fill mushrooms with bean mixture and bake 30 minutes or until tender.
2. Top with cheese and bake 5 minutes more to melt.

Italian Vegetable Filling

Signature Roasted Vegetables   6   tablespoons pasta sauce, divided

¼   cup kalamata olives   1   cup shredded mozzarella cheese

1. Mix vegetables with olives, fill mushrooms and bake 30 minutes or until tender.
2. Top each mushroom with 1½ tablespoons pasta sauce, sprinkle with cheese and bake 5 minutes more.

Artichoke and Asparagus Filling

8   ounces cream cheese, room   ⅓   cup artichoke hearts, drained
    temperature   and chopped
3   tablespoons sour cream   4   asparagus spears, blanched and
2   tablespoons mayonnaise   cut into 2-inch pieces
1½ teaspoons lemon juice   ½   cup crumbled feta or bleu cheese
1½ teaspoons Dijon mustard   2   tablespoons grated Parmesan
2   garlic cloves, minced   cheese
1   teaspoon Worcestershire sauce   1   green onion, finely chopped
⅛   teaspoon hot pepper sauce to taste

1. Beat cream cheese, sour cream, mayonnaise, juice, mustard, garlic and sauces. Fold in artichoke hearts, asparagus and cheeses.
2. Fill mushrooms with mixture and bake 30 minutes or until tender. Top with green onions.

Signature Spanakopita

DAIRY   YIELD: 10 SERVINGS

*O*ur signature recipe for the Greek classic spinach pie is always a hit. Allow two hours for preparation and baking. Serve as a main course, a side dish or appetizer.

2 tablespoons olive oil	3 large eggs
2 cups chopped onions	¾ pound feta cheese, crumbled
7 green onions, finely sliced	¾ cup grated Parmesan cheese
20 ounces frozen chopped spinach, thawed and drained	3 tablespoons chopped fresh parsley
½ teaspoon pepper	½ pound phyllo dough, thawed
1 tablespoon fresh chopped dill	½ cup butter, melted

1. Preheat oven to 400°F. Grease 9 x 13-inch pan.
2. Heat oil in extra large skillet and sauté onions until soft. Add spinach, pepper and dill. Remove from heat and cool 10 minutes.
3. Whisk eggs in large bowl until frothy. Add cheeses, parsley and spinach mixture.
4. Cut phyllo dough if necessary to fit pan and lay six sheets of phyllo in pan, buttering after each sheet.
5. Spread spinach-cheese mixture over phyllo and cover with remaining phyllo, buttering each sheet. Score into diamond shapes through top layers of phyllo using a sharp knife.
6. Bake 50 minutes or until top is puffed and golden.

Substitute 2 pounds fresh spinach, steamed, drained and chopped, for frozen.

If feta cheese is too salty, combine half the feta and substitute remaining quantity with ricotta cheese.

For hors d'oeuvres-size portion, use two 9 x 13-inch pans and 1 pound phyllo with same amount of filling.

How to Work with Phyllo

Phyllo dough is easy to work with if you follow these hints. Relax and be confident!

1. Allow dough to thaw in refrigerator for 2 days, making sure it is sealed and well-wrapped.
2. Prepare a lightly dampened linen towel. Unroll dough and cover immediately. Let stand 15 minutes; moisture makes phyllo easier to handle.
3. Keep remaining phyllo covered with towel as you work.
4. Leftover thawed phyllo will keep 1 month in refrigerator and is preferable to refreezing.

Eggplant Parmesan 👑

DAIRY

YIELD: 8 SERVINGS

It may take a bit of time to prepare, but this marvelous Italian classic, a specialty of Italy's southern regions, can be made in advance — even in bulk — and frozen uncooked or cooked. It reheats directly from the freezer, covered at 350°F. Just uncover for last ten minutes to brown. Substitute zucchini for eggplant.

Sauce

⅓ cup extra virgin olive oil	2 teaspoons dried basil
9 garlic cloves, minced	2 teaspoons dried oregano
8 cups pasta sauce	

1. Heat oil in soup pot and sauté garlic until golden.

2. Remove from heat and add pasta sauce carefully. Return to heat, add basil and oregano and bring to boil. Reduce heat and simmer 20 minutes.

Eggplant

Salt	1 tablespoon dried basil, divided
2½ pounds eggplant, peeled and sliced ½-inch thick	2 large eggs
1½ cups unflavored breadcrumbs	⅓ cup milk
¼ teaspoon pepper	½ cup flour
1 tablespoon dried oregano, divided	3 cups shredded mozzarella cheese
1 tablespoon garlic powder, divided	1 cup grated Parmesan cheese, divided

1. Preheat oven to 375°F. Grease baking sheets and 9 x 13-inch baking pan.

2. Salt eggplant slices lightly and place in colander. Press plate over eggplant and weight down with cans. Drain 30 minutes. Rinse and pat dry with paper towels.

3. Mix breadcrumbs, pepper, ½ teaspoon each oregano, garlic powder and basil. Beat eggs and milk.

4. Dredge eggplant slices in flour. Dip in egg mixture and breadcrumbs. Arrange on sheets, bake 30 minutes or until tender and browned. Reduce oven temperature to 350°F.

Eggplant Parmesan (continued)

5. Combine mozzarella and ¾ cup Parmesan cheese. Add remaining basil, oregano, and garlic powder.

6. Place thin layer of sauce on bottom of pan. Cover with 1 layer of eggplant and sprinkle with cheese mixture. Repeat the layering until all sauce, eggplant and cheese mixtures are used; start and end with sauce. Top with remaining Parmesan cheese. Bake 20 to 25 minutes until eggplant is tender.

Salting, rinsing and draining eggplant removes bitterness and cuts the amount of oil needed.

Eggplant Manicotti

DAIRY   YIELD: 4 TO 6 SERVINGS

*T**his versatile dish is wheat-free and vegetarian-friendly. Use this filling to stuff tomatoes, zucchini or mushrooms.***

Filling

1 large eggplant, peeled and cut lengthwise into ½-inch slices	1 tablespoon lightly toasted pine nuts
1½ cups ricotta cheese	2 garlic cloves
1 tablespoon grated Parmesan cheese	¼ teaspoon pepper
1 cup fresh basil leaves	1 6-ounce jar marinated artichokes, drained
1 cup fresh parsley	2 cups pasta sauce
½ cup fresh spinach, packed and stems removed	½ cup shredded mozzarella cheese

1. Preheat oven to 375°F. Grease cookie sheet and 9 x 13-inch pan.

2. Rinse, drain and pat eggplant slices dry. Roast eggplant on sheet until soft, 8 to 10 minutes, turning once.

3. Purée ricotta, Parmesan, basil, parsley, spinach, nuts, garlic, pepper and artichokes for filling.

4. Pour ½ cup sauce into pan.

5. Spread filling on each eggplant slice and roll. Arrange, seam side down, over sauce. Spoon remaining sauce over rolls and sprinkle with mozzarella. Bake 45 minutes.

 *White Zinfandel*

How to Zebra Stripe Vegetables

• Remove vegetable peel at even intervals with a vegetable peeler.

• Use for vegetables with tough skins.

Baked Eggplant Stack Non-G

PAREVE   YIELD: 6 SERVINGS

Versatile in every way, this dish may be served with any entrée, and used for Passover. Prepare in advance and freeze, baked or unbaked.

Eggplant

2½ pounds eggplant, zebra stripe
      and cut into ½-inch slices

Salt
Olive oil for brushing

1. Preheat oven to 375°F. Grease cookie sheets.
2. Salt eggplant lightly and place in colander. Press plate over eggplant slices and weight down with cans. Drain 30 minutes. Rinse and pat dry with paper towels.
3. Place eggplant slices on sheet, brush with oil and roast until tender but firm.

Sauce

¼ cup extra virgin olive oil
4 garlic cloves, minced

2 cups drained canned tomatoes, chopped

1. Heat oil in medium saucepan and sauté garlic until soft.
2. Add tomatoes and simmer 20 minutes.

Topping

2 tablespoons olive oil
4 garlic cloves, minced
1 large onion, chopped
1¼ cups drained canned tomatoes, chopped
⅔ cup drained pitted black olives, chopped

2 tablespoons finely chopped fresh parsley, divided
¼ teaspoon dried thyme
1 tablespoon lemon juice
   Salt and pepper to taste

1. Heat oil in medium saucepan and sauté garlic and onions until soft. Add tomatoes and olives, reduce heat and simmer uncovered, 15 minutes.
2. Add 4 teaspoons parsley, thyme, juice, salt and pepper.

Assembly

1. Reduce oven temperature to 350°F. Grease cookie sheet.
2. Spoon 2 tablespoons sauce in 6 puddles on sheet. Place large slice of

eggplant over each puddle. Arrange three additional slices slightly overlapping large slice. Repeat on each puddle and top stacks with any remaining eggplant. Cover with topping and remaining sauce. Bake 15 minutes. Sprinkle with remaining parsley before serving.

Hard-Boiled Eggs in Spicy Cream Sauce

DAIRY   YIELD: 10 SERVINGS

These eggs make a wonderful first course for a fish or pasta meal. Use the sauce as an accompaniment to grilled or broiled fish.

3   tablespoons vegetable oil
1   small onion, minced
1½ teaspoons minced fresh
      gingerroot
½   fresh jalapeño pepper, chopped
      fine
1¼ cups heavy cream
1   tablespoon lemon juice
1   teaspoon ground cumin

½   teaspoon cayenne pepper
½   teaspoon salt
¼   teaspoon Garam Masala
2   teaspoons tomato paste
⅔   cup vegetable broth
10 large eggs, hard-boiled, peeled
      and halved lengthwise
1   tablespoon chopped cilantro or
      parsley

1. Heat oil in large skillet and sauté onions until golden. Stir in ginger and jalapeño and sauté 1 minute more.
2. Add cream, juice, cumin, cayenne, salt, Garam Masala, tomato paste and broth. Simmer to thicken sauce, about 10 minutes.
3. Add eggs, cut side up, in single layer and top with sauce. Cook 5 minutes more, spooning sauce over eggs frequently.
4. Place eggs on serving plate and spoon sauce over eggs. Top with cilantro or parsley.

Vegetable Stir-Fry

PAREVE   YIELD: 4 SERVINGS

2	tablespoons vegetable oil	½	cup teriyaki sauce
1	red pepper, julienned	2	cups shredded bok choy
1	green pepper, julienned	1	cup bean sprouts
1	cup thinly sliced red onion	½	cup snow peas
1	cup thinly sliced yellow squash		Salt and pepper to taste
1	cup broccoli florets	2	tablespoons sesame oil
3	garlic cloves, minced		

1. Heat vegetable oil in wok or extra large skillet over high heat until almost smoking. Add peppers and onions, stirring constantly for 2 minutes.

2. Add squash, broccoli, garlic and teriyaki sauce, stirring for another 2 minutes.

3. Add bok choy, sprouts, snow peas, salt and pepper. Cook until crisp-tender, another 2 minutes.

4. Stir in sesame oil, remove from heat and serve.

Add the following to vary your stir-fry: 1 cup julienned carrots, 1 cup green beans, 1 cup sliced mushrooms, 1 sliced green onion and/or 1 tablespoon minced gingerroot.

 White Zinfandel

Chicken, Beef or Tofu Stir-Fry

- For a meat version, stir-fry 1 pound chicken breast halves, skinned and boned or shoulder steak cut into ¼-inch strips in 2 tablespoons vegetable oil. Add to Vegetable Stir-Fry.

- For a pareve version, drain and dry 1 pound firm tofu and cut into chunks. Toss with ¼ cup teriyaki sauce and marinate 30 minutes. Stir-fry in 2 tablespoons vegetable oil. Add to Vegetable Stir-Fry.

Sides

Signature Roasted Vegetables
and Roasted Asparagus

Curried Apple-Squash Rings

DAIRY OR PAREVE   YIELD: 8 SERVINGS

Perfect for fall and winter holidays, this harvest medley of apples and squash savors overnight to an even more flavorful taste. Adjust the amount of curry to your palate.

Filling

6	tablespoons butter for dairy, divided (use margarine for pareve)	2	large Granny Smith apples, peeled and diced
1	large onion, chopped	⅔	cup apple juice
1½	tablespoons curry powder, divided	½	cup dried currants
			Salt and pepper to taste
		2	acorn squash, cut into 1-inch rings and seeded

1. Preheat oven to 350°F. Grease cookie sheets.
2. Heat 1 tablespoon butter or margarine in large skillet and sauté onions until soft.
3. Stir in 1 tablespoon curry powder, apples, juice and currants. Simmer until liquid evaporates. Season with salt and pepper.
4. Melt remaining butter or margarine in saucepan, add remaining curry powder and stir until fragrant, to make curry glaze.
5. Arrange squash rings in single layer on sheets. Sprinkle with salt and pepper.
6. Place scoop of filling into center of each squash ring. Drizzle with curry glaze. Cover with foil and bake until tender, about 45 minutes. Transfer with spatula to serve.

Lower-Salt Tip

• Add fresh aromatic herbs near the end of cooking to enhance the taste of your lower-salt recipes.

Roasted Broccoli with Red Peppers Non-G

PAREVE   YIELD: 6 SERVINGS

1	bunch broccoli, cut into florets	2	garlic cloves, minced
1	red pepper, cut into ½-inch strips		Extra virgin olive oil

1. Preheat oven to 375°F. Prepare ungreased rimmed cookie sheet.
2. Mix vegetables with garlic and toss with oil.
3. Roast 15 to 18 minutes or until tender, stirring occasionally.

Sautéed Spinach with Garlic  Non-G

PAREVE   YIELD: 6 SERVINGS

2   tablespoons extra virgin olive oil
6   garlic cloves, minced
1½ pounds baby spinach leaves

Salt and pepper to taste
½   teaspoon lemon juice

1. Heat oil in large pot and sauté garlic until soft. Add spinach, salt and pepper and cook until spinach is wilted.
2. Transfer to bowl with slotted spoon and toss with juice.

Mexican Hominy and Zucchini

PAREVE OR DAIRY   YIELD: 6 SERVINGS

*H*ominy is the Algonquin name for large kernelled white corn. Hominy is an unusual ingredient but readily found in the ethnic section of the grocery store.

1½ tablespoons vegetable oil
1   medium onion, chopped
2   garlic cloves, minced
1½ pounds zucchini, cut into ½-inch slices
1   15-ounce can hominy, drained and rinsed
1   large tomato, diced

2   tablespoons lime juice
1   tablespoon chili powder
2   tablespoons chopped fresh cilantro
½   cup salsa
½   cup shredded Cheddar cheese for dairy

1. Heat oil in large skillet and sauté onions and garlic until soft.
2. Mix in zucchini and remaining ingredients except cheese. Simmer uncovered, stirring often until zucchini is tender. Add cheese 5 minutes before finished cooking.

Cilantro Facts

• If you have eaten Asian or Mexican food, you have tasted cilantro. Also known as coriander or Chinese parsley, this herb is a mix of parsley and citrus that adds fresh flavor to many dishes. Snip cilantro with kitchen scissors to maintain its bright color.

Roasted Curried Cauliflower

PAREVE   YIELD: 8 TO 10 SERVINGS

This side dish is packed with distinctive flavor, making it a good complement to a mild entrée.

1 teaspoon coriander seeds	1 tablespoon paprika
1 teaspoon cumin seeds	1¾ teaspoons salt
¾ cup olive oil	12 cups cauliflower florets
½ cup red wine vinegar	1 large onion, quartered
3½ teaspoons curry powder	

1. Preheat oven to 450°F. Grease roasting pan.
2. Stir seeds in dry skillet over medium heat, 5 minutes, until fragrant.
3. Combine seeds, oil, vinegar, curry powder, paprika and salt. Toss mixture with cauliflower and onions. Spread in roasting pan.
4. Roast 35 minutes, stirring occasionally until vegetables are just tender.

Cornbread-Stuffed Zucchini Boats

DAIRY   YIELD: 8 SERVINGS

Serve this attractive side dish with any dairy entrée. Homemade cornbread toasted and cut into cubes may be substituted for the prepared stuffing mix.

4 medium zucchinis, halved	1¼ cups shredded Cheddar cheese, divided
2 tablespoons vegetable oil	
½ cup chopped onion	¼ cup cornbread stuffing mix or croutons
1 garlic clove, minced	
1 large egg, slightly beaten	Salt and pepper to taste
1¼ cups shredded Monterey Jack cheese, divided	1 teaspoon chopped parsley

1. Preheat oven to 350°F. Grease 9 x 13-inch baking pan.
2. Scoop out zucchini pulp, leaving ¼-inch thick shell. Heat oil in large skillet and sauté pulp, onions and garlic 5 minutes; drain well.
3. Add egg, 1 cup of each cheese, stuffing mix or croutons, salt and pepper.
4. Fill boats with mixture, place in pan and sprinkle with remaining cheeses.
5. Bake 30 minutes or until zucchini is tender. Sprinkle with parsley.

Spicy Cabbage with Red Pepper Strips

PAREVE   YIELD: 6 TO 8 SERVINGS

The stir-fry method of preparing vegetables seals in fresh flavor, valuable nutrients and tasty juices. Quickly toss the vegetables until they reach desired texture for stir-frying, which is crisp-tender.

2	tablespoons vegetable oil	6	green onions, finely chopped
1	tablespoon peeled and minced fresh gingerroot	1	red pepper, cut into thin strips
2	pounds green cabbage, shredded	1	tablespoon sesame oil
			Salt and pepper to taste

1. Heat vegetable oil in extra large skillet or wok over medium heat and sauté ginger 30 seconds.
2. Add half the cabbage and toss until wilted. Add remaining cabbage, onions, red pepper and sesame oil. Toss until cabbage is crisp-tender. Season with salt and pepper.

Oven-Roasted Tomatoes

PAREVE   YIELD: 6 TO 8 SERVINGS

Magical overnight tomatoes that bake while you sleep. The ultimate solution to summertime garden overages. Any fresh herb may be substituted.

4	large tomatoes or 8 plum tomatoes	3	garlic cloves, minced
	Salt and pepper to taste		Basil leaves or dill sprigs
		2	teaspoons olive oil

1. Preheat oven to 200°F. Grease cookie sheet.
2. Halve large tomatoes widthwise or plum tomatoes lengthwise.
3. Arrange on sheet. Sprinkle with salt, pepper and garlic.
4. Place basil or dill on each tomato half. Drizzle lightly with oil.
5. Bake 12 to 14 hours for large tomatoes or 6 to 8 hours for small ones or until shriveled.

Green Onion Ties

• Blanch green onions for about 20 seconds to make them flexible enough to use for ties around bundles of steamed vegetables.

Grilled Vegetable Stacks Non-G

PAREVE   YIELD: 8 SERVINGS

This recipe comes to us from one of our collaborations with area chefs from whom As You Like It *has learned many culinary tips and techniques.*

Marinade

2	cups vegetable oil	2	tablespoons paprika
1	tablespoon granulated garlic	2	teaspoons salt
1	tablespoon granulated onion	2	teaspoons pepper

1. Combine all ingredients.

Vegetables

2	large Vidalia onions, cut into ½-inch slices	2	red peppers, quartered
		2	green peppers, quartered
1	medium yellow squash, cut into ½-inch diagonal slices	8	Portobello mushrooms, stems removed
1	medium zucchini, cut into ½-inch diagonal slices		

1. Preheat grill, broiler or grill pan. Preheat oven to 325°F. Grease cookie sheet.
2. Dip onion slices in marinade keeping intact and place on sheet. Roast 10 minutes.
3. Dip remaining vegetables in marinade and grill or broil until crisp-tender. Grill marks add visual interest.
4. Pile vegetables on top of onion slices to form stack in following order: zucchini, yellow squash, green pepper, red pepper, mushroom cap. Warm in oven 5 to 8 minutes.

Apricot Chutney

PAREVE   YIELD: 8 SERVINGS

A pickled condiment of Indian origin, chutney has many variations and may be served as a side dish or appetizer. Our apricot chutney may be made one week ahead and stored covered and chilled.

12	ounces dried apricots, chopped fine	1½	tablespoons chopped fresh rosemary
1	large red onion, chopped	3	garlic cloves, finely chopped
1	cup water	2	teaspoons fresh lemon zest
⅔	cup cider vinegar	½	teaspoon salt
⅔	cup brown sugar, firmly packed	⅛	teaspoon cayenne pepper
¾	cup dried tart cherries	½	cup sliced almonds, toasted

Granulated Garlic and Onion Equivalencies

• Granulated garlic is coarse garlic powder that is 5 times stronger than raw garlic, ½ teaspoon equals 1 clove.

• Granulated onion is similar to granulated garlic in texture, 1 tablespoon equals ½ cup fresh chopped onion.

Apricot Chutney (continued)

1. Combine all ingredients except almonds in saucepan. Bring to boil, stirring until sugar dissolves.
2. Reduce heat and simmer until most of the liquid has evaporated and chutney is thick, 25 minutes. Stir in almonds and chill 2 hours.

Cheesy Cauliflower

DAIRY   YIELD: 6 SERVINGS

You may substitute Cheddar or Provolone for the mozzarella.

1 *cauliflower, cut into 1-inch florets*	2 *large eggs*
1 *tablespoon butter*	2 *tablespoons sour cream*
2 *tablespoons unflavored breadcrumbs*	1 *cup shredded mozzarella cheese*

1. Preheat oven to 375°F. Grease 9-inch square baking pan.
2. Steam florets until tender and rinse under cold water. Drain.
3. Heat butter in large skillet and sauté breadcrumbs, stirring until toasted. Stir in cauliflower and remove from heat.
4. Whisk eggs with sour cream and add cheese. Combine with cauliflower mixture and spoon into pan. Bake 25 minutes or until golden brown.

Green Beans with Tahini and Garlic

PAREVE   YIELD: 8 SERVINGS

2½ *pounds fresh green beans, trimmed and cut into 1-inch pieces*	3 *tablespoons tahini*
	¼ *cup finely chopped fresh cilantro*
6 *tablespoons vegetable oil*	⅛ *teaspoon pepper to taste*
2 *teaspoons black mustard seeds*	⅛ *teaspoon cayenne pepper*
9 *garlic cloves, minced*	1 *tablespoon lemon juice*
1 *inch fresh gingerroot, peeled and grated*	

1. Steam beans until tender and bright green, 5 minutes. Drain and rinse under cold water.
2. Heat oil in extra large skillet and sauté beans. Stir in mustard seeds. Add garlic and ginger and brown lightly. Mix in remaining ingredients.

Pecan-Lemon Green Beans

PAREVE   YIELD: 4 SERVINGS

2   tablespoons extra virgin olive oil

1   pound green beans, trimmed

½   cup pecan halves, toasted

2   tablespoons fresh lemon zest to taste

¼   cup packed cilantro, finely chopped

Salt and pepper to taste

1. Heat oil in large skillet and sauté beans until crisp-tender, about 4 minutes.

2. Mix in nuts, zest and cilantro and cook 2 minutes more. Toss gently with salt and pepper.

Irresistible Mushrooms

DAIRY OR PAREVE   YIELD: 4 TO 6 SERVINGS

The mushrooms and peppers will be very dark and evil-looking, but irresistible in flavor and aroma. Prepare pareve *and you can serve them with steak and hamburgers.*

½   cup butter for dairy (use margarine for pareve)

1   onion, chopped

2   tablespoons Dijon mustard

½   cup brown sugar, firmly packed

2   tablespoons Worcestershire sauce

¾   cup dry red wine

Salt and pepper to taste

1   pound mushrooms, halved

2   red or green peppers, cut into 1-inch pieces

1. Heat butter or margarine and sauté onions until soft.

2. Combine mustard, sugar and Worcestershire to form smooth paste. Add wine, salt and pepper.

3. Mix mushrooms and peppers into onions and sauté 2 minutes. Add wine paste.

4. Simmer 45 minutes or until sauce is reduced and thickened.

How to Clean Mushrooms

Mushrooms by their nature are dirty! They are very porous and absorb water easily.

• Rinse mushrooms lightly with a spray of water, pat dry immediately and brush off visible dirt.

Eggplant, Indian Style

PAREVE   YIELD: 8 SERVINGS

A delicious accompaniment for an Indian or Mideastern meal. This vegetable side dish may be served hot, cold or at room temperature.

1   inch fresh gingerroot, peeled and chopped
6   garlic cloves
¼   cup water
1½ cups vegetable oil, divided
1¾ pounds eggplant, peeled and cut into ¾-inch slices
1   teaspoon whole fennel seeds
½   teaspoon whole cumin seeds

¾   pound fresh tomatoes, peeled and chopped fine or 2 cups canned diced tomatoes, drained
1   tablespoon ground coriander seeds
¼   teaspoon ground turmeric
¼   teaspoon cayenne pepper to taste
1¼ teaspoons salt to taste

1. Purée ginger, garlic and water.
2. Heat ½ cup oil in large skillet and fry one layer of eggplant at a time until browned on each side. Drain on paper towels. Continue to add oil as needed.
3. Add 3 tablespoons oil to same skillet and cook fennel and cumin seeds 10 seconds until darkened and fragrant.
4. Add ginger-garlic mixture, tomatoes and remaining ingredients. Cook 5 minutes or until mixture thickens. Add eggplant, stir gently, cover and simmer until tender.

Roasted Onions with Balsamic Glaze  Non-G

PAREVE   YIELD: 6 SERVINGS

T his versatile side dish offers "something extra" to toss over salad, steak or even Kasha Varnishkes. For your garlic lovers, add two additional garlic cloves.

1   garlic clove, minced
¼   cup balsamic vinegar (use K-P balsamic vinegar for Passover)
¼   cup olive oil

⅛   teaspoon salt
⅛   teaspoon pepper
3   red onions, peeled and thinly sliced

1. Preheat oven to 350°F ten minutes before cooking. Grease cookie sheet.
2. Mix garlic with vinegar, oil, salt and pepper. Add onions and toss. Marinate at room temperature 1 hour.
3. Place on sheet and roast 1¼ hours or until tender and caramelized.

Glazed Parsnips with Apricots Non-G

DAIRY OR PAREVE   YIELD: 4 TO 6 SERVINGS

This is an attractive, change-of-pace dish that reheats without losing flavor or texture.

1	pound parsnips, peeled
¾	cup dried apricots
¼	cup sugar to taste
¼	cup orange juice

1	tablespoon butter for dairy (use margarine for pareve)
½	teaspoon salt
⅛	teaspoon pepper

1. Cut parsnips into ¼-inch diagonal slices.

2. Cover parsnips and apricots with water in saucepan. Bring to boil, reduce heat, cover and simmer until tender. Drain and return to saucepan.

3. Add remaining ingredients, bring to boil and remove.

Carrot Pudding

PAREVE   YIELD: 10 SERVINGS

2	pounds carrots, peeled and cooked
6	eggs or 12 ounces egg substitute
¾	cup sugar
6	tablespoons flour (use 4 tablespoons matzoh meal for Passover)

2	teaspoons baking powder (use K-P baking powder for Passover)
2	teaspoons vanilla extract

1. Preheat oven to 325°F. Grease 8 x 8-inch baking pan.

2. Purée carrots.

3. Add remaining ingredients.

4. Pour batter into pan and bake 1 hour or until tester inserted in center comes out clean.

Fill 16 muffin tins for smaller portions.

Signature Roasted Vegetables Non-G

PAREVE   YIELD: 6 TO 8 SERVINGS

This is an As You Like It staple, frequently served and frequently requested. We even sell this packaged for home take-out.

1	green pepper	5	tablespoons olive oil
1	red pepper	10	whole garlic cloves
1	large onion	1	teaspoon dried rosemary
1	sweet potato, peeled	1	teaspoon dried basil
1	medium eggplant, peeled	1	teaspoon dried oregano
2	large carrots, peeled		Salt and pepper to taste
12	ounces button mushrooms, halved		

1. Preheat oven to 400°F. Prepare ungreased rimmed cookie sheet.

2. Cut all vegetables, except mushrooms, into 2-inch pieces. Toss vegetables with oil and spices.

3. Roast on sheet in single layer until tender and caramelized. Stir occasionally.

You may substitute baby vegetables, red onion, yellow and green squash, asparagus, broccoli, cauliflower, Brussels sprouts, fennel, Portobello mushrooms, marinated mushrooms, artichokes, olives and peppers.

How to Seed Peppers

1. Slice off top and bottom of pepper.

2. Cut pepper lengthwise on one side, open pepper flat and remove the bulk of seeds.

3. Run a knife along the inside to remove white membrane and remaining seeds. Rinse.

Cucumber Raita Non-G

DAIRY   YIELD: 6 SERVINGS

Raitas are refreshing, "cool" yogurt and cucumber dishes invented by Indian cooks to relieve the "heat" of spicy foods.

16 ounces plain yogurt	⅛ teaspoon cayenne pepper
1 cucumber, peeled and grated	⅛ teaspoon paprika
1 teaspoon salt	2 tablespoons dried mint leaves
⅛ teaspoon pepper	Paprika and fresh mint
½ teaspoon ground cumin	

1. Beat yogurt at medium speed with electric mixer until smooth and fold in all ingredients except paprika and mint.
2. Serve sprinkled with paprika and topped with mint.

Brussels Sprouts in Lemon Mustard

DAIRY OR PAREVE   YIELD: 4 SERVINGS

This combination of flavors will make you a Brussels sprout fan.

1 pound Brussels sprouts, stems trimmed	1 tablespoon lemon juice
2 garlic cloves, minced	2 teaspoons spicy mustard
2 teaspoons butter for dairy (use margarine for pareve)	

1. Steam sprouts and garlic until tender, about 10 minutes.
2. Melt butter or margarine in small skillet and stir in juice and mustard.
3. Add sprouts and garlic and toss.

Roasted Asparagus  Non-G

PAREVE   YIELD: 6 TO 8 SERVINGS

A must-try alternative to steamed asparagus.

1⅓ pounds asparagus, woody ends   1½ tablespoons olive oil
    removed   Salt and pepper to taste

1. Preheat oven to 375°F. Grease cookie sheet.
2. Lay asparagus on sheet in single layer. Toss with oil, salt and pepper.
3. Roast 15 to 20 minutes or until asparagus are crisp-tender.

Signature Potato Kugel

PAREVE   YIELD: 12 SERVINGS

T his versatile kugel, one of As You Like It's *favorites, is easily adapted for Passover. Try spooning batter into well-greased muffin tins for quicker baking kugelettes.*

4   large eggs, beaten   ½   pound sweet potatoes, peeled
1   teaspoon salt to taste   and shredded
½   teaspoon pepper to taste   1   large onion, finely chopped
½   cup flour (use ⅓ cup matzoh   1   green onion, finely chopped
    meal for Passover)   4   garlic cloves, minced
½   teaspoon baking powder (use K-P   2   tablespoons finely chopped
    baking powder for Passover)   parsley
2½ pounds potatoes, peeled and   2   tablespoons Veggie Schmaltz or
    shredded   olive oil

1. Preheat oven to 350°F. Grease 9 x 13-inch baking pan.
2. Whisk eggs until foamy and add salt and pepper.
3. Combine flour or matzoh meal with baking powder.
4. Drain potatoes and mix with onions, garlic and parsley. Add eggs, schmaltz or oil.
5. Stir in dry mixture and pour into pan, bake 45 minutes or until kugel is firm and golden brown.

Reheat covered in 325°F oven, about 30 minutes.

No-Salt Herb Blend
This versatile blend is better than salt. Use dried herbs.

4 tablespoons
each oregano and
onion powder

2 tablespoons garlic
powder

4 teaspoons each
marjoram, basil
and savory

2 teaspoons each
thyme and rosemary

1 teaspoon each
sage and pepper

• Combine ingredients
and store in tightly
covered jar.

Potatoes and Cauliflower, Indian Style

PAREVE   YIELD: 4 SERVINGS

1	head cauliflower, cut into 2-inch florets	¼	teaspoon cayenne pepper to taste
1	pound potatoes, peeled, cut into ½-inch cubes	¼	teaspoon ground turmeric
3	tablespoons vegetable oil	½	teaspoon ground coriander
½	teaspoon whole fenugreek seeds	1	teaspoon salt to taste
½	teaspoon whole fennel seeds	¼	teaspoon pepper to taste
½	teaspoon whole cumin seeds	½	cup water
		8	ounces canned peas, drained
		½	teaspoon Garam Masala

1. Thinly slice each floret lengthwise. Combine with potatoes and soak 30 minutes in cold water. Drain and dry with paper towels.
2. Heat oil in large skillet over high heat. When oil is smoking, add seeds and cayenne and stir until fragrant. Mix in cauliflower and potatoes and reduce heat.
3. Add turmeric, coriander, salt and pepper and sauté 5 minutes.
4. Add water, cover and steam vegetables until tender. Mix in peas and Garam Masala.

Confetti Hash Brown Potatoes Non-G

PAREVE OR DAIRY   YIELD: 6 SERVINGS

Add two shredded carrots for a confetti effect. Chock-full of flavor and irresistible for brunch.

¼	cup Veggie Schmaltz or vegetable oil for pareve (use butter for dairy)	1	medium onion, diced
		½	red pepper, diced
1½	pounds potatoes, diced, excess liquid squeezed out	½	green pepper, diced
		2	teaspoons salt to taste
		½	teaspoon pepper to taste

1. Preheat oven to 350°F. Grease large roasting pan.
2. Heat schmaltz, oil or butter in pan. Add vegetables and roast until tender and caramelized. Add salt and pepper.

Mashed Potatoes in Crêpe Cups

PAREVE OR DAIRY   YIELD: 6 SERVINGS

A pretty and delicious way to serve mashed potatoes, either white or sweet. Perfect for a birthday or anniversary dinner. Make it extra fancy by piping potatoes into crêpe cups through decorating bag fitted with large star tip.

2   tablespoons Veggie Schmaltz or olive oil
1   small onion, finely chopped
2   tablespoons peeled and finely chopped carrots
4   garlic cloves, minced
1½ pounds potatoes, peeled and cut into ½-inch cubes

½   cup nondairy milk for pareve, warmed (use milk for dairy)
1   tablespoon minced chives
    Salt and pepper to taste
¼   cup Parmesan cheese for dairy
6   6-inch unfilled Crêpes

1. Preheat oven to 350°F. Grease 6 muffin cups.

2. Heat schmaltz or oil in large skillet and sauté onions, carrots and garlic.

3. Boil potatoes until soft. Drain, add nondairy milk or milk and whip at medium speed in electric mixer until fluffy.

4. Add chives, salt, pepper, cheese and sautéed vegetables.

5. Place crêpe in each muffin cup and fill with potato mixture.

6. Bake until hot and crêpe is crispy.

Crusty Roasted Potatoes  Non-G

MEAT OR PAREVE   YIELD: 8 TO 10 SERVINGS

*T*hese spuds could quickly become a family favorite at Passover seders and holiday meals. Whole fingerling potatoes make an elegant presentation.

8   large potatoes (3 pounds), peeled
    and quartered
½   cup Veggie Schmaltz or olive oil

Salt, pepper, onion powder,
    garlic powder to taste
¾   cup chicken broth for meat
    (use vegetable broth for pareve)

1. Preheat oven to 375°F. Prepare large roasting pan.
2. Place potatoes in pan and toss with schmaltz or oil until coated.
3. Sprinkle with seasonings. Roast uncovered 35 to 45 minutes, stirring occasionally. Add broth and roast 20 to 30 minutes more or until browned.

Potato Fans  Non-G

DAIRY OR PAREVE   YIELD: 4 SERVINGS

*U*niquely shaped, just right to accompany any entrée.

4   medium potatoes
    Salt and pepper to taste
3   tablespoons Veggie Schmaltz or
    olive oil
3   tablespoons chopped
    fresh parsley or chives

¼   cup shredded Cheddar cheese for
    dairy
2   tablespoons grated Parmesan
    cheese for dairy

1. Preheat oven to 450°F. Grease baking pan.
2. Slash potatoes three-quarters of the way through at ¼-inch intervals, being careful not to cut all the way.
3. Place potatoes in baking pan, fanning slices slightly.
4. Sprinkle with salt and pepper. Drizzle with schmaltz or oil and top with herbs.
5. Bake potatoes for 50 minutes, sprinkle with cheeses and bake 10 minutes more, or until potatoes are crispy and tender.

Crusty Roasted Potatoes, Italian Style

• For that Italian taste, prepare Crusty Roasted Potatoes adding basil, oregano and rosemary to seasonings.

Lots o' Latkes

Vegetable-Feta Latkes

DAIRY   YIELD: 10 TO 12 LATKES

Surprise your party guests with these crisp vegetable-potato pancakes spiked with the tangy taste of feta cheese.

2½ cups grated zucchini	½ teaspoon pepper
1 cup peeled and shredded potatoes	¾ cup flour (use ½ cup matzoh meal for Passover)
1 cup peeled and shredded carrots	½ cup chopped fresh parsley or dill
Salt to taste	¾ cup crumbled feta cheese
3 large eggs, slightly beaten	Vegetable oil for frying

1. Place zucchini, potatoes and carrots in colander, sprinkle with ½ teaspoon salt and drain 15 minutes. Squeeze out excess liquid and place in bowl.

2. Add eggs, salt and pepper. Stir in flour or matzoh meal, parsley or dill and feta.

3. Heat oil in large skillet. Drop mixture by spoonfuls and fry on both sides until golden brown. Drain on paper towels.

Sweet Potato Latkes

PAREVE OR DAIRY   YIELD: 12 TO 16 LATKES

These pancakes are exotically flavored with ginger and allspice. To ensure even cooking, don't crowd the latkes in the skillet.

4½ cups peeled and shredded sweet potatoes or yams	½ teaspoon pepper to taste
2 large eggs, slightly beaten	½ teaspoon ground cinnamon
½ cup flour (use ⅓ cup matzoh meal for Passover)	¼ teaspoon ground allspice
1 tablespoon brown sugar, firmly packed	⅛ teaspoon ground ginger or cloves
	Vegetable oil for frying
1 teaspoon salt to taste	Applesauce and/or nondairy sour cream for pareve (use sour cream for dairy)

1. Combine potatoes with eggs, flour or matzoh meal, sugar, salt, pepper and spices.

2. Drop mixture by heaping spoonfuls into hot oil in large skillet, turning once after first side is browned. Drain on brown paper or paper towels.

3. Serve with applesauce and sour cream or nondairy sour cream.

Lots o' Latkes (continued on next page)

How to Freeze and Reheat Latkes

1. Stand latkes up in freezable container and cover with foil or plastic wrap.

2. To reheat, place latkes in single layer on cookie sheet and bake at 375°F.

Potato Latkes

PAREVE OR DAIRY   YIELD: 12 TO 16 LATKES

Traditional potato pancakes, always welcome at a meal.

2 pounds peeled white potatoes or unpeeled red skin potatoes	1 teaspoon baking powder (use K-P baking powder for Passover)
2 medium onions	⅓ cup flour (use ¼ cup matzoh meal for Passover)
2 large eggs, slightly beaten	Vegetable oil for frying
1 teaspoon salt to taste	Applesauce
½ teaspoon pepper to taste	Sour cream for dairy

1. Grate or shred potatoes and onions. Squeeze out excess liquid.
2. Add eggs, salt, pepper, baking powder and flour or matzoh meal.
3. Drop mixture by heaping spoonfuls into hot oil in large skillet, turning once after first side is browned. Drain on brown paper or paper towels.
4. Serve with applesauce and/or sour cream.

Tex-Mex Latkes

PAREVE OR DAIRY   YIELD: 24 MINIPANCAKES

One of the most popular hot pass-arounds that As You Like It offers, they freeze and refreeze beautifully. These pancakes may be reheated at 375°F until hot.

1 cup corn	1 teaspoon chopped fresh cilantro
½ cup finely chopped onions	1 teaspoon ground cumin
2 green onions, chopped	1 teaspoon salt to taste
3 tablespoons finely chopped red pepper	½ teaspoon pepper to taste
3 tablespoons finely chopped green pepper	½ cup flour
1 tablespoon grated fresh gingerroot	½ teaspoon baking powder
2 garlic cloves, minced	2 large eggs, separated
1 teaspoon finely chopped fresh dill	Vegetable oil for frying
	Caliente Sour Cream (use nondairy for pareve)

Easy Removal of Corn

• A serrated knife works best for removing kernels from a corn cob.

1. Mix together all ingredients except whites and oil.

2. Beat whites at high speed with electric mixer until stiff and fold into corn mixture.

3. Heat oil in large skillet and spoon batter by tablespoons into oil. Fry until golden brown on each side and drain on paper towels or brown paper.

4. Serve with Caliente Sour Cream.

Fruited Rice Combo

PAREVE   YIELD: 6 SERVINGS

This fruited rice side dish calls for dried cherries or cranberries but apricots and pineapple are alternatives. The sweetness and texture of the fruit melds nicely with the sharper tang of the orange and pineapple juices.

2 cups water	¾ cup thinly sliced mushrooms, optional
½ cup wild rice	½ cup dried cherries or cranberries
1⅓ cups pineapple juice	⅓ cup pine nuts, toasted
½ cup basmati rice	2 tablespoons chopped parsley
2 tablespoons olive oil	⅓ cup orange juice
1 medium onion, finely chopped	Salt and pepper to taste
2 garlic cloves, minced	

1. Preheat oven to 350°F. Grease 8-inch square baking pan.

2. Bring water to boil in saucepan and add wild rice, stir, cover and simmer about 35 minutes or until just tender. Drain excess liquid and transfer to large bowl.

3. Boil pineapple juice in second saucepan and add basmati rice, stir, cover and simmer 20 minutes. Liquid should be totally absorbed and rice tender. Add to wild rice.

4. Heat oil in large skillet and sauté onions, garlic and mushrooms until soft. Combine with rice mixture. Stir in remaining ingredients.

5. Transfer mixture to pan, cover and bake 30 minutes.

Layered Sweet Potatoes and Apples   Non-G

DAIRY OR PAREVE · YIELD: 6 SERVINGS

This lower fat dish is free of added sugar.

3 apples, peeled and thinly sliced
1 tablespoon lemon juice
1½ pounds sweet potatoes, peeled and thinly sliced
¼ cup apple cider
1 tablespoon butter for dairy, melted (use margarine for pareve)

1. Preheat oven to 350°F. Grease 8-inch square pan.
2. Toss apple slices with juice. Arrange alternating layers of potatoes and apples in pan, ending with potatoes.
3. Pour cider and butter or margarine over top. Cover and bake 1 hour.
4. Uncover and bake 15 minutes longer or until tender.

Spicy Indian Rice

PAREVE · YIELD: 8 SERVINGS

2 cups long grain or basmati rice
¼ cup vegetable oil
1 medium onion, cut in thin rings
1 garlic clove, minced
1 teaspoon grated fresh gingerroot
½ teaspoon minced jalapeño pepper or ⅛ teaspoon cayenne pepper
¾ teaspoon Garam Masala
3 cups vegetable broth, warmed
1 teaspoon salt

1. Preheat oven to 325°F. Grease 9-inch square baking pan.
2. Cover rice with water and soak 30 minutes. Drain and leave rice in strainer.
3. Heat oil in large skillet and sauté onions until browned.
4. Add rice, garlic, ginger, pepper and Garam Masala. Sauté until rice is translucent.
5. Add broth and cook 5 minutes, stirring occasionally.
6. Transfer to pan, cover and bake 20 to 25 minutes. Remove from oven and keep covered 10 minutes.

Mushroom Risotto

DAIRY   YIELD: 4 SERVINGS

3   tablespoons butter, divided
1   medium onion, minced
¼   pound porcini mushrooms, stems
    trimmed, thinly sliced
1   pound button or cremini
    mushrooms, stems trimmed,
    thinly sliced

Salt and pepper to taste
2   teaspoons minced fresh oregano
1½ cups Arborio rice
6   cups vegetable broth, warmed
½   cup grated Parmesan cheese,
    plus more for serving on the
    side

1. Melt 2 tablespoons butter in saucepan and sauté onions until soft.
   Add mushrooms and cook until golden brown, about 8 minutes. Add
   salt, pepper and oregano.

2. Stir in rice with wooden spoon and cook 1 minute. Add ½ cup broth
   and cook until rice absorbs liquid, stirring frequently. Continue
   adding broth in ½ cup increments, stirring until rice is creamy and
   soft but still a bit al dente, about 25 minutes.

3. Remove pan from heat and vigorously stir in remaining butter and
   Parmesan. Add salt and pepper. Serve risotto immediately with
   additional Parmesan cheese.

For asparagus risotto, substitute ¾ pound chopped asparagus for the mushrooms.

Coconut Basmati Rice

PAREVE   YIELD: 4 SERVINGS

A fruity, fragrant spiced rice with the golden hue of turmeric.

1   cup basmati rice
1⅓ cups water
¼   cup raisins
½   cup coconut milk

½   teaspoon turmeric
¼   teaspoon salt
1   cinnamon stick

1. Rinse rice and drain well.
2. Boil water in saucepan, stir in rice and remaining ingredients.
3. Return to boil, reduce heat, cover and simmer 20 minutes.
4. Remove from heat and let rest 10 minutes. Fluff rice with fork and
   remove cinnamon stick.

*When is the
Risotto Done?*

When the rice is
almost tender, the
risotto will look
loose. Finished
risotto is tender but
slightly al dente
and creamy.

Fresh Garden Couscous

PAREVE   YIELD: 8 SERVINGS

Fragrantly herbed garden vegetables, at peak season freshness, add color and crunch to the steamed couscous grains. Vary the recipe with other fresh vegetables and herbs.

1 cup couscous	½ cup chopped fresh parsley
1 cup boiling water	2 tablespoons chopped fresh dill
1 15-ounce can black beans, rinsed and drained	2 tablespoons chopped fresh mint
1 celery stalk, diced	2 green onions, chopped
1 red pepper, diced	2 tablespoons lemon juice
2 tomatoes, diced	2 tablespoons olive oil
¼ cup chopped green olives	Salt and pepper to taste

1. Combine couscous and water in bowl. Cover and let stand 15 minutes. Uncover and fluff with fork. Cool.
2. Stir in remaining ingredients. Cover and chill 1 hour.

Polenta Wedges

DAIRY OR PAREVE   YIELD: 4 SERVINGS

A traditional Italian favorite, polenta is a popular alternative to pasta. Our polenta wedges are a versatile side dish to a wide variety of main dishes. They make a summertime hit served with Grilled Vegetable Stacks or topped with salsa or bruschetta topping.

4 cups vegetable broth	2 tablespoons butter for dairy (use margarine for pareve)
Salt to taste	
1⅓ cups polenta cornmeal	2 tablespoons olive oil for frying

1. Grease 8-inch square baking pan.
2. Boil broth and add salt. Beat in polenta slowly, stirring until mixture is thick and free of lumps, about 5 minutes. Mix in butter or margarine and remove from heat.
3. Spoon polenta into pan. Chill 1 hour.
4. Cut into ½-inch slices. Cut each slice diagonally to form wedge. Heat olive oil in medium skillet and fry wedges until golden brown on both sides. Drain on paper towels.

Kasha Varnishkes

PAREVE   YIELD: 10 SERVINGS

The classic Eastern European dish beloved by young and old. Served with gravy, it is a traditional complement to a brisket main dish.

3 tablespoons vegetable oil	1 large egg, slightly beaten
¾ cup chopped onions	1 cup buckwheat groats (kasha)
1 carrot, peeled and chopped	2 cups vegetable broth, warmed
2 garlic cloves, minced	8 ounces small bow tie pasta, cooked and drained
1 teaspoon salt	
¼ teaspoon pepper	

1. Heat oil in medium skillet and sauté onions, carrots and garlic until onions are soft. Add salt and pepper and set aside.

2. Combine egg with kasha in large dry skillet. Cook on low heat, stirring constantly, until egg has dried and kasha has separated.

3. Add onion mixture to kasha and stir in broth, reduce heat and cover. Steam kasha 15 to 20 minutes or until tender and liquid is absorbed. Add more broth if needed.

4. Fluff with fork and combine with pasta. Serve warm.

Garam Masala

PAREVE   YIELD: 3 TABLESPOONS

Every home in India or Pakistan probably has its own handed-down recipe for this aromatic mixture of spices. Used as a flavoring agent, it is supposed to "heat" the body.

1 tablespoon cardamom seeds	1 teaspoon whole cloves
1 inch stick of cinnamon	1 teaspoon black peppercorns
1 teaspoon whole black cumin seeds or regular whole cumin seeds	⅓ whole nutmeg or 1 teaspoon ground nutmeg

1. Grind all ingredients together in electric spice mill or coffee grinder until powdery.

Egg Barley with Vegetables

MEAT OR PAREVE   YIELD: 6 SERVINGS

 versatile accompaniment to a Shabbat meal.

8	ounces egg barley	4	garlic cloves, minced
2	tablespoons olive oil	8	ounces mushrooms, optional
½	cup diced onions	1	cup chicken broth for meat
1	celery stalk, diced		(use vegetable broth for pareve)
1	red pepper, diced		Salt and pepper to taste

1. Preheat oven to 350°F. Grease 8-inch baking pan.
2. Cook barley according to package directions.
3. Heat oil in large skillet and sauté vegetables until tender. Add broth and simmer 2 minutes.
4. Add barley, salt and pepper. Place in pan and bake covered 30 minutes.

Savory Challah Stuffing

PAREVE   YIELD: 8 SERVINGS

Use this savory recipe to stuff a chicken or turkey.

8	cups cubed challah, hard crust removed	1	cup finely chopped green pepper
3	cups vegetable broth, warmed	1	cup finely chopped red pepper
¼	cup olive oil	1	teaspoon ground sage
½	cup finely chopped onion	1	teaspoon pepper
4	cloves garlic, minced	1	large egg
			Salt to taste

1. Preheat oven to 350°F. Prepare ungreased cookie sheet. Grease 9-inch square pan.
2. Toast challah on sheet in oven, stirring occasionally. Remove to large bowl.
3. Cover challah with broth and mash, leaving some cubes visible.
4. Heat oil in large skillet and sauté onions, garlic and peppers until soft. Mix in spices and egg.
5. Combine bread with onion mixture and place into pan. Bake 30 minutes until set and browned.

Perfect Slicing

Use an egg slicer to cut perfect mushroom, strawberry and kiwi slices.

Chocolate-Orange Cake

Heavenly Desserts and Signature Desserts

*D*essert lovers will agree: a truly "divine" meal ends with a "heavenly" dessert. *Some might even say that everything beforehand is only prelude to dessert, and the more delicious the meal, the more excited the palate becomes in anticipation of dessert.* Divine Kosher Cuisine *does not disappoint! For the well-tempered palate that savors a lush ending to a luscious meal, we have loaded two entire sections with a treasure trove of dessert recipes. Heavenly Desserts presents a bonanza of tried and true family desserts contributed by our congregants. It is followed by Signature Desserts, which features the signature recipes that have brought fame to As You Like It Kosher Catering. Our catering company is renowned for its lavishly decorated desserts, pies, cakes, bars, cookies and fancy pick-up pastries. These fabulous desserts have the touch of elegance and the imprint of the home baker, having always been baked from scratch in our synagogue kitchen by our army of expert volunteer bakers, who lovingly devote untold hours to their creation.*

Sour Cream Pound Cake

DAIRY   YIELD: 10 TO 12 SLICES

*E*veryone has a sour cream cake recipe but this rich, moist version is guaranteed to be your favorite.

1 cup butter, room temperature	1 teaspoon baking powder
2 cups sugar	¼ teaspoon salt
2 large eggs	4 teaspoons sugar
1 cup sour cream	1 cup chopped pecans
½ teaspoon vanilla extract	1 teaspoon ground cinnamon
2 cups flour	

1. Preheat oven to 350°F. Grease Bundt pan or 9-inch tube pan.
2. Cream butter and 2 cups sugar at medium speed with electric mixer until light and fluffy. Beat in eggs 1 at a time.
3. Fold in sour cream and vanilla. Mix in flour, baking powder and salt.
4. Combine remaining sugar, pecans and cinnamon.
5. Place one-third batter in pan. Sprinkle with three-quarters pecan mixture and spoon in remaining batter. Sprinkle with remaining pecan mixture.
6. Bake 1 hour or until tester inserted in center comes out clean.

Sour Cream Chocolate Cake

DAIRY OR PAREVE   YIELD: 12 SERVINGS

A moist chocolate cake spiked with a hint of coffee and the slight piquancy of sour cream.

Cake

2	cups flour	1	cup sour cream for dairy (use nondairy sour cream for pareve)
2	cups sugar	⅓	cup butter for dairy, room temperature (use margarine for pareve)
2	teaspoons instant coffee powder		
4	ounces unsweetened chocolate, melted and cooled	1¼	teaspoons baking soda
2	tablespoons cocoa powder, sifted	½	teaspoon baking powder
3	large eggs	1	teaspoon salt
1	cup water	1	teaspoon vanilla extract

1. Preheat oven to 350°F. Grease two 9-inch round pans.
2. Beat all ingredients 30 seconds on low speed with electric mixer. Increase speed to high and beat 3 minutes more.
3. Divide batter evenly between pans and bake 30 to 35 minutes or until tester inserted in center comes out clean. Prepare Sour Cream Chocolate Frosting while cake cools.

Sour Cream Chocolate Frosting

⅓	cup butter for dairy, room temperature (use margarine for pareve)	2⅔	cups confectioners' sugar
		½	cup sour cream for dairy (use nondairy sour cream for pareve)
3	ounces unsweetened chocolate, melted and cooled	2	teaspoons vanilla extract

1. Beat butter or margarine with chocolate at medium speed with electric mixer. Add sugar.
2. Add sour cream or nondairy sour cream and vanilla, beating until fluffy.
3. Spread frosting between layers and over cake.

Jam-Filled Graham Cracker Nut Loaf

DAIRY   YIELD: 16 SLICES

Use any fruit jam or preserves in this recipe. If you don't cut the cake in half, spread jam on top as frosting.

⅔ cup flour	⅓ cup butter, room temperature
½ teaspoon salt	1 teaspoon vanilla extract
1 tablespoon baking powder	2 large eggs
2 cups graham cracker crumbs	⅓ cup evaporated or whole milk
⅔ cup finely chopped nuts	⅓ cup apple juice
1 cup brown sugar, firmly packed	1 cup strawberry jam

1. Preheat oven to 375°F. Grease 9 x 5 x 3-inch loaf pan.
2. Beat all ingredients except jam at medium speed with electric mixer. Pour mixture into pan.
3. Bake 50 minutes until lightly browned and tester inserted in center comes out clean. Cool. Remove from pan.
4. Cut cake in half horizontally, spread jam over bottom layer and top with remaining layer.

Pareve Pumpkin Pie

PAREVE   YIELD: 8 SERVINGS

3 cups canned pumpkin	¼ teaspoon ground allspice
1 cup sugar	4 large eggs, slightly beaten
1 teaspoon salt	¼ cup margarine, melted
1 teaspoon ground nutmeg	9-inch deep-dish unbaked pie shell
1 teaspoon ground cinnamon	Liquid nondairy whipped
1 teaspoon ground ginger	topping, whipped
¼ teaspoon ground cloves	

1. Preheat oven to 450°F.
2. Combine pumpkin, sugar, salt, nutmeg, cinnamon, ginger, cloves and allspice.
3. Add eggs and margarine and stir until smooth.
4. Pour into shell and bake 10 minutes. Reduce oven temperature to 350°F and bake 40 minutes more or until center is set. Chill. Serve with whipped topping.

Pie Shell Tip

• Place a store-bought pie shell into an empty ungreased metal or glass pie pan for stability when baking.

Chocolate-Orange Cake

DAIRY OR PAREVE   YIELD: 8 SERVINGS

A creamy, crunchy chocolate cake, textured with ground almonds and challah crumbs, fragrant with orange flavor and, finally, bathed with a bittersweet, honey chocolate icing.

Cake

2 slices challah, lightly toasted	1 cup ground almonds
½ cup butter for dairy, room temperature (use margarine for pareve)	3 large eggs
	2 tablespoons fresh orange zest
⅔ cup sugar	¾ cup chocolate chips, melted

1. Preheat oven to 350°F. Grease 8-inch round pan and line with parchment paper.

2. Trim crusts from challah and discard. Grind remainder into crumbs to measure ¼ cup.

3. Cream butter or margarine with sugar at medium speed with electric mixer. Add almonds and challah crumbs. Add eggs, 1 at a time, beating well after each. Add zest and chocolate.

4. Pour into pan and bake 30 to 35 minutes or until tester inserted in center comes out clean. Prepare Honey-Chocolate Icing while cake cools.

Honey-Chocolate Icing

2 tablespoons honey	1½ ounces chocolate chips
2 ounces bittersweet chocolate	¼ cup butter for dairy (use margarine for pareve)

1. Melt all ingredients.

2. Pour warm icing over cake. Chill.

Successful Baking

• Recipes indicate estimated baking times.

• The appearance and texture of the baked item is just as important as the length of time it is baked.

• Check smaller items five minutes before the designated baking time has elapsed and ten minutes earlier for larger items.

Eggless Chocolate Cake

PAREVE   YIELD: 10 SERVINGS

*Y*ou won't miss the egg in this moist novel cake. For a Mexican variation with "heat," add ¼ teaspoon cayenne or chili powder to dry ingredients.

Cake

1½	cups flour	¼	cup vegetable oil
1	cup sugar	1	teaspoon vanilla extract
½	cup cocoa, sifted	1	cup cold water
1	teaspoon baking soda	1	tablespoon balsamic vinegar
¼	teaspoon salt		Confectioners' sugar for dusting

1. Preheat oven to 350°F. Grease 8-inch round cake pan.
2. Combine dry ingredients. Mix in oil, vanilla and water.
3. Add vinegar and pour batter immediately into pan.
4. Bake 25 to 30 minutes or until cake springs back when touched.
5. Cool 10 minutes and remove from pan. Cool completely before dusting with confectioners' sugar or frost with Mocha Glaze.

Mocha Glaze

1	cup confectioners' sugar	1	tablespoon coffee liqueur
½	cup cocoa, sifted	10	strawberries for garnish
5	tablespoons hot water		

1. Whisk sugar, cocoa, water and liqueur until smooth.
2. Dip strawberries into glaze and place on wax or parchment paper.
3. Pour remaining glaze over cooled cake and arrange strawberries. Chill 30 minutes.

Southern Lemon Pound Cake

DAIRY   YIELD: 10 SLICES

*T*his is a true Southern pound cake, spiked with generous splashes of vanilla and lemon flavoring. This cake freezes very well. Cover with plastic wrap and then foil.

Cake

½	cup solid vegetable shortening	¼	teaspoon salt
1	cup butter	1½	teaspoons baking powder
3	cups sugar	1	cup milk
6	large eggs	2	tablespoons vanilla extract
3¼	cups flour	2	tablespoons lemon extract

Buttermilk Substitute

• Place 1 tablespoon white vinegar in a 1-cup glass measure and pour milk up to the 1-cup line. Stir.

1. Preheat oven to 300°F. Grease Bundt pan or two 8½ x 4½ x 2½-inch loaf pans.
2. Cream shortening, butter and sugar at medium speed with electric mixer. Beat in eggs, 1 at a time.
3. Combine flour with salt and baking powder. Add to batter, alternating with milk. Mix in extracts.
4. Pour into pan and bake 1½ hours or until tester inserted in center comes out clean. Cool 20 minutes. Remove cake from pan and top with Lemon Glaze.

Lemon Glaze

6   tablespoons lemon juice   1¾ cups confectioners' sugar, sifted

1. Beat ingredients at medium speed with electric mixer until smooth.

Chocolate Melting Cakes

DAIRY OR PAREVE   YIELD: 8 SERVINGS

These "melting" chocolate cakes, which can be dusted with confectioners' sugar, are a chocoholic's dream! The secret to this recipe's success is to not over bake it. The center should be gooey.

10 ounces bittersweet chocolate, chopped
¼   cup butter for dairy (use margarine for pareve)
5   large eggs
½   cup sugar
1   teaspoon vanilla extract

¾   cup flour
1½ teaspoons baking powder
⅛   teaspoon salt
½   cup chocolate chips
    Confectioners' sugar for dusting, optional

1. Preheat oven to 325°F. Grease 8-inch pan or 8 small custard or soufflé cups.
2. Melt chopped chocolate with butter or margarine and stir until smooth. Cool.
3. Beat eggs and sugar at high speed with electric mixer until light and fluffy. Stir in vanilla.
4. Combine flour, baking powder and salt and beat into egg mixture. Add melted chocolate mixture. Fold in chocolate chips.
5. Divide batter evenly into pan or cups.
6. Bake 15 minutes until cakes have just cooked through, a top crust has formed and center is gooey. Cool 5 minutes and dust with confectioners' sugar. Cakes may be reheated in 325°F oven.

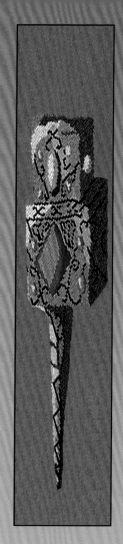

Cake Flour Substitute

1 cup flour minus 2 tablespoons

2 tablespoons cornstarch

• Combine flour and cornstarch.

Spiked Honey Cake

PAREVE   YIELD: 24 SERVINGS

An aromatic, deep brown colored and densely textured classic festival honey cake. A splash of brandy or whiskey further spikes the flavor and aging only improves the taste.

½	cup vegetable oil	2½	cups flour
¾	cup sugar	1½	teaspoons baking soda
1	cup honey	1½	teaspoons ground cinnamon
1	tablespoon vanilla extract	1½	teaspoons ground ginger
2	large eggs	½	cup coffee
1	tablespoon brandy or whiskey	½	cup chopped walnuts
1	tablespoon anise seed	¼	cup raisins
6	tablespoons orange marmalade or apricot preserves	2	tablespoons maraschino cherries, chopped

1. Preheat oven to 350°F. Grease Bundt pan or two 8½ x 4½ x 2½-inch loaf pans.
2. Mix oil, sugar, honey and vanilla at medium speed with electric mixer. Beat in eggs.
3. Add brandy or whiskey, anise seed and marmalade or preserves.
4. Combine flour, baking soda, cinnamon and ginger. Add to batter, alternately, with coffee.
5. Fold in nuts and fruit, and pour batter into pan. Bake 50 minutes or until tester inserted in center comes out clean. Tent with foil while baking if top gets too dark.

Peanut Butter Swirl Bars

DAIRY   YIELD: 24 BARS

½	cup crunchy peanut butter	2	teaspoons vanilla extract
⅓	cup butter, room temperature	1	cup flour
¾	cup brown sugar, firmly packed	1	teaspoon baking powder
¾	cup sugar	¼	teaspoon salt
2	large eggs	12	ounces chocolate chips

1. Preheat oven to 350°F. Grease 9 x 13-inch baking pan.
2. Cream peanut butter, butter and sugars at medium speed with electric mixer. Beat in eggs and vanilla.
3. Combine flour, baking powder and salt and mix into peanut butter mixture. Spread in pan.

4. Sprinkle chocolate chips over surface and bake 5 minutes. Remove from oven and swirl a knife through batter to marbleize. Bake 20 to 25 minutes more. Cool before cutting.

Hungarian Meringue Lattice Bars

DAIRY OR PAREVE   YIELD: 18 BARS

1¼ cups butter for dairy (use margarine for pareve)	1 cup sugar
2½ cups flour	1 cup ground blanched almonds
1½ cups confectioners' sugar	½ cup grated bittersweet chocolate
¾ teaspoon salt	1 teaspoon vanilla extract
2½ teaspoons fresh lemon zest	1 cup apricot preserves
3 tablespoons lemon juice	1 large egg yolk
4 large eggs, separated	1 teaspoon water

1. Preheat oven to 350°F. Grease 9 x 13-inch baking pan.

2. Cut butter or margarine into flour until crumbly.

3. Mix in confectioners' sugar, salt, zest, juice and 4 yolks. Cover and chill 30 minutes.

4. Press two-thirds dough on bottom and sides of pan and bake 10 minutes. Cool. Cover and chill remaining dough until ready to use.

5. Beat whites and sugar at medium speed with electric mixer until foamy. Increase speed and beat on high speed until stiff and glossy. Fold in almonds, chocolate, and vanilla to make filling.

6. Spread preserves on crust and top with filling.

7. Roll remaining dough ⅛-inch thick and cut into ½-inch wide strips. Lay half the strips 1-inch apart horizontally and arrange remaining strips diagonally to form diamond-shaped pattern. For a fancier lattice, twist strips.

8. Beat remaining yolk with water and brush pastry. Bake 30 to 35 minutes or until firm to touch and lattice is golden brown. Cool before cutting.

Hungarian Kipfel

DAIRY   YIELD: 100 COOKIES

This recipe makes a lot of cookies so you may want to freeze some dough for later use.

Rolling Mixture

1   cup flour   1   cup confectioners' sugar

1. Combine ingredients.

Filling

1   large egg white   1   cup ground walnuts

1   cup sugar   1   teaspoon vanilla extract

1. Combine ingredients.

Dough

4   cups flour   1   teaspoon vanilla extract
4½ teaspoons yeast   ½   teaspoon salt
1½ cups butter, cut into 1-inch chunks   1   cup sour cream
3   large egg yolks, beaten   Confectioners' sugar for dusting

1. Preheat oven to 350°F ten minutes before baking. Grease cookie sheets.
2. Combine flour and yeast with butter at medium speed with electric mixer until mixture resembles coarse meal.
3. Mix egg yolks with vanilla and salt and add to dough. Beat in sour cream. Dough should be smooth. Add additional flour if needed.
4. Divide into 10 pieces. Chill 1 hour.
5. Roll each ball into circle ⅛-inch thick on lightly floured surface using Rolling Mixture. Cut into 10 wedges. Work with 1 piece of dough at a time, keeping remainder chilled.
6. Spread ½ teaspoon filling on wide end of each triangle and roll up. Place on sheet and bake 25 minutes or until just golden brown.
7. Cool and dust with confectioners' sugar.

Cookie Dusting Tip

• Place confectioners' sugar in small wire sieve and lightly shake over cookies to coat.

Caraway Cookies

DAIRY OR PAREVE   YIELD: 48 COOKIES

*T*he caraway seeds in this unusual recipe add a pleasant pungency to this mildly sweet, biscuit-like cookie. A clever complement to a sweet dessert wine.

2	cups flour	½	cup butter for dairy, room temperature (use margarine for pareve)
1	tablespoon caraway seeds		
1	teaspoon baking powder	1	cup sugar
¼	teaspoon baking soda	2	large eggs
¼	teaspoon salt		

1. Preheat oven to 375°F ten minutes before baking. Grease cookie sheets.
2. Combine flour, caraway seeds, baking powder, baking soda and salt.
3. Cream butter or margarine at medium speed with electric mixer until fluffy. Add sugar. Beat in eggs, 1 at a time. Add dry ingredients.
4. Cover dough with plastic wrap. Chill 3 hours or overnight.
5. Divide dough in half and roll each piece on lightly floured surface ⅛-inch thick. Cut out decorative 2½-inch shapes and place 2 inches apart on sheets.
6. Bake 6 to 8 minutes or until edges are golden brown.

 Muscat

Poppy Seed Cookies

DAIRY   YIELD: 48 COOKIES

1	cup butter	2½	cups flour
9	tablespoons sugar	½	teaspoon ground cinnamon
1	large egg	¼	teaspoon ground ginger
⅛	teaspoon salt	⅓	cup chopped pecans
1	teaspoon vanilla extract	¼	cup poppy seeds
½	teaspoon almond extract		

1. Preheat oven to 350°F. Grease cookie sheets.
2. Cream butter with sugar at medium speed with electric mixer. Beat in egg, salt and extracts.
3. Mix in flour, spices, nuts and seeds.
4. Roll dough into 6 logs, 1½ inches in diameter. Chill 30 minutes. Cut into ¼-inch thick diagonal slices. Place on sheets.
5. Bake 10 to 12 minutes until lightly browned.

Chocolate-Dipped Peanut Balls

PAREVE   YIELD: 48 BALLS

A marriage made in heaven — chocolate-dipped peanut balls. These no-bake cookies are an easy crowd pleaser.

1   cup peanut butter
1   cup confectioners' sugar
1   cup ground walnuts

1   cup finely chopped dates
2   cups chocolate chips

1. Line cookie sheet with parchment paper.
2. Cream peanut butter with sugar at medium speed with electric mixer and add walnuts and dates.
3. Shape into balls, using 1½ teaspoons dough per cookie.
4. Melt chocolate chips and keep over container of hot water.
5. Dip balls into chocolate and place on sheet. Chill to set.

White Chocolate Chip-Orange Cookies

DAIRY   YIELD: 36 COOKIES

2¼ cups flour
¾   teaspoon baking soda
½   teaspoon salt
1   cup butter, room temperature
½   cup sugar

½   cup brown sugar, firmly packed
1   large egg
1   tablespoon fresh orange zest
2   cups white chocolate chips

1. Preheat oven to 350°F. Grease cookie sheets.
2. Combine flour, baking soda and salt.
3. Cream butter and sugars at medium speed with electric mixer. Beat in egg and zest and gradually beat in flour mixture. Stir in white chocolate chips.
4. Drop dough by rounded tablespoons onto sheets. Bake 10 to 12 minutes until edges are golden brown.

How to Bake Cookies Evenly

1. Position 2 racks in upper and lower thirds of oven.

2. Bake cookies for half the time, then switch positions from top to bottom.

3. It also helps to turn sheets 180° so front is in back.

Giant Chocolate Chip Cookie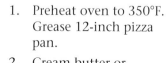

DAIRY OR PAREVE   YIELD: 12 TO 16 SERVINGS

½   cup butter for dairy, room
     temperature (use margarine for
     pareve)
⅓   cup brown sugar, firmly packed
¼   cup sugar
1   large egg

1   teaspoon vanilla extract
1⅓ cups flour
½   teaspoon baking soda
¼   teaspoon salt
½   cup chocolate chips
¼   cup chopped nuts

1. Preheat oven to 350°F. Grease 12-inch pizza pan.
2. Cream butter or margarine with sugars at medium speed with electric mixer. Beat in egg and vanilla.
3. Mix in flour, baking soda and salt. Fold in chocolate chips and nuts.
4. Spread into pan and bake 15 to 20 minutes until golden brown.
5. Frost and decorate if desired. Cut into wedges or break into pieces.

Sandwich Cookie Truffles

DAIRY   YIELD: 30 TRUFFLES

The best thing to ever happen to a chocolate, cream-filled sandwich cookie!

18 ounces chocolate cream-filled
     sandwich cookies
8   ounces cream cheese, room
     temperature

12 ounces chocolate chips
2   tablespoons vegetable oil

1. Process cookies until fine. Add cream cheese and blend until mixture holds together. Cover and chill 2 hours.
2. Roll dough into 1-inch balls.
3. Melt chocolate chips with oil and stir until smooth. Dip balls into warm chocolate and place on parchment or wax paper-lined cookie sheet. Chill to set.

Decorating Icing

2 cups confectioners' sugar

½ teaspoon vanilla extract

2 tablespoons milk, as needed

Food coloring

1. Beat sugar, vanilla and milk at medium speed with electric mixer until smooth. Thin frosting with additional milk as needed.

2. Tint frosting with food coloring.

Beignets with Chocolate-Bourbon Sauce

DAIRY   YIELD: 30 PASTRIES

Teaming chocolate with cayenne or other chili pepper dates back to the ancient Aztec and Mayan civilizations — where the cocoa plant originated. The tradition survives in creative baking around the world. Mound these wonderful fried sweet rolls around a bowl of chocolate dipping sauce spiked with bourbon and cayenne.

Beignets

Vegetable oil for frying	1 large egg
1 cup flour	½ cup buttermilk
1 teaspoon baking powder	½ teaspoon vanilla extract
¼ teaspoon baking soda	¼ cup flour for kneading and rolling
½ teaspoon salt	
1½ tablespoons sugar	1 cup confectioners' sugar
1 tablespoon instant rapid rise yeast	1 teaspoon ground cinnamon

1. Preheat oil to 365°F in deep heavy skillet 10 minutes before frying.
2. Combine flour, baking powder, baking soda, salt, sugar and yeast.
3. Mix egg, buttermilk and vanilla into flour mixture to form sticky dough.
4. Place on lightly floured surface and knead until smooth but slightly sticky to touch, adding more flour as needed.
5. Transfer to lightly floured bowl. Cover with plastic wrap and let rest until doubled in size, 1½ to 2 hours.
6. Punch down dough, turn onto lightly floured surface, pat down into rectangle, ¼-inch thick. Cut into 1½-inch squares.
7. Pour oil ¾-inch deep into skillet and fry dough in batches 1 minute on each side or until evenly golden brown. Do not crowd pan. Drain on paper towels. Sprinkle with mixture of confectioners' sugar and cinnamon.
8. Serve with Chocolate-Bourbon Sauce.

Check oil temperature with candy thermometer to maintain even temperature.

Chocolate-Bourbon Sauce

⅔ cup heavy cream	⅛ teaspoon ground mace
4 ounces bittersweet chocolate, melted	⅛ teaspoon cayenne pepper
	1 teaspoon instant coffee granules or espresso powder
1 tablespoon bourbon	
1 teaspoon fresh minced gingerroot	

1. Heat cream in saucepan until it just starts to boil. Stir chocolate into cream.
2. Add bourbon and remaining ingredients, stirring until smooth.
3. Pour chocolate mixture into fondue pot and keep warm.

Delicate Chocolate Cups

DAIRY OR PAREVE   YIELD: 12 MINICUPS

Create delicate chocolate cups to hold an array of fillings. Fill with Quick White Chocolate Mousse, Chocolate Mousse, Custard Filling or assorted puddings.

6 ounces chocolate chips	2 tablespoons butter or margarine

1. Line minimuffin tin with baking papers.
2. Melt chocolate chips with butter or margarine and stir until smooth.
3. Spread chocolate mixture with back of spoon to coat inside of each baking paper to ⅛-inch thickness. Chill to set.

Quick White Chocolate Mousse

DAIRY   YIELD: 6 SERVINGS

2¼ cups heavy cream, divided	8 ounces white chocolate, finely chopped
2 tablespoons honey	1 tablespoon vanilla extract

1. Bring 1¾ cups cream to boil. Stir in honey and remove from heat.
2. Stir in chocolate until melted and mixture is smooth and transfer to bowl.
3. Chill 2 hours. Add remaining cream and vanilla.
4. Beat with whisk attachment of electric mixer until soft peaks form. Do not over whip because mixture thickens as it chills.

Apple-Honey Dessert Pizza

PAREVE   YIELD: 12 SLICES

A pretty-as-a-picture pizza pie to wow the kids — and the kid in you — this gorgeous apple and honey dessert cleverly blends the traditional Rosh Hashanah symbol foods. A fun and versatile recipe, so easy to prepare that kids love to make it.

	9-inch unbaked pie shell	⅓	cup ground nuts
	Flour for dusting	¼	cup raisins
¼	cup honey	¼	cup sugar
1	cup applesauce	½	teaspoon ground cinnamon
2	medium apples, peeled and thinly sliced		

1. Preheat oven to 400°F. Grease cookie sheet or pizza pan.

2. Remove pie crust from foil pan, dust lightly with flour and roll into 12-inch circle directly on sheet or pan.

3. Crimp edge of dough to form rim, prick with fork and brush with honey.

4. Cover with applesauce to rim. Top with apple slices in concentric circles.

5. Sprinkle with nuts and raisins. Combine sugar and cinnamon and sprinkle over top. Bake 20 minutes or until crust is firm and golden brown. Cut into wedges.

Add chocolate minichips, nuts or finely chopped maraschino cherries.

Flaky Pie Crust may be substituted.

Streusel-Topped Apple Pie

DAIRY OR PAREVE   YIELD: 8 SERVINGS

Jazz up this all-American classic with our tasty topping.

Streusel Topping

1½ tablespoons sugar
1   tablespoon brown sugar, firmly
    packed
⅛   teaspoon salt
¼   teaspoon ground cinnamon

½   cup flour
2   tablespoons butter for dairy,
    room temperature
    (use margarine for pareve)

1. Combine dry ingredients and cut in butter or margarine until crumbly.

Pie and Crust

½   cup sugar
⅓   cup brown sugar, firmly packed
2   tablespoons flour
½   teaspoon ground cinnamon
¼   teaspoon ground nutmeg
¼   teaspoon ground coriander
¼   teaspoon salt
2   tablespoons butter for dairy
    (use margarine for pareve)

3   pounds apples, peeled and thinly
    sliced
1   recipe Double Crust Flaky Pie
    Crust
    Flour for rolling
1   recipe Streusel Topping
    Vanilla ice cream for dairy
    (use nondairy ice-cream for
    pareve)

1. Preheat oven to 375°F. Grease 9-inch deep-dish pie pan.
2. Combine sugars, flour, cinnamon, nutmeg, coriander and salt. Cut in butter or margarine until pieces are size of large peas. Toss with apples.
3. Roll 1 disk of dough out onto lightly floured surface to 11-inch circle. Fit into pan. Spoon apple mixture into shell. Trim dough to rim of pan.
4. Roll remaining disk out on lightly floured surface to 12-inch circle and fit over filling. Cut slits for steam to escape. Form ridge by tucking top edge of pastry under bottom edge. Flute, if desired. Sprinkle with Streusel Topping.
5. Cover edge with foil and bake 25 minutes. Remove foil and bake additional 25 to 30 minutes until crust is golden brown and apples are tender.
6. Serve warm with vanilla ice cream or nondairy ice cream.

Substitute prepared pie shell for Flaky Pie Crust.

Apple Cream Cheese Torte

DAIRY

YIELD: 10 TO 12 SERVINGS

Crust

½ cup butter
⅓ cup sugar

¼ teaspoon vanilla extract
1 cup flour

1. Preheat oven to 450°F. Grease 10-inch springform pan.
2. Cream butter, sugar and vanilla at medium speed with electric mixer until smooth. Add flour to form dough.
3. Pat dough on bottom and sides of pan.

Filling

8 ounces cream cheese, room temperature
¾ cup sugar, divided
1 large egg

½ teaspoon vanilla extract
¾ teaspoon ground cinnamon
4 tart apples, peeled and sliced
¼ cup slivered almonds

1. Beat cheese and ¼ cup sugar at medium speed with electric mixer. Add egg and vanilla, beating until smooth. Pour over crust.
2. Toss remaining sugar and cinnamon with apples. Arrange apples over cheese filling and sprinkle with almonds.
3. Bake 10 minutes, reduce oven temperature to 400°F and bake 35 minutes more or until apples are tender. Serve chilled.

Dates and Nuts Non-G

PAREVE

YIELD: 24 PIECES

Serve as pastry or candy.

Stuffed Dates

24 dates, pitted

24 whole blanched almonds, unsalted

Sugar for rolling

1. Stuff almond into each date where pit was removed.

2. Roll in sugar and set aside to dry.

Date Nut Roll

1 pound dates, pitted
1½ cups plus ⅔ cup pecans, divided

1. Process dates and 1½ cups pecans until mixture holds together. Shape into log on wax or parchment paper.
2. Process remaining pecans until fine. Roll log over nuts to coat completely.
3. Chill 2 hours. Cut into ½-inch rounds.

Fresh Peach Cobbler

DAIRY OR PAREVE   YIELD: 6 SERVINGS

1 cup flour	4 cups peeled and sliced fresh peaches
¾ cup sugar	1 tablespoon lemon juice
1 teaspoon baking powder	⅓ cup butter for dairy, melted (use margarine for pareve)
½ teaspoon salt	Ice cream for dairy (use nondairy ice cream for pareve)
1 large egg	
1 tablespoon cornstarch	
⅓ cup sugar	

1. Preheat oven to 350°F. Grease 8-inch round baking pan.
2. Mix flour, ¾ cup sugar, baking powder, salt and egg until crumbly.
3. Combine cornstarch with ⅓ cup sugar and stir into peaches. Add juice.

4. Arrange peaches in pan, top with flour mixture and drizzle with butter or margarine.
5. Bake until bubbly and crust is browned, 30 minutes. Serve with ice cream or nondairy ice cream.

Substitute pears for peaches.

Citrus and Grapes in Muscat Wine Non-G

PAREVE   YIELD: 6 SERVINGS

Serve this light refreshing dessert as a finale to a meat dinner, in individual portions or from an attractive fruit bowl. Any sweet wine may be used.

3 navel oranges, sectioned	1 cup red or green seedless grapes
3 tangerines, sectioned	¼ cup sugar or honey
2 red grapefruit, sectioned	1 cup Muscat wine

1. Place fruit in bowl and stir in sugar or honey. Chill 1 hour.
2. Combine fruit with Muscat.

Simple Fruit Sorbet

PAREVE   YIELD: 4 SERVINGS

Sorbets are basically sherbets with a French accent. These icy, finely textured fruit desserts are refreshing and palate-cleansing. Vary this sorbet to suit the season or your taste. If you use berries that have seeds, force them through a sieve. Try using figs or plums. You may substitute lemon or orange juice for the liqueur. If you use fruit in light syrup, the sorbet will be icier, like an Italian granita.

1   15-ounce can apricots or peaches   2   tablespoons almond or other
      in heavy syrup   liqueur

1. Freeze can of fruit at least 12 hours.
2. Warm frozen can in hot water 2 minutes. Carefully remove top and bottom lids (may spurt) and pour contents into processor or blender. Add liqueur and purée.
3. Serve immediately or form balls with cookie scoop and freeze.

Use any 15 to 16-ounce canned fruit in heavy syrup and mix and match flavorings.

• *Pears with orange liqueur or Port wine*

• *Plums with raspberry or currant liqueur*

• *Figs with Marsala wine*

• *Grapefruit sections or Mandarin oranges with rum or orange liqueur.*

• *Reduce sweetness by adding 1 teaspoon lemon juice.*

Piña Colada Sorbet

1 20-ounce can crushed pineapple in heavy syrup

2 tablespoons canned cream of coconut

• Follow directions for Simple Fruit Sorbet.

Mango Sorbet

PAREVE   YIELD: 4 SERVINGS

2   large ripe mangoes   ¼   cup light corn syrup
6   tablespoons sugar

1. Peel mangoes and remove flesh from pit. Purée in processor or blender until smooth. Mix in sugar and corn syrup. Chill 1 hour.
2. Place mixture into ice cream maker and follow manufacturer's directions. Or, freeze mixture in metal tray and beat vigorously as it starts to freeze and again just before it sets.

Strawberry Sorbet

Sorbet

1   quart strawberries, hulled
½   cup sugar, pulverized in blender

3   tablespoons lemon juice

1. Purée berries in processor or blender and place in small bowl. Stir in sugar and juice.
2. Fill large bowl with ice and sprinkle with 1½ tablespoons salt for ice bath.
3. Place smaller bowl of purée into ice bath. Beat mixture at medium speed with electric hand mixer until sugar completely dissolves.
4. Place mixture in freezer. When it begins to freeze, beat vigorously to break up ice crystals and beat again just before it is set.
5. Serve with Strawberry Garnish.

If you use an ice cream machine, follow manufacturer's directions.

Strawberry Garnish

½   pint strawberries, hulled
1   tablespoon sugar

½   teaspoon red wine vinegar

1. Slice strawberries and add sugar and vinegar, tossing gently to completely coat.

Granola Ice Cream Bar Pie

Prepare this crust ahead of time for a child's birthday party and invite the kids to help with the toppings.

½   cup butter, melted
1½ cups granola
⅓   cup chopped nuts

3   tablespoons brown sugar, firmly packed
Ice cream, toppings, and candy

1. Grease 8-inch pie pan.
2. Mix butter, granola, nuts and brown sugar. Press into pan and chill 1 hour.
3. Fill with scoops of ice cream, toppings and candy.

Banana Crisp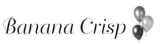

DAIRY OR PAREVE   YIELD: 6 SERVINGS

Bananas transform this traditional crisp into a unique dessert. Serve with dairy or nondairy whipped cream.

6	cups sliced bananas	1¼	cups flour
1	cup sugar	1	cup rolled oats
¼	teaspoon ground nutmeg	½	teaspoon salt
½	teaspoon ground cinnamon	¾	cup butter for dairy
1	cup chocolate chips, divided		(use margarine for pareve)
½	cup brown sugar, firmly packed		

1. Preheat oven to 375°F. Grease 8-inch square pan.
2. Combine bananas, sugar, nutmeg and cinnamon. Place in pan and sprinkle with half the chocolate chips.
3. Mix sugar, flour, oats and salt. Cut in butter or margarine until it forms crumbs. Add remaining chocolate chips. Scatter mixture over batter and bake 40 minutes or until browned.

Marinated Fresh Fruit Salad   Non-G

PAREVE   YIELD: 12 SERVINGS

Substitute citrus fruits for summer seasonal fruit in the winter and adjust sweetness.

½	pineapple, cut into 1-inch pieces	2	peaches, cut into 1-inch pieces
½	large honeydew melon, cut into 1-inch pieces	2	plums, cut into 1-inch pieces
½	large cantaloupe, cut into 1-inch pieces	2	kiwis, cut into 1-inch pieces
½	pint strawberries, hulled and quartered	¼	cup red wine or cranberry juice
½	pint raspberries	2	tablespoons fruit preserves, warmed
½	pint blueberries	1	tablespoon lemon juice to taste
1	cup cherries, pitted and cut in half	2	tablespoons chopped fresh mint leaves to taste

1. Combine fruit in large bowl.
2. Mix wine or cranberry juice with preserves and lemon juice. Pour over fruit and stir in mint. Cover and chill.

Poached Pears
with Raspberry Coulis  Non-G

PAREVE   YIELD: 4 TO 8 SERVINGS

This very light fruit dessert is an elegant finish to a meat meal. Serve a half or a whole pear, sliced and fanned out, over a pool of Raspberry Coulis. Substitute fresh peaches, plums or apricots for pears.

Pears

4	Anjou, Comice or Bartlett pears
2	teaspoons lemon juice
1	teaspoon fresh lemon zest
2½	cups dry white wine, white grape juice or orange juice

2½	cups water
1	tablespoon vanilla extract
⅔	cup sugar

1. Peel pears, halve lengthwise and remove cores and pits. Sprinkle with lemon juice.
2. Combine zest, wine, grape or orange juice, water, vanilla and sugar in saucepan. Bring to boil and simmer until sugar dissolves.

3. Add pears, cover and simmer until pears are just tender, 15 minutes.
4. Remove pears from poaching liquid. Boil poaching liquid until thick. Pour over pears and chill. Serve with Raspberry Coulis.

Raspberry Coulis

12	ounces frozen raspberries, thawed and drained, or 1 cup fresh raspberries
¼	cup sugar

1	tablespoon lemon juice
1	tablespoon raspberry liqueur, optional

1. Purée fruit over sieve by pushing pulp through with back of spoon. Discard seeds.
2. Heat fruit and sugar in saucepan, stirring constantly until sugar dissolves. Do not let mixture boil.
3. Remove from heat and stir in juice and liqueur. Cool.

*How to
Poach Fruit in the
Microwave*

• Submerge fruit in poaching liquid, cover and microwave on high power, 15 minutes or until fruit is tender.

Meringue-Topped Apples Non-G

DAIRY OR PAREVE   YIELD: 6 TO 8 SERVINGS

This dish makes good use of freshly picked apples during the fall harvest season. Serve this dessert directly from the oven to the table.

4   tart cooking apples, peeled and
      thinly sliced
3   tablespoons butter for dairy,
      melted (use margarine for
      pareve)
6   tablespoons sugar, divided

¼   cup raisins
1   tablespoon apple liqueur,
      optional
3   large egg whites
¼   teaspoon cream of tartar

1. Preheat oven to 350°F. Grease 8-inch baking pan or 8 soufflé cups.

2. Arrange apples in pan or cups, drizzle with butter or margarine and sprinkle with 2 tablespoons sugar, raisins and liqueur. Cover and bake 30 minutes or until apples are tender.

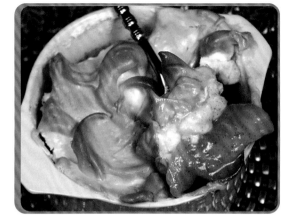

3. Beat whites with cream of tartar at medium speed with electric mixer until foamy. Beat in remaining sugar, 1 tablespoon at a time. Continue beating on high speed until stiff and glossy. Spread meringue over apples.

4. Bake 12 to 15 minutes until meringue is golden brown.

Carob Gorp

PAREVE   YIELD: 6½ CUPS

Prepare this recipe for Tu B'Shevat.

1   cup carob chips
1   cup crispy rice cereal
1   cup toasted oat cereal
½   cup thin pretzel sticks
½   cup cashews

½   cup pecans
½   cup raisins
½   cup banana chips
1   cup peanuts, unsalted

1. Mix ingredients in plastic bag and shake gently.

Cream of Tartar Substitute

Great for Passover recipes.

• Use 1 teaspoon lemon juice for ½ teaspoon cream of tartar.

Star of David Pavlova

The Signature Desserts

*H*ere they are! Our highly sought after, never before revealed, signature desserts — desserts that made As You Like It Kosher Catering *famous. A treasure trove from which to choose happy endings for every meal and great beginnings for any gathering that calls for festive desserts. Ranging from old-fashioned Oodles of Strudels and Mix and Match Rugelach, to gourmet Trifle Our Way and Signature Triple-Layer Chocolate Mousse Cake, these treasured desserts are the best-of-the-best.*

Cocoa Balls

DAIRY   YIELD: 36 COOKIES

*T*he basic recipe produces a satisfying chocolate-nut cookie. Moved up to its truffle version, it becomes positively addictive.*

1 cup butter	1 teaspoon vanilla extract
1 cup confectioners' sugar	2 cups flour
½ cup cocoa, sifted	1 cup finely chopped pecans
1 teaspoon water	Confectioners' sugar for rolling

1. Preheat oven to 350°F. Grease cookie sheets.

2. Cream butter and sugar at medium speed with electric mixer. Beat in cocoa, water and vanilla. Add flour and pecans and mix until soft dough forms. Add
   ¼ teaspoon additional water at a time until mixture holds together

3. Shape into 1-inch balls and place 1 inch apart on sheets. Bake 12 minutes until set and lightly brown. Cool 2 minutes and roll in sugar.

For a truffle version, skip sugar rolling and dip into Dipping Chocolate.

Signature Almond Horns 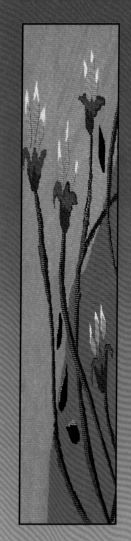 Non-G

PAREVE   YIELD: 36 COOKIES

*T*he most sought after cookie recipe we make, they sell by the thousands! These crescent shaped marvels, bursting with almond flavor, have chocolate-dipped tips. Featured at Carrot Festival, they sell faster than we can bake them.

1   pound almond paste, crumbled
1   cup sugar
⅔   cup confectioners' sugar, sifted
      (use K-P confectioners' sugar for
      Passover)

5   large egg whites, divided
2½ cups sliced almonds

1. Preheat oven to 300°F. Line cookie sheets with parchment or brown paper.
2. Beat almond paste with sugars at medium speed with electric mixer. Add 3 whites and beat 2 minutes. Dough will be very sticky. Chill 1 hour.
3. Roll tablespoons of dough into balls and place on sheets.

4. Roll balls between palms to form logs, about 3 inches long. Keep center of log a little thicker. Dip logs in slightly beaten remaining whites and roll in almonds.
5. Return to sheets and shape into crescents. Chill 15 minutes.
6. Bake 15 to 18 minutes, or just golden brown. Slide parchment or brown paper off sheets and cool. You may freeze almond horns at this point.

7. Dip 1 end of horn in Dipping Chocolate. Place on sheet and chill 10 minutes until chocolate is set.

Slightly oil hands when rolling dough.

Dipping Chocolate

PAREVE OR DAIRY

1 cup pareve chocolate chips (use dairy chocolate chips for dairy

1 tablespoon vegetable oil

• Melt chocolate with oil in microwaveable container for 30 seconds. Stir. Continue to microwave for additional 30 second intervals, stirring each time. Stop melting when a few small chunks are visible. Stir until smooth.

Almond-Cinnamon Crescents

DAIRY OR PAREVE   YIELD: 24 COOKIES

These light, melt-in-your-mouth cookies, delicately flavored with almonds and cinnamon, are terrific as is or you can dress them up by dipping ends of crescents in warmed apricot jam and then into nuts or toasted coconut.

½ cup butter for dairy (use margarine for pareve)	¼ teaspoon salt
15 tablespoons confectioners' sugar, divided	⅓ cup chopped almonds
¾ cup flour	1¼ teaspoons ground cinnamon, divided

1. Preheat oven to 325°F. Grease cookie sheets.
2. Cream butter or margarine with 3 tablespoons sugar at medium speed with electric mixer until light and fluffy. Blend in flour, salt, almonds and ¾ teaspoon cinnamon.
3. Cover and chill dough 30 minutes. Shape dough into crescents. Bake 2 inches apart 18 minutes or until set and lightly brown. Cool 2 minutes.
4. Combine remaining sugar and cinnamon and roll crescents in mixture. Cool.

Chocolate Shortbread Hearts

DAIRY OR PAREVE   YIELD: 30 COOKIES

Chocolate makes these shortbread cookies special and heart shapes make them festive.

2 cups flour	1 cup butter for dairy, room temperature (use margarine for pareve)
¼ teaspoon salt	
½ cup cocoa, sifted	1 cup confectioners' sugar
¼ teaspoon baking soda	1¼ teaspoons vanilla extract

1. Preheat oven to 325°F. Grease cookie sheets.
2. Combine flour, salt, cocoa and baking soda.
3. Cream butter or margarine with sugar at medium speed with electric mixer. Beat in vanilla and add flour mixture, half at a time, to form dough. Cover and chill dough 2 hours.
4. Divide dough in half and roll each between sheets of wax or parchment paper. Cut heart shapes with cookie cutter and arrange on sheets 2 inches apart.
5. Bake 16 to 18 minutes or until set.

Brownie in a Cup

DAIRY OR PAREVE   YIELD: 16 SERVINGS

Each delicate crust holds a thick, rich brownie, delicious as is, or decorate with nut halves or maraschino cherries.

Crust

1 cup flour	⅓ cup butter for dairy
¼ teaspoon salt	*(use margarine for pareve)*
1 large egg	

1. Preheat oven to 350°F. Grease 16 minimuffin tins.
2. Combine all crust ingredients.
3. Place walnut-size ball of dough in each cup. Press down with lightly floured spoon to form even crust on bottom and three-fourths up sides.

Filling

1 cup chocolate chips	1 large egg, beaten
⅓ cup sugar	*Walnut or pecan halves or*
1 tablespoon butter for dairy	*maraschino cherries, drained,*
(use margarine for pareve)	*optional*
1 teaspoon vanilla extract	

1. Melt chocolate chips and mix in sugar, butter or margarine and vanilla.
2. Remove from heat and stir in egg.
3. Fill crusts with brownie mixture. Decorate with nut half or cherry.
4. Bake 25 minutes or until firm.

An Edible Cookie Bowl

*Your cookie jar will never be empty with this clever edible.
Use also to hold candy, fruit and ice cream. Make any size or shape,
as long as you use an ovenproof container. Wonderful idea for a
child's birthday party and as a house or teacher's gift.*

1. Preheat oven to 350°F. Wrap outside of ovenproof loaf pan or mixing bowl with foil. Grease foil.
2. Prepare favorite roll-out cookie dough and roll to ⅛-inch thickness.
3. Cut shapes with decorative edge cookie cutter. When using a loaf pan, use a 1½-inch cookie cutter. Smaller containers require smaller cutters.
4. Cover prepared pan or bowl with cutouts, overlapping them slightly. Bake upside down until cookies are firm. Cool.
5. Lift cookie bowl from container carefully and peel away foil. Freezes well.

Meringue Drops   Non-G

PAREVE   YIELD: 48 COOKIES

Kids love these easy to make featherweight cookies.

½   cup egg whites (about 4 large),
       room temperature
½   teaspoon cream of tartar

13   tablespoons sugar
2   teaspoons vanilla extract
1   cup chocolate chips, chopped

1. Preheat oven to 275°F.
    Line cookie sheets with
    parchment or brown
    paper.
2. Beat egg whites at high
    speed with electric
    mixer until foamy. Add
    cream of tartar and beat
    until smooth.
3. Continue beating,
    gradually adding sugar
    until stiff peaks form.
    Fold in vanilla and
    chocolate.

4. Drop batter onto sheets by heaping teaspoons or pipe with decorating
    bag fitted with a star tip.
5. Bake 20 minutes. Turn off oven. Let rest in oven 1 hour.
6. Remove cookies carefully with spatula as they break easily.

Egg Tips

• Eggs separate best
  when cold.

• Egg whites beat
  with more volume
  when they are at
  room temperature.

Meringue Variations

• Nut Meringues: substitute 1 cup chopped nuts for chocolate chips.

• Nut and Raisin Meringues: substitute ½ cup chopped nuts and ¼ cup raisins
   for chocolate chips.

• Mocha Meringues: add 2 tablespoons finely crushed instant coffee granules.

• Chocolate Meringues: use 1 teaspoon vanilla extract and 3 tablespoons
   sifted cocoa.

• Chocolate Cinnamon Meringues: use 1 teaspoon vanilla extract,
   2½ tablespoons sifted cocoa and 1 teaspoon ground cinnamon.

• Peppermint Meringues: substitute 1 teaspoon mint extract for vanilla, add
   ¼ cup finely crushed peppermint candy and reduce chocolate chips to ½ cup.

Chocolate-Filled Lace Sandwich Cookies

DAIRY OR PAREVE   YIELD: 36 SANDWICH COOKIES

These fragile cookies are a delight to the eye and a treat to the taste buds.

½	cup butter for dairy, melted (use margarine for pareve)	1	cup flour
⅔	cup brown sugar, firmly packed	1	cup walnuts, chopped
½	cup corn syrup	1	teaspoon vanilla extract
		6	ounces chocolate chips

1. Preheat oven to 325°F ten minutes before baking. Line cookie sheet with parchment paper.

2. Melt butter or margarine in saucepan and mix in sugar and corn syrup. Bring to boil and remove from heat.

3. Stir in flour, walnuts and vanilla, mixing well after each addition.

4. Cover dough with plastic wrap and chill overnight or freeze 30 minutes.

5. Wet hands and roll dough into ½-inch balls. Place 3 inches apart on sheet and bake 8 to 10 minutes or until golden brown.

6. Cool 1 minute. Remove from sheet and turn face down on foil or parchment paper to cool.

7. Melt chocolate chips and place thin layer between pairs of cookies. Or, dip each cookie halfway into chocolate. Chill to set.

If using margarine, increase the vanilla extract to 2 teaspoons.

Custard Filling

DAIRY OR PAREVE   YIELD: 4½ CUPS

½	cup sugar	4	cups milk for dairy (use liquid nondairy whipped topping for pareve)
¼	cup cornstarch		
4	large egg yolks	2	teaspoons vanilla extract

1. Combine sugar and cornstarch in saucepan. Whisk in yolks and milk or nondairy topping.

2. Cook, stirring constantly, until mixture thickens, about 25 minutes. Transfer to bowl and stir in vanilla.

3. Cover custard with plastic wrap so skin won't form. Chill 2 hours.

Storing Chocolate

• Chocolate that has been exposed to excessive heat and humidity may "bloom." This refers to a dull look or grayish-white streaks on the chocolate. It doesn't affect the taste or texture.

Chocolate Chip Sandwich Cookies

DAIRY OR PAREVE   YIELD: 48 SANDWICH COOKIES

Cookie Dough

1¼ cups brown sugar, firmly packed
½ cup butter for dairy, room temperature (use margarine for pareve)
1 large egg

1¼ cups flour
¼ teaspoon baking soda
⅛ teaspoon salt
1 cup chocolate minichips

1. Preheat oven to 350°F. Grease cookie sheets.
2. Cream sugar, butter and egg at medium speed with electric mixer.
3. Mix in flour, baking soda and salt. Fold in chocolate chips.
4. Drop dough by level teaspoons onto sheet 2 inches apart.
5. Bake 8 to 10 minutes until golden brown. Cool 2 minutes and remove from sheet to cool completely. Spread with choice of filling.

Chocolate Filling

2 ounces unsweetened baking chocolate
2 tablespoons butter for dairy (use margarine for pareve)

2 cups confectioners' sugar
3 tablespoons hot water

1. Melt chocolate and butter or margarine in saucepan.
2. Stir in sugar and water until smooth and spreading consistency.
3. Spread 1 teaspoon filling on smooth sides of half the cookies. Cover with remaining cookies, pressing sides together.

Vanilla Cream Filling

¼ cup butter for dairy, room temperature (use margarine for pareve)

¼ cup solid vegetable shortening
2⅓ cups confectioners' sugar, sifted
1 tablespoon vanilla extract

1. Cream butter or margarine with vegetable shortening at medium speed with electric mixer. Beat in sugar and vanilla until fluffy.
2. Spread 1 teaspoon of filling on smooth sides of half the cookies. Cover with remaining cookies and press together.

Truffles from Scraps

What to do with leftover bits, pieces and dried edges of brownies and/or cookies? Form those humble scraps into elegant truffle balls.

4 cups brownie and/or cookie scraps, including frosting, coarsely crumbled

2 tablespoons preserves or jam
2 tablespoons liquid or more as needed (choose from brandy, rum or juice)

1. Mix all ingredients adding sufficient liquid to bind mixture and shape rounded teaspoons into balls.

2. For a glossy covering, dip balls into Dipping Chocolate and remove with fork. Drip off the excess. Place balls on parchment or wax paper, decorate with sprinkles, nuts or coconut and chill until set.

For a sweet surprise, tuck a piece of maraschino cherry inside the ball.

Thumbprint Cookies

DAIRY OR PAREVE   YIELD: 30 COOKIES

Make your mark on these nutty, fruity mouthfuls by varying the basic recipe. Use jam instead of fruit preserves or fill cavity with a chocolate star or kiss. For a colorful cookie platter, use a variety of jams.

1 cup butter for dairy (use margarine for pareve)
½ cup brown sugar, firmly packed
2 large egg yolks
1 teaspoon vanilla extract

2 cups flour
¼ teaspoon salt
2 large egg whites, slightly beaten
2½ cups finely chopped walnuts
1 cup fruit preserves

1. Preheat oven to 325°F. Grease cookie sheets.
2. Cream butter or margarine with sugar at medium speed with electric mixer. Beat in yolks and vanilla.
3. Combine flour and salt and add to batter, forming dough. Add water, ¼ teaspoon at a time, if dough does not stick together.
4. Shape dough into 1-inch round balls. Roll balls in whites and then in nuts.
5. Place balls on sheet. Make deep depression in center of each with end of wooden spoon. Bake 15 to 17 minutes or until lightly browned. Cool.
6. Warm preserves and fill depressions.

Is Your Oven Telling the Truth?

- Correct oven temperature is essential for successful baking.

- A reliable oven thermometer is a baker's best friend.

- Use a thermometer to make sure your oven is calibrated correctly.

Chocolate-Dipped Peppermint Patties

PAREVE   YIELD: 24 PATTIES

The exhilarating duo of fragrant peppermint and sweet chocolate combine to make these patties truly flavorful but they owe their texture to a secret ingredient that will amaze everyone...read on.

Patties

2½ tablespoons mashed baked potato (nothing added)	2 teaspoons mint extract
2 cups confectioners' sugar	1 recipe pareve Dipping Chocolate

1. Prepare ungreased cookie sheet covered with parchment or wax paper.

2. Cream cooled potato, sugar and extract at medium speed with electric mixer to form dough. Add water, ¼ teaspoon at a time, as needed, until mixture holds together.

3. Form into quarter-size patties and place on sheet. Chill 10 minutes.

4. Dip each patty into Dipping Chocolate using candy fork or plastic fork, allowing excess chocolate to drip off. Place on sheet, chill to set, about 30 minutes. Chilling is essential.

Chocolate-Cherry-Almond Mandelbrot

DAIRY OR PAREVE   YIELD: 48 COOKIES

Decorate these versatile pareve cookies by dipping one end into melted chocolate or vary the flavor by replacing almonds with walnuts, pecans, pistachios or macadamia nuts. For a dairy version, melt white chocolate chips for dipping. These cookies freeze well.

½ cup butter for dairy, melted
   (use margarine for pareve)
½ cup cocoa, sifted
1 cup sugar
1¼ cups brown sugar, firmly packed
3 large eggs
1 teaspoon vanilla extract
1 teaspoon almond extract

2¼ cups flour
¼ teaspoon salt
1½ teaspoons baking powder
¼ teaspoon baking soda
1½ cups chocolate chips
1 cup almonds, coarsely chopped
1 cup maraschino cherries, patted
   dry

1. Preheat oven to 350°F. Grease cookie sheet.

2. Mix butter or margarine with cocoa in large bowl. Add sugars. Mix in eggs and extracts.

3. Combine flour, salt, baking powder and baking soda. Stir dry ingredients into wet batter. Fold in chocolate chips, nuts and cherries.

4. Shape dough on sheet into 2 oblong loaves, each 3 inches wide by 8 inches.

5. Bake 25 to 35 minutes until top is firm. Cool 15 minutes. Transfer to cutting surface and cut on diagonal into ¾-inch thick wedges.

6. Reduce oven to 325°F. Return cookies to sheet and bake 8 to 10 minutes on each side, or until dry. Cookies are dark, so when they are almost dry to the touch, they're done.

Mandelbrot or Biscotti Cutting

Pinwheel Mandelbrot

DAIRY OR PAREVE   YIELD: 50 SLICES

*T*his recipe makes two loaves of **mandelbrot**. *Make them one at a time or in tandem. Serve plain or frost with dairy or pareve version of Chocolate Ganache.*

Orange Dough

2   tablespoons butter for dairy,
      room temperature
      (use margarine for pareve)
6   tablespoons sugar
½   teaspoon vanilla extract
1   teaspoon baking powder

Zest and juice of small orange
2   large eggs
⅛   teaspoon salt
2   cups flour
¼   teaspoon baking soda

1. Combine all ingredients at medium speed with electric mixer, adding extra juice as needed to form soft dough. Divide in half and set aside.

Chocolate Dough

2   tablespoons butter for dairy,
      room temperature
      (use margarine for pareve)
¾   cup brown sugar, firmly packed
½   teaspoon vanilla extract
⅛   teaspoon salt

¾   teaspoon baking soda
2   large eggs
1¼ cups flour
1   teaspoon baking powder
¼   cup cocoa, sifted
     Water, about 2 to 4 tablespoons

1. Combine all ingredients at medium speed with electric mixer, adding water as needed to form soft dough. Divide in half and set aside.

Cinnamon-Sugar Mixture

¼   cup sugar

½   teaspoon ground cinnamon

1. Combine sugar and cinnamon and set aside.

Assembly

1. Preheat oven to 350°F. Grease cookie sheet.
2. Lightly flour parchment or wax paper or surface. Using palm of hand or rolling pin, flatten each Orange Dough portion and shape into rectangle, ¼-inch thick.

3. Prepare 2 rectangles Chocolate Dough as in step 2.

4. Flip each chocolate dough rectangle onto each orange dough rectangle. Press with rolling pin or hands until dough adheres. Roll up like jelly roll.

5. Place rolls on sheet, seam side down. Sprinkle with Cinnamon-Sugar Mixture.

6. Bake 45 minutes or until browned and firm. Cool and cut into diagonal ½-inch slices.

Chocolate Chip Mandelbrot

PAREVE   YIELD: 36 COOKIES

*L*oaded with nuts and spices and flavors, these chocolate chip goodies are irresistible. Vary the recipe by substituting chopped dried cherries, raisins and different chopped nuts.

Topping

1 teaspoon ground cinnamon	5 tablespoons sugar

1. Combine ingredients.

Dough

1 cup vegetable oil	½ teaspoon ground coriander
1 cup sugar	½ teaspoon almond extract
3 large eggs	½ teaspoon vanilla extract
1 tablespoon fresh orange zest	½ teaspoon salt
3 cups flour	1 cup finely chopped pecans
2 teaspoons baking powder	½ cup chocolate chips
5 teaspoons ground cinnamon	

1. Preheat oven to 375°F. Grease cookie sheets.

2. Beat oil, sugar, eggs and zest in large bowl.

3. Combine flour, baking powder, cinnamon, coriander, extracts and salt.

4. Gradually add 2 cups flour mixture to sugar mixture and fold in pecans and chocolate chips. Mix in remaining flour mixture and chill 30 minutes.

5. Shape dough on sheets into 2 loaves, each 3 inches wide and ¾-inch high. Oil hands when forming loaves for easier handling.

6. Sprinkle topping over loaves. Bake 20 minutes or until golden brown.

7. Remove from oven and cool 5 minutes. Cut into ½-inch diagonal slices, turn cut side up, bake again until toasted, about 10 minutes.

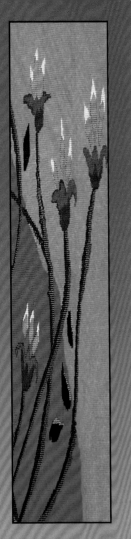

Brown Sugar Shortbreads

DAIRY OR PAREVE   YIELD: 30 COOKIES

1 cup butter for dairy, room temperature (use margarine for pareve)	¾ cup brown sugar, firmly packed
	2 teaspoons vanilla extract
	2 cups flour

1. Preheat oven to 325°F. Grease cookie sheets.
2. Cream butter or margarine and sugar at medium speed with electric mixer. Mix in vanilla and flour.
3. Shape level tablespoons of dough into 1-inch balls and form into logs, 2 inches long and 1-inch wide. Place 2 inches apart on sheets.
4. Bake 17 to 19 minutes or until golden brown. Cool.

Topping

1 tablespoon butter for dairy (use margarine for pareve)	Colored sprinkles
	Apricot or raspberry preserves or coconut, optional
6 ounces chocolate chips	
1 cup pecans, finely chopped	

1. Melt butter or margarine with chocolate. Stir until smooth.
2. Dip 1 tip of each cookie into Dipping Chocolate, then into chopped nuts or sprinkles. To vary, dip cookies into warmed apricot or raspberry preserves and in nuts or coconut.
3. Place cookies on wax or parchment paper and chill to set.

Double Almond Biscotti

DAIRY OR PAREVE   YIELD: 22 BISCOTTI

*O*odles of almonds make this biscotti *doubly delicious.*

7 ounces almond paste	¼ teaspoon salt
½ cup cold butter for dairy (use margarine for pareve)	1 cup slivered almonds
	4 large egg whites
1¾ cups flour	½ teaspoon vanilla extract
½ cup sugar	Flour for rolling
1 teaspoon baking powder	

1. Preheat oven to 350°F. Prepare ungreased or parchment-lined cookie sheets.
2. Crumble almond paste and mix at medium speed with electric mixer. Beat in butter or margarine.

How to Make a Clever Cooling Rack

• If you don't have a wire rack, place chopsticks on surface and place cookie sheets on top of them. This allows air to circulate underneath to speed cooling.

3. Add flour, sugar, baking powder and salt until crumbly. Fold in almonds.

4. Whisk whites and vanilla in small bowl until frothy. Add to almond mixture and mix until dough holds together. Turn out onto lightly floured surface and shape into 2-inch thick log. Cut in half and roll each piece 10 inches long and ¾-inch thick.

5. Transfer to sheet and bake 35 minutes or until golden. Cool 10 minutes. Cut into diagonal ¾-inch slices and turn cut side down. Bake 12 minutes. Flip and bake 12 minutes more. Cool.

Schnecken

DAIRY   YIELD: 48 MINIROLLS

To vary this recipe, use any fruit preserves or jam. In place of coconut or currants, use nuts. Try adding chocolate minichips or finely chopped chocolate bits.

Dough

1 cup butter, room temperature	2 cups flour
8 ounces cream cheese, room temperature, cut into small pieces	¼ teaspoon salt

1. Cream butter and cheese at medium speed with electric mixer. Add flour and salt to form dough. Cover with plastic wrap and chill overnight.

Filling

Flour for rolling	½ cup sweetened grated coconut
1 cup raspberry jam	¼ cup sugar
½ cup currants, finely chopped	½ cup butter
	½ cup brown sugar

Assembly

1. Preheat oven to 350°F. Grease 48 minimuffin tins.

2. Divide dough into 4 pieces. Roll each into rectangle on lightly floured surface to ¼-inch thick.

3. Spread with raspberry jam. Sprinkle with currants, coconut and sugar.

4. Roll into log and place seam side down. Chill 30 minutes.

5. Place ½ teaspoon each, butter and brown sugar in each tin.

6. Slice each log into 12 pieces. Place cut side down over butter-sugar mixture. Bake 20 to 25 minutes or until golden brown. Turn out immediately to cool.

Oodles of Strudels

DAIRY OR PAREVE

Three doughs and two fillings to mix and match; variety galore! Make dough ahead and chill overnight. Look in Carrot Festival for additional strudel recipes.

Basic Cream Cheese Dough

DAIRY   YIELD: 48 COOKIES

2   cups butter, room temperature   1   teaspoon salt
1   pound cream cheese, room   4½ cups flour, divided
      temperature   ½   cup confectioners' sugar

1. Preheat oven to 350°F ten minutes before baking. Grease cookie sheets.
2. Beat butter and cream cheese at medium speed with electric mixer until smooth.
3. Gradually add salt and 4 cups flour. Beat until dough forms ball.
4. Divide into 4 parts, flatten into disks, cover with plastic wrap and chill overnight.
5   Combine remaining flour with sugar and lightly dust work surface. Roll each dough portion into ¼-inch thick rectangle.
6. Spread with any filling and roll up like jelly roll. Place on sheets, seam side down.
7. Bake 30 minutes or until golden brown. Cut each strip into 12 diagonal pieces.

Traditional Dough

DAIRY   YIELD: 48 PASTRIES

14 tablespoons butter   ¼   cup ice water
1   cup sugar, divided   Flour for dusting
2   cups flour   ½   cup graham cracker crumbs
½   teaspoon salt   ½   teaspoon ground cinnamon
1   teaspoon vanilla extract

1. Preheat oven to 350°F ten minutes before baking. Grease cookie sheets.
2   Cream butter with ½ cup sugar at medium speed with electric mixer. Mix in flour, salt and vanilla.
3. Add ice water by tablespoons, while mixing, until dough forms ball.
4. Divide into 3 portions and form each into a log about 14 inches long. Flatten the log to 1-inch, cover with plastic wrap and chill 2 hours.
5. Roll each flattened log into ¼-inch thick rectangle on flour-dusted surface.

6. Spread with any filling and sprinkle with graham cracker crumbs. Roll up like jelly roll and place on sheet, seam side down.
7. Combine cinnamon with remaining sugar and sprinkle over roll.
8. Bake 30 minutes or until golden brown. Cut each strip into 12 diagonal pieces.

Basic Pareve Dough

PAREVE   YIELD: 36 PASTRIES

8   ounces nondairy cream cheese, room temperature
1   cup margarine, room temperature

2½ cups flour, divided
½   cup confectioners' sugar

1. Preheat oven to 350°F ten minutes before baking. Grease cookie sheets.
2. Beat nondairy cream cheese and margarine at medium speed with electric mixer.
3. Add 2 cups flour and mix until dough forms ball.
4. Divide into 3 balls. Flatten into disks, cover with plastic wrap and chill overnight.
5. Continue with steps 5 through 7 as for Basic Cream Cheese Dough.

Work with 1 ball at a time. Keep remaining dough chilled until ready to roll.

Cheese Filling

DAIRY

1   pound cream cheese, room temperature
2   teaspoons vanilla extract
1   teaspoon lemon juice

½   cup sugar
2   tablespoons butter, room temperature

1. Beat all ingredients at medium speed with electric mixer until smooth.

Old-Fashioned Fruit Filling

PAREVE

2½ cups baking apples, peeled and diced
1½ cups crushed pineapple, drained
1   cup apricot preserves
1   cup chopped nuts
¾   cup grated coconut

½   cup raisins
2   tablespoons chopped maraschino cherries
½   cup brown sugar, firmly packed
½   cup sugar

1. Combine all ingredients.

More Strudel Ideas

• Toasted and crumbled challah makes wonderful breadcrumbs.

• For more color and flavor, add two tablespoons cooked, mashed carrots to apple and fruit fillings.

• Substitute any flavor jams, preserves or nuts.

• Coil puff pastry strudels into 8-inch rounds and bake. See Festival Apple Strudel.

Fluden

PAREVE   YIELD: 30 PIECES

Fluden is a multilayered cookie dough pastry of Eastern European origin. Filled with fruit and nuts, it is appropriate for Sukkot and good to eat anytime of the year.

Dough

4½ cups flour	1⅛ cups solid vegetable shortening
2¼ teaspoons baking powder	4 large eggs
1⅛ cups sugar	2½ tablespoons ice water
¼ teaspoon salt	

1. Mix flour, baking powder, sugar, salt and shortening at medium speed with electric mixer to form dough.
2. Add eggs, 1 at a time, and blend well. Mix in ice water until dough forms ball. If dough is dry, add additional ice water by teaspoonfuls.
3. Divide dough into 4 balls and cover with plastic wrap while preparing filling.

Filling

3 tablespoons lemon juice	16 ounces fruit preserves
1 tablespoon fresh lemon zest	1 cup raisins
10 large apples, peeled and grated	1 cup chopped nuts
¼ cup bread or graham cracker crumbs	

1. Toss juice and zest with apples.
2. Add crumbs, preserves, raisins and nuts.

Topping

⅓ cup sugar
1 teaspoon ground cinnamon

1. Combine sugar and cinnamon.

Assembly

Flour for rolling

1. Preheat oven to 350°F. Grease 9 x 13-inch baking pan.
2. Roll out 1 ball of dough to rectangle the size of pan on lightly floured wax or parchment paper. Flip into pan and firmly press down. Top with one-third filling.
3. Repeat twice with dough and filling, topping with last dough sheet.
4. Sprinkle with topping. Bake 45 minutes or until golden brown. Cut into squares in pan and return to oven additional 10 minutes.

Align dough directly with edge of baking pan before flipping.

Miniature Sour Cream Coffee Cakes

DAIRY OR PAREVE   YIELD: 64 MINICAKES

Topping

½   cup sugar
1½ teaspoons ground cinnamon
1½ teaspoons cocoa, sifted

1½ cups chopped walnuts
1½ cups chocolate minichips

1. Combine all ingredients.

Cake

¾   cup butter for dairy
      (use margarine for pareve)
1½ cups sugar
3   large eggs
2½ cups flour, sifted

2¼ teaspoons baking powder
1½ teaspoons baking soda
1½ cups sour cream for dairy (use
      nondairy sour cream for pareve)
1½ teaspoons vanilla extract

1. Preheat oven to 350° F. Grease 64 minimuffin tins.

2. Cream butter or margarine and sugar at medium speed with electric mixer until fluffy. Add eggs, 1 at a time, beating well after each addition.

3. Mix flour with baking powder. Stir baking soda vigorously into sour cream or nondairy sour cream just before using.

4. Beat one-third flour mixture into batter, then one-third sour cream mixture. Alternate flour and sour cream, one-third at a time, until both mixtures are incorporated, scraping sides of bowl often. Add vanilla.

5. Spread 1 rounded tablespoon batter in bottom of each muffin tin and sprinkle with ½ teaspoon topping. Repeat once more. Fill all tins.

6. Bake 12 to 15 minutes or until tester inserted in center comes out clean. Cool. Run a knife around tin to remove.

Sour Cream Coffee Cake

DAIRY   YIELD: 16 SERVINGS

This is a tube pan version of the Miniature Sour Cream Coffee Cakes.

1. Preheat oven to 350°F. Grease 10-inch tube pan.

2. Prepare Miniature Sour Cream Coffee Cakes recipe.

3. Place half of the batter in pan and sprinkle with half of the topping mixture.

4. Repeat with remaining batter and topping. Bake 50 to 55 minutes or until tester inserted in center comes out clean.

5. Cool in pan. Run knife around edges and remove tube from pan; cake will be attached to tube. Loosen bottom of cake from tube but don't turn pan upside down. Use spatulas to gently lift cake from tube portion of pan.

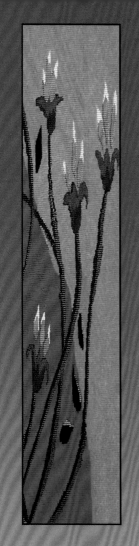

Mix and Match Rugelach

DAIRY OR PAREVE

Mix and match these three dough options and fill with one or two of five fillings. Some dough recipes need to be chilled overnight. Follow diagram for rolling and filling.

Sour Cream Dough

DAIRY OR PAREVE   YIELD: 36 COOKIES

1	cup butter for dairy, room temperature (use margarine for pareve)	1	large egg yolk
2	cups flour	½	cup sour cream for dairy (use nondairy sour cream for pareve)
½	teaspoon salt		Flour for rolling

1. Preheat oven to 375°F ten minutes before baking. Grease cookie sheets.
2. Cream butter or margarine at medium speed with electric mixer. Beat in flour and salt.
3. Add yolk and sour cream or nondairy sour cream and mix until dough forms sticky ball. Cover and chill overnight. Prepare filling.
4. Divide dough into 3 portions. Roll each portion on lightly floured surface into 8-inch round, ⅛-inch thick.
5. Top dough with filling and cut into 12 wedges. Roll up each wedge, shape into crescent and place on sheet with point down. Bake 25 minutes until golden brown.

Cream Cheese Dough

DAIRY   YIELD: 36 COOKIES

1	cup butter, room temperature	½	teaspoon salt
8	ounces cream cheese, room temperature		Sugar for sprinkling
2	cups flour		Flour for rolling

1. Preheat oven to 350°F. Grease cookie sheets.
2. Cream butter and cream cheese at medium speed with electric mixer. Beat in flour and salt gradually, until dough forms ball. Chill 1 hour and divide dough into 2 portions. Roll as Sour Cream Dough.
3. Sprinkle rugelach lightly with sugar. Bake 15 to 18 minutes or until golden brown.

Pareve Yeast Dough

PAREVE   YIELD: 48 COOKIES

2¼ teaspoons active dry yeast	2 large eggs, beaten
4 teaspoons sugar, divided	1 cup margarine, melted
¼ cup warm water	¾ cup sugar for topping
3 cups flour	1 teaspoon ground cinnamon
1 teaspoon salt	Flour for rolling

1. Preheat oven to 350°F ten minutes before baking. Grease cookie sheets.
2. Dissolve yeast with 1 teaspoon sugar in warm water. Set aside 5 minutes.
3. Mix flour, salt and 1 tablespoon sugar at medium speed with electric mixer. Beat in eggs and margarine. Mix in yeast. Divide dough into 4 parts. Cover and chill overnight.
4. Combine ¾ cup sugar and cinnamon for topping.
5. Roll as Sour Cream Dough. Bake 15 to 18 minutes or until golden brown.

Cinnamon-Sugar Nut Filling

PAREVE

½ cup sugar	1 cup nuts, finely chopped
½ cup brown sugar, firmly packed	1 cup raisins, plumped in rum
1 teaspoon ground cinnamon	

1. Combine all ingredients.

Rugelach Rolling

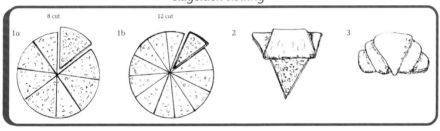

Mix and Match Rugelach (continued on next page)

Yeast Packet

• A packet of yeast contains 2¼ teaspoons.

Meringue Filling

PAREVE

3   large egg whites
¾   cup sugar
1   teaspoon vanilla extract

1   cup finely chopped nuts or
    chocolate minichips

1. Beat whites at high speed with electric mixer until soft peaks form.
2. Gradually add sugar until whites are stiff and glossy. Fold in vanilla and nuts.

Apricot-Nut Filling

PAREVE

1   cup dried apricots
1   cup apricot preserves
1   teaspoon lemon juice

½   cup ground nuts, toasted
⅓   cup graham cracker crumbs

1. Cover apricots with water and simmer 10 minutes. Drain liquid and finely chop.
2. Add preserves and juice. Mix in nuts and crumbs.

Pistachio Filling

PAREVE

¼   recipe Baklava Filling

1. Prepare filling as directed.

Strawberry Jam Filling

PAREVE

½   cup ground almonds

½   cup strawberry preserves or jam

1. Combine ingredients.

Almond Tart Dough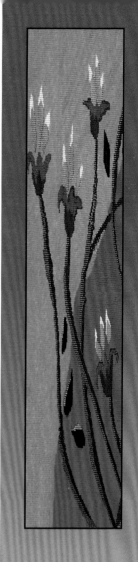

DAIRY OR PAREVE

YIELD: 18 MINITARTS OR
ONE 10-INCH TART PLUS 6 MINITARTS

Almond dough makes an excellent alternative to your regular pie crust.

10 tablespoons butter, room
   temperature (use margarine for
   pareve)
¾ cup sugar
1 cup finely ground almonds

1 large egg
1½ teaspoons almond extract
1½ cups flour
¾ teaspoon baking powder

1. Preheat oven to 350°F ten minutes before baking. Grease desired pans and prepare sheet pan.

2. Cream butter or margarine with sugar at medium speed with electric mixer. Blend in almonds. Mix in egg and extract.

3. Combine flour and baking powder and add to mixture, beating until dough forms. Cover with plastic wrap and chill 4 hours.

4. Press thin layer of dough evenly into bottom and sides of pans.

5. Place minitart pans on sheet and large tart pan directly on oven shelf. Bake 12 to 15 minutes for minitarts, and 15 to 18 minutes for large tart pan, or until golden brown.

6. Cool, wrap and freeze until firm, preferably overnight. This makes it much easier to remove from individual tart pans.

Fill tarts with prepared lemon curd, prepared pudding or Custard Filling. Decorate top with fresh fruit. For a shiny glaze, warm currant or apple jelly in microwave until spreading consistency and brush fruit.

Signature Brownies — As Good As It Gets

DAIRY OR PAREVE   YIELD: 36 BARS

Decadently delicious fudgy brownies — as good as it gets! For fabulous variations, decorate frosted brownies with icing roses, add a cream cheese topping, marble the brownies or add a praline crust.

Brownie

1   cup butter for dairy
      (use margarine for pareve)
2⅓ cups chocolate chips, divided
3   ounces unsweetened chocolate
4   large eggs
1½ tablespoons instant coffee
      granules

1   tablespoon vanilla extract
½   teaspoon salt
1⅛ cups sugar
10 tablespoons flour, divided
1½ teaspoons baking powder
1½ cups chopped walnuts, optional

1. Preheat oven to 350°F. Grease 9 x 13-inch baking pan.

2. Melt butter or margarine with 1⅓ cups chocolate chips and unsweetened chocolate. Cool slightly.

3. Combine eggs, coffee, vanilla, salt and sugar.

4. Add chocolate mixture to egg mixture and cool.

5. Combine ½ cup flour with baking powder and stir into chocolate mixture.

6. Toss remaining chocolate chips and nuts with remaining flour and add to chocolate batter. Spread evenly into pan.

7. Bake 12 minutes. Bang pan against oven shelf to release trapped air between pan and batter. Bake about 8 minutes more, until just set. Do not over bake! Cool.

8. Cover with Chocolate Glaze and chill to set. Cut into squares, diamonds or rectangles.

Chocolate Glaze

DAIRY OR PAREVE

1½ tablespoons butter for dairy (use margarine for pareve)
¼ cup chocolate chips
1⅓ cups confectioners' sugar, sifted

1 teaspoon vanilla extract
3 tablespoons strong hot coffee or boiling water

1. Melt butter or margarine with chocolate chips.
2. Combine sugar, vanilla and coffee or water at medium speed with electric mixer. Add chocolate mixture gradually, beating until smooth.

Cream Cheese-Topped Brownie

DAIRY

*P*repare Signature Brownies, omit nuts and top with cheese mixture before baking.

12 ounces cream cheese, room temperature
¾ cup sugar
¾ teaspoon vanilla extract

3 large eggs
1½ tablespoons flour
¼ teaspoon fresh orange zest, optional

1. Beat cream cheese at medium speed with electric mixer until fluffy. Add sugar, vanilla, eggs, flour and zest, 1 item at a time, beating well to incorporate.
2. Pour cheese mixture evenly over top of unbaked brownie layer. Bake 30 minutes.
3. Chill 1 hour before cutting.

For a marbleized effect, gently swirl a knife through batter before baking.

Minty Frosting and Glaze

½ cup butter for dairy, room temperature (use margarine for pareve)
1 cup confectioners' sugar, sifted
2 tablespoons mint extract or liqueur
Milk for dairy (use nondairy milk for pareve)

1 recipe Chocolate Glaze, substitute mint extract or liqueur for vanilla extract and use boiling water instead of coffee

1. Cream butter or margarine at medium speed with electric mixer. Add sugar and mint. Thin to spreading consistency with milk or nondairy milk.
2. Spread frosting over brownies, follow with glaze.

Praline Brownie

DAIRY OR PAREVE

Prepare and bake Signature Brownies, omitting optional nuts.

¼ cup butter for dairy, melted (use margarine for pareve)

1 cup brown sugar, firmly packed

1 cup chopped pecans

• Combine all ingredients and sprinkle mixture over baked brownies and bake 5 minutes more. It will set as it cools. Cut.

Sour Cream-
Yeast Dough Hamantaschen

DAIRY OR PAREVE   YIELD: 25 LARGE PASTRIES

Buoyant and beautifully browned, these large hamantaschen make tasty pockets for your favorite Purim fillings.

Dough

2¼ teaspoons dry yeast
¼   cup lukewarm milk for dairy
     (use nondairy milk for pareve)
½   cup sugar, divided
2   cups flour, divided
½   cup butter for dairy
     (use margarine for pareve)

½   cup sour cream for dairy (use
     nondairy sour cream for pareve)
2   large eggs, beaten well
¼   teaspoon salt
     Poppy seed, prune, apricot,
     cherry, raspberry or Double-
     Chocolate Filling

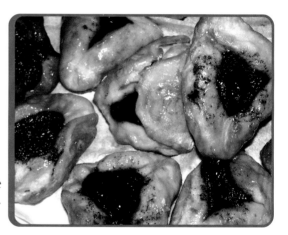

1. Preheat oven to 350°F ten minutes before baking. Line cookie sheets with parchment paper.

2. Make mixture from yeast, milk or nondairy milk, ¼ teaspoon sugar and ¼ cup flour. Allow to sit 20 minutes.

3. Cut butter or margarine into flour in large bowl.

4. Add yeast mixture and remaining ingredients. Mix to smooth dough, adding flour until dough is no longer sticky. Cover with plastic wrap and chill overnight.

5. Roll out ¼-inch thick on floured surface, fold into thirds and roll out again. Fold and roll twice more. This makes a very rich, flaky, but not sweet pastry.

6. Roll out, cut with 3½-inch cookie cutter and fill.

7. Fold up sides in a triangle, leaving almost no filling exposed. The cookies will open as they proof and bake. Brush liberally with Egg-Honey Wash. Cover and let rise 30 minutes. Bake 15 to 20 minutes until golden brown. Cool.

8. Store in airtight container for up to 2 days. May be frozen.

For a just baked taste, warm hamantaschen in 300°F oven for 10 to 15 minutes to freshen.

Egg-Honey Wash

2   large eggs   ½   cup honey

1. Beat eggs with honey and brush tops of unbaked yeast hamantaschen.

Folding Hamentaschen

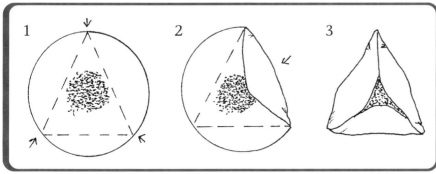

Cookie Dough Hamantaschen

DAIRY OR PAREVE   YIELD: 44 COOKIES

*A*s Purim *approaches, Jewish bakers around the world make their version of* Haman's *pockets. At* Congregation Agudat Achim, *a large baking crew gathers annually to bake 4,000* hamantaschen, *to fill* shaloach manot *package orders.*

1   cup butter for dairy   ½   teaspoon salt
       (use margarine for pareve)   4   cups flour
2   cups sugar   Flour for rolling
3   large eggs, divided   Prune, poppy seed, apricot,
2   teaspoons vanilla extract   raspberry, cherry, or Double
3½ tablespoons orange juice   Chocolate Filling
1   teaspoon baking powder

1. Preheat oven to 350°F. Grease cookie sheets.
2. Cream butter or margarine and sugar at medium speed with electric mixer. Beat in 2 eggs, vanilla and juice.
3. Combine baking powder and salt with flour and gradually add to creamed mixture. Dough will be sticky.
4. Divide dough into 4 balls and cover with plastic wrap. Chill 4 hours.

Cookie Dough Hamantaschen (continued on next page)

5. Roll each ball on lightly floured surface to ¼-inch thickness. Cut 3-inch circles with cookie cutter.

6. Beat remaining egg with 1 teaspoon water. Brush rim of circle with egg wash and place 1 teaspoon of filling in center. Pinch edges together to form triangle, leaving center open slightly to expose filling.

7. Place on sheets and bake 15 to 18 minutes until lightly browned. Freezes well.

Double Chocolate Filling

4 ounces dairy or pareve pound or chiffon cake	1 large egg yolk
3 tablespoons sugar	½ teaspoon vanilla extract
3 tablespoons cocoa, sifted	2 tablespoons chocolate syrup
1 tablespoon butter for dairy, melted (use margarine for pareve)	1 tablespoon orange juice
	⅓ cup chocolate minichips

1. Process cake into fine crumbs and mix in sugar and cocoa. Add butter or margarine.

2. Beat in egg yolk and vanilla. Add chocolate syrup and juice. Fold in chocolate chips.

3. Fill hamantaschen or other cookies, strudel or Danish.

Raspberry-Oatmeal Squares

DAIRY OR PAREVE   YIELD: 32 BARS

This recipe calls for raspberry preserves but you may vary it with any fruit preserves or jam.

2 cups flour	½ cup chopped nuts
1 teaspoon baking soda	1¼ cups butter for dairy, melted (use margarine for pareve)
¼ teaspoon salt	
1½ cups brown sugar, firmly packed	⅓ cup raisins
1 cup rolled oats	¾ cup raspberry jam

Raspberry-Oatmeal Squares (continued)

1. Preheat oven to 350°F. Grease 9 x 13-inch pan.
2. Combine flour, baking soda, salt, sugar, oats and nuts and stir in melted butter or margarine. Press half the mixture into pan.
3. Combine raisins and preserves and cover oat mixture. Crumble remaining oat mixture over top.
4. Bake 30 minutes or until browned. Cool before cutting.

Lemon Squares

DAIRY OR PAREVE   YIELD: 48 BARS

These squares have a delicate texture that exudes a fresh lemon flavor. One of the most beloved and most requested desserts for As You Like It's buffet lunches. Over the last 10 years, we have baked thousands of them. Dress them up with a fresh raspberry and mint leaf.

Crust

2 cups flour
½ cup confectioners' sugar
⅛ teaspoon salt

1 cup butter for dairy, room temperature
(use margarine for pareve)

1. Preheat oven to 350°F. Grease 9 x 13-inch pan.
2. Combine flour, sugar and salt at medium speed with electric mixer. Add butter or margarine and mix to consistency of meal.
3. Press dough into pan and bake 20 minutes, or until edges are golden brown. Prepare filling while crust bakes.

Filling

4 large eggs
2 cups sugar
⅔ cup lemon juice

1½ teaspoons fresh lemon zest
¼ cup flour
Confectioners' sugar for dusting

1. Beat eggs at medium speed with electric mixer. Add sugar and beat until light and fluffy.
2. Mix in juice, zest and flour. Pour over crust and bake 20 minutes or until golden brown and set.
3. Cool and dust with confectioners' sugar. Cut into squares.

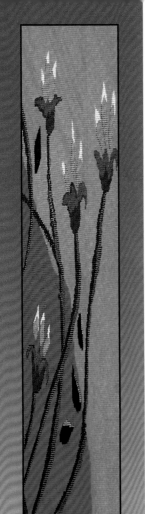

Apricot Delights

DAIRY OR PAREVE   YIELD: 36 BARS

Moist and luscious, these bars add tart lemon and sweet apricot flavors to a crunchy walnut texture.

Crust

½   cup butter for dairy   1   cup flour
    (use margarine for pareve)   1   cup sugar

1. Preheat oven to 350°F. Grease 9-inch square pan.
2. Melt butter or margarine. Mix in flour and sugar. Press into pan and bake 20 minutes or until golden brown.

Filling

¾   cup dried apricots   ¼   teaspoon salt
2   large eggs   2½   teaspoons fresh lemon zest
1   cup brown sugar, firmly packed 2½   tablespoons lemon juice
⅓   cup flour   ½   cup chopped walnuts
½   teaspoon baking powder

1. Cover apricots with water in saucepan and bring to boil. Reduce heat and simmer 10 minutes.
2. Drain, cool and purée apricots.
3. Beat eggs at medium speed with electric mixer and add sugar.
4. Combine flour, baking powder and salt and add to egg and sugar mixture.
5. Mix in zest and juice. Fold in nuts and apricots and pour filling over crust. Bake 35 minutes. Cool 10 minutes.
6. Run knife around edges to loosen from pan. Chill thoroughly before cutting into squares.

Coconut-Walnut Squares

DAIRY OR PAREVE   YIELD: 36 SQUARES

A chewy coconut-walnut concoction sure to please. Great for bake sales and they freeze and travel well.

Crust

1	cup flour
2	tablespoons brown sugar, firmly packed

½ cup butter for dairy, melted (use margarine for pareve)

1. Preheat oven to 350°F. Grease 9-inch square pan.
2. Mix flour with sugar at medium speed with electric mixer. Add butter or margarine and combine to form dough.
3. Press dough into pan and bake 20 minutes or until golden brown. Prepare filling while crust bakes.

Filling

2   large eggs
1¼ cups brown sugar, firmly packed
2   tablespoons flour
1   teaspoon vanilla extract

¼   teaspoon salt
¾   cup chopped walnuts
½   cup shredded coconut

1. Beat eggs at medium speed with electric mixer. Mix in sugar and flour. Beat in vanilla and salt. Add nuts and coconut.
2. Pour filling over crust and bake 30 to 35 minutes or until tester inserted in center comes out clean.
3. Cool 10 minutes and run knife around edges to loosen sides. Cool completely before cutting into squares.

Glass Rolling Pin

Sometimes a full-size rolling pin is not what you need.

• For those hard to reach corners inside a baking pan, use a smooth juice glass or small jar as a rolling pin.

Baklava

DAIRY OR PAREVE   YIELD: 36 PIECES

Baklava is the crown jewel of classic Greek pastry. Here is the traditional recipe as well as a novel variation for a minitart, plus a contemporary cherry-pistachio version. All freeze well.

Traditional Syrup

1	cup honey		1	cinnamon stick
1	cup sugar		½	teaspoon fresh orange zest
1	cup water		½	teaspoon vanilla extract

1. Combine all ingredients except vanilla in saucepan. Bring to boil, reduce heat and simmer 10 minutes.
2. Remove from heat, stir in vanilla and cool.

Traditional Nut Filling

2	cups walnuts		1	teaspoon ground cinnamon
2	cups pistachio nuts		½	teaspoon ground allspice
⅓	cup sugar		⅛	teaspoon ground cloves

1. Process nuts, sugar and spices until fine.

Assembly

¾	cup butter for dairy, melted (use margarine for pareve)	½ pound phyllo dough, thawed

1. Preheat oven to 400°F. Brush 9 x 13-inch pan with melted butter or margarine.

2. Cut phyllo dough if necessary to fit pan. Lay five sheets of phyllo in pan, brushing with butter or margarine after each sheet. Sprinkle one-third nut mixture over phyllo. Repeat layering of phyllo and filling, 2 more times, top with remaining phyllo and brush.
3. Cut into diamond shapes through all layers using sharp knife.
4. Bake 1 hour or until top is golden brown.
5. Pour syrup immediately over baklava. Chill at least 2 hours. Freezes well.

Baklava Tartlets

YIELD: 15 TARTLETS

¼ recipe Traditional Nut Filling   15 store-bought phyllo minitarts

¼ recipe Traditional Syrup,
   divided

1. Preheat oven to 350°F. Line cookie sheet with parchment paper.

2. Mix nut filling with half the syrup and fill phyllo cups to top. Place on pan
    and bake about 8 minutes or until filling is bubbly.

3. Pour remaining syrup over baked tarts. Chill 2 hours.

Dried Cherry and Pistachio Baklava

Cherry-Almond Syrup

2 cups sugar   ¼ cup dried cherries

2 cups water   ½ teaspoon almond extract

1. Combine sugar, water and cherries in saucepan. Heat until sugar
    dissolves, stirring constantly. Bring to boil. Remove from heat.

2. Strain cherries and set aside for filling. Add extract to syrup and cool.

Cherry-Pistachio Filling

3   cups unsalted pistachio nuts   1⅓ cups dried cherries

1   cup chopped walnuts   4   large egg yolks

⅔ cup sugar

1. Coarsely process nuts with sugar.

2. Combine dried cherries, reserved cherries and yolks and process until
    moist clumps form.

Assembly

1 cup butter for dairy, melted   ½ pound phyllo dough, thawed
   (use margarine for pareve)

1. Preheat oven to 400°F. Brush 9 x 13-inch pan with melted butter or
    margarine.

2. Follow assembly directions for Baklava substituting Cherry-Pistachio
    Filling and Cherry-Almond Syrup.

Peanut Butter-Chocolate Cream Torte

DAIRY   YIELD: 12 SERVINGS

An imaginative, impressive dessert, this spectacular torte makes a dramatic presentation at the dinner table.

Crust

2¼ cups graham cracker crumbs
6   tablespoons butter, melted

6   tablespoons smooth peanut butter

1. Preheat oven to 350°F. Grease 10-inch springform pan.
2. Combine all ingredients. Press mixture into bottom of pan and 1-inch up sides.
3. Bake until golden brown, about 6 to 8 minutes. Cool.

Filling

12   ounces cream cheese, room temperature
1⅛ cups confectioners' sugar
6   tablespoons smooth peanut butter
4½ ounces chocolate, melted and cooled
¼   cup milk

3   tablespoons chopped roasted peanuts
6   cups heavy cream, whipped
1½ cups chocolate sauce
¾   cup roasted peanuts, chopped for topping
¾   cup Chocolate Curls

How to Melt Chocolate in Microwave

1. Place chocolate in container and microwave 30 seconds. Stir.

2. Continue to microwave at 30 second intervals, stirring each time. Stop melting when a few small chunks are still visible. Stir until smooth.

1. Beat cream cheese with sugar at medium speed with electric mixer until smooth. Mix in peanut butter and melted chocolate. Add milk and 3 tablespoons chopped peanuts and beat well.

2. Fold half the whipped cream into peanut butter mixture and pour into crust.
3. Cover with plastic wrap and chill until firm, about 2 hours.
4. Spoon remaining whipped cream over torte. Drizzle with chocolate sauce. Top with peanuts and chocolate curls.

Floating Sandwich Cookie Cake

DAIRY   YIELD: 12 TO 14 SLICES

A party pleaser par excellence! You'll need a box of store-bought, cream-filled sandwich cookies, vanilla, chocolate or chocolate mint. During baking, the cookie tidbits float in the batter. Glaze this cake with fudgy chocolate and decorate with more cookie morsels.

Cake

25	cream-filled chocolate sandwich cookies
3	cups flour
1½	cups sugar
1¼	cups milk

1	cup solid vegetable shortening
2½	teaspoons baking powder
1	teaspoon salt
1	teaspoon vanilla extract
4	large eggs

1. Preheat oven to 350°F. Grease 9-inch tube or Bundt pan.

2. Cut each cookie into quarters.

3. Beat remaining ingredients at low speed with electric mixer. Increase speed to high and beat 2 minutes more.

4. Pour ¾ cup batter into pan. Gently fold cookies into remaining batter and spoon into pan.

5. Bake 50 minutes or until cake springs back when lightly touched and top is golden. Cool.

Glaze

24	ounces chocolate chips
¾	cup solid vegetable shortening
¼	cup milk

2	tablespoons corn syrup
6	cream-filled chocolate sandwich cookies

1. Melt chocolate, shortening, milk and syrup in microwave or saucepan and stir until smooth.

2. Pour warm glaze over top and sides of cake.

3. Cut cookies in half and insert into top of cake at even intervals while glaze is warm. Chill until glaze is set.

Signature Triple-Layer Chocolate Mousse Cake

DAIRY OR PAREVE   YIELD: 12 SERVINGS

*A*s You Like It's *most popular decorated layer cake, it appears on all our Viennese tables and serves as the base for our in-house special-occasion cakes. It is as* good pareve *as it is dairy.*

Cake

1¾ cups flour
2   cups sugar
¾   cup cocoa, sifted
1½ teaspoons baking soda
1½ teaspoons baking powder
1   teaspoon salt
2   large eggs, room temperature

1   cup milk for dairy, room temperature (use nondairy milk for pareve)
½   cup vegetable oil
2   teaspoons vanilla extract
1   cup boiling water

1. Preheat oven to 350°F. Grease bottom and sides of three 9-inch round baking pans.

2. Combine dry ingredients at low speed with electric mixer. Increase speed to medium and beat in eggs, milk, oil and vanilla, about 2 minutes.

3. Reduce speed to low and add boiling water; mixture will be very thin.

4. Divide evenly among pans and bake 25 to 30 minutes or until tester inserted in center comes out clean.

5. Cool pans 10 minutes, run knife around edges and cool completely.

Is It Done Yet?

• A tester such as a wooden toothpick or commercial metal tester is essential for determining doneness in baked goods.

• Items that indicate doneness by springing back should be touched lightly in the center of the item.

• Pulling away from the pan is another indicator of doneness.

Chocolate Mousse

8   ounces heavy cream for dairy
     (use liquid nondairy whipped
     topping for pareve)

⅓   cup sugar
⅓   cup cocoa, sifted
1   teaspoon liqueur of your choice

1. Beat cream or nondairy topping at medium speed using wire whisk attachment of electric mixer until fluffy. Increase speed to high and beat until peaks form.
2. Add sugar and cocoa and whip until thick.
3. Fold in liqueur.

Chocolate Icing

2   tablespoons butter for dairy
     (use margarine for pareve)
4½ ounces chocolate

6   tablespoons heavy cream for
     dairy (use liquid nondairy
     whipped topping for pareve)
1¼ cups confectioners' sugar, sifted
1   teaspoon vanilla extract

1. Whisk all ingredients in saucepan over medium heat until smooth. Cool 2 minutes.

Assembly

1. Place 1 cake layer on serving plate and spread with half the Chocolate Mousse. Top with another layer, spread with remaining mousse. Top with last cake layer.
2. Pour Chocolate Icing over assembled cake, allowing icing to dribble over edges.

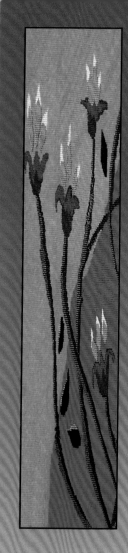

Variations on a Cheesecake

DAIRY   YIELD: 16 SERVINGS

Queen of the custard cakes, a silky cheesecake is always a hit. Here are our recipes for a basic cheesecake and several variations. Cheesecakes are delicate, apt to crack, so follow our directions and never worry. Just bake with a pan of water on the rack beneath the cheesecake and after baking, allow the cake to cool in the turned-off oven for 1 hour.

Traditional Cheesecake

Graham Cracker Crust

2	cups graham cracker crumbs	½	cup butter, melted
5	tablespoons granulated sugar		

1. Preheat oven to 425°F ten minutes before baking. Grease 10-inch springform pan.
2. Combine crumbs with sugar and mix in butter. Press on bottom and two-thirds up sides of pan. Freeze while preparing filling.

Cheesecake Filling

40	ounces cream cheese, room temperature	1	teaspoon fresh orange zest
		⅛	teaspoon salt
1⅔	cups sugar	5	large eggs
2½	tablespoons flour	3	tablespoons milk
1	teaspoon fresh lemon zest	1	teaspoon vanilla extract

1. Beat cream cheese at medium speed with electric mixer until fluffy. Add sugar, flour, zests and salt.
2. Add eggs 1 at a time, beating well after each. Mix in milk and vanilla.
3. Pour into crust and bake 15 minutes. Reduce heat to 250°F and bake 45 to 55 minutes more.
4. Turn off oven and leave cake in oven with door ajar to cool 1 hour. Chill overnight. Decorate with Fresh Fruit Topping and chill 2 hours.

Mint-Chocolate Cheesecake

Chocolate Crust

2	cups chocolate cookie crumbs	6	tablespoons butter, melted
3⅓	tablespoons brown sugar, firmly packed	3⅓	tablespoons cocoa, sifted
		3⅓	tablespoons green mint liqueur

Crust Variations

• Vanilla wafers, chocolate cookies or chocolate sandwich cookies may be used instead of graham crackers.

• Place a wafer in the bottom of muffin tin, fill to the with batter and bake.

• Place ½ teaspoon batter in minimuffin tin, top with chocolate peanut butter minicup and fill to top with additional batter. Bake and dust with ground chocolate.

1. Preheat oven to 425°F ten minutes before baking. Grease 10-inch springform pan.
2. Combine crumbs and sugar and mix in butter. Add cocoa and liqueur.
3. Press crumbs on bottom and two-thirds up sides of pan. Freeze while preparing filling.

Mint Filling

40 ounces cream cheese, room temperature
1⅔ cups sugar
2½ tablespoons flour

⅛ teaspoon salt
5 large eggs
3 tablespoons green mint liqueur
1 tablespoon peppermint extract

1. Follow directions for Cheesecake Filling. Use mint flavorings instead of zest and milk. Fill crust and bake.

Minicheesecakes

YIELD: 48 MINICHEESECAKES

1 recipe Graham Cracker Crust
1 recipe Cheesecake Filling

½ cup fruit preserves, warmed

1. Preheat oven to 350°F. Grease minimuffin tins or line with papers.
2. Prepare Graham Cracker Crust according to directions and press 1 teaspoon crumbs onto bottom of each muffin tin.
3. Prepare Cheesecake Filling and spoon 3 tablespoons over each crust. Bake 20 minutes or until set. Cool and chill.
4. Top with fruit preserves. Before serving, decorate with strawberry or kiwi slice.

I Can't Believe
It's Not Cheese, Cheesecake

PAREVE   YIELD: 16 SLICES

Our pareve cheesecake, indistinguishable from its dairy counterpart, is a treasured recipe for anyone with lactose intolerance.

Graham Cracker Crust

2 cups graham cracker crumbs
5 tablespoons sugar

½ cup margarine, melted

Variations on a Cheesecake – I Can't Believe It's Not Cheese, Cheesecake (continued on next page)

1. Preheat oven to 375°F. Grease 10-inch springform pan.
2. Combine crumbs and sugar and mix in melted margarine.
3. Press crumbs into bottom and three-fourths up sides of pan. Freeze while preparing filling.

Filling

50 ounces nondairy cream cheese, room temperature	1½ teaspoons fresh orange zest
2 cups sugar	4 large eggs
⅛ teaspoon salt	1 tablespoon liquid nondairy whipped topping
3 tablespoons flour	1½ teaspoons vanilla extract
1½ teaspoons fresh lemon zest	

1. Preheat oven to 375°F.
2. Whip nondairy cream cheese until fluffy. Combine sugar, salt, flour, and zests and beat into cheese.
3. Add eggs 1 at a time, beating well after each. Beat in nondairy topping and vanilla. Pour filling into pan.
4. Bake 12 minutes. Reduce heat to 250°F and bake 50 to 55 minutes.
5. Turn oven off and let cake rest 1 hour in oven with door ajar. Chill cake 6 hours or overnight.
6. Decorate with Fresh Fruit Topping.

Additional Fresh Fruit Toppings

• Thinly slice any of the following whole fruit: peaches, nectarines, plums, pears, mangoes, star fruit, kiwi or clementines.

Fresh Fruit Topping

1½ cups apricot preserves, warmed	½ pint raspberries
1½ tablespoons lemon juice to taste	1 pint strawberries
½ pint blueberries	

1. Purée apricot preserves and add juice.
2. Spread ¼ cup purée over top of cake and allow to set.
3. Wash and dry berries. Cut strawberries in half, reserving 1 large strawberry for top. Stems add interest; use if desired.
4. Decorate with fruit and drizzle with remaining purée.

Party Cake Cones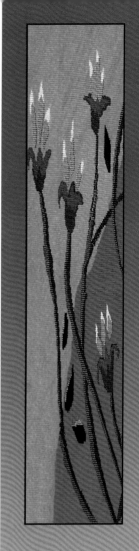

DAIRY OR PAREVE   YIELD: 24 CONES

These cake cones are always a hit with the youngsters. No forks or plates make for quick cleanup. Be careful placing cones in the oven; they may wobble. Don't worry if batter drips out of cones while baking. It looks like melted ice cream. Use nondairy ingredients for a pareve version.

1 cake mix yielding 5½ cups batter	16 ounces prepared frosting
24 flat-bottomed ice cream cones	Sprinkles and candy decorations

1. Preheat oven to 350°F. Prepare ungreased muffin tins.
2. Prepare cake mix as directed on package.
3. Fill ice cream cones with batter to 1-inch from top. Place cones in muffin tins, spacing them so they do not touch each other. Bake 23 to 25 minutes or until tester inserted in center comes out clean. Cool.
4. Frost and decorate with sprinkles and candy.

Frostings on the Cake

As You Like It's premier bakers share their delicious frosting recipes, dairy and pareve. More frosting recipes accompany specific cake recipes in the index. Leftover frosting freezes well. Recipes yield about two cups, except where noted.

Cream Cheese Frosting

DAIRY

8	ounces cream cheese, room temperature	3	cups confectioners' sugar, sifted
¾	cup butter, room temperature	1	teaspoon vanilla extract
		½	teaspoon lemon juice

1. Beat cream cheese and butter at medium speed with electric mixer. Slowly add sugar and beat until smooth.
2. Stir in vanilla and juice.

Pareve Cream Cheese Frosting

PAREVE

4	ounces nondairy cream cheese	1	teaspoon lemon juice
¼	cup margarine, room temperature	2½	cups confectioners' sugar, sifted
½	teaspoon vanilla extract		Nondairy milk

1. Beat nondairy cream cheese and margarine at medium speed with electric mixer until smooth. Add vanilla and juice.
2. Mix in sugar and add nondairy milk by teaspoons until spreading consistency.

Mocha Frosting

DAIRY OR PAREVE

6	tablespoons strong hot coffee	6	tablespoons cocoa, sifted
6	tablespoons butter for dairy (use margarine for pareve)	1	teaspoon coffee liqueur
		2	cups confectioners' sugar, sifted

1. Blend coffee, butter or margarine and cocoa at medium speed with electric mixer.
2. Mix in liqueur and gradually beat in sugar.

Orange Cream Cheese Frosting

DAIRY

1	tablespoon butter	1	teaspoon fresh orange zest
3	ounces cream cheese, room temperature	2½	cups confectioners' sugar, sifted
		1	tablespoon orange juice

Pareve Orange Frosting

PAREVE

1 tablespoon margarine

2 cups confectioners' sugar, sifted

⅓ cup orange juice

1 tablespoon fresh orange zest

• Cream margarine and sugar at medium speed with electric mixer and add juice and zest, beating until smooth.

1. Beat butter and cream cheese at medium speed with electric mixer and add zest.
2. Add sugar and juice, alternately, beating until smooth.

Pareve Chocolate Fudge Frosting

PAREVE

2   cups solid vegetable shortening or margarine
6   ounces chocolate chips, melted
2   cups confectioners' sugar, sifted, divided

1   teaspoon vanilla extract
¼   cup liquid nondairy whipped topping or strong coffee

1. Beat shortening or margarine and chocolate at medium speed with electric mixer until creamy. Add 1 cup sugar and continue beating.
2. Add vanilla and whipped topping or coffee and beat until smooth. Beat in remaining sugar until spreading consistency.

Buttercream Frosting

DAIRY

1   cup butter
1   cup solid vegetable shortening
2   teaspoons vanilla extract

2   cups confectioners' sugar, sifted
6   tablespoons milk

1. Cream butter and shortening at medium speed with electric mixer and add vanilla.
2. Beat in sugar alternately with milk, adding more milk until spreading consistency.

Chocolate Ganache

DAIRY OR PAREVE   YIELD: ABOUT 1½ CUPS

½   cup heavy cream for dairy (use liquid nondairy whipped topping for pareve)
2   tablespoons sugar

8   ounces bittersweet chocolate, finely chopped
1   tablespoon butter for dairy (use margarine for pareve)

1. Boil cream or whipped topping and sugar in saucepan, whisking until sugar dissolves. Remove from heat.
2. Mix in chocolate and butter or margarine. Cover 5 minutes or until chocolate melts. Whisk mixture until shiny and smooth. Use immediately.

If prepared ahead of time, reheat on low until spreading consistency.

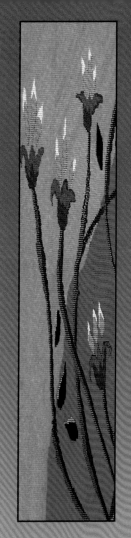

Orange or Lemon Glaze

DAIRY OR PAREVE
YIELD: ABOUT 1½ CUPS

1½ cups confectioners' sugar, sifted
1 tablespoon butter for dairy (use margarine for pareve)
½ teaspoon fresh orange or lemon zest
3 tablespoons orange or lemon juice

• Cream sugar with butter or margarine at medium speed with electric mixer. Add zest and enough juice to make slightly runny glaze.

Star of David Pavlova

DAIRY OR PAREVE   YIELD: 10 SERVINGS

This is not as difficult as it may seem. It makes a dramatic presentation and a memorable centerpiece for any dessert table. For a simpler version, shape meringue into a circle or rectangle.

Meringue

PAREVE

2 cups sugar	6 large egg whites
2 tablespoons cornstarch	

1. Preheat oven to 250°F. Draw 10-inch circle on parchment paper. Draw six pointed star within the circle. Flip paper over on greased baking sheet making certain image is visible.

2. Combine sugar and cornstarch.

3. Beat whites at high speed with electric mixer to form soft peaks. Add sugar-cornstarch mixture gradually to whites, 1 tablespoon at a time, beating well after each addition. Whites will become stiff and glossy.

4. Spoon batter within the outlines of star, using back of spoon to ensure uniform thickness.

5. Bake 1 to 1½ hours until meringue is dry but not brown. Cool completely.

6. Remove meringue carefully to serving platter using spatulas. Star may be brittle.

7. Cover with topping choices 10 minutes before serving.

Pipe meringue onto outline with decorating bag fitted with large star tip.

Toppings

Dairy options

- 2 cups sweetened whipped cream flavored with 2 tablespoons liqueur and topped with 2 cups fresh fruit.
- 2 cups chocolate pudding covered with 2 cups fresh strawberries and drizzled with ¼ cup chocolate sauce.
- 2 cups vanilla pudding covered with 2 cups fresh tropical fruit such as mango, pineapple, papaya and kiwi.

Pareve options

- 2 pints assorted fresh berries or 4 cups sliced fresh fruit mixed with either ¼ cup seedless raspberry jam or 2 tablespoons confectioners' sugar. Garnish with mint sprig.
- 2 cups nondairy whipped topping flavored with 2 tablespoons liqueur and topped with 2 cups fresh fruit.
- 2 cups pareve Chocolate Mousse covered with 2 cups strawberries and drizzled with ¼ cup chocolate sauce.
- 2 cups pareve Custard Filling covered with 2 cups fresh tropical fruit such as mango, pineapple, papaya and kiwi.

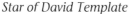

Star of David Template

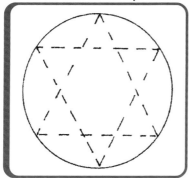

Pareve Chocolate Sauce   Non-G

YIELD: ABOUT 2 CUPS

6 tablespoons water	¼ cup margarine
6 tablespoons sugar	1⅓ cups chocolate chips

1. Bring water, sugar and margarine to boil in medium saucepan.
2. Remove from heat and stir in chocolate chips. Whisk until smooth. Cool.

Signature Bread Pudding

DAIRY OR PAREVE   YIELD: 16 SERVINGS

Here are three fabulous versions of our famous Bread Pudding.

Topping

1 cup pecan pieces, toasted	2 tablespoons butter for dairy, melted (use margarine for pareve)
½ cup brown sugar, firmly packed	
1 tablespoon ground cinnamon	½ cup pure maple syrup

1. Combine all ingredients.

Pudding

4 cups heavy cream for dairy (use liquid nondairy whipped topping for pareve)	1½ cups sugar
	2 teaspoons ground cinnamon
9 cups cubed challah, toasted dry	1⅓ tablespoons vanilla extract
4 large eggs	Whipped cream for dairy, optional (use nondairy whipped topping for pareve)
2 tablespoons butter for dairy, melted (use margarine for pareve)	

1. Preheat oven to 350°F. Grease 9 x 13-inch pan.
2. Pour cream or nondairy topping over bread cubes, let stand 10 to 15 minutes or until bread is soft.
3. Whisk eggs, butter or margarine, sugar, cinnamon, and vanilla in large bowl. Stir in bread mixture.
4. Pour into pan. Spread topping evenly over pudding.
5. Bake in water bath about 30 minutes or until knife inserted in center comes out clean.

Bread Pudding freezes well.

Safe Water Bath Handling

• To avoid splattering boiling water, place filled baking pan into empty larger pan on partially pulled out oven rack. Carefully pour boiling water to half the height of the filled pan. Gently push in rack.

Sweet Matzoh Pudding

DAIRY   YIELD: 16 SERVINGS

1. Substitute 10 cups matzoh farfel for challah and follow recipe for Signature Bread Pudding.

Lime Tart

DAIRY OR PAREVE   YIELD: 8 TO 10 SERVINGS

Fresh lime juice is essential.

1 cup heavy cream for dairy (use liquid nondairy whipped topping for pareve)	1 cup orange juice
¼ cup cornstarch	½ cup butter for dairy (use margarine for pareve)
4 large eggs	¼ cup fresh lime zest
12 large egg yolks	9-inch baked deep-dish pie or tart shell
1½ cups sugar	Sugared Lime Peel, optional
1½ cups lime juice	

1. Whisk cream or whipped topping with cornstarch in bowl. Let stand 1 minute. Whisk again to blend. Mix in eggs and yolks.

2. Combine sugar, juices and butter or margarine in saucepan and heat. Stir until sugar dissolves and butter or margarine melts. Bring to boil and remove from heat.

3. Whisk juice mixture into egg mixture, a little at a time. Return to saucepan and boil 1 minute, whisking constantly. Strain into bowl. Cool slightly.

4. Add zest and spoon filling into crust. Chill overnight.

5. Decorate with Sugared Lime Peel.

Sugared Lime Peel

1. Peel narrow strips of lime skin. Avoid white pith.

2. Roll in sugar.

3. Substitute lemon or orange peel.

Bourbon-Pecan Pie

DAIRY OR PAREVE   YIELD: 8 SERVINGS

A classy, classic Southern custard pie with a shot of Bourbon to pique the pecans for maximum flavor. Kick it up a notch with a Bourbon or orange-flavored liqueur whipped cream topping.

9-inch deep-dish pie shell, unbaked	2½ tablespoons flour
1½ cups pecan halves	3 tablespoons Bourbon
3 large eggs	⅛ teaspoon salt
2½ tablespoons butter for dairy, melted (use margarine for pareve)	½ cup brown sugar, firmly packed
	1½ cups corn syrup
	1½ tablespoons orange zest, optional

1. Preheat oven to 450°F.
2. Sprinkle nuts over bottom of crust.
3. Beat eggs at medium speed with electric mixer and add remaining ingredients. Pour mixture over nuts and bake 10 minutes.
4. Reduce heat to 325°F and bake about 35 minutes or until tester inserted in center comes out clean. Cool. Serve pie at room temperature.

Bourbon or Orange Whipped Cream

1 cup heavy cream for dairy (use liquid nondairy whipped topping for pareve)	2 tablespoons granulated sugar
	1 tablespoon Bourbon or orange-flavored liqueur

1. Whip cream or whipped topping, sugar and Bourbon or liqueur at medium speed with electric mixer until cream begins to hold its shape. Increase speed to high and beat until stiff peaks form.

Mississippi Mud Pie

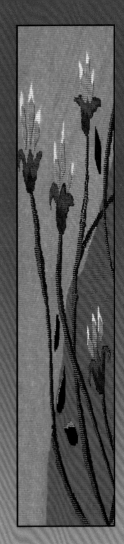

DAIRY

YIELD: 8 SERVINGS

An exuberantly chocolate delight, from crust to filling to chocolate curls luxuriating on the whipped cream topping.

Chocolate Crust

2	cups flour	⅔	cup butter
¼	cup cocoa, sifted	2	tablespoons sugar

1. Preheat oven to 375°F. Grease 9-inch deep-dish pie pan.
2. Combine flour and cocoa. Cut in butter until mixture is crumbly.
3. Stir in sugar and cold water, 1 teaspoon at a time, to form soft dough. Cover with plastic wrap and chill 15 minutes.
4. Press dough into pan. Cover dough with foil and weight down with dried beans. Bake 15 minutes. Remove foil and beans and bake another 10 minutes until browned.

Filling and Topping

¾	cup butter	5½	ounces bittersweet chocolate, melted
1½	cups brown sugar, firmly packed	1¼	cups milk
4	large eggs, slightly beaten	1¾	cups heavy cream, whipped
¼	cup cocoa, sifted		Chocolate Curls

1. Lower oven temperature to 325°F.
2. Cream butter and sugar at medium speed with electric mixer. Gradually beat in eggs and cocoa. Add melted chocolate and milk.
3. Pour mixture into pie shell and bake 45 minutes or until filling is set. Cool.
4. Top pie with whipped cream. Decorate with Chocolate Leaves or Chocolate Curls.

Chocolate Curls

4 ounces thick bar chocolate

1. Warm chocolate in microwave 15 to 20 seconds or until slightly soft.

2. Shave chocolate with vegetable peeler, pressing hard to peel large curls.

3. Place curls on chilled, wax-or parchment paper-lined cookie sheet. Chill to keep chocolate firm.

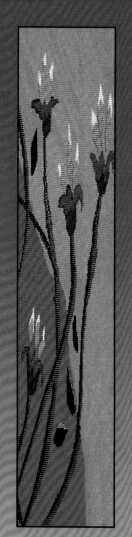

Flaky Pie Crust

DAIRY OR PAREVE   YIELD: ONE 9-INCH PIE CRUST

Every great pie begins with a successful pie crust. Here are our never-fail recipes for creating flaky single and double-crust pie pastry, with directions for processor and by-hand preparation.

Single Crust (standard or deep-dish)

1½	cups flour	9	tablespoons butter, chilled and cut into 9 pieces (use margarine for pareve)
¼	teaspoon salt		
		3	tablespoons ice water

Double Crust

2¼	cups flour	13½	tablespoons butter for dairy, chilled, cut into 14 pieces (use margarine for pareve)
½	teaspoon salt		
		4½	tablespoons ice water

Food Processor Method

1. Preheat oven to 400°F. Grease 9-inch pie pan.

2. Process flour and salt 20 seconds. Distribute butter or margarine evenly over flour and pulse until mixture resembles coarse meal, about 20 seconds.

3. Pour ice water in steady stream through feed tube with processor running until dough comes together.

4. Remove from processor and knead on lightly floured surface 1 minute. Shape into 1 disk for single crust or 2 disks for double crust. Cover with plastic wrap and chill 1 hour.

5. Roll dough into circle 2 inches larger than circumference of pie pan and ⅛-inch thick. Press crust gently into pan and smooth with fingers. Do not stretch dough.

6. For single-crust pie, tuck excess dough under and finish edge decoratively. For two-crust pie, trim bottom crust so it overlaps edge of pan by ¼ inch; fill pie and cover with top crust, making a finished edge. Cut slits in top crust before baking.

7. Chill 30 minutes if baking unfilled. Prick crust with fork in several places on bottom and sides. Line crust with greased foil or parchment paper and fill with dried beans or pie weights to keep crust from shrinking.

8. Bake until edge is golden and sides are firm, 15 minutes. Remove weights and foil or parchment paper and continue to bake until bottom is golden brown, about 5 minutes.

Enhance Pie Crust Flavor

• Replace water with apple juice.

Flaky Pie Crust (continued)

Hand Method

1. Combine dry ingredients.
2. Rub butter or margarine into flour mixture with fingertips or cut in with pastry blender.
3. Sprinkle water over dough while mixing with fork. Continue with step 4.

How to Roll Pie Crust

1. Place dough between two sheets of plastic wrap, wax or parchment paper.

2. Roll from center to edge, moving evenly around circle.

3. Remove top paper and place it back on dough, flip crust and repeat with bottom paper. This step releases the dough and enables you to roll again to maintain an even circle. Repeat rolling and paper removal until circle is size desired.

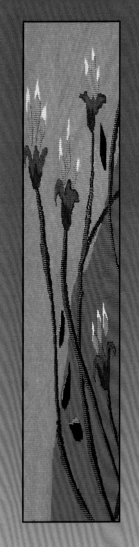

Fresh Blueberry Pie

DAIRY OR PAREVE   YIELD: 10 SERVINGS

An easy-to-fix, single-crust pie that will delight blueberry lovers. Decorate with whipped cream or serve with vanilla ice cream or use nondairy version for pareve.

10-inch deep-dish pie crust, baked	Juice of 1 lemon to taste
7 cups blueberries, divided	Whipped cream or ice-cream for dairy, optional (use nondairy whipped topping or pareve ice cream for pareve)
14 tablespoons water	
¾ cup sugar	
3 tablespoons tapioca, or 2 tablespoons cornstarch	

1. Combine 2 cups blueberries, water, sugar and tapioca or cornstarch in saucepan and bring to boil. Reduce heat and simmer until thick and glossy, stirring often, about 5 minutes. Cool. Add juice.
2. Fold remaining blueberries into cooked filling. Mound into crust. Chill until set.

Trifle Our Way ♛

DAIRY OR PAREVE   YIELD: 16 TO 20 SERVINGS

A trifle it isn't! Perhaps naming it so was simply British understatement. This classic layered dessert combines wine drenched cake slices with sweetened raspberry sauce afloat in meandering waves of cream filling.

1 pound dairy or pareve sponge or pound cake	4 cups vanilla pudding for dairy (use nondairy Custard Filling for pareve)
24 ounces unsweetened frozen raspberries, thawed	1 cup Marsala wine, rum or brandy
3 tablespoons sugar, divided	1 cup fresh raspberries
1½ cups heavy cream for dairy, divided (use liquid nondairy whipped topping for pareve)	

1. Prepare 12-cup trifle dish, wide-mouthed clear glass bowl, or individual glasses.

2. Cut cake into 1 x 2-inch slices.

3. Combine raspberries with 2 tablespoons sugar.

4. Beat ¾ cup heavy cream or nondairy topping at medium speed with electric mixer until thick. Increase speed to high and whip until stiff peaks form. Fold into pudding or pareve Custard Filling.

5. Cover bottom of serving dish with cake slices and sprinkle with ½ cup Marsala, rum or brandy. When using individual glasses, divide all ingredients equally.

6. Spoon half the raspberry mixture over cake. Gently nudge cake away from sides so raspberry mixture can dribble.

7. Spread half the pudding mixture over raspberry layer and smooth top.

8. Layer remaining ingredients. Chill at least 4 hours.

9. Whip remaining cream or nondairy topping and sugar at medium speed with electric mixer until thick. Increase speed to high and whip until stiff peaks form. Decorate with cream and fresh raspberries.

Spoon whipped cream into pastry bag fitted with large star tip and pipe over trifle or drop dollops of whipped cream with spoon.

Brunch

Herb and Onion Bread

Brunch, Simple to Lavish

There are as many reasons for choosing to serve brunch as there are occasions for getting together with family, friends and colleagues. Falling into the gray area between breakfast and lunch, brunch can be as simple or as lavish as you wish, one of the many reasons for its enduring popularity.

Blintzes or Crêpes — What's in a Name?

Blintz or crêpe in any culture is a leaf of dough, usually filled, and cooked. Fry these in butter or margarine in a skillet or bake in a greased pan in 375°F oven, about 10 to 12 minutes, after brushing lightly with butter or margarine. For a lower fat option, use cooking spray.

Blintzes/Crêpes

DAIRY OR PAREVE   YIELD: 12 TO 16 BLINTZES/CRÊPES

2   large eggs
1   cup milk for dairy
    (use nondairy milk for pareve)
½   teaspoon vanilla extract
    (omit for potato filling)

¼   cup flour
⅛   teaspoon salt
    Butter for dairy for frying
    (use margarine for pareve)

1. Whisk eggs, milk and vanilla in bowl. Add flour and salt gradually until smooth. Do not use blender, mixer or processor to mix batter.

2. Grease 6-inch skillet and heat. Add enough batter to coat pan bottom, returning excess to batter bowl. Fry until edges and center are dry. Flip onto dish towel.

3. Repeat with remaining batter. Do not stack crêpes until they are cool.

Cheese Filling

DAIRY

8   ounces farmer cheese
8   ounces cream cheese
2   tablespoons sour cream
    Sugar and cinnamon to taste

1. Combine all ingredients.

2. Place a heaping tablespoon of filling in center of each crêpe, fold in ends and roll up like jelly roll. Fry or bake as desired.

Serve with sour cream or Fruit Sauce.

Potato Filling

PAREVE

4	medium potatoes, peeled and chunked	2	medium onions, chopped
1	tablespoon Veggie Schmaltz or olive oil	2	garlic cloves, minced
		1	large egg
			Salt and pepper to taste

1. Boil potatoes until tender. Cool and mash.
2. Heat schmaltz or oil in medium skillet and sauté onions and garlic. Cool.
3. Combine all ingredients. Fill and fry or bake as above.

Serve with nondairy sour cream.

Apple Filling

DAIRY

½	cup butter	3	Granny Smith apples, peeled and thinly sliced
1	cup brown sugar, firmly packed	½	cup raisins
½	teaspoon ground cinnamon		Apple liqueur or brandy to taste, optional
¼	teaspoon ground nutmeg		
1	cup coarsely chopped walnuts		

1. Melt butter in saucepan, stir in sugar, cinnamon and nutmeg. Cook mixture to dissolve sugar.
2. Add walnuts, apples and raisins, cooking until apples are tender.
3. Remove from heat. Add liqueur or brandy. Fill and fry or bake as above.

Spread crêpe with scoop of ice cream. Roll and freeze 1 hour. Top with apple filling just before serving.

Blintz or Crêpe Tips

- Crêpes may be frozen before frying. Separate layers of crêpes with wax or parchment paper.
- When cooking for a crowd, fry crêpes until golden and keep warm in 350°F oven on cookie sheets until ready to serve.
- Lower fat substitutions for dairy: reduced fat cream cheese, yogurt instead of sour cream, reduced fat milk.
- For a lower fat version, use a nonstick pan and reduce shortening.

Orange Muffins

DAIRY   YIELD: 12 MUFFINS

Topping

¼   cup sugar
1   tablespoon flour

1   tablespoon butter, room
    temperature
½   teaspoon ground cinnamon

1. Combine all ingredients.

Muffins

2   cups flour
⅓   cup sugar
1   tablespoon baking powder
½   teaspoon salt
⅓   cup chopped pecans
1   large egg

½   cup orange juice
¼   cup milk
½   cup vegetable oil
1   tablespoon fresh orange zest
½   cup orange marmalade

1. Preheat oven to 375°F. Grease muffin tins or line with papers.
2. Combine flour, sugar, baking powder, salt and pecans.
3. Mix egg, juice, milk, oil, zest and marmalade in another bowl.
4. Add flour mixture to egg mixture. Mix gently until moistened.
5. Fill muffin cups two-thirds full and sprinkle each with topping.
6. Bake 20 to 25 minutes until golden brown or tester inserted in center comes out clean.

Fresh Cherry Muffins

DAIRY   YIELD: 24 MUFFINS OR 60 MINIMUFFINS

½   cup butter, room temperature
2   large eggs
1½ cups sugar
3   cups flour
2   teaspoons baking powder

½   teaspoon salt
⅛   teaspoon baking soda
1   teaspoon vanilla extract
1   cup milk
2   cups fresh cherries, pitted

1. Preheat oven to 400°F. Grease muffin tins or line with papers.
2. Cream butter, eggs and sugar in large bowl. Combine flour, baking powder, salt and baking soda in separate bowl. Add vanilla to milk.
3. Add milk and flour mixtures, alternately, to butter mixture.
4. Fold cherries into batter and spoon into tins, two-thirds full.
5. Bake 15 to 20 minutes or until tester inserted in center comes out clean.

Muffin Mixing Magic

Follow these tips for success.

• Don't overmix.

• Lumpy is better than smooth.

• Use batter immediately because baking powder loses its potency once combined with wet ingredients.

Orange Corn Bread

PAREVE OR DAIRY   YIELD: 12 SERVINGS

The big surprise in this recipe is the unpeeled orange.

1 cup plus 3 tablespoons flour	½ cup margarine for pareve (use butter for dairy)
½ teaspoon salt	
4 teaspoons baking powder	1 large egg
¾ cup cornmeal	1¼ cups nondairy milk for pareve (use milk for dairy)
3½ tablespoons sugar	
1 orange	

1. Preheat oven to 375°F. Grease 9-inch square pan.
2. Combine dry ingredients.
3. Zebra stripe orange, quarter and seed. See How to Zebra Stripe.
4. Process margarine or butter with egg, nondairy milk or milk and orange.
5. Add dry ingredients in batches blending only until flour is combined.
6. Pour batter into pan. Bake 45 minutes or until tester inserted in center comes out clean.
7. Cut bread into squares or triangles. Serve warm.

Apple Fritters

DAIRY   YIELD: 40 FRITTERS

Light, flavorful, perfect for Chanukah.

1 cup milk	1 teaspoon vanilla extract
1 large egg, beaten	3 cups flour
¼ cup butter, melted	2 teaspoons baking powder
½ cup sugar	½ teaspoon salt
1 orange, juice and zest	Vegetable oil for deep frying
1 cup peeled and chopped apple	Confectioners' sugar

1. Preheat oil to 350°F in deep fryer or deep pot.
2. Whisk milk, egg and melted butter in bowl. Add sugar, juice, zest, apple and vanilla.
3. Combine flour, baking powder and salt. Stir dry mixture into milk mixture until moistened.
4. Drop tablespoons of batter into hot oil. Fry until golden, turning to brown evenly. Remove and drain on paper towels. Cool and sprinkle with confectioners' sugar.

Successful Frying Tip

• To monitor oil temperature when frying, attach a candy thermometer to the side of the pan.

Chocolate Chip-Orange Scones

DAIRY   YIELD: 8 SCONES

Buttery, floury, moist mouthfuls. Eat them warm with butter and jam.

2   cups flour
⅓   cup sugar
2   teaspoons baking powder
½   teaspoon salt
½   cup butter, chilled, cut into
      ½-inch pieces
2   large eggs

¼   cup orange juice
1   teaspoon vanilla extract
½   teaspoon fresh orange zest
¾   cup chocolate minichips
1   large egg white mixed with
      ½ teaspoon water

1. Preheat oven to 425°F. Grease cookie sheet.

2. Combine flour, sugar, baking powder and salt in large bowl. Cut butter into flour until mixture resembles coarse crumbs.

3. Mix eggs, juice, vanilla and zest in another bowl.

4. Combine egg and flour mixtures. Dough will be sticky.

5. Lightly flour hands and knead in chocolate chips. Pat dough into 8-inch circle in center of cookie sheet and brush dough with egg white mixture. Cut into 8 wedges with serrated knife.

6. Bake 20 to 25 minutes or until tester inserted in center comes out clean.

7. Remove from sheet and cool 10 minutes. Recut wedges if necessary. Serve warm. Freezes well.

Savory Cheese Scones

DAIRY   YIELD: 8 SCONES

2   cups flour
2   teaspoons baking powder
¼   teaspoon salt
⅛   teaspoon ground cayenne pepper
½   teaspoon garlic powder
1½   cups shredded Cheddar cheese

3   tablespoons grated Parmesan
        cheese
⅓   cup butter, chilled, cut into
        ½-inch pieces
⅓   cup milk
2   large eggs

Desalt Salted Butter

• If a recipe calls for unsalted butter and you have only salted, know that ½ pound salted butter contains ¾ teaspoon salt. Accordingly reduce the salt requirement in the recipe.

Savory Cheese Scones (continued)

1. Preheat oven to 400°F. Grease cookie sheet.

2. Combine flour, baking powder, salt, cayenne and garlic powder in large bowl.

3. Stir in cheeses and cut butter into mixture until it resembles coarse crumbs.

4. Whisk milk and eggs in another bowl. Add to flour mixture and stir until moistened.

5. Pat dough into 8-inch circle in center of cookie sheet. Cut into 8 wedges with serrated knife.

6. Bake 15 to 17 minutes or until top is lightly browned and tester inserted in center comes out clean.

7. Remove from cookie sheet and cool 5 minutes. Recut wedges if necessary. Serve warm with butter. Freezes well.

Apple-Apricot Kugel

PAREVE   YIELD: 8 TO 10 SERVINGS

Laced with apricot preserves and fresh apple chunks, this noodle pudding is an instant hit.

12 ounces wide egg noodles	2 tablespoons sugar
¼ cup margarine, melted	1 teaspoon ground cinnamon
4 large eggs	¾ cup golden raisins
12 ounces apricot preserves	2 teaspoons sugar for topping
2 apples, peeled and chopped	½ teaspoon ground cinnamon for
1 teaspoon salt	topping

1. Preheat oven to 350°F. Grease 9 x 13-inch pan.

2. Cook noodles al dente. Drain, rinse with cold water and drain again. Stir in margarine.

3. Combine remaining ingredients except topping and mix into noodles. Pour into pan, cover and bake 45 minutes.

4. Combine topping ingredients and sprinkle over kugel. Bake 15 minutes more or until tester inserted in center comes out clean.

Signature Noodle Kugel

DAIRY   YIELD: 12 SERVINGS

Topping

½   cup slivered almonds   1   teaspoon ground cinnamon
¼   cup brown sugar, firmly packed

1.   Combine all ingredients.

Kugel

½   pound medium egg noodles   ¼   cup sugar
4   large eggs   ¼   cup butter, melted
8   ounces cream cheese, room   ½   teaspoon salt
      temperature   1   cup crushed pineapple, drained
1½ cups cottage cheese   Sour cream or Fruit Sauce
1   cup sour cream

1.   Preheat oven to 375°F. Grease 9 x 13-inch baking pan.
2.   Cook noodles al dente. Drain and rinse with cold water.
3.   Beat eggs, cream cheese, sour cream, sugar, butter and salt at medium speed with electric mixer, 5 minutes.
4.   Combine pineapple, noodles and egg mixture and pour into pan. Bake 30 minutes.
5.   Remove kugel from oven and sprinkle with topping. Bake 15 minutes more or until set and golden brown.
6.   Serve with sour cream or Fruit Sauce.

Freezes well. Thaw and reheat covered in 325°F oven 30 to 40 minutes. Uncover last 10 minutes.

Kugel Variations

• Add ¾ cup golden raisins.

• Substitute 3 apples, peeled and chunked, for pineapple.

• Substitute ¼ cup toasted cake crumbs for half the almonds.

Signature Cheese Blintz Soufflé

DAIRY   YIELD: 10 SERVINGS

*As You Like It's **tried and true** Kiddush **favorite. We've probably made a million portions to date.***

Batter

½	cup butter, room temperature	1½	cups sour cream
⅓	cup sugar	½	cup orange juice
¼	teaspoon salt	1	cup flour
6	large eggs	2	teaspoons baking powder

1. Beat all ingredients at medium speed with electric mixer until smooth.

Filling

8	ounces cream cheese, cubed	1	teaspoon vanilla extract
2	cups cottage cheese	1	tablespoon sugar
2	large egg yolks		

1. Beat all ingredients at medium speed with electric mixer until smooth.

Assembly

Sour cream or Fruit Sauce

1. Preheat oven to 350°F. Grease 9 x 13-inch baking pan.
2. Pour half the batter into pan and pour filling over batter, spreading evenly. Top with remaining batter. Bake uncovered 50 to 60 minutes or until puffed and golden brown. Freezes well.
3. Serve with sour cream or Fruit Sauce.

Fruit Sauce
PAREVE
1 cup fruit preserves

2 tablespoons orange juice

• Warm preserves and mix in orange juice. Cool.

Cheddar-Potato Kugel   Non-G

DAIRY   YIELD: 12 SERVINGS

This quick and easy kugel *wonderfully complements fish. You may substitute any cheese or combination of cheeses for variety.*

3 pounds potatoes, peeled and shredded	½ teaspoon paprika
4 large eggs	5 tablespoons olive oil
Salt and pepper to taste	1 onion, chopped
¼ teaspoon white pepper	3 garlic cloves, minced
	2½ cups shredded Cheddar cheese

1. Preheat oven to 350°F. Grease 9 x 5 x 3-inch loaf pan.
2. Drain potatoes, squeezing out excess liquid.
3. Combine eggs, salt, peppers, paprika, oil, onions and garlic.
4. Fold in potatoes and cheese. Pour mixture into pan and bake 1 hour.
5. Increase temperature to 450°F and bake 10 minutes more or until browned.

Nova Smoked Salmon Platter

PAREVE   YIELD: 10 SERVINGS

1   pound Nova smoked salmon, presliced

1   cucumber, scored and sliced

1   medium red onion, sliced

¼   cup capers, rinsed

2   lemons, sliced

2   large tomatoes, sliced

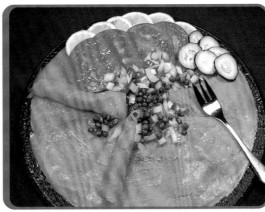

1. Arrange Nova on platter.
2. Decorate with cucumbers, onions, capers, lemon and tomatoes.

Allow 1 ounce per person for a Kiddush Buffet Lunch and Evening Cocktail Hour and 1½ ounces per person for a Breakfast Buffet where Nova is featured.

Chocolate-Streusel French Toast

DAIRY   YIELD: 8 SERVINGS

This streusel-topped French toast melds a surprising combination of buttermilk, cinnamon, nutmeg and chocolate and is served with maple syrup or warm strawberry sauce.

5	large eggs	⅛	teaspoon salt
1¼	cups buttermilk	⅓	cup sugar
⅓	teaspoon ground cinnamon	1	pound unsliced challah
⅛	teaspoon ground nutmeg		Maple syrup for topping

1. Preheat oven to 350°F ten minutes before baking. Grease cookie sheet.

2. Combine eggs, buttermilk, cinnamon, nutmeg, salt and sugar.

3. Cut challah into ¾-inch thick diagonal slices. Thoroughly soak in egg mixture and place on sheet. Cover and chill 1 hour. Prepare Chocolate-Streusel Topping and Strawberry Sauce.

4. Sprinkle streusel over each slice. Bake 18 to 20 minutes or until lightly brown.

5. Serve with maple syrup and/or Strawberry Sauce.

Chocolate-Streusel Topping

½	cup flour	¼	cup butter
⅓	cup brown sugar, firmly packed	½	cup chocolate minichips or grated chocolate
½	teaspoon ground cinnamon		

1. Combine flour, sugar and cinnamon. Cut in butter until mixture resembles coarse crumbs. Add chocolate.

Warm Strawberry Sauce

1	pint strawberries, hulled	2	tablespoons sugar

1. Combine strawberries with sugar and let rest 1 hour.

2. Warm in microwave and serve.

Stale challah makes excellent French toast but requires increasing buttermilk to 2 cups and using 7 eggs. The challah will take longer to absorb the egg mixture.

If not serving immediately, French toast may be chilled or frozen.

Reheating Frozen French Toast

What to do with leftover slices of French toast.

1. Layer parchment or wax paper between toast slices and wrap each with plastic wrap and then foil.

2. To reheat, unwrap and heat for 10 to 12 minutes on baking sheet in 350°F oven.

Strata with Fresh Herbs

DAIRY   YIELD: 12 SERVINGS

*F*resh herbs differentiate this layered brunch favorite from all the rest. This dish requires overnight chilling before baking.

1½ tablespoons butter	2 tablespoons finely chopped fresh parsley
¾ cup thinly sliced green onions	
4 cups shredded Cheddar cheese	½ teaspoon pepper to taste
8 large eggs, beaten	½ teaspoon salt to taste
2½ cups milk	⅛ teaspoon cayenne to taste
½ teaspoon onion powder	1 pound challah, sliced, crusts removed
½ teaspoon garlic powder	
2 tablespoons finely chopped fresh dill	

1. Preheat oven to 350°F ten minutes before baking. Grease 9 x 13-inch pan.
2. Heat butter in small skillet, sauté onions and cool. Mix with cheese.
3. Combine eggs, milk, herbs and spices.
4. Layer half the challah in pan followed by half the cheese mixture, repeat. Press down to compact layers and top with egg-milk mixture. Cover and chill overnight.
5. Bring to room temperature before baking. Bake 1 hour uncovered until puffed and browned. Allow to rest 10 minutes before cutting.

Nova and Egg Strata

DAIRY   YIELD: 12 SERVINGS

A lush layered nova and egg dish, floating in a golden, cheesy custard. This recipe requires chilling overnight.

¼ cup butter, melted	¼ cup snipped fresh chives
8 cups challah, cut into small pieces	8 large eggs, beaten
	2 cups milk
4 ounces sliced Nova smoked salmon, cut into small pieces	1 cup cottage cheese
	½ teaspoon pepper
2 cups shredded Swiss or Monterey Jack cheese	

1. Preheat oven to 350°F ten minutes before baking. Grease 9 x 13-inch pan.

Nova and Egg Strata (continued)

2. Place challah in pan and top with Nova, cheese and chives.

3. Combine eggs and remaining ingredients and pour over Nova mixture.

4. Press ingredients down, to moisten thoroughly. Cover and chill overnight.

5. Bake uncovered 40 to 45 minutes or until set and edges are puffed and golden. Let stand 10 minutes before cutting.

Pizza Dough Fold-Overs

DAIRY   YIELD: 4 SERVINGS

It is ready to bake by the time the oven preheats. A neat group activity for kids' parties.

Unbaked pizza dough, enough for 2 crusts, divided in half	1 cup shredded Cheddar cheese
	1 cup pizza sauce
1 cup shredded mozzarella cheese	⅔ cup sliced mushrooms

1. Preheat oven to 450°F. Grease cookie sheets.

2. Roll dough into 12-inch circle on sheet.

3. Combine and place half the cheeses in center of dough followed by half the mushrooms. Top with half the sauce.

4. Gently stretch dough over filling and press edges together with fork to seal, forming semicircle. Repeat with remaining dough.

5. Cut 4 slits in tops and bake 10 minutes or until puffed and golden brown.

Add sautéed onions, garlic, peppers or sliced olives.

Sprinkle filling with garlic powder, dried oregano and/or dried basil.

French Toast with Apples and Raisins

DAIRY   YIELD: 6 TO 8 SERVINGS

This French toast is baked upside down; apples and raisins are the surprise on the bottom. Perfect for the Break-Fast meal after Yom Kippur.

½	cup butter, melted	½	cup raisins, dried cranberries or chopped dried apricots
1	cup brown sugar, firmly packed		
3	teaspoons ground cinnamon, divided	1	pound challah, cut into 1-inch slices
3	tart apples, peeled and thinly sliced	6	large eggs
		1½	cups milk
		1	tablespoon vanilla or rum extract

1. Preheat oven to 375°F ten minutes before baking. Grease 9 x 13-inch pan.
2. Combine butter, sugar and 1 teaspoon cinnamon. Add apples and dried fruit.
3. Spread mixture in pan and arrange challah on top.
4. Mix eggs, milk, vanilla or rum and remaining cinnamon.
5. Pour mixture over bread, soaking bread completely. Cover and chill 4 hours or overnight.
6. Bake covered 40 minutes. Uncover and bake 5 minutes more. Remove from oven and let stand 5 minutes. Serve warm.

Blueberry Bread Pudding

DAIRY   YIELD: 12 SERVINGS

Perfect for holiday brunching, fresh blueberries take it up a notch but you may also use frozen berries.

Blueberry Sauce

1	cup sugar	1	cup fresh blueberries
1	cup water	1	tablespoon butter
2	tablespoons cornstarch		

1. Combine sugar, water and cornstarch and cook 5 minutes, stirring until thickened.
2. Add berries and simmer 10 minutes. Stir in butter until melted. Remove from heat.

Blueberry Bread Pudding (continued)

Bread Pudding

1	pound challah, torn into small pieces	12	large eggs
8	ounces cream cheese, cut into cubes	½	cup sugar
		⅓	cup maple syrup
2	cups fresh blueberries	1	tablespoon vanilla extract
		2	cups half-and-half

1. Preheat oven to 350°F ten minutes before baking. Grease 9 x 13-inch baking pan.
2. Place half of the challah pieces in pan.
3. Scatter cream cheese and blueberries over bread. Top with remaining challah.
4. Combine remaining ingredients and pour over bread.
5. Cover with plastic wrap and chill overnight.
6. Bake uncovered until golden brown and puffed, 45 to 55 minutes.
7. Serve with blueberry sauce.

Pizza Bagels

DAIRY   YIELD: 24 PIECES

Pizza bagels are one of the most popular offerings at As You Like It's *Kiddush buffets, appealing to young and old. You may prepare these ahead of time, freeze and bake before serving.*

2	cups shredded mozzarella cheese	¼	teaspoon pepper
¼	cup grated Parmesan cheese	¾	teaspoon garlic powder
½	teaspoon dried oregano	¾	cup pasta sauce
½	teaspoon dried basil	1	dozen minibagels, split in half

1. Preheat oven to 350°F. Grease cookie sheets.
2. Mix cheeses with herbs and spices.
3. Place bagel halves cut side up on sheet, spread with sauce and sprinkle with cheese mixture.
4. Bake until golden brown, about 10 minutes.

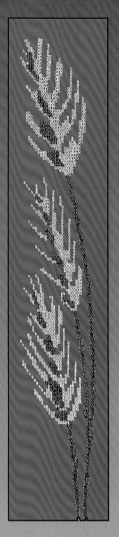

Herb and Onion Bread

DAIRY OR PAREVE   YIELD: 1 LOAF

½   cup milk for dairy (use nondairy   2¼ teaspoons dry yeast
    milk for pareve)
1½ teaspoons sugar
1   teaspoon salt
1   tablespoon butter for dairy
    (use margarine for pareve)

2¼ teaspoons dry yeast
½   cup warm water
2¼ cups flour
½   small onion, minced
½   teaspoon dried dill
1   teaspoon dried rosemary

1. Preheat oven to 350°F ten minutes before baking. Grease 9 x 5 x 3-inch loaf pan or cookie sheet.

2. Combine milk or nondairy milk, sugar, salt and butter or margarine in saucepan and heat until sugar dissolves. Cool to lukewarm.

3. Dissolve yeast in warm water in large bowl and add milk mixture, flour, onions, dill and rosemary. Mix until it forms soft dough.

4. Cover bowl with towel and let rise in warm place until triple in bulk, 1 to 1½ hours.

5. Punch down and knead a few minutes, transfer into pan or shape into round loaf and place on sheet.

6. Cover and let bread rest in warm place 10 minutes.

7. Bake 1 hour or until bread pulls away from side of pan and sounds hollow when tapped on bottom or until crust is browned.

Freshening Bread

No need to throw hardened bread to the birds.

• Preheat oven to 350°F. Place bread in paper bag and close completely. Sprinkle bag with water and place directly on oven rack. Heat 5 to 10 minutes until bread is soft. Eat immediately.

Shabbat Challah

PAREVE   YIELD: 2 LOAVES

*T*he queen of the **Shabbat** *dinner table. This recipe makes two glorious breads. For a more nutritious bread, substitute with 3 cups whole wheat flour in step 3.*

8 cups flour or bread flour, divided	½ cup vegetable oil
¼ cup sugar	4 large eggs, beaten, reserve
1 tablespoon salt	3 tablespoons for egg wash
4½ teaspoons dry yeast	*Flour for rolling*
1½ cups hot water	*Vegetable oil for greasing dough*
(between 115°F and 130°F)	*Sesame seeds or poppy seeds, optional*

1. Preheat oven to 350°F ten minutes before baking. Prepare cookie sheet covered with parchment paper or grease 2 loaf pans.

2. Combine 3 cups flour with sugar, salt and yeast. Mix in water, oil and eggs.

3. Add remaining flour as needed to form stiff dough.

4. Knead dough on floured surface, sprinkling with additional flour as needed. Dough should be elastic and surface blistered.

5. Place dough in large lightly oiled bowl, turning once to coat. Cover with damp towel. Let rise until double in bulk, about 1 hour. Dough is ready when indentation remains after touching.

6. Punch dough down on floured surface and divide in half. Divide each half into thirds or number of braids you need.

7. Roll each portion on floured surface into long rope, keeping middle of each roll thicker than ends. Braid challah and pinch ends together tucking under to secure. Place on sheet or in pan.

8. Mix 1 teaspoon water into reserved egg and brush tops of bread. Sprinkle with seeds. Allow to rise 1 hour. Bake 30 minutes or until crust is browned. Cool.

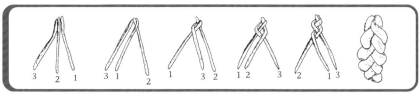

3 Strand Challah Braiding

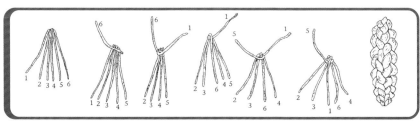

6 Strand Challah Braiding

What is Challah?

• Challah is a rich, yeast egg bread that is slightly sweeter than most breads.

• Traditionally challah is served at a Sabbath or festival meal.

• For a recipe using challah, you may substitute an enriched egg bread.

Soufflé Roll with Mushroom or Nova Filling

DAIRY   YIELD: 8 SERVINGS

The soufflé roll makes an elegant presentation at a brunch or lunch. It may also be rolled for small hors d'oeuvres-size pieces.

Soufflé Batter

¼	cup butter	⅛	teaspoon cayenne pepper
½	cup flour	4	large eggs, separated
½	cup milk, room temperature	¾	cup breadcrumbs for turning out
½	teaspoon salt		

1. Preheat oven to 375°F. Grease jelly roll pan, line with parchment and grease again.

2. Melt butter in saucepan over medium heat and blend in flour. Remove from heat and add milk, salt and cayenne, whisking until smooth.

3. Return to heat and cook until mixture thickens, reduce heat and simmer 1 minute.

4. Whisk yolks in bowl and stir in one-third warm mixture. Combine egg mixture with remaining flour mixture in saucepan. Stir until smooth, about 1 minute. Remove from heat, transfer to large bowl and cool 10 minutes.

5. Beat whites at medium speed with electric mixer until frothy. Increase speed to high and beat until stiff. Stir one-fourth whites into cooled mixture. Fold in remaining whites.

6. Spread soufflé batter evenly in pan and bake 35 to 45 minutes until golden.

7. Sprinkle large towel with breadcrumbs. Loosen edges of soufflé with spatula or knife and turn out onto towel. Roll up like jelly roll from the short side for a brunch or lunch portion and the long side for hors d'oeuvres.

Mushroom Filling

2	tablespoons butter	3	tablespoons sour cream
1	pound mushrooms, sliced	¼	teaspoon pepper
1	tablespoon lemon juice	½	teaspoon salt
1	cup chopped onions	⅛	teaspoon cayenne pepper, optional
8	ounces cream cheese, room temperature		Fluted mushrooms, optional
			Carrot curls, optional

1. Heat butter in large skillet and sauté mushrooms until soft. Remove from pan with slotted spoon, add lemon juice and set aside.

2. Sauté onions in same skillet until soft and add to mushrooms.
3. Beat cream cheese and sour cream at medium speed with electric mixer. Add salt, pepper and cayenne.
4. Drain liquid from mushroom-onion mixture and fold into cream cheese.
5. Unroll soufflé and spread with filling mixture. Roll up like jelly roll and place seam side down on oven proof platter. Use two large spatulas to move and position roll.
6. Decorate roll with extra filling and keep warm in 250°F oven 20 minutes.
7. Garnish with fluted mushrooms and/or carrot curls.

Nova Filling

½ *pound Nova smoked salmon, minced*

1. Prepare Mushroom Filling substituting Nova for mushrooms.
2. Add Nova to skillet after onions are soft and continue recipe.

Deviled Eggs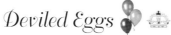

PAREVE   YIELD: 8 SERVINGS

8 *large hard-boiled eggs, peeled*	¼ *teaspoon garlic powder*
¼ *cup mayonnaise*	¼ *teaspoon onion powder*
1 *teaspoon Dijon mustard*	*Paprika for decoration*
Salt to taste	1 *tablespoon chopped fresh dill*
⅛ *teaspoon white pepper*	2 *tablespoons red or black caviar*

1. Cut eggs in half lengthwise and remove yolks.

2. Beat yolks with mayonnaise, mustard and seasonings at medium speed with electric mixer until smooth.
3. Fill whites with yolk mixture. Sprinkle with paprika.
4. Top with dill and/or caviar.

Yolk mixture may be piped through a decorating bag.

How to Make a Decorating Bag

• Use pinking shears to cut tip off one corner of plastic bag. Opening should be large enough to allow mixture to flow easily.

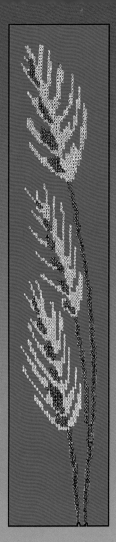

Olive Baguette

PAREVE   YIELD: 2 LOAVES

*W*e prepare this bread using a rapid mix method. Kalamata olives, garlic and shallot filling creates a scrumptious appearance.

Olive Filling

2   garlic cloves, minced   2   cups chopped kalamata olives
2   tablespoons minced shallots   1   teaspoon fresh lemon zest

1. Combine ingredients.

Dough

1   tablespoon active dry yeast   1½ cups hot water
2   tablespoons olive oil   Olive oil for greasing bowl
2   teaspoons salt   Cornmeal
3   cups flour or bread flour, divided

1. Preheat oven to 400°F ten minutes before baking. Grease cookie sheet.
2. Place yeast, oil, salt and 1 cup flour in large bowl. Add hot water and beat with electric mixer dough hook or by hand until smooth.
3. Turn dough out onto lightly floured surface and knead in remaining flour ½ cup at a time, until dough is springy and smooth, about 5 minutes. Add additional flour as needed, 1 tablespoon at a time.
4. Place in greased bowl, turn once to grease top and cover with plastic wrap. Let rise in warm place until triple in size, about 1 hour.
5. Gently punch down dough, turn out onto lightly floured surface and divide in half. Roll or pat each section into large rectangle.
6. Spread each rectangle with half the filling and roll up like jelly roll from long edge. Pinch seams and sides. Place loaves on cornmeal dusted sheets.

7. Cover loosely with plastic wrap and allow to rise until double, about 25 minutes. Remove plastic wrap and slash tops with serrated knife. Bake 25 to 35 minutes until browned.

Carrot Festival

Carrot Festival Tzimmes

The Incomparable Carrot Festival

Begun in 1978 as a modest farmers market, the annual autumn Carrot Festival at *Congregation Agudat Achim* has evolved into a mega-harvest fair with a happy carnival air that draws huge crowds from all over New York and surrounding states. For 27 years, every aspect of the Carrot Festival has been organized and run by succeeding generations of volunteers. Preparations for set-up, execution and cleanup, for musical entertainment, local radio broadcasting, children's games and activities, and participating merchants, begin months in advance. A multigenerational army of volunteers crowds the synagogue's kosher kitchen to join *As You Like It Kosher Catering* in cooking, baking and packaging a voluminous number of foods and dishes that will be snapped up on festival day. All day long, waves of enthusiastic visitors of all ages, religions and backgrounds spill across the synagogue's expansive front lawn. They sample delicious food cooked *al fresco*, stroll among numerous stalls filled with unique handiwork of local artists and crafters, and shop the display tables piled high with succulent harvest produce, trucked in from nearby Schoharie Valley farms. They queue up in long lines at a central food court, manned by volunteer servers, to buy all the tasty delicacies and main-course dishes, constantly replenished from the feverishly busy synagogue kitchen. They bring their plates to tables and chairs set up in a shady spot of the lawn. They feast on Festival Carrot Tzimmes, Potato Latkes with applesauce, Fragrant Carrot Soup with Indian Spices, Signature Chicken Soup with *matzoh* balls and sliced carrots, Garlicky Portobello Mushrooms, Black Bean-Corn Salad

and Falafel in pita garnished with Israeli Salad and Tahini Sauce. From among the dinner dishes there is Chicken Schwarma, Double Marinated Chicken Wings, Signature Roasted Chicken and Signature Brisket. Then of course, there are the desserts to die for — always a sell out — which we prepare in single portions and package for take-home. These include our incomparable slate of carrot-based baked goods, crowned by a heavenly two-layer, praline-filled Signature Carrot Festival Cake. Also our Carrot-Applesauce Snack Cake, Banana-Chocolate Chip Carrot Cake, Zucchini-Carrot Loaf, Streusel-Topped Pineapple-Carrot Cake, Carrot Strudel, as well as Festival Apple Strudel and Chunky Apple Cake. All these recipes appear in *Divine Kosher Cuisine*.

Festival Apple Strudel

3½ cups canned apple slices, diced or fresh apples, peeled and diced

½ cup peeled, cooked and mashed carrots

3 tablespoons sugar

1½ tablespoons golden raisins, plumped in hot water

1½ tablespoons chopped walnuts

1 teaspoon ground cinnamon

½ teaspoon ground ginger

⅛ teaspoon ground cloves

½ teaspoon ground coriander

½ teaspoon ground allspice

1 tablespoon lemon juice

1 teaspoon fresh lemon zest

⅓ cup strawberry preserves

⅓ cup breadcrumbs made from toasted challah

⅔ cup sugar for topping

2 teaspoons ground cinnamon for topping

1 sheet puff pastry, cut in half lengthwise

Flour for rolling

2 tablespoons melted margarine

Confectioners' sugar

1. Preheat oven to 400°F. Grease two 8-inch round baking pans.

2. Combine apples with carrots, sugar, raisins and nuts.

3. Mix in spices, juice and zest. Moisten with preserves and fold in breadcrumbs.

4. Combine sugar and cinnamon for topping. Divide into thirds.

5. Roll 1 piece of pastry on lightly floured surface, brush with margarine and sprinkle with one-third topping mixture.

6. Place half the apple mixture at one end of long side of pastry and roll up like jelly roll. Coil to fit pan. Repeat with remaining pastry.

7. Brush with margarine and sprinkle strudel with remaining topping. Let rest at room temperature 20 minutes.

8. Bake until strudel is golden and pastry puffs, about 25 minutes. Cool. Freezes well. Cut strudel just before serving and sprinkle with confectioners' sugar.

Strudel may be formed into a long strip and baked on greased cookie sheet.

Signature Carrot Festival Cake

DAIRY   YIELD: 16 TO 18 SERVINGS

Here is our never revealed recipe for carrot cake, kept secret for more than 20 years. This recipe produces a moist layered cake with buttery pecan filling, crowned with a luscious cream cheese frosting, sprinkled with toasted shredded coconut. It is very rich so serve small slices. Carrot Festival attendees stand in line to purchase this cake. We sell more than 1,500 servings at Carrot Festival. The cake may be refrigerated for 3 days or frozen.

Festival Cake

1¼	cups vegetable oil	1	teaspoon salt
2	cups sugar	4	large eggs
2	cups flour	4	cups peeled and grated carrots
2	teaspoons ground cinnamon	1	cup chopped pecans
2	teaspoons baking powder	1	cup raisins
1	teaspoon baking soda	1¼	cups shredded coconut, toasted

1. Preheat oven to 350°F. Grease two 9-inch baking pans.
2. Beat oil and sugar at medium speed with electric mixer. Combine dry ingredients and divide in half. Beat half into oil-sugar mixture.

3. Mix in eggs, one at a time, and beat in remaining dry ingredients.
4. Fold in carrots, nuts and raisins. Fill pans.
5. Bake 40 to 45 minutes or until tester inserted in center comes out almost clean. Cool and remove from pans. Cake may be frozen at this point.
6. Place 1 layer upside down on cake plate and spread with room temperature Buttery Pecan Filling. Top with second layer right side up.
7. Frost cake with Festival Cream Cheese Frosting, pat coconut on sides of cake and sprinkle lightly over top. Chill to set frosting but serve at room temperature.

How to Toast Coconut

1. Preheat oven to 300°F. Prepare ungreased cookie sheet.

2. Toast coconut on sheet in oven 10 to 12 minutes, stirring occasionally until golden. Cool.

Buttery Pecan Filling

1½ cups sugar	¾ cup butter, cut into 1-inch pieces
¼ cup flour	1¼ cups chopped pecans
¾ teaspoon salt	2 teaspoons vanilla extract
1½ cups heavy cream	

1. Blend sugar, flour and salt in large pot and gradually stir in cream and then butter.
2. Stir over low heat until butter melts. Simmer 20 to 30 minutes until golden brown, stirring constantly.
3. Cool to lukewarm and stir in nuts and vanilla. Chill overnight. May be frozen at this point.

Festival Cream Cheese Frosting

1 cup butter, room temperature	3¾ cups confectioners' sugar
8 ounces cream cheese, room temperature	1 teaspoon vanilla extract

1. Cream butter and cream cheese at medium speed with electric mixer and beat in sugar. Stir in vanilla.

Zucchini-Carrot Loaf

PAREVE   YIELD: 20 SLICES

3 large eggs	3 cups flour, divided
2 cups sugar	1 teaspoon salt
1 cup vegetable oil	½ teaspoon baking powder
1 teaspoon ground cinnamon	1 teaspoon baking soda
1 teaspoon ground nutmeg	2 cups grated unpeeled zucchini
1 cup chopped walnuts	1 cup peeled and shredded carrots
1 cup raisins	1 tablespoon vanilla extract

1. Preheat oven to 350°F. Grease two 8½ x 4½ x 2½-inch loaf pans.
2. Beat eggs with sugar at medium speed with electric mixer until fluffy. Mix in oil, cinnamon and nutmeg.
3. Combine nuts with raisins and coat with 2 tablespoons flour.
4. Beat remaining flour, salt, baking powder and baking soda into egg mixture. Mix in zucchini, carrots and vanilla. Fold in raisin-nut mixture.
5. Pour into pans and bake 50 to 60 minutes or until tester inserted in center comes out clean.

The carrot is the second most popular vegetable in the world after the potato.

Carrot Strudel

PAREVE

YIELD: 30 SLICES

½	cup margarine	1	cup grape jelly, warmed
1	cup sugar, divided	½	cup crushed cornflakes
2	large eggs	1	cup golden raisins
½	cup peeled and grated carrots	½	cup chopped walnuts
2	teaspoons baking powder	1½	teaspoons ground cinnamon
2	cups flour		Flour for rolling and kneading
⅛	teaspoon salt	1	tablespoon margarine, melted for brushing

1. Preheat oven to 375°F ten minutes before baking. Grease cookie sheet.
2. Cream ½ cup margarine with ½ cup sugar at medium speed with electric mixer. Mix in eggs, carrots, baking powder, flour and salt. Cover dough with plastic wrap and chill overnight.
3. Combine jelly, cornflakes, raisins and nuts for filling. Mix cinnamon with remaining sugar for topping.
4. Divide dough into 3 pieces. Knead in additional flour until dough is no longer sticky. Roll 1 piece dough into ¼-inch thick rectangle and spread with one-third filling and sprinkle with one-fourth topping. Roll up like jelly roll. Repeat.
5. Brush strudel with margarine and sprinkle with remaining topping. Place on sheet and bake 25 minutes or until golden. Cool before cutting into slices. Freezes well.

Carrot-Applesauce Snack Cake

PAREVE

YIELD: 20 SLICES

We tested this recipe with a sugar substitute for baking with resounding success but it must be served at room temperature for best flavor.

2¾	cups flour	2	cups sugar
1	tablespoon baking soda	1	teaspoon vanilla extract
½	teaspoon salt	2	cups applesauce
1	tablespoon ground cinnamon	3	cups peeled and grated carrots
1	teaspoon ground nutmeg	1	cup golden raisins
4	large eggs	1	cup chopped walnuts
¾	cup vegetable oil	½	recipe Streusel Topping, optional

1. Preheat oven to 375°F. Grease two 9 x 5 x 3-inch loaf pans.
2. Combine flour, baking soda, salt, cinnamon and nutmeg.

3. Beat eggs at medium speed with electric mixer and add oil, sugar, vanilla, applesauce and carrots.

4. Stir in flour mixture just to moisten and fold in raisins and nuts. Pour batter into pans. Sprinkle streusel over batter.

5. Bake 40 to 45 minutes or until tester inserted in center comes out clean.

Frost cake with Orange Glaze instead of streusel.

Banana-Chocolate Chip Carrot Loaf

DAIRY OR PAREVE   YIELD: 10 SLICES

½   cup butter for dairy
     (use margarine for pareve)
1   cup brown sugar, firmly packed
2   large eggs
2   cups flour
1   teaspoon baking soda
½   teaspoon baking powder

½   teaspoon ground cinnamon
¼   teaspoon salt
1   cup mashed ripe bananas
1   teaspoon vanilla extract
1   cup peeled and grated carrots
9   ounces chocolate chips, divided

1. Preheat oven to 350°F. Grease 9 x 5 x 3-inch loaf pan.

2. Cream butter or margarine and sugar at medium speed with electric mixer until light and fluffy. Beat in eggs.

3. Combine flour, baking soda, baking powder, cinnamon and salt. Mix flour mixture and bananas alternately into egg mixture.

4. Add vanilla and fold in carrots and 6 ounces chocolate chips. Pour batter into pan and sprinkle top with remaining chocolate chips.

5. Bake 50 to 60 minutes or until tester inserted in center comes out clean. Cool 10 minutes, remove from pan and cool completely. Freezes well.

Streusel-Topped Pineapple-Carrot Cake

PAREVE   YIELD: 20 SLICES

A mixture of complementary flavors and textures characterize this carrot cake. The sharper tang of the pineapple enhances the sweetness of the carrots, while the crushed pineapple pulp plays against the chopped, crunchy nuts.

Cake

3	cups flour	1½	cups vegetable oil
2	cups sugar	2	teaspoons vanilla extract
2	teaspoons baking powder	3	large eggs
1	teaspoon baking soda	1	cup crushed pineapple, undrained
1	teaspoon ground cinnamon	1	cup peeled and grated carrots
½	teaspoon salt	½	cup chopped pecans or walnuts

1. Preheat oven to 350°F. Grease two 8½ x 4½ x 2½-inch loaf pans.
2. Combine dry ingredients.
3. Beat oil, vanilla and eggs at medium speed with electric mixer. Stir in pineapple and carrots. Mix in dry ingredients and add nuts.
4. Pour into pan, cover with Streusel Topping. Bake 50 minutes or until tester inserted in center comes out clean. Cool 15 minutes. Freezes well.

Bake in a 10-inch tube pan as an option.

Streusel Topping

6	tablespoons sugar	½	teaspoon ground cinnamon
¼	cup brown sugar, firmly packed	2	cups flour
¾	teaspoon salt	½	cup margarine

1. Combine all dry ingredients.
2. Cut margarine into dry mixture to make crumbly topping. Freezes well.

Chunky Apple Cake

PAREVE   YIELD: 12 SERVINGS

4	cups apples, peeled and diced	1	cup vegetable oil
2	cups sugar	2	large eggs, beaten
3	cups flour	2	teaspoons vanilla extract
2	teaspoons baking soda	1	cup finely chopped walnuts
1	teaspoon salt		

1. Preheat oven to 350°F ten minutes before baking. Grease 9 x 13-inch pan.
2. Mix apples and sugar and set aside at room temperature 1 hour.
3. Combine flour, baking soda and salt in large bowl.
4. Mix oil, eggs and vanilla and add to dry ingredients. Fold in apple mixture and nuts.
5. Pour batter into pan and bake 50 to 60 minutes or until tester inserted in center comes out clean.

Iced Carrot Cake

PAREVE   YIELD: 10 SERVINGS

A bouquet of sweet spices permeates this moist and marvelous carrot cake.

1	cup flour	½	cup vegetable oil
½	teaspoon baking powder	2	large eggs
½	teaspoon baking soda	⅓	teaspoon salt
⅛	teaspoon ground nutmeg	1½	cups peeled and grated carrots
¼	teaspoon ground cinnamon	2	tablespoons raisins
⅛	teaspoon ground allspice	½	cup chopped walnuts, optional
1	cup sugar		Pareve Cream Cheese Frosting

1. Preheat oven to 350°F. Grease 9-inch square pan.
2. Combine flour, baking powder, baking soda and spices.
3. Beat sugar, oil, eggs and salt at medium speed with electric mixer. Mix in carrots.
4. Add flour mixture and beat. Stir in raisins and walnuts.
5. Pour batter into pan and bake 35 to 40 minutes or until tester inserted in center comes out clean. Cool and frost.

Festival Carrot Tzimmes   Non-G

PAREVE   YIELD: 10 SERVINGS

Our carrot tzimmes is a medley of harvest staples. Carrots, sweet potatoes and butternut squash blend with raisins, prunes and dates in a tangy orange sauce.

3	large sweet potatoes, peeled and chunked	2	tablespoons fresh orange zest
4	large carrots, peeled and sliced	1	orange, juiced
1	small butternut squash, peeled, seeded and chunked	2	tablespoons brown sugar, firmly packed
¼	cup raisins	¼	cup honey or maple syrup
¼	cup pitted prunes, cut in half		
¼	cup chopped dates		

1. Preheat oven to 350°F. Grease 9 x 13-inch pan.
2. Combine all ingredients and place in pan.
3. Bake covered 1½ to 2 hours or until tender. Freezes well.

Garlicky Portobello Mushrooms   Non-G

PAREVE   YIELD: 4 SERVINGS

Roasted, grilled or Italianized, these meaty mushrooms may be served as a vegetarian main course or as a side dish.

½	cup olive oil	4	large Portobello mushrooms, stems removed
2	tablespoons lemon juice	½	teaspoon dried oregano
6	garlic cloves, minced	½	teaspoon dried basil
	Pepper to taste		

1. Preheat grill or oven to 425°F ten minutes before cooking. Grease 9 x 13-inch baking pan.
2. Whisk oil, juice, garlic and pepper. Place mushrooms in pan and brush tops. Turn mushrooms over and top with remaining marinade. Sprinkle with herbs and cover. Marinate 2 to 3 hours at room temperature.
3. Remove from marinade and grill or roast in oven, basting occasionally until tender, 8 to 12 minutes.

Portobello Mushroom Parmesan

DAIRY

6 Portobello mushrooms

• Follow directions for Eggplant Parmesan substituting grilled or roasted Portobello mushrooms for eggplant. Do not bread mushrooms.

Fragrant Carrot Soup with Indian Spices

PAREVE   YIELD: 12 SERVINGS

Delight your guests on Rosh Hashanah with fragrant carrot soup. An aromatic blend of Indian spices makes this harvest pareve soup a downright spicy first course to any menu.

½   cup olive oil
2   large onions, chopped
2   tablespoons brown sugar, firmly packed
1   teaspoon ground coriander
2   tablespoons curry powder
½   teaspoon ground cardamom
⅛   teaspoon ground nutmeg

2   pounds carrots, peeled and chopped
4   medium potatoes, peeled and chopped
3   quarts vegetable broth
    Salt and pepper to taste
    Cilantro, mint leaves or nondairy sour cream for garnish

1. Heat oil in soup pot and sauté onions until soft but not browned. Add sugar and spices and cook 1 minute.

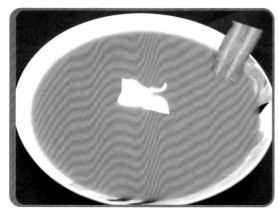

2. Add carrots, potatoes and broth and bring to boil. Reduce heat and simmer 30 minutes or until vegetables are soft. Add salt and pepper. Cool and purée.

3. Serve soup hot or at room temperature and garnish.

For a lower fat version, reduce oil to ⅓ cup.

Did You Know?

- 900-1000 AD: Purple and yellow carrots spread from Afghanistan to eastern Mediterranean.

- 1300s: Purple and yellow carrots appear in Western Europe and China.

- 1600s: Yellow carrots appear in Japan.

- 1700s: White carrots appear in Europe and orange in the Netherlands.

- Today: Orange carrots predominate worldwide.

Grinding Spices

Fresh ground spices have the most potency.

• Use a spice mill, coffee grinder or blender for good results.

Hot Off the Grill at Carrot Festival 🎈 👑

MEAT   YIELD: 8 SERVINGS

All barbecue items are meat. Marinades are pareve and suitable for fish and vegetables.

Grilled Chicken Sandwiches

2   pounds chicken breast halves, boned and skinned
8   hamburger buns or hard rolls

2   large tomatoes, sliced for garnish
1   medium onion, sliced for garnish

1.   Preheat grill 10 minutes before cooking.
2.   Cut chicken into 3½-ounce portions, pound to flatten.
3.   Marinate in Carrot Festival Vinaigrette Marinade overnight.
4.   Discard marinade and brush with Bourbon Grill Glaze before and during cooking. Grill until tender. Warm buns or rolls on grill and serve with tomatoes and onions.

Hamburgers

2   pounds ground beef
8   hamburger buns or hard rolls
     Salt, pepper and garlic powder to taste
2   large tomatoes, sliced for garnish

1   medium onion, sliced for garnish
2   large kosher pickles, cut ½-inch thick
¾   cup deli mustard
½   cup ketchup

1.   Preheat grill 10 minutes before cooking.
2.   Shape hamburgers using ¼ pound for each patty and season with salt, pepper and garlic powder.
3.   Grill meat to desired doneness. Warm buns or rolls and serve with tomatoes, onions and condiments.

Hot Dogs

8   hot dogs
8   hot dog buns
¾   cup mustard
¾   cup ketchup
1   medium onion, chopped
½   cup relish
½   cup fresh sauerkraut

1.   Preheat grill 10 minutes before cooking.
2.   Grill hot dogs. Warm buns and serve with condiments, onions, relish and sauerkraut.

Double Marinated Chicken Wings

6 pounds chicken wings, tips discarded	¼ cup jellied cranberry sauce
	¼ cup chili sauce

1. Preheat grill or broiler 10 minutes before cooking.
2. Cut wings in half, place in Carrot Festival Vinaigrette Marinade and chill overnight.
3. Thicken Bourbon Grill Glaze by adding sauces and simmering 10 minutes. Cool.
4. Remove chicken from marinade and brush with glaze before and during cooking.

Carrot Festival Vinaigrette Marinade

*C**arrot Festival's grilled chicken and chicken wings marinate in this oil and vinegar combo sparked with glorious garlic and soy sauce. This recipe will marinate 6 whole chicken breasts, 3 pounds London broil or 2 pounds fish.*

¼ cup olive oil	6 garlic cloves, minced
¼ cup red wine vinegar	Pepper to taste
⅓ cup soy sauce	

1. Whisk all ingredients. Pour marinade into plastic bag, add chicken or beef and marinate for 2 hours or overnight. Marinate fish only 30 minutes. Discard marinade.

Bourbon Grill Glaze

*B**rush this sauce on chicken or beef in the last few minutes of grilling to create a fragrant glaze. It may also be warmed and passed as an accompaniment to roasted meats.*

1 tablespoon olive oil	1⅓ cups brown sugar, firmly packed
12 garlic cloves	3 tablespoons lemon juice
⅔ cup water	3 tablespoons minced onion
1 cup pineapple juice	1 tablespoon Bourbon Whiskey
¼ cup teriyaki sauce	1 tablespoon crushed pineapple
1 tablespoon soy sauce	¼ teaspoon cayenne pepper to taste

1. Preheat oven to 325°F.
2. Drizzle oil over garlic and wrap in foil. Roast 45 to 50 minutes or until soft. Cool and mash.
3. Heat water, pineapple juice, sauces and sugar. Stir occasionally until mixture boils.
4. Reduce heat and stir in garlic and remaining ingredients. Simmer 40 to 50 minutes or until sauce is reduced by about half and is thick.

How to Measure Reduced Liquid

• Place handle of wooden spoon in the liquid and mark the level. As mixture reduces, measure again.

Chicken Schwarma

MEAT   YIELD: 4 SERVINGS

Our version of schwarma *is a sell-out item at Carrot Festival. Reportedly originating in Lebanon as a lamb dish,* schwarma *has many variations and its popularity is worldwide. This recipe requires an overnight marinade. May also be grilled on skewers with vegetables.*

¼   teaspoon pepper
¼   teaspoon ground cinnamon
¼   teaspoon ground allspice
¼   teaspoon ground cloves
1   teaspoon ground cardamom
¼   teaspoon cayenne pepper
4   teaspoons lemon juice, divided
1   pound chicken breast halves,
       boned and skinned
5   garlic cloves

⅓   teaspoon salt
7   tablespoons olive oil, divided
½   pound red peppers, cut into
       1-inch cubes
½   pound onions, cut into 1-inch
       cubes
2   tablespoons vegetable oil
⅔   pound tomatoes, cut into 1-inch
       cubes
4   pita breads with pocket

1. Combine pepper, cinnamon, allspice, cloves, cardamom, cayenne and 3 teaspoons juice for spice rub. Set aside one-fourth of mixture.

2. Cut chicken into 1-inch pieces and toss with remaining rub. Cover and chill overnight.

3. Process garlic with salt and add rest of juice to form paste. Add 6 tablespoons olive oil in slow stream with processor running until sauce is consistency of mayonnaise for garlic sauce. Chill.

4. Coat peppers and onions with remaining spice rub and set aside at room temperature 1 hour. Heat rest of olive oil in large skillet and sauté peppers and onions until soft. Remove from skillet.

5. Heat vegetable oil in same skillet and sauté chicken until tender.

6. Toss cooked vegetables with chicken and fold in tomatoes. Stuff in pita pockets and drizzle with garlic sauce.

 *Gewürztraminer*

Dr. Ruth's Favorite Passover Nut Torte

Cooking for Passover*

*P*assover, the Festival of Freedom that commemorates the Exodus from Egypt, is as unique as the first of the four questions asked at the *Seder* table implies, why is this night different from all other nights? With its special requirements and challenges, cooking for Passover has developed into a kosher subcategory, to which *Divine Kosher Cuisine* now adds a sterling new chapter. We approach cooking for Passover with special care and pay attention to the spirit of the holiday and observance of the common dietary prohibitions. There are differing traditions — some are briefly listed here — but for more insight into this area, we refer readers to their local *Kashrut* authority. Over the years, cooking for Passover has eased a great deal, as more and more kosher for Passover foods have become commercially available. To those, we add our recipes for Confectioners' Sugar and Passover Flour to simplify your Passover meal planning. In select recipes throughout the collection, a *matzoh* symbol indicates that it is also suitable for Passover. When Passover recipes call for ingredients that have been altered to make them suitable for Passover, these ingredients carry the symbol K-P. Suggestions for your *Seder* table appear in Passover *Seder* Menus.

Best of the Best, Non-g'brochts

Fig-Nut Chopped Chicken Liver

Signature Whitefish Salad

Apple Brie Soup

Artichoke-Potato Soup

Feta-Pear Layered Salad

Marinated Grilled Salmon

Meat Balls with Sauerkraut

Baked Eggplant Stack

Potato-Cheese Lasagna

Grilled Chicken Breast with Tomato Salsa

Fruited Quinoa Primavera

Layered Sweet Potatoes and Apples

Sautéed Spinach with Garlic

Roasted Onions with Balsamic Glaze

Apricot-Macaroon Cheesecake

Citrus and Grapes in Muscat

Dr. Ruth's Favorite Passover Nut Torte

Meringue Topped Apples

Signature Almond Horns

Preparing for Passover

Extensive preparation centers on the complete removal of *chometz* from home and diet. This involves a complete change of dishes, utensils, and silverware, with separate meat and dairy sets. *Chometz* includes any food made from wheat, oats, barley, rye or spelt, except *matzoh*. *Matzoh* is baked for 18 minutes, which prevents the flour-water mixture from rising. Some people also avoid legumes, peanuts, rice, corn and chickpeas, as a class of foods called *kitniots*. Our Passover recipes exclude all the items commonly considered *kitniots*.

Differing Traditions

However, some traditions prohibit foods that mix baked *matzoh* with water, known as *g'brocht* foods. Non-*g'brocht* Passover recipes, wherever they appear in our collection, are identified by the key, "Non-G." Non-*g'brochts* here means K-P, with no *matzoh* or *matzoh* by-products used. In our collection, you will find some 70 *non-g'brochts*. From among these we have compiled the "Best of the Best," recipes that encompass a full range of foods and courses, traditional to contemporary, sufficient to delight your family and friends throughout the Passover festival. For more details on differing traditions, consult your local *Kashrut* authority. For a complete listing of *non-g'brochts*, see index.

* Use only Kosher for Passover foods and ingredients when preparing the recipes recommended for Passover.

Chocolate Truffle Cake

DAIRY OR PAREVE   YIELD: 12 SERVINGS

A rich, velvety chocolate cake doused with a shimmering chocolate glaze.

12 ounces semisweet chocolate,
    chopped, divided

3 ounces bittersweet chocolate,
    chopped

1½ cups butter for dairy, cut into
    pieces, divided (use margarine
    for pareve)

13 tablespoons sugar, divided

1½ cups heavy cream for dairy,
    divided (use liquid nondairy
    whipped topping for pareve)

1 tablespoon vanilla extract

6 large eggs

1. Preheat oven to 350°F. Grease 9-inch round pan, line bottom with parchment and grease again.

2. Melt 6 ounces semisweet chocolate with bittersweet chocolate, 1 cup butter or margarine, 12 tablespoons sugar and ½ cup cream or nondairy topping, stirring frequently until smooth. Cool slightly and stir in vanilla.

3. Beat eggs at medium speed with electric mixer 1 minute. Beat chocolate mixture into eggs until smooth.

4. Pour batter into pan and tap gently on work surface to break any large air bubbles.

5. Place pan into larger pan. Pour water into larger pan, filling about ¾ of an inch up sides of cake pan to create water bath.

6. Bake 25 to 30 minutes until edges of cake are set but center is still soft. Remove pan from water bath. Cool. Cake will sink a little in center and may crack slightly.

7. Turn cake over onto rack placed over cookie sheet. Remove pan and paper.

8. Melt remaining chocolate and butter or margarine stirring until smooth for glaze. Pour over cake, spreading with spatula. Allow to set.

9. Whip remaining cream or nondairy topping with remaining sugar and serve with cake.

How to Make Your Own Passover Vanilla

Better than the imitation vanilla available.

• Break up 2 ounces vanilla beans and add to 3⅛ cups (750 ml) Passover vodka. Store in a dark place for 2 months.

Apricot-Macaroon Cheesecake Non-G

DAIRY   YIELD: 24 SERVINGS

A spectacular, three-level cheesecake sure to please everyone.

Macaroon Crust

1	cup dried apricots	4	egg whites
½	cup water	3½	cups shredded coconut, divided
¾	cup sugar		

1. Preheat oven to 425°F ten minutes before baking. Grease 10-inch springform pan.
2. Bring apricots and water to boil, reduce heat and simmer 5 minutes. Cover and remove from heat. Let stand 30 minutes until fruit is soft.
3. Drain apricots and purée with sugar, egg whites and ½ cup coconut.
4. Fold in remaining coconut. Cover with plastic wrap and freeze 20 minutes.
5. Press mixture evenly over bottom and 2 inches up sides of pan. Chill.

Filling

2½	pounds cream cheese, room temperature	½	teaspoon fresh lemon zest
		½	teaspoon fresh orange zest
1⅔	cups sugar	5	large eggs
⅛	teaspoon salt	¼	cup milk
2	tablespoons potato starch	1	teaspoon vanilla extract

1. Whip cream cheese at medium speed with electric mixer until fluffy.
2. Combine sugar, salt, potato starch and zest. Mix into cheese.
3. Add eggs one at a time, beating after each.
4. Add milk and vanilla and beat until smooth.
5. Pour over crust and bake 15 minutes. Reduce heat to 250°F and bake for an additional 40 minutes or until tester inserted in center comes out almost clean.
6. Turn oven off and leave cake in oven with door ajar. Allow to cool 1 hour.
7. Spread Apricot Topping over cheesecake and decorate with sliced almonds. Chill.

Apricot Topping

1	cup dried apricots	2	teaspoons fresh lemon zest
⅓	cup white wine or water	1½	teaspoons lemon juice
1½	cups apricot preserves	1¼	cups sliced almonds, lightly toasted for topping
1	tablespoon fresh orange zest		

1. Combine dried apricots and wine or water. Bring to boil, remove from heat and let stand until liquid is absorbed. Purée.
2. Add preserves, zests and juice. Cool.

Charoset Non-G

PAREVE   YIELD: ABOUT 3 CUPS

Ashkenazi

2 apples, peeled and chopped
1 cup walnuts, toasted and
    chopped

3 tablespoons sweet Concord grape
    wine
1 teaspoon ground cinnamon
1 tablespoon honey, optional

1. Combine all ingredients adding honey for a sweeter taste.
2. Cover and chill.

Greek

1¼ cups dates, finely chopped
1 large orange
½ cup honey or sugar
    Ground cinnamon to taste
    Ground cloves to taste

½ cup almonds, finely chopped
½ cup walnuts, finely chopped
½ cup sweet Concord grape wine to
    taste

1. Peel orange and cut into pieces, removing seeds. Add dates and mash into paste.
2. Cook paste and honey in top of double boiler over gently simmering water and stir constantly with wooden spoon until quite thick, about 20 minutes.
3. Add cloves, cinnamon and wine and simmer until very thick.
4. Remove from heat and stir in nuts. Cool.

Sephardic Date

1 cup dates, pitted
1 cup raisins
½ cup walnuts
1 medium apple, peeled and diced

1 teaspoon ground cinnamon
¼ teaspoon ground ginger
3 tablespoons sweet Concord grape
    wine to taste

1. Process all ingredients until finely chopped adding additional wine if needed.

Passover Chocolate Roll

PAREVE   YIELD: 14 TO 16 SLICES

Filling

6   large egg yolks   8   ounces bittersweet chocolate
10 tablespoons margarine

1. Beat yolks at high speed with electric mixer 10 minutes or until thick and lemon colored.
2. Melt margarine with chocolate. Stir until smooth and cool slightly.
3. Add chocolate to yolks and beat until thick.

Cake

7   large eggs, separated   ½   cup cocoa powder, sifted
14 tablespoons K-P confectioners' 1   teaspoon K-P baking powder
    sugar, divided   ½   teaspoon salt
6   tablespoons potato starch   Cocoa, K-P confectioners' sugar
                                        and potato starch for rolling

1. Preheat oven to 350°F. Grease 12 x 18 x 1-inch baking pan. Line with parchment paper and grease again.
2. Beat yolks on high speed with electric mixer 10 minutes until thick and lemon colored. Add 8 tablespoons sugar.
3. Combine potato starch, cocoa and baking powder. Fold mixture into yolks.
4. Whip whites with salt in separate bowl on high speed with electric mixer until foamy. Add remaining sugar and continue beating until stiff peaks form.
5. Fold whites gently into chocolate mixture and spread into pan.
6. Bake 6 minutes, rotate pan 180° and bake additional 5 to 6 minutes or until cake pulls away from sides. Cool 2 minutes and run knife along sides of pan.

Cake Roll

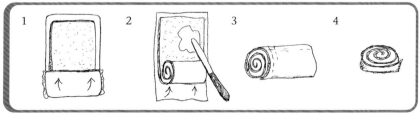

1. Unroll cake.   3. Roll-up cake, placing seam side down.
2. Spread with filling.   4. Slice cake roll.

Confectioners' Sugar Substitute for Passover

• When a non-Passover recipe calls for confectioners' sugar, on Passover you can replace the sugar by mixing 1 cup, less 1 tablespoon of sugar, with 1 tablespoon of potato starch. Pulverize in blender.

7. Spread large dampened linen towel or tablecloth on surface and sprinkle with equal amounts of cocoa, sugar and potato starch. Remove parchment and roll from 18-inch side. Cool slightly.

8. Unroll cake, cut away any hard edges, and spread with three-fourths filling, leaving ½-inch border on sides and 1-inch at top. Roll-up cake and decorate with remaining filling. Chill and slice when filling is firm. Freezes well.

Fruit-Filled Jelly Roll  Non-G

PAREVE   YIELD: 20 SLICES

A jelly roll for Passover and beyond. So good that you will make this all year round.

6 large eggs, separated	⅛ teaspoon salt
1 large egg	Potato starch and pulverized sugar for turning cake out
1½ cups sugar	
1½ tablespoons lemon juice	1 cup apricot or raspberry preserves, warmed
1½ teaspoons fresh lemon zest	
¾ cup potato starch, sifted twice	

1. Preheat oven to 350°F. Grease 12 x 18 x 1-inch pan, line with parchment paper and grease again.

2. Beat yolks and whole egg at medium speed with electric mixer until thick.

3. Add sugar, juice and zest, beating constantly. Add potato starch gradually.

4. Whip whites with salt at high speed in separate bowl with clean beaters until stiff. Fold into batter.

5. Pour into pan and bake 10 to 12 minutes or until cake springs back when lightly touched. Rotate pan after 6 minutes to insure even baking. Do not over bake.

6. Dampen linen towel and sprinkle lightly with mixture of potato starch and pulverized sugar.

7. Run knife around sides of pan and turn cake onto towel. Let rest 2 minutes and remove parchment.

8. Spread with warmed preserves. Cut in half down center, making 2 equal jelly rolls 9 x 12 inches. Roll each from 12-inch long side. Wrap in clean towels and cool.

9. Slice into 1-inch thick diagonal pieces.

The jelly roll may be frozen in 1 piece and cut while still frozen, 2 hours before serving.

Traditional Passover Sponge Cake

PAREVE

Yield: 12 servings

1. Preheat oven to 350°F. Prepare ungreased 10-inch tube pan.

2. Prepare Fruit-Filled Jelly Roll cake batter and pour into pan.

3. Bake 50 minutes or until cake comes away from sides of pan. Cool.

Dr. Ruth's
Favorite Passover Nut Torte  Non-G

DAIRY   YIELD: 10 TO 12 SERVINGS

A frequent visitor over the years to her local family who belong to Congregation Agudat Achim, Dr. Ruth Westheimer calls this nut torte her Passover favorite.

Cake

Potato starch for dusting pan
12 large eggs, separated
1½ cups plus 2 tablespoons sugar

2 tablespoons lemon juice
3 cups finely ground walnuts

1. Preheat oven to 325°F. Grease three 9-inch round cake pans, line with parchment paper, grease again and dust with potato starch.

2. Beat yolks on high speed with electric mixer until thick. Add sugar and lemon juice and beat until light yellow. Mix in nuts.

3. Beat whites in separate bowl at high speed with electric mixer until stiff peaks form. Fold gently into yolk mixture.

4. Divide batter into pans and bake 25 to 30 minutes or until golden brown or until tester inserted in center comes out mostly clean but moist. Loosen edges with knife immediately after removing pans from oven.

5. Cool completely. Remove from pans and peel off parchment.

Frosting 1

16 ounces heavy cream

4 teaspoons sugar

1. Whip cream at high speed with electric mixer until soft peaks form. Add sugar and beat until stiff peaks form.

Frosting 2

8 ounces heavy cream
2 tablespoons sugar

2 tablespoons cocoa, sifted
1 teaspoon instant coffee granules

Dr. Ruth's Favorite Passover Nut Torte (continued)

1. Combine all ingredients and whip at high speed with electric mixer until stiff peaks form.

Assembly

Chocolate Curls

1. Place 1 cake layer on plate and top with scant half of Frosting 1.
2. Top with 2nd layer and spread with Frosting 2. Top with 3rd layer.
3. Frost top and sides with remainder of Frosting 1. Decorate with Chocolate Curls and chill until serving.

Fruit-Nut Passover Mandelbrot

PAREVE   YIELD: 24 SLICES

This dough requires overnight chilling. It may be made in advance and frozen for later use.

3	large eggs, slightly beaten
¾	cup vegetable or walnut oil
½	teaspoon salt
1	cup sugar
2	tablespoons matzoh meal
1	cup cake meal
½	cup potato starch

2	teaspoons fresh orange zest to taste
1	cup coarsely chopped walnuts or pecans
½	cup chopped dates
2	tablespoons ground cinnamon for topping
3	tablespoons sugar for topping

1. Preheat oven to 350°F ten minutes before baking. Grease cookie sheet.
2. Mix eggs with oil and add salt, 1 cup sugar, matzoh and cake meals and potato starch. Fold in zest, nuts and dates. Cover with plastic wrap and chill overnight.
3. Form two 3-inch wide logs, 15 inches long. Bake 25 minutes or until bottom is slightly browned and top is dry.
4. Cut into ½-inch wide diagonal slices and place, cut side up, on sheet. Combine topping ingredients and sprinkle over slices.
5. Reduce oven temperature to 325°F and bake 20 minutes more or until slices are browned.

Apricot and Linzer Tarts

PAREVE   YIELD: 2 TARTS

*T*hese two tarts are an unusual departure from typical Passover desserts. They are filled with fruit flavors and redolent of the ever popular Passover nut, almonds. Make ahead and freeze for easy company entertaining.

Pesach Almond Tart Dough for Two Tarts

½	cup margarine	¼	cup potato starch
1	large egg	½	cup matzoh meal
½	cup sugar	½	cup cake meal
1	tablespoon fresh lemon zest	½	teaspoon ground cinnamon to taste
½	cup ground almonds		

1. Cream margarine with egg and sugar at medium speed with electric mixer. Add zest.
2. Combine almonds, potato starch, matzoh and cake meal and cinnamon and mix into margarine mixture until dough holds together.
3. Divide into 2 balls and cover with plastic wrap. Chill 2 hours.

Frangipane Filling

6	tablespoons margarine	¾	cup ground almonds
⅓	cup sugar	1	teaspoon almond extract
1	large egg	1	teaspoon lemon juice

1. Cream margarine with sugar at medium speed with electric mixer. Add remaining ingredients.

Pesach Apricot Almond Tart

½	recipe Pesach Almond Tart Dough	1	cup apricot preserves, warmed
		1	teaspoon lemon juice, optional

1. Preheat oven to 375°F. Grease 8-inch tart or springform pan.
2. Press dough on bottom and ½-inch up sides of pan. Cover dough with foil or parchment and weight down crust. Bake 10 minutes.
3. Mix preserves with juice and spread over partially baked crust.
4. Top with Frangipane Filling.
5. Bake 35 to 45 minutes until set. Cool and remove from pan.

Linzer Tart

1	recipe Pesach Almond Tart Dough	2	teaspoons lemon juice to taste
2	cups raspberry preserves, warmed	¾	cup sliced almonds, divided
			Fresh raspberries

1. Preheat oven to 375°F. Grease 8-inch tart or springform pan.
2. Press 1 ball of dough on bottom and half inch up sides of pan. Cover dough with foil or parchment and weight down crust. Bake 10 minutes.
3. Mix preserves with juice and spread filling over partially baked crust. Sprinkle ½ cup almonds over filling.
4. Form second ball of dough into eight quarter-inch ropes, 9 inches long and lay over preserves to form lattice pattern.
5. Bake 35 to 45 minutes until lightly browned. Cool and remove from pan.
6. Decorate with remaining almonds and fresh raspberries.

Versatile Passover Pie Crust

DAIRY OR PAREVE

1 cup matzoh cake meal

1 cup finely ground toasted nuts, cookie or cake crumbs

1 teaspoon ground cinnamon

¼ cup brown sugar, firmly packed

¼ cup butter for dairy, melted (use margarine for pareve)

• Combine ingredients and press into greased 9-inch pie shell.

Passover Chocolate Chip Cookies

DAIRY OR PAREVE   YIELD: 60 COOKIES

These cookies were created especially for the 1981 Congregation Agudat Achim Passover Food Sale. Irresistible to young and old alike, best you hide them until the Seder. Dough requires overnight chilling.

14 *tablespoons butter for dairy (use margarine for pareve)*
1⅓ *cups brown sugar, firmly packed*
2 *large eggs*
1 *tablespoon vanilla extract*
6 *tablespoons cake meal, sifted*

14 *tablespoons potato starch*
1 *teaspoon K-P baking powder*
½ *teaspoon salt*
1½ *cups chopped walnuts or pecans*
12 *ounces chocolate chips*

1. Preheat oven to 350°F ten minutes before baking. Grease cookie sheets.
2. Cream butter or margarine with sugar at medium speed with electric mixer. Add eggs and vanilla.
3. Combine dry ingredients and add gradually to creamed mixture.
4. Fold in nuts and chocolate chips. Cover and chill overnight.
5. Roll dough into walnut-size balls and space 2 inches apart on sheet or use 1½-inch cookie scoop.
6. Bake 9 minutes. Cool 3 minutes and remove from sheets.

Granulated sugar may be substituted for brown sugar.

Cookie Baking Tips

- For uniform cookies, use cookie scoop.
- For even baking, position oven racks one-third and two-thirds up from bottom. Bake 1 sheet half the time on upper rack, move it to lower rack and put new sheet on upper rack. Continue until all cookies are baked.
- If cookie sheets are hot when ready to re-use, run backs under cold water to cool.
- Store cookies in containers with tight-fitting lids.

Chocolate-Chocolate Chip
Macaroons Non-G

PAREVE   YIELD: 24 COOKIES

Moist, chewy and chocolaty, the staple Passover macaroon has never been better.

16 ounces chocolate chips, divided
2   large egg whites
½   cup sugar
¼   teaspoon salt
½   teaspoon vanilla extract
1¼ cups shredded coconut

1. Preheat oven to 350°F. Line cookie sheets with parchment or brown paper.
2. Melt 12 ounces chocolate chips and cool.
3. Beat whites at high speed with electric mixer until foamy. Add sugar gradually and beat until stiff peaks form. Add salt and vanilla.
4. Fold in melted chocolate, remaining chocolate chips and coconut.
5. Drop by teaspoons on sheets and bake 15 to 20 minutes. Cookies may look soft but will get firm. Do not over bake!

Chocolaty Crispy Bars

DAIRY   YIELD: 24 BARS

The chocolate-nut-raisin bars meld beautifully with the marshmallow. For an extra treat, add 3 ounces of chocolate chips to the marshmallow mixture. Wrap each bar in colored plastic wrap for kid appeal.

¼   cup butter
3½ cups marshmallows
4   cups matzoh farfel
1   cup raisins
1   cup nuts, chopped and divided
½   teaspoon ground cinnamon
6   ounces chocolate chips, melted

1. Grease 9 x 13-inch pan.
2. Melt butter in soup pot and add marshmallows. Stir until smooth and remove from heat.
3. Add farfel, raisins, ½ cup nuts and cinnamon. Mixture will be sticky.
4. Pat into pan with moistened hands. Drizzle chocolate over top and sprinkle with remaining nuts. Chill before cutting into bars. Keep covered with plastic wrap.

Matzoh Farfel Substitute

• Three crumbled matzohs equals 2 cups matzoh farfel.

Fudgy Passover Brownies

DAIRY OR PAREVE   YIELD: 16 SQUARES

Luscious basic recipe you can build on. Add ½ cup coarsely chopped nuts to the batter and top with broken pieces of a chocolate bar while brownies are hot. Cover brownies with cookie sheet for 5 minutes to melt chocolate pieces, then spread evenly over brownies.

¼ cup cocoa, sifted	½ cup brown sugar, firmly packed
½ cup chocolate chips, melted and cooled	2 large eggs
	¼ cup potato starch
½ cup butter for dairy (use margarine for pareve)	¼ cup matzoh cake meal
	1 teaspoon vanilla extract
½ cup sugar	

1. Preheat oven to 350°F. Grease 8-inch square baking pan.

2. Cream cocoa, chocolate, butter or margarine and sugars at medium speed with electric mixer until smooth.

3. Beat in eggs. Mix in potato starch, cake meal and vanilla. Pour into pan.

4. Bake 25 minutes or until tester inserted in center comes out nearly clean. Cool before cutting into squares.

Orange Marmalade Bars

DAIRY OR PAREVE   YIELD: 16 SQUARES

5 tablespoons butter for dairy, divided, room temperature (use margarine for pareve)	2 large eggs
	1 cup orange juice
1 cup sugar, divided	⅓ cup orange marmalade
1 cup cake meal	1 teaspoon ground cinnamon
9 tablespoons potato starch	¼ cup chopped nuts

1. Preheat oven to 350°F. Grease 9-inch square baking pan.

2. Cream 4 tablespoons butter or margarine with ¾ cup sugar at medium speed with electric mixer until light and fluffy.

3. Mix cake meal with potato starch and add to creamed mixture. Beat in eggs and orange juice.

4. Pour half the batter into pan. Top with marmalade, and remaining batter.

5. Melt remaining butter or margarine and combine with cinnamon, nuts and remaining sugar. Sprinkle over top.

6. Bake 30 minutes or until light brown. Cool in pan before cutting.

Unsweetened and Semisweet Chocolate Substitutes

• For unsweetened chocolate, use 3 tablespoons cocoa mixed with 1 tablespoon vegetable oil or melted margarine.

• For semisweet chocolate, add 3 tablespoons sugar to above mixture.

Passover Lemon Bars

DAIRY OR PAREVE   YIELD: 32 BARS

Finish these rich lemon bars with a dusting of our snowy Passover confectioners' sugar.

Crust

¾	cup potato starch	¼	teaspoon salt
½	cup cake meal	14	tablespoons butter for dairy, room temperature (use margarine for pareve)
½	cup K-P confectioners' sugar		

1. Preheat oven to 350°F. Grease 9 x 13-inch pan.
2. Combine potato starch, cake meal, sugar and salt.
3. Cream butter or margarine at medium speed with electric mixer. Add dry ingredients and mix until consistency of meal. Press into pan. Bake 20 minutes or until crust is lightly browned around edges.

Filling

5	large eggs	6	tablespoons potato starch
2½	cups sugar		K-P confectioners' sugar or raspberry preserves, optional
¾	cup lemon juice		
2	teaspoons fresh lemon zest		

1. Beat eggs at medium speed with electric mixer. Add sugar, juice and zest. Mix in potato starch and pour over crust.
2. Bake 15 to 20 minutes or until tester inserted in center comes out clean. Cool. Cut into squares and sprinkle with confectioners' sugar or dollop with raspberry preserves.

Flour Substitutes for Passover

When a non-Passover recipe calls for flour, on Passover you can replace 1 cup of all-purpose flour, with:

- ⅝ cup of potato starch.

- ⅝ cup of *matzoh* cake meal.

- A mixture of potato starch and *matzoh* cake meal that equals ⅝ cup.

Strawberry Muffins

PAREVE   YIELD: 16 MUFFINS

It is the fresh fruit that enlivens these muffins. Substitute any fresh berries. Also try chopped, peeled apples, pears or peaches.

Topping

½ teaspoon ground cinnamon	2 tablespoons sugar or vanilla sugar

1. Combine ingredients.

Batter

½ cup vegetable oil	¼ teaspoon salt
1 cup sugar	½ teaspoon vanilla extract
3 large eggs	¼ teaspoon ground cinnamon
½ cup cake meal	1½ cups sliced fresh strawberries
¼ cup potato starch	

1. Preheat oven to 325°F. Grease muffin tins or line with papers.
2. Cream oil with sugar and add eggs, beating well.
3. Mix in cake meal, potato starch, salt, vanilla and cinnamon.
4. Fold in strawberries. Fill tins to top with batter.
5. Sprinkle with topping and bake 40 minutes or until golden brown and top is firm. Muffins will be moist.

Banana-Nut Muffins

PAREVE   YIELD: 12 TO 15 MUFFINS

Great for Passover breakfast or brunch. Vary recipe by using leftover charoset in place of some or all of the mashed bananas. Raisins plumped in boiling water may replace nuts.

½ cup walnut or vegetable oil	½ cup potato starch
¾ cup sugar	¾ cup cake meal
2 large eggs	1 teaspoon K-P baking powder
1⅓ cups mashed banana	1 teaspoon baking soda
¾ cup finely chopped walnuts or pecans	¾ teaspoon ground cinnamon

1. Preheat oven to 350°F. Grease muffin tins or line with papers.
2. Beat oil with sugar at medium speed with electric mixer. Add eggs 1 at a time.
3. Mix banana with nuts and fold into batter.
4. Combine dry ingredients and stir into batter. Do not over mix.
5. Spoon batter into muffin tins, filling ¾ full. Bake 20 to 25 minutes until top is browned and tester inserted in center comes out clean.

Passover Granola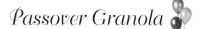

DAIRY OR PAREVE   YIELD: 5 CUPS

Great for a snack or as cereal with milk. Substitute your favorite nuts, dried fruit or add chocolate chips.

¼ cup butter for dairy (use margarine for pareve)	½ cup chopped walnuts
½ cup vegetable oil	1 teaspoon ground cinnamon
½ cup water	½ cup raisins
½ cup brown sugar, firmly packed	½ cup flaked coconut
1 cup matzoh farfel	½ cup chopped dates

1. Preheat oven to 350°F. Grease rimmed cookie sheet.
2. Melt butter or margarine with oil, water and brown sugar in soup pot. Mix in remaining ingredients.
3. Spread on sheet and bake 25 minutes, stirring occasionally. Cool.

Passover Lasagna, Two Ways

Vegetable Lasagna

DAIRY   YIELD: 10 SERVINGS

6   matzohs
16 ounces sour cream
2   large eggs, slightly beaten
16 ounces cottage cheese
8   ounces Cheddar cheese, shredded
8   ounces Swiss or mozzarella
      cheese, shredded
½   cup grated Parmesan cheese
1   pound fresh spinach, steamed
      and chopped

2   bunches green onions, sliced
6   garlic cloves, minced
1   cup minced fresh parsley
2   teaspoons dried oregano
2   teaspoons dried basil
    Pepper to taste
6   cups pasta sauce, divided
    Grated Parmesan cheese

1. Preheat oven to 375°F. Grease 9 x 13-inch pan.
2. Moisten each matzoh under hot running water and set aside. Do not soak.
3. Combine sour cream, eggs and cheeses. Mix in spinach, onions, garlic, parsley, herbs and pepper.
4. Cover bottom of pan with ¼ cup sauce. Top with 2 matzohs, half the cheese mixture and one-third the sauce. Repeat layering, matzohs, cheese and sauce and end with remaining matzohs and sauce.
5. Sprinkle with additional Parmesan cheese and bake 45 minutes. If top becomes too brown, tent with foil loosely. Remove from oven and allow to rest 10 minutes before cutting.

Meat Lasagna

MEAT   YIELD: 10 SERVINGS

1½ pounds ground beef,
      lamb, chicken or turkey,
      browned and drained

1. Substitute ground meat for dairy products and follow directions for Vegetable Lasagna.

Potato-Cheese Lasagna Non-G

DAIRY   YIELD: 6 TO 8 SERVINGS

4   garlic cloves, minced
1   cup shredded Cheddar cheese,
      divided
1   cup shredded mozzarella cheese,
      divided
¼   cup grated Parmesan cheese
    Salt and pepper to taste

2   large baking potatoes, peeled and
      thinly sliced
¼   cup olive oil
2   large sweet potatoes, peeled and
      thinly sliced
2   large red-skin potatoes, peeled
      and thinly sliced

1. Preheat oven to 350°F. Grease 9-inch square pan.
2. Combine garlic, cheeses, salt and pepper.

3. Cover bottom of pan with baking potatoes, overlapping slightly.
4. Drizzle with one-third oil and sprinkle with one-third cheese mixture.
5. Top with sweet potatoes and one-third oil and cheeses. Repeat with red-skin potatoes and cheeses. Cover and bake 1 hour or until potatoes are tender.

Nut Butter Non-G

PAREVE   YIELD: 2 CUPS

2   cups unsalted cashews or
      almonds
3   tablespoons vegetable oil,
      divided

¼   teaspoon salt
1   teaspoon sugar or honey,
      optional

1. Process nuts, 2 tablespoons oil, salt and sugar or honey 30 seconds.
2. Purée to spreading consistency adding remaining oil if needed. Store in airtight container in refrigerator.

Pineapple Pudding

PAREVE OR DAIRY   YIELD: 8 TO 10 SERVINGS

Crushed pineapple tidbits enhance both taste and texture of this lush Passover pudding.

Topping

¼   cup sugar   1   teaspoon ground cinnamon

1. Combine ingredients.

Pudding

½   cup margarine for pareve, melted
      (use butter for dairy)
⅔   cup sugar
¾   teaspoon vanilla extract
4   large eggs, beaten

2¾ cups matzoh farfel
1⅔ cups canned crushed pineapple,
      drained
1   teaspoon ground cinnamon

1. Preheat oven to 350°F. Grease 9 x 13-inch pan.
2. Cream margarine or butter with sugar. Stir vanilla into beaten eggs and add to creamed mixture.
3. Pour hot water over farfel to cover and let rest 5 minutes. Squeeze out excess liquid and fold into creamed mixture. Add pineapple and cinnamon. Pour into pan and sprinkle with topping.
4. Bake 30 to 40 minutes or until set and lightly browned.

Carrot-Apple Pudding

PAREVE   YIELD: 4 TO 6 SERVINGS

The apple adds complementary tartness to sweet, nutty savor of the carrots, raisins and toasted nuts.

3 large eggs, separated	½ cup raisins
¾ cup slivered almonds or pecans, toasted and divided	½ cup matzoh meal
	½ cup sugar
1 large tart apple, peeled and grated	3 tablespoons lemon juice
	1 teaspoon ground cinnamon
1 cup peeled and grated carrots	½ cup margarine, melted

1. Preheat oven to 375°F. Grease 8-inch round baking pan.
2. Beat whites at high speed with electric mixer until stiff.
3. Combine yolks, ½ cup nuts and remaining ingredients.
4. Fold whites into yolk mixture and pour into pan. Top with remaining nuts and bake 40 minutes or until browned and set.

European Fruit Pudding

PAREVE   YIELD: 6 TO 8 SERVINGS

This versatile Old World style pudding may be served for breakfast or used as a side dish for lunch or dinner. It also makes a lovely fruit dessert. Choose a combination of prunes, peaches and apricots for the dried fruit.

6 large eggs	3 large apples, peeled and sliced
1 cup vegetable oil	½ cup raisins
1 cup sugar	1½ cups dried fruit soaked in water 1 hour, drained and diced
1 cup cake meal	1 teaspoon ground cinnamon

1. Preheat oven to 350°F. Grease 9 x 13-inch pan.
2. Beat eggs and add oil, sugar and cake meal. Fold in apples, raisins and dried fruit. Pour mixture into pan and sprinkle with cinnamon.
3. Bake 40 to 45 minutes or until golden brown.

Popovers with Roasted Garlic Bulb

PAREVE

YIELD: 12 LARGE POPOVERS OR
30 SMALL POPOVERS

These light and fluffy popovers are great for sandwich-making. Serve the smooth roasted garlic right in the bulb with the popovers. Why not try the sweet popover variation or use minimuffin tins for bite-size popovers?

Roasted Garlic Bulb

1	tablespoon olive oil	1	large garlic bulb

1. Preheat oven to 375°F.
2. Cut ½-inch off top of bulb and drizzle with oil. Wrap in foil and roast until soft, about 30 minutes.

Popovers

½	cup oil	½	teaspoon pepper
1	teaspoon garlic powder	2	cups matzoh meal
1	teaspoon onion powder	2	teaspoons dried basil, oregano or dill, optional
2	cups water		
1	teaspoon salt	6	large eggs

1. Preheat oven to 400°F. Grease cookie sheet or minimuffin tins.
2. Combine oil, garlic and onion powder, water, salt and pepper in large saucepan and bring to boil. Mix in matzoh meal and herbs. Remove from heat and quickly beat in eggs 1 at a time.
3. Spoon 2½-inch rounded mounds of batter for large popovers on sheet 3 inches apart. Fill minimuffin tins for small popovers.
4. Bake 40 to 50 minutes or until golden brown and firm. Small popovers will bake in less time.

Fresh Garlic Tips

• Garlic bulbs should be large, firm and tight-skinned. Store garlic in dark, cool, dry place up to one month for peak freshness. Do not chill.

Sweet Popovers

½	cup sugar	1	teaspoon ground cinnamon

• Prepare Popover recipe. Add sugar and substitute cinnamon for garlic and onion powder, pepper and dried herbs.

Broccoli-Feta Cheese Pie

DAIRY

YIELD: 4 MAIN COURSE OR
6 TO 8 SIDE DISH SERVINGS

1½ matzohs, broken into small pieces
3 large eggs, divided
Salt and pepper to taste
1 head broccoli, broken into florets
1 tablespoon olive oil
1 medium onion, diced
4 green onions, finely sliced

3 garlic cloves, minced
2 tablespoons chopped fresh parsley
1 teaspoon dried dill
7 ounces feta cheese, crumbled
¼ cup grated Parmesan cheese, divided

1. Preheat oven to 375°F. Grease 10-inch pie pan.
2. Soak matzohs in boiling water 1 minute and drain.
3. Beat 1 egg with salt and pepper and combine with matzohs.
4. Press into pan to form crust and bake 10 minutes.
5. Steam broccoli 4 minutes.
6. Heat oil in large skillet and sauté onions and garlic until soft. Mix in parsley, dill, and broccoli. Combine with feta, eggs and 2 tablespoons Parmesan.
7. Spread mixture over crust and sprinkle with remaining Parmesan. Bake 15 to 20 minutes or until filling is bubbly.

For a double recipe, use 9 x 13-inch pan and bake 20 to 25 minutes.

Matzoh Pizza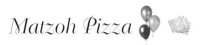

DAIRY   YIELD: 4 SERVINGS

The all-time kids' favorite Passover lunch, and one they can help prepare.

4   matzohs
½   teaspoon each garlic powder,
       dried oregano and dried basil
¾   cup tomato sauce

12   ounces mozzarella cheese,
        shredded
¼   cup grated Parmesan cheese

1. Preheat oven to 400°F. Grease cookie sheet.
2. Moisten matzoh under running water a few seconds and place on sheet in single layer.
3. Mix garlic powder, oregano and basil into sauce and spread on matzohs.
4. Combine cheeses and sprinkle over sauce. Bake 10 to 12 minutes until cheese is bubbly.

Basic Matzoh Stuffing

MEAT OR PAREVE   YIELD: 8 SERVINGS

This is a basic Passover stuffing for turkey and chicken. For a side dish, bake in 8-inch square pan at 350°F for 20 to 30 minutes until golden brown.

¼   cup vegetable oil
¼   cup chopped onion
1   cup diced celery
4   cups matzoh farfel
1   cup chicken broth for meat
      (use vegetable broth for pareve)

1   teaspoon paprika
¼   cup chopped fresh parsley
1   large egg, beaten
    Salt and pepper to taste

1. Heat oil in large skillet and sauté onions and celery until soft. Add farfel and sauté until toasted.
2. Combine broth with paprika and parsley and add to mixture. Cool 5 minutes and add egg, salt and pepper.

Fluffy Matzoh Brie

DAIRY   YIELD: 6 SERVINGS

The perennial Passover dish with variations.

4   matzohs, broken into small
      pieces
⅔   cup milk, warmed
3   large eggs, slightly beaten
½   teaspoon salt to taste

3   tablespoons butter or vegetable oil
      Melted butter, applesauce,
      honey, maple syrup, marinated
      fruit compote, fresh fruit or
      preserves for topping

1. Cover matzoh with boiling water, 5 minutes. Drain. Add milk and let
     stand 5 minutes.
2. Mix in eggs and salt.
3. Heat butter or oil in extra-large skillet and add matzoh mixture.
4. Fry until golden on both sides. Serve with toppings.

Matzoh Brie Variations

- Add ¼ cup mushrooms, 2 tablespoons onions and 1 minced garlic clove
  sautéed in 1 tablespoon butter or oil.
- Add ½ teaspoon ground cinnamon or ½ teaspoon vanilla with 2 tablespoons
  sugar or honey.
- Add 1 tablespoon fresh herbs.
- Add ½ cup shredded cheese, ¼ cup grated Parmesan cheese or ⅓ cup feta cheese.
- Add ⅓ cup minced Nova smoked salmon and 2 tablespoons chopped onions.

Cheese Pancakes

DAIRY   YIELD: 8 TO 10 PANCAKES

*Apple is a pleasant surprise in these cheese pancakes. Serve with jam or maple
syrup.*

8   ounces cottage cheese
4   large eggs, beaten
1   tablespoon sugar
½   cup matzoh meal

½   teaspoon salt
½   teaspoon ground cinnamon
1   apple, peeled and chopped
     Oil for frying

1. Combine cheese and eggs. Slowly stir in sugar, matzoh meal, salt and
     cinnamon. Fold in apples.
2. Heat oil in large skillet and drop batter by tablespoons. Fry until
     browned on both sides, turning once.

Kugelach — Not Just for Soup

PAREVE OR MEAT   YIELD: 24 PIECES

*S*mall **kugelach** *are great in soup as an alternative to* matzoh *balls. Add sautéed onions or garlic for extra flavor. For a meat version, add cooked beef or poultry. They are a delicious snack eaten either hot or at room temperature. Freezes well.*

6 cups matzoh farfel	½ cup Veggie Schmaltz or solid shortening, room temperature
6 large eggs	
1 teaspoon salt	½ cup cooked beef or poultry for meat

1. Preheat oven to 375°F. Grease muffin tins generously.
2. Place farfel in colander and dampen with boiling water.
3. Beat eggs with salt and add schmaltz or shortening. Mix in farfel and cooked meat.
4. Heat tins 5 minutes. Pour batter into hot tins, two-thirds full. Bake 20 minutes or until browned.

Vegetarian Kishke

PAREVE   YIELD: 24 SLICES

*O*ur contemporary spin on grandma's stuffed **kishke,** *as flavorful as its progenitor and just as irresistible.*

½ cup peeled and grated carrots	2 large eggs, beaten
1 large onion, finely chopped	1 cup Veggie Schmaltz or margarine, melted
½ cup finely chopped celery	
2 cloves garlic, minced	1 teaspoon salt
3 cups finely crushed egg matzoh	¼ teaspoon pepper
	2 tablespoons olive oil

1. Preheat oven to 350°F. Prepare ungreased cookie sheet.
2. Combine all ingredients except oil.

3. Cut two 20-inch pieces of foil and grease with oil. Divide mixture in half and shape each into log on foil, 2 inches in diameter. Loosely wrap each log and place on sheet.

4. Bake 45 minutes. Chill 1 hour. Remove from foil and cut into 1-inch slices. Reheat loosely covered, on sheet in 325°F oven.

Fruited Quinoa Primavera Non-G

PAREVE   YIELD: 4 TO 6 SERVINGS

This "spring style" Italian dish combines the classic primavera veggies with apricots and cranberries mixed with quinoa (keenwa), a creamy white grain. This South American product has a light texture and delicate flavor.

2 cups vegetable broth	1 small red onion, thinly sliced
1 bay leaf	2 garlic cloves, minced
1 teaspoon salt	1 tablespoon lemon juice
1 cup quinoa	½ cup dried apricots, diced
3 tablespoons olive oil, divided	½ cup dried cranberries
1 small zucchini, thinly sliced	½ cup chopped fresh parsley
1 small yellow squash, thinly sliced	¼ cup chopped fresh dill
½ cup sliced mushrooms	Salt and pepper to taste

1. Bring broth, bay leaf and salt to boil in soup pot.

2. Add quinoa and return to boil, cover, reduce heat and simmer 20 minutes or until quinoa absorbs liquid. Remove from heat, discard bay leaf and cool.

3. Heat 2 tablespoons oil in large skillet and sauté vegetables until lightly browned. Add to quinoa.

4. Drizzle remaining oil and juice over mixture. Stir in fruit, herbs, salt and pepper.

Quinoa Stuffed Acorn Squash

PAREVE   YIELD: 4 SERVINGS

2 large acorn squash, halved and seeded	¼ cup olive oil

1. Preheat oven to 350°F. Grease 9 x 13-inch pan.

2. Prepare Fruited Quinoa Primavera.

3. Cut ½-inch off bottoms of squash. Brush inside with oil.

4. Stuff each half generously with quinoa mixture and place in pan. Cover and bake 45 minutes or until squash is tender.

Potato-Cheese Kugel

DAIRY   YIELD: 6 TO 8 SERVINGS

An easy-to-fix, cheesy potato kugel to grace any dairy Passover meal.

3 large eggs	16 ounces cottage cheese
2 cups water	¾ cup sour cream
1 6-ounce package K-P potato pancake mix	2 teaspoons minced fresh parsley
	Sour cream

1. Preheat oven to 350°F. Grease 8-inch square pan.
2. Combine eggs, water and pancake mix. Set aside to thicken.
3. Stir in cheese, sour cream and parsley. Let rest 2 minutes.
4. Pour into pan and bake 1 hour until edges begin to brown. Serve with sour cream.

Potato-Vegetable Patties

PAREVE   YIELD: 6 TO 8 SERVINGS

Sautéed or baked, these patties always please. To bake patties, put them on a lightly greased baking sheet and place in 350°F oven for about 12 minutes; turn the patties and bake for another 12 minutes.

1 tablespoon olive oil	1 pound potatoes, boiled and mashed
1½ cups minced red or yellow peppers, or combination	6 tablespoons grated onion
1½ cups peeled and grated carrots	3 large eggs, slightly beaten
2 cups chopped fresh spinach, tightly packed, coarse stems removed	1½ teaspoons salt
	Pepper to taste
	1 cup matzoh meal
	Vegetable oil for frying

1. Heat oil in large skillet and sauté peppers until soft. Remove from heat.
2. Add all remaining ingredients except frying oil to pepper mixture and let stand 30 minutes.
3. Form patties using ¼ cup mixture for each.
4. Flatten patties slightly and fry in oil, browning both sides. Drain on paper towels.

Made-to-Order

W̲e all have times in the kitchen when no one-size-fits-all solution will do. This section provides novel answers for those moments. Make the kids happy with recipes tailored to their tastes. Give yourself a well-earned breather with our quick-prep recipes. Turn to our equivalents and substitutions guides when you suddenly find you've run out of a recipe ingredient. And, don't forget your out-of-country family and friends. Send them a copy of Divine Kosher Cuisine. It travels with its very own oven temperature and metric conversion charts!

Contents

Kid-Friendly Food

Quick-Prep Recipes for All Occasions

What to Do In a Pinch

Pizza Dough Foldovers

Party Cake Cones

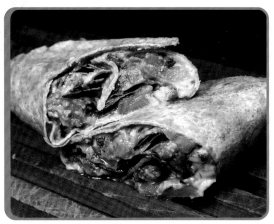

It's a Wrap

Kid-Friendly Food

We take great interest in a child's developing palate. Some tips on how to appeal to younger eaters: make it colorful, make it fun and when possible, make it together. Self-serve, bite-size pieces tend to be child pleasers. More adventuresome kids also go for spice and tang.

All recipes on this page appear in the index.

A Sundry of Salsas
Artichoke Jack Tartlets
Asian Salad Bar
Baked Brie in Bread Bowl
Banana-Nut Muffins
Basic Salad Bar
Beef Chili with Pasta
Blintzes or Crêpes — What's in a Name?
Blueberry Bread Pudding
Cheddar-Potato Kugel
Cheese Pancakes

Desserts Galore

You will find many tasty treats suitable for kids in the Heavenly Desserts, Signature Desserts and Passover sections.

Cookies on Demand

Most cookie dough can be prepared in advance. Just cover with plastic wrap, chill or freeze and bake as needed.

Chicken Satay with Spicy Dipping Sauce
Chocolate-Streusel French Toast
Deviled Eggs
Dress Up Your Bagel
Eggplant Parmesan
English Muffin-Spinach Tarts
Falafel Bar
Fluffy Matzoh Brie
Fresh Tomato Salsa with tortilla chips
Fresh Vegetables with Spinach Dip
Fruit Nut Granola
Giant Stuffed Hamburger
Hot Off the Grill at Carrot Festival
It's a Wrap
Layered Sweet Potatoes and Apples

Marinated Vegetables
Matzoh Pizza
Mozzarella Sticks
Nut Butter
Passover Granola
Passover Popovers
Pasta Bar
Pastry-Wrapped Hot Dog
Pineapple Chicken
Pineapple Pudding
Pink Lemonade Punch
Pita Crisps
Pizza Bagels
Pizza Dough Foldovers
Potato Latkes
Potato Skin Bar
Potato-Cheese Lasagna
Signature Cheese Blintz Soufflé
Signature Egg Salad
Signature Sesame Noodles
Six-Fruit Soup
Strawberry Muffins
Sweet Potato Latkes
Tuna Fish Salad with a Twist
Yakatori Chicken Skewers

Giant Chocolate Chip Cookie

Quick-Prep Recipes for All Occasions

***B**usy cooks appreciate timesaving recipes that they can assemble or make in advance, in whole or in part, and quickly finish just before mealtime. Check out these suggestions in the index for their ease of preparation.*

Starters

Black Bean Salsa
Chicken Satay with
   Spicy Dipping Sauce
Curry Dip
English Muffin-Spinach Tarts
Marinated Vegetables
Olive Tapenade
Pita Crisps
Roasted Red Peppers with Garlic
Spiced Iced Tea
Spinach Dip

Soups

Black Bean Salsa Soup
Chilled Cherry Soup
No-Fail Matzoh Balls
Quick and Delicious
   Vegetable Soup

Salads

Caesar Salad
Chickpea Salad
Dress Up Your Salad
Herbed White Bean-Artichoke
   Salad
Mango Salad with
   Red Onion and Lime
Marinated Cucumbers with Dill
Signature Mixed Green Salad
Tuna Fish Salad with a Twist

Meat

Brisket with Burgundy-Orange
   Sauce
Garlic-Dijon Encrusted London
   Broil
Marinated London Broil
Signature Brisket
Sweet and Sour Glazed
   Corned Beef
Sweet and Sour Short Ribs
Veal Meatloaf

Poultry

Dijon-Tarragon Grilled Chicken
Grilled Chicken Breast with
   Fresh Tomato Salsa
Italian Roasted Chicken
Pineapple Chicken
Signature Roasted Chicken
Yakatori Chicken Skewers

Fish

Salmon with Mustard-Chive Butter
Basil Marinated Scrod
Crumb-Topped Baked Fish
Cucumber Dill Sauce
Marinated Grilled Salmon
Salmon with Maple Syrup and
   Toasted Almonds
Seared Tuna with Wasabi Sauce
Sesame Salmon with Spinach-
   Watercress Sauce

Vegetarian

Garbanzo Bean Burgers
Presto Pasta Sauce
Tamale Pie

Side Dishes

Brussels Sprouts in Lemon Mustard
Crusty Roasted Potatoes
Oven-Roasted Tomatoes
Potato Fans
Roasted Asparagus
Roasted Broccoli with Red Peppers
Roasted Onions with Balsamic
   Glaze
Spicy Indian Rice

Brunch

Chocolate Chip-Orange Scones
Dress Up Your Bagel
Fresh Cherry Muffins
Orange Cornbread
Orange Muffins
Pizza Bagels
Pizza Dough Fold-Overs
Savory Cheese Scones

Passover

Banana-Nut Muffins
Fluffy Matzoh Brie
Matzoh Pizza
Nut Butter
Popovers with Roasted Garlic Bulb
Potato-Cheese Kugel
Strawberry Muffins

Quick Cookies

You can prepare dough in advance for most cookies. Cover with plastic wrap and chill or freeze. Bake as needed.

Desserts

Apple-Honey Dessert Pizza
Eggless Chocolate Cake
Bittersweet Chocolate Fondue Bar
Carob Gorp
Citrus and Grapes in Muscat Wine
Meringue Drops
Pareve Chocolate Sauce
Quick White Chocolate Mousse
Simple Fruit Sorbet

Versatile Flavor Enhancer

Veggie Schmaltz

With a little advance planning, you can create impressive meals that fit your busy life and crowded schedule, and allow you more time to socialize with your family and guests.

What to Do in a Pinch

*I*t happens to the wisest cooks with the most well stocked cupboards. You reach for a recipe ingredient and come up bare. Or, a recipe calls for shredded cups of cabbage or cheese, and you're left wondering what chunk size that denotes. Not to worry! We've been there too. Here is a potpourri of equivalents and substitutions to the rescue. And, for our international readers, a special guide to convert our Fahrenheit oven temperatures to your Celsius scale.

What Equals What?

Ingredient	Amount	Equivalent Amount
• berries	1 quart	3½ cups
• bread	2 slices	1 cup soft breadcrumbs
• bread, toasted	4 to 5 slices	1 cup fine dry breadcrumbs
• butter	1 pound	2 cups
• cheese	1 pound	4 cups, shredded
• cream, heavy	½ pint	2 cups whipped
• egg yolks	1 cup	12 to 14 egg yolks
• egg whites	1 cup	8 to 10 egg whites
• lemon	1	3 to 4 tablespoons juice 1 teaspoon grated zest
• mushrooms	½ pound	3 cups, sliced
• nuts	¼ pound	1 cup, chopped
• onion, medium	1	½ cup, chopped
• orange	1	6 to 7 tablespoons juice 2 teaspoons grated zest

What's in a Cup?

1 cup of crumbs equals:
22 salted crackers
14 graham crackers
22 vanilla wafers
19 chocolate wafers
15 gingersnaps

What Substitutes for What?

Ingredient	Amount	Substitute
• baking powder	1 teaspoon	¼ teaspoon baking soda plus ½ teaspoon cream of tartar
• buttermilk or sour milk	1 cup	1 cup minus 1 tablespoon milk, plus 1 tablespoon white vinegar or lemon juice
• cornstarch	1 tablespoon	2 tablespoons flour
• cream of tartar	1 teaspoon	½ teaspoon lemon juice
• garlic	1 clove	⅛ teaspoon garlic powder
• ginger, fresh	1 tablespoon	1 teaspoon ground ginger
• milk, whole	1 cup	½ cup evaporated milk plus ½ cup water
• mustard, prepared	1 tablespoon	1 teaspoon ground dry mustard
• sugar, light brown	1 cup	½ cup dark brown sugar plus ½ cup granulated sugar
• vinegar, white	1 teaspoon	2 teaspoons lemon juice

Metric Conversions

Weight Equivalents

These are not exact weight equivalents, but have been rounded up or down slightly to make measuring easier.

American	Metric	American	Metric	American	Metric
¼ ounce	7 grams	8 ounces (½ pound)	225 grams	16 ounces (1 pound)	450 grams
½ ounce	15 grams	9 ounces	250 grams	1 pound 2 ounces	500 grams
1 ounce	30 grams	10 ounces	300 grams	1½ pounds	750 grams
2 ounces	60 grams	11 ounces	325 grams	2 pounds	900 grams
3 ounces	90 grams	12 ounces	350 grams	2¼ pounds	1 kilogram
4 ounces	115 grams	13 ounces	375 grams	3 pounds	1.4 kilograms
5 ounces	150 grams	14 ounces	400 grams	4 pounds	1.8 kilograms
6 ounces	175 grams	15 ounces	425 grams		
7 ounces	200 grams				

Volume Equivalents

These are not exact volume equivalents, but have been rounded up or down slightly to make measuring easier.

American	Metric	Imperial
¼ teaspoon	1.25 milliliters	
½ teaspoon	2.5 milliliters	
1 teaspoon	5 milliliters	
½ tablespoon (1½ teaspoons)	7.5 milliliters	
1 tablespoon (3 teaspoons)	15 milliliters	
¼ cup (4 tablespoons)	60 milliliters	2 fluid ounces
⅓ cup (5 tablespoons)	75 milliliters	2½ fluid ounces
½ cup (8 tablespoons)	125 milliliters	4 fluid ounces
⅔ cup (10 tablespoons)	150 milliliters	5 fluid ounces (¼ pint)
¾ cup (12 tablespoons)	175 milliliters	6 fluid ounces (⅓ pint)
1 cup (16 tablespoons)	250 milliliters	8 fluid ounces
1¼ cups	300 milliliters	10 fluid ounces (½ pint)
1½ cups	350 milliliters	12 fluid ounces
1 pint (2 cups)	500 milliliters	16 fluid ounces
2½ cups	625 milliliters	20 fluid ounces (1 pint)
1 quart (4 cups)	1 litre	1¾ pints

Oven Temperature Equivalents

Oven	°Fahrenheit	°Celsius	Gas Mark
very cool	250-275	130-140	½-1
cool	300	150	2
warm	325	170	3
moderate	350	180	4
moderately hot	375	190	5
moderately hot	400	200	6
hot	425	200	7
very hot	450	230	8
very hot	475	250	9

Catering to Family & Friends

Catering To Family and Friends

*L*ife is with people! Food serves a significant role whenever family and friends gather in the intimacy of someone's home, whether it is to celebrate good times or share life's sadder moments. Feeding a houseful of guests with ease and elegance need not be any harder to accomplish than entertaining a smaller gathering. This section guides you through step-by-step preparations that ensure hassle-free home entertaining for 10 to 60 guests for a variety of self-serve buffets covering all occasions. We eliminate the need to calculate how much food to prepare for a specific number of guests. We simply provide easy-to-read, scale-to-order menu grids, based on our professional catering experience, that do the calculations for you. We provide advance plan-and-prep guidelines to get a head start on party preparations. Furthermore, simple instructions and photographs show you remarkably easy ways to set up elegant, multilevel displays for your buffet platters. You won't believe how easy it is to create beautiful food garnishes that add drama to your table. We offer time and work saving tips at each turn because, ultimately, the goal of home entertaining is to create a memorable event to be enjoyed as much by the host as the guests. Like all menus in this cookbook, those in this section offer suggestions for recipes from which to choose — to mix and match — according to your personal likes and interests. We have varied our suggestions to give you a large pool of ideas, ranging from traditional to contemporary, to spark your culinary imagination and inspire you to create a dining experience for your guests that is truly your own.

Getting Down to Scaling Up for All Occasions in 10 Easy Segments

Sweet and Savory Spreads

Dress Up Your Bagels

Favorite Food Bars:
• Potato Skin • Basic Salad • Pasta • Asian Style Salad
• Falafel • Ice Cream Sundae
• Bittersweet Chocolate Fondue

Create a Dramatic Presentation:
• Fruit Platter with Two Dips
• Fresh Vegetables for Dipping
• Decorative Cheese Display

Commercial Sheet Pan Recipes: Large-scale baking

Multilevel Displays: Construct showcases
for your buffet table

Disposable Paper and Plastic Party Supplies:
Attractive and reliable throwaways

Dressing the Table

Garnish Magic: The final flourish to an elegant table

Planning the Larger Gathering:
• Dairy Kiddush Luncheon and Meat Dinner
• Dinner Buffets: Meat and Dairy
• Grazing Buffets with Viennese Table: Meat and Dairy
• Dessert Displays to Viennese Table
• The *Shivah* Meal: Traditional first Meal of Condolence
• Keeping Your Spirits Up: Dining with spirits
• International Coffee Bar:
A gourmet accompaniment to dessert

Sweet and Savory Spreads

PAREVE OR DAIRY   YIELD: 16 SERVINGS

Serve these spreads with a bread basket of minimuffins, flat breads and assorted rolls.

Sweet Strawberry Spread

8	ounces margarine for pareve, room temperature (use butter for dairy)	1	cup coarsely chopped fresh strawberries
		2	tablespoons honey

1. Whip margarine or butter at medium speed with electric mixer until creamy. Fold in remaining ingredients.

Garlic Herb Spread

½	teaspoon olive oil	1½	tablespoons minced fresh dill
3	garlic cloves, minced	1½	tablespoons minced fresh parsley
8	ounces margarine for pareve, room temperature (use butter for dairy)		

1. Heat oil in small skillet and sauté garlic. Cool.
2. Whip margarine or butter at medium speed with electric mixer until creamy. Fold in garlic-oil and remaining ingredients.

Lime Chive Spread

Jazz up an ear of corn. The lime juice makes the corn even sweeter.

1	cup margarine for pareve, room temperature (use butter for dairy)	2	teaspoons fresh lime zest
		1	teaspoon salt
⅔	cup finely snipped chives	½	teaspoon paprika
4	teaspoons lime juice	¼	teaspoon cayenne pepper to taste

1. Combine all ingredients.

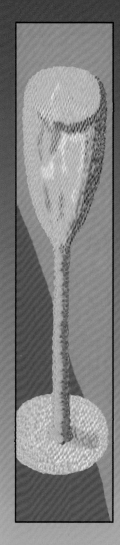

How to Pipe Rosettes

• Pipe individual margarine portions through a decorating bag fitted with a large star tip to form rosettes and place on lemon leaves to serve. Chill.

Dress Up Your Bagels

DAIRY   YIELD: 1 DOZEN BAGELS

Dress up your bagels with homemade spreads made with a variety of herbs, vegetables and Nova smoked salmon, whipped into cream cheese. Be creative and mix and match ingredients. Two recipes will cover a dozen bagels.

Plain Spread

8   *ounces cream cheese, room
      temperature*
    Milk to soften

1. Whip cream cheese at medium speed with electric mixer, adding milk to soften.

Herb Spread

½   *teaspoon olive oil*
3   *garlic cloves, minced*
8   *ounces cream cheese, room
      temperature*

1½ *tablespoons minced fresh dill*
1½ *tablespoons minced fresh parsley*

1. Heat oil in small skillet and sauté garlic. Cool.
2. Whip cream cheese at medium speed with electric mixer and fold in garlic and herbs.

Nova Smoked Salmon Spread

8   *ounces cream cheese, room
      temperature*
    Milk to soften

4   *ounces Nova smoked salmon,
      minced*
1½ *tablespoons chopped dill or
      chives, snipped or chopped*

1. Whip cream cheese at medium speed with electric mixer, adding milk to soften.
2. Fold in Nova with dill or chives.

Vegetable Spread

2	radishes, chopped	½	carrot, peeled and shredded
½	red pepper, chopped	8	ounces cream cheese, room temperature
¼	green pepper, chopped		
2	green onions, thinly sliced	2	tablespoons minced fresh dill

1. Drain vegetables in colander.
2. Whip cream cheese at medium speed with electric mixer and fold in vegetables and dill.

Strawberry Spread

8	ounces cream cheese, room temperature	¼	cup chopped pecans
		2	tablespoons honey
1	cup coarsely chopped fresh strawberries	⅛	teaspoon ground ginger

1. Whip cream cheese at medium speed with electric mixer and fold in remaining ingredients.

Pareve Spreads
Perfect for the lactose intolerant and those who follow a vegan diet.

- Substitute nondairy versions of cream cheese and milk in any of the spreads in Dress Up Your Bagels.

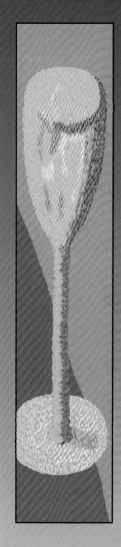

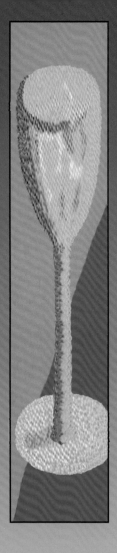

Favorite Food Bars

Our food bar recipes raise the bar a notch to provide you with a versatile group of foods that make an engaging display for self-service dining.

Potato Skin Bar

DAIRY, MEAT OR PAREVE   YIELD: 20 SERVINGS

A potato skin bar offers a fun alternative to a brunch gathering or a kids' birthday party.

Potatoes

10 Idaho or russet potatoes
¼   cup butter for dairy,
     melted (use olive oil for
     pareve)
     Salt and pepper to taste

1. Preheat oven to 400°F. Grease cookie sheet.

2. Bake potatoes on sheet 1 hour or until soft.

3. Cool, cut in half and scoop out flesh to leave ¼-inch shell, reserving flesh for another use.

4. Brush inside of skins with butter or oil. Season with salt and pepper.

5. Reduce oven temperature to 375°F and bake skins 10 to 12 minutes or until crisp and browned. Serve with topping suggestions.

Dairy Toppings

1 cup sliced black olives	1½ cups shredded Cheddar cheese
1 cup salsa	½ cup minced hot peppers
4 green onions, thinly sliced	1 cup Refried Beans
1 cup sour cream	1 cup guacamole

Meat Toppings

1 cup sliced black olives	1 cup guacamole
1 cup salsa	2 cups browned chopped ground beef, turkey or chicken, seasoned to taste with ground cumin, onion, garlic and chili powder
4 green onions, thinly sliced	
½ cup minced hot peppers	
1 cup Refried Beans	

Potato Skin Bar (continued)

Pareve Toppings

2	cups Signature Roasted Vegetables	1	cup chopped red pepper
1	cup corn mixed with 1 tablespoon fresh chopped cilantro	1	cup salsa
		½	cup minced hot peppers
1	cup sliced black olives	1	cup Refried Beans
		1	cup guacamole
		1	cup nondairy sour cream

Assembly

1. Place toppings in individual dishes for condiment bar.
2. Keep potato skins warm in chafing dish or on hot plate.

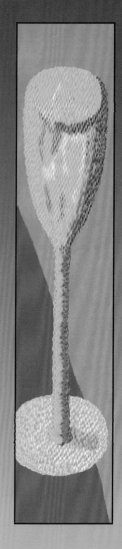

Basic Salad Bar

PAREVE OR DAIRY   YIELD: 10 SERVINGS

Punch up this basic salad with any of the following items: marinated artichokes and green beans, roasted red peppers, pimento-stuffed green olives, raisins, nuts and seeds, diced dried fruit, pickled hot peppers, chopped hard-boiled eggs and shredded cabbage.

3	romaine lettuce hearts, torn into bite-size pieces	3	celery stalks, diced
1	head iceberg lettuce, torn into bite-size pieces	1	cup thinly sliced radishes
		1	red pepper, thinly sliced
10	ounces mesclun greens	1	green pepper, thinly sliced
2	cups peeled and shredded carrots	2	cups chickpeas
2	cucumbers, peeled and thinly sliced	1	cup black olives
		1	cup prepared croutons
1	pint yellow or red grape tomatoes	1	cup shredded Cheddar cheese or crumbled feta or bleu cheese for dairy
1	large red onion, thinly sliced		

1. Combine all greens in large salad bowl.
2. Place each remaining ingredient in its own serving dish and arrange around greens.
3. Serve with 2 choices of salad dressing from Dress Up Your Salad.

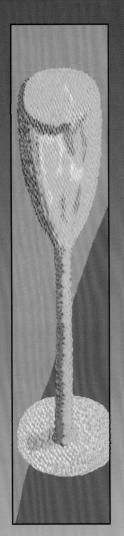

Pasta Bar

PAREVE OR DAIRY

YIELD: 20 BUFFET OR
10 ENTRÉE SERVINGS

This feature offers three topping choices with pasta, each scaled for twenty guests. Each recipe is suitable for a one-choice pasta station. If offering two or three choices on a pasta bar, prepare one half of each recipe. This recipe is designed for a cocktail hour format and not a main course event. The Pesto Pasta and Fresh Tomato Pasta are traditional everyday fare, while the creamed salmon version is for special occasions.

Pesto Pasta

DAIRY

4½ cups packed fresh basil	1 cup olive oil
¼ cup pine nuts, toasted	1 cup grated Parmesan cheese
6 garlic cloves, minced	2½ pounds linguine
Salt and pepper to taste	Parmesan cheese for serving

1. Mince basil, pine nuts and garlic in processor and add salt and pepper. Add oil with machine running and process until blended. Add 1 cup cheese.
2. Cook pasta al dente and drain, reserving 1 cup liquid.
3. Thin basil mixture with enough reserved liquid to make sauce. Toss with pasta.
4. Serve additional cheese on the side.

Pasta with Nova Smoked Salmon in Cream Sauce

DAIRY

2½ pounds bow-tie pasta	2 cups heavy cream
½ cup butter	Pepper to taste
1 pound Nova smoked salmon, cut into ¼-inch strips	Parmesan cheese

1. Cook pasta al dente and drain.
2. Heat butter in large skillet and sauté Nova until opaque. Add cream and warm. Toss with pasta and add pepper. Add additional cream if more sauce is needed.
3. Serve with additional cheese on side.

Fresh Tomato Pasta

PAREVE OR DAIRY

8 garlic cloves	Pepper to taste
¼ cup extra virgin olive oil	2½ pounds ziti or rotelle pasta
4 pounds ripe tomatoes, chunked	2 cups pitted kalamata olives
¼ cup packed fresh basil	Grated Parmesan cheese for dairy
¼ teaspoon salt	

1. Mince garlic in processor with oil. Add tomatoes and basil and coarsely chop.
2. Spoon tomato mixture into large bowl and season with salt and pepper.
3. Cook pasta according to package directions. Drain and mix with sauce and olives.
4. Serve at room temperature with cheese on the side.

Asian Style Salad Bar

MEAT OR PAREVE   YIELD: 10 SERVINGS

Five-Spice Powder Dressing

¼ cup sesame oil	¾ cup sugar
½ cup vegetable oil	2 teaspoons five-spice powder
1 cup cider vinegar	4 garlic cloves, minced
½ cup soy sauce	¼ cup toasted sesame seeds

1. Combine all ingredients. Let stand at room temperature 1 hour.

Salad Bar

5 cups cooked cubed chicken or	1 cup of each of the following: thinly sliced celery, slivered almonds, thinly sliced, canned water chestnuts, thinly sliced radishes, thinly sliced green onions, thinly sliced green pepper, broccoli florets, julienned carrots, sliced mushrooms
5 cups cooked pepper steak strips or 5 cups cubed browned tofu	
1 large zucchini or cucumber, julienned	
1 large head iceberg lettuce, shredded	
15 wonton wrappers, cut into strips, deep-fried and drained	

1. Toss chicken, beef or tofu with 1 cup Five Spice Powder Dressing.
2. Arrange all items in separate serving bowls.
3. Serve buffet style with remaining dressing.

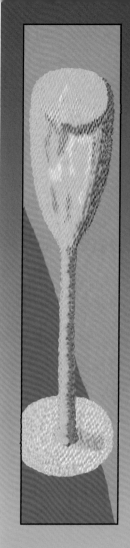

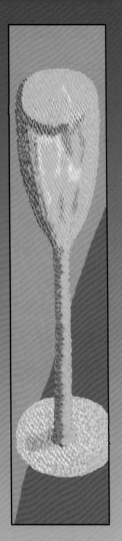

Falafel Bar

PAREVE   YIELD: 10 SERVINGS

Spicy falafel balls stuffed into warm pita pockets, doused with a lemon-garlicky tahini sauce and served with a zesty, colorful Israeli Salad. Display this marvelous Mideastern fare buffet-style or treat family and guests to individual portions.

Tahini Sauce

3 garlic cloves, minced	¼ cup lemon juice
½ cup tahini	¼ teaspoon salt to taste
¼ cup water	

1. Purée all ingredients.

Israeli Salad

2 cucumbers, seeded and finely diced	2 tablespoons finely chopped fresh parsley
2½ pounds tomatoes, finely diced	1 teaspoon salt
1 red pepper, finely diced	1 teaspoon pepper
1 green pepper, finely diced	2½ tablespoons extra virgin olive oil
1 medium onion, finely diced	1 tablespoon lemon juice
4 green onions, finely sliced	½ teaspoon fresh lemon zest
3 tablespoons finely chopped black olives	

1. Combine vegetables, olives and parsley. Add salt and pepper.
2. Toss with oil, juice and zest. Marinate 1 hour.

Assembly

20 prepared falafel balls
10 pitas with pocket

1. Preheat oven to 375°F. Grease cookie sheet.
2. Heat falafel balls and warm pita. Cut 1-inch off top of pita to open pocket and stuff with two balls. Serve with Tahini Sauce and Israeli Salad.

Ice Cream Sundae Bar

DAIRY   YIELD: 10 SERVINGS

Ice cream bars are enjoyed by all generations and make any occasion festive. A sundae bar is always a welcome addition to a Viennese Table.

3   pints ice cream
15   maraschino cherries
1½   cups whipped cream

½   cup of each of the following: chocolate sprinkles, colored sprinkles, chocolate syrup, caramel syrup, chopped nuts, cookie crumbs, chocolate minichips, crushed chocolate coated candy pieces

1. Remove ice cream from freezer 5 minutes before serving allowing it to soften. Wrap bottom of ice cream containers with foil and place in bowl of crushed ice while serving.
2. Fill individual serving bowls with toppings and arrange around ice cream container.

Bittersweet Chocolate Fondue Bar

DAIRY OR PAREVE   YIELD: 10 SERVINGS

A creamy, orange-tinged and liqueur-laced chocolate sauce, gently warming in a fondue pot, surrounded by a variety of bite-size cake and fruit dippers.

Fondue Bar

1   dairy or pareve pound cake, cut into 1-inch cubes
½   dairy or pareve angel food cake, cut into 1-inch cubes
10   strawberries, hulled
2   kiwi, peeled and sliced

1   pear, cut into 1-inch pieces
1   banana, sliced
1   orange, peeled and sectioned
10   dried figs
10   dried apricot halves

Bittersweet Chocolate Orange Fondue

⅓   cup heavy cream for dairy (use liquid nondairy whipped topping for pareve)
1½   teaspoons fresh orange zest

8   ounces bittersweet or semisweet chocolate, finely chopped
3   tablespoons orange liqueur, divided

1. Boil cream or nondairy topping with zest, reduce heat and simmer 2 minutes. Whisk in chocolate and 1 tablespoon liqueur. Remove from heat and add remaining liqueur.
2. Transfer mixture to fondue pot to keep warm. Serve with Fondue Bar items.

Substitute almond or raspberry liqueur for orange liqueur.

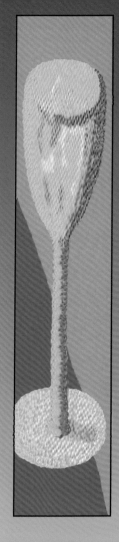

Pareve Sundae Bar

• Use nondairy ice cream and *pareve* toppings to serve a *pareve* sundae bar.

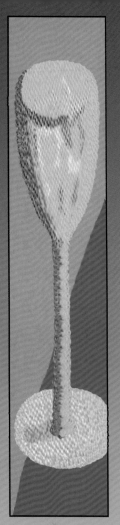

Fruit Platter with Two Dips

DAIRY OR PAREVE   YIELD: 12 SERVINGS

Fruit Plate

1 large pineapple	½ large honeydew melon, peeled
½ cup maraschino cherries	1 kiwi, peeled and sliced
Frilled toothpicks	1 pint strawberries, with hulls
½ large cantaloupe, peeled	½ pound grapes

1. Cut pineapple in quarters, leaving crown attached for an attractive presentation. Cut under flesh and slice. Fasten cherries to pineapple with toothpicks.

2. Cut melons in slices or chunks.

3. Cut small bunches of grapes.

4. Arrange fruit attractively on large platter and serve with Almond Dip or Ginger Syrup.

Almond Dip

1 cup yogurt or sour cream for dairy (use nondairy sour cream for pareve)	¼ cup brown sugar, firmly packed
	1 tablespoon almond liqueur
	¼ cup crushed almond-flavored cookies

1. Combine all ingredients and allow to sit 2 hours.

Tips for Using Fresh Mint

• Sprinkle coarsely chopped mint over fresh fruit.

• Add mint to hot or iced tea.

Ginger Syrup

1½ cups water
1 cup sugar

1 cup thinly sliced fresh gingerroot, unpeeled

1. Boil water with sugar and ginger, stirring until sugar dissolves. Reduce heat and simmer 10 minutes, stirring occasionally. Remove from heat and let steep 15 minutes.
2. Pour syrup through sieve, discarding ginger. Chill 2 hours. Covered and chilled, syrup keeps 2 weeks.

Decoratively Cut Your Pineapple

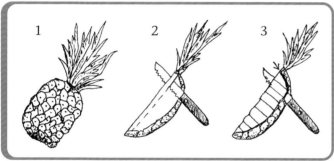

- Quarter pineapple carefully, cutting through leafy fronds.
- Remove tough core.
- Slice flesh from rind. Cut into wedges.

Fresh Vegetables for Dipping

PAREVE   YIELD: 10 SERVINGS OR 1 PLATTER

Sticks of raw ivory colored jicama and orange disks of peeled sweet potatoes add more interest.

2 cups broccoli florets
2 cups cauliflower florets
3 carrots, peeled and cut into sticks
1 red pepper, cut into ½-inch strips
1 green pepper, cut into ½-inch strips

1 pint cherry tomatoes
3 celery stalks, cut into sticks
½ pound snow peas, trimmed
1 recipe pareve Spinach Dip or Curry Dip

1. Arrange all vegetables on serving platter. Place dip in center of display.

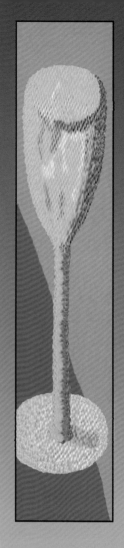

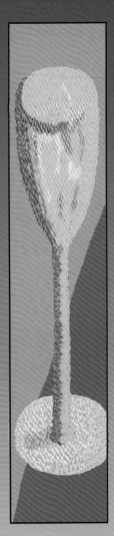

Decorative Cheese Display ♛

DAIRY   YIELD: 20 SERVINGS

Estimate 1 ounce of cheese per person at a buffet.

Mock Boursin

1 ounce feta cheese, finely diced	½ teaspoon minced garlic
4 ounces cream cheese, room temperature	¼ teaspoon dried oregano
¾ teaspoon milk	1¼ teaspoons chopped fresh dill

1. Beat feta with cream cheese and milk at medium speed with electric mixer until smooth.
2. Fold in herbs.

Double Salmon Spread

8 ounces whipped cream cheese	1 tablespoon chopped fresh chives, divided
1½ tablespoons milk	
2 ounces Nova smoked salmon, cut into ½-inch slices	¼ teaspoon pepper
	1 ounce red salmon caviar

1. Beat cream cheese with milk at medium speed with electric mixer until smooth.
2. Mix in Nova, 1½ teaspoons chives and pepper.
3. Fold in caviar. Cover and chill 2 hours.
4. Sprinkle with remaining chives and serve chilled.

Decorated Brie

4   ounces Brie
2   teaspoons apricot or
      raspberry preserves,
      warmed
1   teaspoon sliced almonds,
      toasted
1   teaspoon capers, drained
      and dried

1. Cut off top rind of cheese and spread with preserves. Decorate with nuts and/or capers.

Decorative Cheese Display (continued)

Assembly

1	Decorated Brie	4	ounces grapes
½	pound Cheddar or Swiss cheese, cubed	½	pint strawberries Kale
½	pound Havarti or yogurt cheese, sliced	½	pound assorted crackers or 1 sliced party-size rye or pumpernickel
1	recipe Mock Boursin or 1 recipe Double Salmon Spread		

1. Arrange cheeses and spreads on large platter. Decorate with grapes, strawberries and kale. Serve with crackers and party breads.

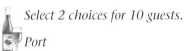 *Select 2 choices for 10 guests.*

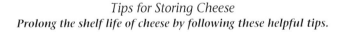 Port

Tips for Storing Cheese
Prolong the shelf life of cheese by following these helpful tips.

- Always rewrap cheese in aluminum foil, parchment or wax paper to avoid cheese from drying out or picking up refrigerator flavors. Place wrapped cheese in an airtight container or bag.

- The recommended temperature for storing cheese is between 35°F and 45°F. Your vegetable/fruit bin is ideal.

- Double wrap pungent cheese to prevent its aromas from permeating other foods.

- Never freeze natural cheese as it may lose its texture and flavor, however frozen cheese may be used for cooking.

Commercial Sheet Pan Recipes

Baking for a crowd? If you can arrange to use a commercial oven, preparing these scaled-up, party-size dessert bar recipes are great timesavers. Full-sheet pans measuring 18 x 26 inches will turn out bars that you can cut into upwards of 100 pieces. These four dairy or pareve recipes are perennial crowd pleasers at our congregational Kiddushim and dinners.

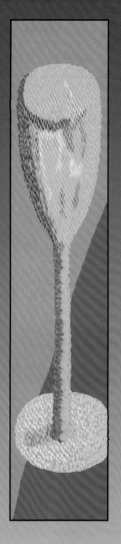

Dried Fruit Dipped in Chocolate

PAREVE

1 recipe Dipping Chocolate

Dried fruit

• Dip fruit half way into chocolate and place on wax or parchment paper. Allow to set. Store covered. Add to a cookie platter.

Kiddush Favorites

Coconut-Walnut Squares

Lemon Squares

Raspberry-Oatmeal Squares

Signature Brownies

Raspberry Oatmeal Squares

(full sheet pan)

DAIRY OR PAREVE   YIELD: 100 SQUARES

A different flavor jam varies the recipe.

8 cups flour	2 pounds nuts, chopped
1 tablespoon baking soda	3 pounds butter for dairy, melted
6 cups brown sugar, firmly packed	(use margarine for pareve)
½ teaspoon salt	2⅛ pounds raspberry jam
4½ cups rolled oats	1½ cups raisins

1. Preheat oven to 350°F. Grease 18 x 26-inch sheet pan.
2. Combine flour, baking soda, sugar, salt, oats and nuts at medium speed with electric mixer. Mix in butter or margarine.
3. Press half the mixture into pan. Cover with jam and sprinkle with raisins.
4. Crumble remaining oat mixture on top. Bake 45 minutes until browned. Cool completely before cutting.

Coconut-Walnut Squares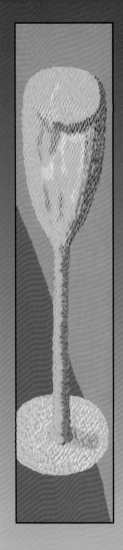

(full sheet pan)

DAIRY OR PAREVE   YIELD: 144 SQUARES

Crust

7   cups flour
1   cup brown sugar minus 2
    tablespoons, firmly packed

1¾ pounds butter for dairy, melted
    (use margarine for pareve)

1. Preheat oven to 350°F. Grease 18 x 26-inch sheet pan.
2. Combine flour and brown sugar at medium speed with electric mixer. Add butter or margarine to form dough.
3. Press dough into pan and bake 20 minutes or until golden. Prepare filling while crust is baking.

Filling

14 large eggs
8¾ cups brown sugar, firmly packed
1   cup flour minus 2 tablespoons
2½ tablespoons vanilla extract

1¾ teaspoons salt
5¼ cups chopped walnuts
3½ cups shredded coconut

1. Beat eggs at medium speed with electric mixer. Add sugar and flour. Beat in vanilla and salt. Add nuts and coconut.
2. Pour filling over crust and bake 30 to 35 minutes or until tester inserted in center comes out clean.
3. Cool 10 minutes and run knife around edges to loosen. Cool completely before cutting into squares.

Bar Cutting Made Easy

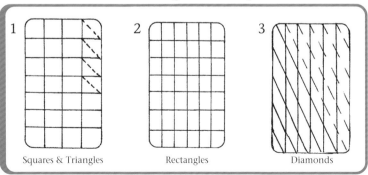

1 Squares & Triangles   2 Rectangles   3 Diamonds

Different shapes add interest to your cookie platters.

Lemon Squares
(full sheet pan)

DAIRY OR PAREVE   YIELD: 100 SQUARES

Crust

7   cups flour
1¾ cups confectioners' sugar, sifted
½   teaspoon salt

1¾ pounds butter for dairy, room temperature (use margarine for pareve)

1. Preheat oven to 350°F. Grease 18 x 26-inch sheet pan.
2. Combine flour, sugar and salt at medium speed with electric mixer. Add butter or margarine and mix to consistency of meal. Press into pan and bake 20 minutes or until edges are golden brown.
3. Prepare filling while crust bakes.

Filling

17   large eggs
10   cups sugar
3¼ cups lemon juice

2½ tablespoons fresh lemon zest
2½ cups flour
       Confectioners' sugar for dusting

1. Beat eggs at medium speed with electric mixer. Add sugar and beat until light and fluffy. Mix in juice, zest and flour.
2. Pour filling over crust and bake 15 to 20 minutes more, until set and golden brown.
3. Cool and chill before cutting. Dust with confectioners' sugar.

Chocolate Dipped Fresh Fruit

PAREVE

1 recipe Dipping Chocolate

Strawberries, pineapple chunks, grapes

1. Wash fruit and pat very dry.

2. Dip fruit half way into chocolate and place on wax or parchment paper. Allow to set. Chill.

Signature Brownies –
As Good As It Gets *(full sheet pan)*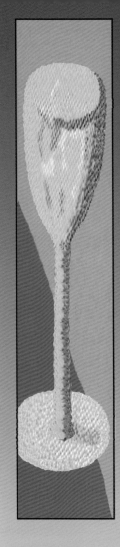

DAIRY OR PAREVE   YIELD: 120 SQUARES

Brownies

2 pounds butter for dairy (use margarine for pareve)	¼ cup vanilla extract
	4½ cups sugar
9⅓ cups chocolate chips, divided	2 teaspoons salt
12 ounces unsweetened chocolate	2½ cups flour, divided
16 large eggs	2 tablespoons baking powder
6 tablespoons instant coffee granules	6 cups chopped walnuts, optional

1. Preheat oven to 350°F. Grease 18 x 26-inch sheet pan.
2. Melt butter or margarine with 5⅓ cups chocolate chips and unsweetened chocolate. Cool slightly.
3. Combine eggs, coffee, vanilla, sugar and salt. Add chocolate mixture and cool to room temperature.
4. Combine 2¼ cups flour with baking powder and stir into chocolate mixture.
5. Toss remaining chocolate chips and nuts with remaining flour and add to chocolate batter. Spread evenly into pan.
6. Bake 20 minutes. Bang pan against oven shelf to force air to escape. Bake 10 minutes more, or until just set. Do not over bake! Cool.
7. Cover with Chocolate Glaze and chill to set. Cut into squares, diamonds or rectangles and decorate with icing flowers.

Chocolate Glaze

4½ ounces butter for dairy (use margarine for pareve)	1½ tablespoons vanilla extract
	¾ cup strong hot coffee or boiling water
6 ounces chocolate chips	
1½ pounds confectioners' sugar, sifted	

1. Melt butter or margarine with chocolate chips.
2. Combine sugar, vanilla and coffee or water at medium speed with electric mixer. Add chocolate mixture gradually and beat until smooth. Cool 5 minutes.

Multilevel Displays

*P*resentation is everything! Take a note from As You Like It Kosher Catering's bag of tricks. Don't risk flattening the impact of all those marvelous dishes you've prepared for your self-serve buffet by lining them up side-by-side across a banquet table. Lift those luscious platters and raise the drama, literally. It is so easy to build up platforms of varying heights — that will be hidden by artfully draped table linens — to create elevated displays, on which to showcase your food. All you need are flat, hard-surfaced items and stable holders on which to balance them. Most of these items you have around the house. Trays, baking pans and cutting boards of various shapes and sizes can be securely balanced over unopened cans of food and sections of PVC pipes, which you can buy in any size at any hardware store. Reflecting mirrored trays holding any platter add dazzling color refraction. Study the photographs for more ideas.

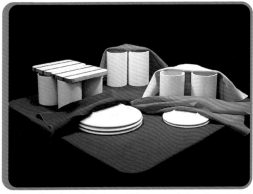 

These 3 pairs of photos utilize a variety of materials for building multilevel displays. The photos on the left suggest ways to construct platforms of varying heights. The photos on the right disguise the platforms with table linens to make attractive display bases.

Disposable Paper and Plastic Party Supplies

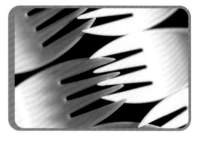

*T*oday's throwaway party supplies are so sturdy and attractive that they enhance your table setting as much as they simplify table set-up and clean-up chores. A wide variety of paper and plastic disposables lets you coordinate your color scheme and choose just the right style and quality for your particular menu. This guide indicates the minimum number of place settings per guest you will need for a typical meal, along with our recommendations, based on As You Like It Kosher Catering's long experience. Always have extras on hand, and for that special party, consider using the clear, crystal-like plates.

Per Person:	**Recommendations:**
• 3 cocktail/dessert size plates	Plates with a well to hold a cup or glass will free up one hand.
• 1 dinner size plate	Heavy gauge quality is most reliable and worth the price.
• 2 forks, 1 knife and 2 spoons	Sturdy flatware is most reliable and worth the price.
• 1 coffee stirrer	Saves on spoons.
• 3 cold cups	Translucent cold cups let guests see what they are drinking. Gauge cup size to beverage and reasonable serving amount.
• 1 fluted champagne glass and/or wine glass with stem	These hard plastic glasses add elegance to your table setting.
• 1 hot cup	Hard plastic coffee cups with a handle are elegant and easiest to use. Wax-coated paper cups work well, but provide 2 per person, as you may need to double them up for easier handling. Styrofoam is least expensive.
• 4 cocktail/dessert napkins 2 large dinner napkins	Linen-like quality absorbs well and is most elegant.
• Table covers	Plastic or plastic-backed paper is easier to wipe off. It is available in rolls or individual packages. Linen-like covers are more elegant but more expensive.

Product list provided by Hill & Markes, Inc., Amsterdam, New York

Dressing the Table

Dinner is cooking, the wine is breathing and your table is dressed with a lovely tablecloth and napkins, elegant dishes, sparkling stemware and gleaming silverware. You can be as creative with your table dressings as with your menu.

Table Dressings

- Lift the napkins off the tablecloth, fold or twist them into interesting shapes and arrange them in the wine glasses or water goblets.
- Use a different napkin color to contrast with the tablecloth color.
- Alternate napkin colors at each place setting.

Centerpieces

You can't go wrong with flowers as a centerpiece, but you can create your own, original centerpiece, one that reflects your mood, the time of year, or the style, menu or theme of the evening, especially if you are celebrating a specific occasion. The possibilities are endless.

Multi level candle centerpiece

- **Flowers and More:** Combine flowers and sprigs from your own garden. Add leaves, branches, acorns and berries.
- **Candles Plus:** Arrange a composite of various size and height candles and holders.
- **International Menus:** As an example, for an Italian meal, mound on a plate or in a see-through bowl, some recipe ingredients, like pasta, a bottle of olive oil, a can of tomato sauce, zucchini, eggplant and breadsticks.
- **Autumn and Festivals:** For *Sukkot,* combine harvest fruits and vegetables, spilling out of a cornucopia. Scatter autumn leaves.
- **Holidays:** For *Chanukah,* decorate with cookie cutter cookies, foil-covered *gelt* and *dreidels.* For *Purim,* use masks and noise makers. Scatter confetti and make good use of children's art.
- **Sculpted Garnishes:** Incorporate any of the decorative fruit and vegetable garnishes which appear in Garnish Magic.

Displaying Food with Artistic Flair

In searching for clever, artistic ways to display food you need go no farther than your own home. Got a favorite glass-covered photograph, lithograph or print hanging on a wall? Something whose color, texture or subject matter either ties in or contrasts with a particular dish, food or cuisine you're planning to serve? Take it down, dust it off and use it for a platter, as we did with the cookies arranged in photo 1. The cheese platter in photo 2 is displayed on a mirror. Hunt through the house for ideas and don't overlook the kids' toy box, your jewelry chest or your garden.

Photo 1

Photo 2

Garnish Magic

*H*and-sculpted garnishes let you play with your food! It's way more than turning a turnip into a flower or a parsnip into a tree or melted chocolate into a petal. Clever, beautiful garnishes are edible works of art that appeal to the eye as much as they whet the palate. They are the finishing flourishes to a lovely table, the signature of the chef-artist who created them.

Turnip Flowers

*M*ake one day ahead and keep chilled. Use as a garnish. Always wear disposable gloves when working with food coloring and protect work area with plastic covering.

Petals

1. Peel turnip and score deep ridges to make a scalloped edge.
2. For flexibility, cut into slices no thicker than ⅛ inch, using a sharp mandoline or meat slicer. Average size turnip yields 6 to 8 slices.
3. Submerge 6 to 8 slices — do not crowd — in large bowl containing highly concentrated solution of a specific food coloring. Paste coloring offers more color selections and yields more intense color than liquid variety. Add 3 drops of paste at a time to 1 quart of water, until desired hue develops. If using liquid coloring, add ¼ teaspoon at a time, until desired hue develops. Chill overnight. Create as many different color baths for slices as petal colors desired. For a bouquet effect, slice 3 to 4 turnips and match color assortment to your color scheme.
4. Remove from refrigerator, drain in colander, place on parchment paper to air dry.
5. With a Q-tip or a gloved finger, you can tint each petal for contrast and accent colors as desired.

Assembly

1. Arrange 3 or 4 petals artfully in the shape of a flower.
2. Turn petals over and secure with two wooden toothpicks, forming an "X."
3. Wind a rubber band around the toothpicks for additional support.
4. Turn over and decorate center with slices of green beans, red pepper, carrot or other colored vegetables.

Turnip Leaves

1. Cut leaf shapes from turnip leaves and cut notches. Tint edges.

Garnish Magic (continued on next page)

Parsnip and Green Pepper Palm Tree

1. Slice off root end of unpeeled parsnip to form a flat base and nip off pointed end for trunk.

2. Cut vertical, angled notches with a paring knife, to resemble a palm tree trunk. Place parsnip in cold water to open the cuts.

3. Use green pepper to form top of tree. With stem down, cut each rounded section into scallop curves to resemble foliage. Cut small "V" notches in edges to create palm fronds effect. Remove core and seeds.

4. Connect pepper to small end of parsnip with a toothpick.

5. Cut medium-size potato in half, lengthwise, and use as a base.

6. Turn base cut side down, push toothpick in center of base and skewer tree.

Mushroom Garnish

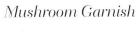

1. Pierce a decorative pattern of puncture marks into each mushroom head, using a punch can opener.

2. Soak mushrooms in 1 cup water mixed with 1 tablespoon lemon juice, to bring out the design.

Red Cabbage Anthuriums

1. Slice bottom of cabbage head and remove leaves carefully to keep them intact.

2. Notch the core end and fashion each leaf into a heart shape.

3. Insert 6-inch bamboo skewer, ½-inch above the notch from the back.

4. Skewer a green bean, baby carrot or canned baby corn.

Garnish Magic (continued on next page)

Eggplant Vase

1. Cut off rounded bottom of eggplant to form flat base.

2. With a metal skewer, puncture holes into eggplant and fill each opening with a skewered anthurium.

Chrysanthemum Onion

1. Choose a large white or red onion. Place root side down.

2. With a sharp pairing knife, make even cuts about half way in center of onion.

3. Place onion in hot water for 5 minutes to remove onion odor, then soak onion cut side down, in colored ice water to open petals.

Zucchini Rose

1. Trim ¼-inch off one end of zucchini.

2. With a potato peeler, make a slice from trimmed end to the other end.

3. Starting from uncut end, roll peel up onto itself to form rose. Spread outer edges to form petals.

Zucchini Tie

1. Follow steps 1 and 2 for Zucchini Rose.

2. Cut slice into ¼-inch lengthwise strips. Cut off green peel and use as a decorative tie around vegetables.

Zucchini Rose, Zucchini Tie and Turnip Leaves

Garnish Magic (continued on next page)

Green Onion Brushes

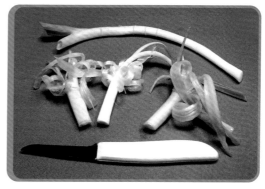

1. Make a bowl of ice water.

2. Trim onion to 5-inch length, strip off unattractive outer leaves and cut ¼-inch off root.

3. Insert knife tip into middle of onion shaft, about 2 inches from cut end. Using a smooth stroke, make a straight shallow cut through to the root end. Do not cut all the way through the onion. Rotate onion slightly and make a second cut, parallel to first and about ⅛-inch from it. Continue rotating onion and making parallel cuts until you have gone all around the onion shaft. Make as many slices as possible.

4. Place in ice water and chill for 2 hours. Onion will curl. Drain and pat dry.

A Rose is a Rose, Unless It's a Tomato!

Garnish almost any dish with a tomato flower and it screams royalty. Psssst! It's easier to make than you imagine. Follow these simple instructions and sculpt a perfect rose-shaped tomato.

1. Use a medium-size tomato.

2. Using a paring knife, start at the stem end and cut a 4-inch long piece of peel as thin as possible. Cut a second strip 3-inches long.

3. Coil first strip tightly and wind second strip loosely around the first. Adjust peels to form a rose.

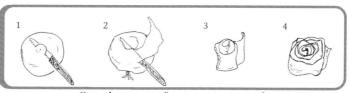

Creating a rose from a tomato peel.

Chocolate Leaves

12 TO 14 LEAVES

1   *Recipe Dipping Chocolate*
14   *lemon leaves*

1. Brush chocolate onto back of leaves with small paint brush, ⅛-inch thick.

2. Chill 15 minutes. Carefully peel leaf from chocolate. Chill until ready to use.

Planning the Larger Gathering

Use the grids to determine how many times to multiply the basic recipe per number of guests.

Dairy Kiddush Luncheon Menu

A popular, self-serve way to celebrate significant events at home. Suitable for a birthday, anniversary, engagement, b'nai mitzvah, graduation, testimonial, brit milah or baby naming.

Number of Guests						Recipes
10	20	30	40	50	60	
1	2	2	3	3	3	Challah
1	2	3	3	4	4	Dress Up Your Bagel with Spreads
1	2	2	3	4	4	Sliced tomatoes, onions and cucumbers
1	2	3	4	4	5	Nova Smoked Salmon Display
1	2	3	3	4	4	Tuna Fish Salad with a Twist
1	2	3	3	4	4	Deviled Eggs
1	2	3	3	4	4	Caesar Salad
1	2	2	3	3	4	Signature Noodle Kugel
1	2	2	3	3	3	Signature Sesame Noodles
1	1	2	2	3	3	Fruit Platter
1	2	3	4	5	6	Pink Lemonade Punch
						Heavenly Desserts and Signature Desserts**

Substitutions

To vary your Kiddush **offerings substitute:**

- Herring Antipasto or Signature Whitefish Salad for Nova Smoked Salmon Display
- Blintz Soufflé or Wild Mushroom Tart for Noodle Kugel
- Hummus with Parsley Drizzle and Pita for Sesame Noodles
- Basic Salad Bar for Caesar Salad
- Cheese Display for Deviled Eggs

Beverages

Wine and Grape Juice

- Provide sufficient Concord grape wine and grape juice to fill each guest's 1-ounce paper or plastic cup at the ratio of 60% wine to 40% juice.

L'Chaim

- For shot glass servings, set out bottles of scotch, rye or vodka.
- Regular and decaf coffee
- Ice water

Meat Dinner Menu

Number of Guests						Recipes
10	20	30	40	50	60	
1	2	2	3	3	4	Vegetarian Chopped Liver
1	2	2	3	3	4	Quick and Delicious Vegetable Soup
1	2	2	3	3	4	Signature Mixed Green Salad
1	2	3	4	4	5	Signature Brisket
						Vegetarian Stuffed Cabbage or Peppers*
1	2	3	4	4	5	Crusty Roasted Potatoes
1	2	3	4	5	6	Roasted Broccoli with Red Peppers
						Heavenly Desserts and Signature Desserts**
						Coffee and Tea***

Use basic recipes yield to accommodate your number of vegetarian guests

**See Dessert Display-Viennese Table for quantity and recommendations*

***See International Coffee Bar*

Buffet Dinners Scaled for 20, 40 and 60 Guests

Use the grids to determine how many times to multiply the basic recipe per number of guests. To pair your menu with beverages appropriate to starters, main courses and desserts, see Dining with Wine, Alcohol Bar and/or International Coffee Bar.

Meat Buffet Menu

Guests			Recipes
20	40	60	
1	2	3	Champagne Punch
1	2	3	Potato and Cauliflower, Indian Style Wontons
2	4	5	Pastry Wrapped-Hot Dog Medallions
2	3	4	Sweet and Sour Meatballs with rice
2	4	5	Artichoke-Potato Soup
2	4	5	Carrot-Mango Soup
2	3	3	Herb and Onion Bread with Margarine Rosettes
3	5	6	Mesclun Salad with Roasted Asparagus
2	4	6	Marinated London Broil
2	4	5	Chicken with Chickpeas, Olives and Tomatoes on rice
3	5	6	Baked Eggplant Stack
4	5	7	Irresistible Mushrooms
3	4	5	Roasted Onions with Balsamic Glaze
3	5	6	Crusty Roasted Potatoes
			See Dessert Displays to Viennese Table
			Coffee and Tea

Dairy Buffet Menu

Guests			Recipes
20	40	60	
2	4	6	Piña Colada Punch
1	2	3	Sun-Dried Tomato and Black Olive Bruschetta
2	3	4	Olive Tapenade Wrap
2	4	6	Tex-Mex Latke
2	3	4	Fragrant Carrot Soup with Indian Spices
2	3	4	Six-Fruit Soup
2	3	4	Sweet and Savory Salad
2	4	5	Savory Cheese Scones with Whipped Butter
2	3	4	Orange Cornbread
2	3	4	Marinated Grilled Salmon
1	2	2	Pesto Pasta
2	3	4	Spanakopita
3	5	7	Eggplant, Indian Style
3	5	7	Roasted Asparagus
2	4	6	Fresh Garden Couscous
			See Dessert Displays to Viennese Table
			Coffee and Tea

Three-Tier Cookie Display

Grazing Buffets with Viennese Table*

To calculate how much food to prepare per number of guests, multiply the basic recipe by the number directly beneath 20, 40 or 60 guests.

Meat Buffet Menu

Guests			Recipes
20	40	60	
2	4	6	Pink Lemonade Punch
3	3	4	Meringue Baked Pecans
			Soup Station
4	5	6	Six-Fruit Soup
2	4	5	Moroccan Chickpea Soup
			Cold Station
			Vegetable Antipasto including:
2	3	4	Zesty Eggplant Slices
2	3	4	Roasted Red Peppers
2	3	4	Marinated Mushrooms
2	3	3	Hummus with Parsley Drizzle and Pita Crisps
2	3	3	Olive Tapenade
2	3	4	Fig and Walnut Chopped Chicken Liver
3	4	5	Signature Sesame Noodles
			Hot Station
			Carving Station
2	4	6	Sweet-and-Sour Glazed Corned Beef
			Chafing Dish
4	6	7	Veal and Peppers with rice
4	5	6	Baked Eggplant Stack
3	5	6	Falafel Bar
			Hot Pass-Arounds (Choose three.)
2	4	5	Chicken Satay with Spicy Dipping Sauce
2	4	5	Tex-Mex Latkes
2	4	5	Pastry-Wrapped Hot Dog Medallions
2	4	5	Potato and Cauliflower, Indian Style Wontons
2	4	5	Glazed Pastrami Rollups
			Viennese Table*

See Dessert Displays to Viennese Table

Dairy Buffet Menu

Guests			Recipes
20	40	60	
2	4	6	Piña Colada Punch
3	3	4	Baked Meringue Pecans
			Soup Station
4	5	6	Carrot Mango Soup
4	5	6	Chilled Cherry Soup
			Cold Station
2	3	4	Goat Cheese Terrine
2	3	4	Layered Taco Salad
2	3	4	Vegetarian Chopped Liver
3	4	5	Signature Sesame Noodles
3	4	5	Smoked Salmon Nigirizushi
2	3	4	Fresh Vegetables with Spinach Dip
			Hot Station
			Carving Station
3	5	7	Seared Tuna with Wasabi Sauce
			Chafing Dish
4	5	6	Mozzarella Sticks
			Hot Pass-Arounds (Choose three.)
2	4	5	Potato-Cheese Wontons
2	4	5	Artichoke Jack Tartlets
3	4	5	Asparagus and Pesto Palmiers
3	4	5	Porcini-Stuffed Mushrooms
3	4	5	Vegetable-Feta Latke
			Viennese Table*

See Dessert Displays to Viennese Table

Trifle Our Way

Dessert Displays to Viennese Table

Getting a head start on baking and dessert preparation is a great timesaver. This grid indicates how far in advance you can start a sampling of our desserts. Use any combination of recipes and see index for more choices. Check the timing for each recipe and plan accordingly.

A: Bake cakes and pies up to two weeks ahead, cool completely, and cover with plastic wrap and foil. Make fillings and frostings. Freeze separately. Thaw in refrigerator a day before use.

B: Prepare or bake one day ahead of use.

C: Assemble day of use.

How to Calculate

Setting out a self-serve display of assorted sweet treats is an elegant way to offer dessert. A dessert display becomes a Viennese Table as you increase the number and variety of desserts. Choose any combination in our collection. Consider adding a Fruit Platter or a pareve or dairy Ice Cream Sundae Bar.

Here is As You Like It Kosher Catering's formula for calculating the number of desserts per guest.

- 10 guests: prepare 2 desserts
- 20-30 guests: prepare 3 desserts
- 40-50 guests: prepare 4 desserts
- 60 guests: prepare 5 desserts
- In addition, prepare 3 bite-size bars or cookies per guest for the Finger Pastry Assortment*
- Offer an International Coffee Bar.

Lavish fruit display

A	B	C	Pareve Desserts
√		√	Signature Triple-Layer Chocolate Mousse Cake
√		√	Chocolate-Orange Cake
√			Streusel-Topped Apple Pie
	√		Fresh Peach Cobbler
√			Pareve Pumpkin Pie
√			Simple Fruit Sorbet
	√	√	Poached Pears with Raspberry Coulis
√			Bourbon-Pecan Pie
	√		Fresh Blueberry Pie
√		√	Pareve Cheesecake
	√	√	Star-of-David Pavlova
		√	Trifle-Our-Way
√		√	Bittersweet Chocolate Fondue Bar
	√		Meringue Drops
	√		Chocolate Melting Cakes
√		√	Lemon Chiffon Cake with Raspberry Cream
√			Banana Crisp
	√		Citrus and Grapes with Muscat Wine
√			Finger Pastry Assortment*

See Heavenly Desserts and Signature Desserts

A	B	C	Dairy Desserts
√		√	Signature Carrot Festival Cake
√		√	Signature Triple-Layer Chocolate Mousse Cake
√			Apple Cream Cheese Torte
√		√	Chocolate-Orange Cake
√			Streusel-Topped Apple Pie
	√		Fresh Peach Cobbler
√			Simple Fruit Sorbet
√		√	Poached Pears with Raspberry Coulis
√			Buttery Sour Cream Coffee Cake
√		√	Variations on a Cheese Cake
√			Bourbon-Pecan Pie
	√		Fresh Blueberry Pie
√			Floating Sandwich Cookie Cake
√		√	Mississippi Mud Pie
√			Peanut Butter-Chocolate Cream Torte
√		√	Star of David Pavlova
		√	Trifle-Our-Way
√		√	Bittersweet Chocolate Fondue Bar
	√		Meringue Drops
√			Finger Pastry Assortment*

See Heavenly Desserts and Signature Desserts

The Shivah Meal

Shivah, *the Hebrew word for seven, has come to refer to the first seven days of mourning the death of a parent, sibling, child or spouse. The grieving family returns home from the funeral to sit* shivah *and to receive condolence visits from relatives and friends. The first "meal of condolence" is served when the family returns from the burial. Buffet-style is the most common way to serve this meal, and using disposable place settings, the most convenient. Arrange the food on platters and allow the guests to choose from among the offerings. This grid calculates the shopping list for our suggested menu, according to the number of expected guests.*

Shopping List

Food	Amount	10	20	30	40	50	60
Eggs	1 dozen	2	3	4	4	5	5
Cream Cheese	8 ounces	2	3	4	5	6	7
Milk	1 quart	1	1	1	2	2	2
Cottage Cheese	16 ounces	1	1	2	2	3	3
Horseradish	6 ounces	1	1	1	2	2	2
Gefilte Fish Balls	24 ounces	2	2	3	3	4	4
Herring	8 ounces	1	2	3	4	5	6
Minced Nova	Ounces	4	6	8	10	12	14
Tuna Fish	6 ounces	4	7	10	14	17	20
Mayonnaise	16 ounces	1	1	2	2	3	3
Rye Bread	1 pound	1	1	2	2	3	3
Finger Pastries*	3 per guest						
Coffee	1 pound	1	1	1	2	2	2
Tea	Bags	4	8	12	16	20	24
Sugar/Substitutes	½ cup/6 packs	1	2	3	4	5	6
Soft Drinks	1 liter	2	3	4	5	6	7
Ice	6 pounds	1	1	2	2	3	3
Lettuce	1 head	1	1	1	1	1	1
Tomatoes	1 large	2	3	4	5	6	7
Green/Red Pepper	1 large	1	1	2	2	3	3
Cucumbers	1 large	1	2	3	3	4	4
Celery	1 bunch	1	1	1	1	1	1
Salad Dressing	1 cup	1	1	2	2	3	3
Bagels	1 dozen	1	2	3	4	5	6
Scotch, Blended Whiskey or Vodka	Choose 2 kinds	1	1	1	1	1	1

See Heavenly Dessert and Signature Desserts

For your disposable table needs, see Disposable Paper and Plastic Party Supplies.

Shivah Menu

Scotch, Blended Whiskey or Vodka for *L'Chaim*

Hard-boiled eggs, served whole

Signature Egg Salad

Tuna Fish Salad with a Twist

Cottage cheese

Herring in wine or cream sauce

Gefilte fish balls with horseradish

Dress up Your Bagels with Plain and Nova Smoked Salmon Spread

Rye bread

Sliced tomatoes, cucumbers and peppers, on bed of lettuce

Celery sticks

Thousand Island Dressing

Finger Pastries

Coffee, tea, soda and ice water

Directions

- Hard boil eggs. Serve 6 whole eggs for 10 to 20 guests; 8, for 30 to 40; and 10, for 50 to 60.

- Use the remainder in Signature Egg Salad.

- Use celery for Tuna Fish Salad with a Twist. Cut remainder into sticks.

- Use half the cream cheese for Nova Smoked Salmon Spread. Serve the balance plain.

- Cut bagels in half. Serve with cream cheese spreads.

- Slice tomatoes, cucumbers and peppers. Place on bed of lettuce.

- Provide ice water

Keeping Your Spirits Up

*W*hen family and friends get together to celebrate and have a good time, raising a glass to good cheer is part of the convivial feeling. Taken in moderation, wines and spirits relax the mood and spark the appetite. These grids provide a full bar, self-serve set up, offering guests a wide range of drinks. For a limited set up, reduce the choices to fit your needs.

Hints

*O*ur calculations draw on our experience, both in the catering hall and private homes, catering parties and weddings that typically last from four to six hours.

- Allow from two to four drinks per adult depending on the length of the party and your guests' drinking habits.
- Provide sufficient soft drinks for nondrinkers.
- Consider hiring a professional bartender for parties of 40 or more guests. Aside from operating the bar, the bartender will help you plan for the needs of your guests.
- Recently beer has been included at the most sophisticated of parties. Regional preferences abound so serve the most popular beers for your area.
- Check with your liquor store regarding their return policy for unopened spirits.

Type of Spirits	Number of Guests					
	10	20	30	40	50	60
Scotch	1	1	1	2	2	2
Rye (Blended Whiskey)	1	1	1	1	2	2
Vodka	1	1	1	2	2	2
Gin	1	1	1	1	1	2
Bourbon	1	1	1	1	1	1
Tequila	1	1	1	1	1	1
Rum	1	1	1	1	1	1
Dry White Wine	2	2	3	3	4	4
Semi-Dry White Wine or Rose	1	1	2	2	3	3
Red Wine	2	2	3	3	4	4
Champagne	2	2	3	3	4	4
Crème de Cassis	1	1	1	1	1	1
Raspberry Liqueur	1	1	1	1	1	1
Almond Liqueur	1	1	1	1	1	1
Coffee Liqueur	1	1	1	1	1	1
Orange-Chocolate Liqueur	1	1	1	1	1	1

Brunch Drinks

*F*or a breakfast or brunch, consider offering Mimosas (orange juice and champagne), Bloody Marys and/or Piña Coladas. Each of these cocktails can be pre-mixed, and served, either in frosty pitchers or in pre-poured glasses. For those guests who prefer to mix their own cocktails, provide bottled cocktail mixes along with orange juice, tomato juice and champagne. Garnish Bloody Marys with a leafy celery stick, Mimosas with an orange slice and Piña Coladas with a wedge of fresh pineapple.

Freezer Ready Cubes for Bloody Marys

Freeze vegetable broth in ice-cube containers and add desired quantity to a pitcher of Bloody Marys.

Bar Condiments

Item	Number of Guests					
	10	20	30	40	50	60
Lemons	1	2	2	3	4	4
Oranges	1	1	1	2	2	2
Limes	1	2	2	3	4	4
Maraschino cherries, jar	1	1	1	1	1	1
Grenadine, bottle	1	1	1	1	1	1
Bloody Mary Mix, bottle	1	1	1	1	2	2
Sour Mix, bottle	1	1	1	1	2	2
Orange juice, cups	2	3	4	5	6	6
Cranberry juice, cups	1	2	3	4	5	6

Item	Number of Guests					
	10	20	30	40	50	60
Coffee creamer, cups	½	1	2	2	3	3
Cola, regular, liter	2	3	4	5	6	7
Cola, diet, liter	2	3	4	5	6	7
Lemon-Lime, regular, liter	1	2	2	3	4	4
Lemon-Lime, diet, liter	1	1	2	2	3	3
Ginger Ale, liter	1	1	2	2	3	3
Seltzer water, liter	2	3	3	4	4	5
Tonic water, liter	1	1	1	2	2	2
Ice, pounds	8	16	24	32	40	48

Cocktails for the Lighter Palate

Cosmopolitan

Mix 2 ounces citron vodka, 1 ounce orange liqueur, ½ ounce lime juice and 1 ounce cranberry juice. Shake over ice and strain into chilled cocktail glass. Garnish with lime wedge.

Kir

Pour 3 ounces dry white wine over ice in an old-fashioned glass. Add a splash of *crème de cassis,* a twist of lemon, and stir.

Mimosa

Pour equal amounts of chilled champagne and orange juice into a stemmed glass.

Pineapple Cooler

Dissolve ½ teaspoon powdered sugar in 2 ounces each, pineapple juice and dry white wine. Pour into ice-filled Collins glass. Fill with seltzer. Add orange or lemon peel.

Bitters Highball

Fill highball glass with ¾ ounce bitters, ice cubes and sugar-free ginger ale or seltzer. Serve with twist of lemon.

White Wine Spritzer

Pour 3 ounces chilled dry white wine into highball glass or wine glass filled with ice cubes. Add seltzer and stir gently.

Red Wine Cooler

Pour 3 ounces dry red wine into wine glass with ice cubes. Fill with sugar-free lemon-lime soda or seltzer, and stir.

Tools of the Trade

Ice bucket, cooler chest
Corkscrew
Bottle opener
Can opener
Ice tongs
Shot glasses for measuring

Small sharp knife and cutting board
Long-handled spoon to mix drinks
Cocktail napkins
Cocktail shaker
Drink stirrers

Yields

- The average bottle of wine (26 ounces/750 ml) yields 5 glasses.
- The average bottle of champagne yields 6 glasses.
- A case of champagne yields 72 glasses.
- A 26-ounce (750 ml) bottle of spirits yields 17 glasses of 1½ ounces (45 ml) each.

International Coffee Bar

The perfect complement to a Dessert Display or Viennese Table. Offer guests liqueurs, sweet condiments and creams to add to their coffee. It's a good time to use your fine china.

Set Up

Coffee: regular and decaffeinated

Liqueurs: at least 2 varieties, such as Almond, Raspberry, Orange, Cherry, Currant, Mint, Orange-Chocolate or Coffee and Brandy or Rum

Condiments: such as cocoa and/or cinnamon in a small shaker, cinnamon sticks and rock candy sticks

Creams: whipped cream for dairy or whipped liquid nondairy topping for *pareve*

Frozen Flower Vase

PAREVE

1 *attractive freezable glass container*	1 *bunch flowers with leaves*
1 *bottle Vodka*	*Water*

1. Fill container with water two-thirds full. Place bottle of Vodka in container and arrange flowers and leaves around it. Freeze.

2. Remove from container when ready to serve. Serve accompanied by slices of lemon dipped in sugar.

Our Treasured Volunteers and Contributors

No all-volunteer kosher catering service could have achieved the professional stature of As You Like It Kosher Catering *without the consistently reliable support of hundreds of helpers. No project of the scope required to produce this cookbook could have been accomplished without the devotion and labor of a multitude of volunteers. To all our participants, contributors, supporters, promoters and well-wishers,* yasher koach! *This cookbook is the fruit of all our labor.*

Risé Routenberg and Barbara Wasser

Steering Committee

Risé Routenberg, Chairperson
Barrie Handelman and Ann Zonderman, Fundraising Co-chairs
Sharon Kasman and Este Sylvetsky, Marketing Co-chairs
Risé Routenberg and Barbara Wasser, Production Co-chairs
Paul Fraster and Mike Brilliant, Co-treasurers
Jane Israel, Webmaster and Marketing
Eileen Handelman, Marketing and Fundraising
Marvin Israel, Marketing and Fundraising
Stephen Wasser, Distribution

Editorial Production
Annette Keen, Text Author and Editor
Roger Keen, Editorial Assistant

Visuals Production
Harvey Mendelson, Photographer
Deb Friedson, Artistic Design
Steve Schmidt, Companion Disc/Website
Reed Corderman, Companion Disc Assistant
Robert Woll
Marsha Jaros
Monika Woll
Mishka Luft
Arlene Mendelson
Risé Routenberg
Barbara Wasser

Recipe Technical Production
Arlene Mendelson, Recipe Coordinator
Susan Braiman, Typing Coordinator
Risé Routenberg, Editor
Barbara Wasser, Editor

Menu Planning
Susan Bell
Susan Braiman
Marilyn Elson
Daniela Sciaky
Monika Woll
Risé Routenberg
Barbara Wasser

Fundraising Secretary
Marcia Snyder

Our Volunteers

We gratefully acknowledge the hundreds of recipes our devoted congregants submitted. Choosing from among such marvelous recipes was one of our toughest jobs, and only space limitation prevented us from using all of them. We sincerely hope that we have not overlooked anyone. Many congregants wore several hats, participating in many ways in the production of this cookbook. Their names are listed with contribution keys.

C=Recipe Testing Captain   W=Copy Writer
RT=Recipe Tester   P=Production
RC=Recipe Contributor   F=Fundraising
T=Typist   M=Marketing
PR=Proof Reader

RC Helen Aberbach
RT Shelley Altman
RT/PR/M Janet Altschuller
RT/RC Hilary Anapolsky
RC Jayne Architzel
RT Fran Aronowitz
RT Howard Axelrod
RT/RC/F Susan Axelrod
RT Jeffrey Backer
RC Anita Behn
P Alan Bell
RT/RC/P Susan Bell
RT Roberta Berk
F Mikhail Borodulin
RT/RC/T/P Susan Braiman
RT/RC Melissa Routenberg Breaud
RT/RC/T/PR Arleen Brilliant
F Mike Brilliant
RT/RC Valerie Brooks
RC/P Naomi Bristol
RT David Brown
RC Edwin Brown
RT/RC Joan Brown
RC Judith Brown
RC/RT/T Jill Bucinell
RC Pearl Clevenson
RT Kim Cohen
RC Shirley Cohen
RT/F Steve Cohen
RT Michael Consolo
P Reed Corderman
M Steven Cramer
RC Ceil Diamond

RC Edna Doigan
RC Barbara Dworkin
RC Susan Edelheit
RC Esther Eisner
RC Lin Eisner
RC/P/M Marilyn Elson
RT/RC Lynell Engelmyer
RT/W Kathy Englebardt
RT/RC Celia Epstein
F Susan Farber
RC Evy Farbstein
P Mona Feingold
RC Joseph Finkelstein
RC Sharon Finkelstein
P Roslyn Foote
RC Terre Foreman
RC/RT/T/PR Randy Fox
F Rob Fox
RT Diane Frank
F Paul Fraster
RC Ruth Fraster
RT/RC/PR Elissa Freedman
RT Ellin Friedman
RT Art Friedson
RT/RC/M/P Deb Friedson
M Phyllis Friedson
RC/F Marvin Garfinkel
RC Cecelia Garfinkel
RT Sara Gavens
RC Marilyn Glass
RC Judith Gilbert
RT/F Laurey Goldberg
RC Barbara Goldstein

PR Deborah Goldstein
RT Cherrie Goodcoff
RT/M Evelyn Greenstein
RT/F Mery Gross
RC Sue Ann Grosberg
RT/RC/PR/F Barrie Handelman
RT/M/F Eileen Handelman
RT/F Jeffrey Handelman
P/F Mark Handelman
RC Ruth Happ
RC/T Barby Harris
RT/RC Adriane Hertzendorf
T Natalie Hyman
RT/RC/M Jane Israel
RT/RC/F/M Marvin Israel
RC Iris Israel
M Jimmy Israel
PR/M Laurie Jaffe
PR Sam Jaffe
RT/PR Marsha Jaros
F Murray Jaros
RT/C/RC Susan Jarrett
RT/RC Lorraine Kaplan
RT Emily Kasman
RT/RC/PR/W Rabbi Robert Kasman
RT/RC/PR/M/F Sharon Kasman
RC/P/PR/M Annette Keen
PR Roger Keen
RT/RC Josie Kivort
RC Lilly Klein
T Edith Kliman
RC Rena Konheim
M/F Carl Korn

RT Cara Korn

RT Helene Kossoff

RC Barbara Kramer

RC Sharon Kundin

RT/RC/PR/M Bette Kraut

RT Brenda Larkin

RC Sandy Leibson

RC Elaine Lefkowitz

RC/RT/T Joan Levine

RC Marilyn Levine

RT/C Norman Levine

RC Patricia Levinson

RC Louise Lewis

RT/RC/M Yaffa Lown

RC/M Ava Lubert

RT Elaine Lubert

RT Marvin Lubert

RT/RC/P Mishka Luft

RC Jeffry Luria

RC/RT/PR/M/F Susan W. Luria

RT Debye Lurie

RT/PR/M Rosalind Marx

RC Angelo Mazzone

RC/M Esther Meiselman

RT/RC/PR/P/M Arlene Mendelson

P/M Harvey Mendelson

RT/RC Lois Mendelson

RT Shari Mendelson

RT/F Barbara Miller

RT/RC Jackie Mitnick

RT/RC Sally Moise

RC Karen Moldveen

RT/RC Bobbie Moses

RT Gilah Moses

RT Glynes Mountford

M Denise Naparstek

P Rick Nathan

RC/PR Natalie Oshins

RC Anne Paktor

RT/RC Karen Pearlman

RC Rina Perry

RT/C/RC/PR Ann Posner

RT Eric Posner

P/M Gert Prager

RC Sheila Praskin

RC Scott Raplee

RC/M Cheryl Ratner

RT Lauren Kaplan Rieger

RC/P Fran Rosen

M Arlene Rosenberg

RT Carole Rosenkrantz

T Elaine Rotman

RC Annette Routenberg

P Larry Routenberg

RT/RC/PR/P/T/M/F Risé Routenberg

RC/T Barbara Rowen

RC/M Alice Rubenfeld

RC/W Rosette Rubins

P Judith Ruthberg

RT/T Bonnie Schaffer

RT/C Ellie Schantz

RT/RC/M Robin Scharf

F Ron Scharf

RT Zoe Scharf

RT/RC Alexandra Schmidt

RT/RC/P Stephen Schmidt

RT/RC/PR/W/M Sadie Schneider

RC Polly Schwartz

RT/RC/P/M Daniela Sciaky

RT Pat Seftel

RC Joanne Seltzer

RT/W/M Ricki Shapiro

RC Diana Siegel

RT/RC Sharon Silverman

RT/RC Amy Wasser-Simpson

RT/RC Chuck Simpson

RT Esta Skoburn

RT/P Henry Skoburn

RT/C/RC/T/F Marcia Snyder

RT/RC Marilyn Soffer

RC Betty Spigel

RC Bernice Stark

PR Valerie Stark

RT/RC/W/M Linda Woodward Stein

RT/RC/M Roberta Steiner

RT/RC/M/F Este Sylvetsky

RC/P Ruth Talmon

RT/RC/M Cynthia Tepper

RT Amy Tombank

RT/RC/T Bruce Trachtenberg

RT/RC/PR/P/T/M/F Barbara Wasser

RC Eve Wasser

RC David Wasser

RT/RC Scott Wasser

P/W/M Stephen Wasser

RT/T Tammy Weingarten

F Paul Westheimer

RC/F Rose Westheimer

RT/C/RC Ellen Wexler

RC/W Anita Wigler

RT/RC/PR/M Sylvia Winer

RC/T/F Sharon Wohl

P Robert Woll

RC/RT/P Monika Woll

RT/RC Debbie Happ Yablon

F Jay Yablon

RT/C Ellen Zirin

RT/RC/PR/M/F Ann Zonderman

Catering Leadership in Chronological Order

Sandy Leibson

Sharon Kundin

Sheila Seras and Esther Eisner

Penny Buckwalter Wallace

Natalie Oshins

Roberta Steiner and Emily Sondheimer

Emily Sondheimer and Risé Routenberg

Risé Routenberg and Barbara Wasser

Anita Merims

Our Contributors

Five Star Diamond

Helene Kossoff and Jeffrey Backer
Roberta and Stephen Berk
Julia Eddy and Dan Mayer
Susan and Lonnie Edelheit
Marilyn and Clifford Elson
Kathy and Carl Englebardt
Susan and Martin Farber
Linda and Dan Finkle
Ruth and Paul Fraster
Cecelia and Marvin Garfinkel
Deborah and Gary Goldstein
Herschel Graubart

Barrie and Mark Handelman
Eileen and Jeffrey Handelman
Jane and Marvin Israel
Judith and Israel Jacobs
Marsha and Murray Jaros
Bette and Stuart Kraut
Susan and Jeffry Luria
Esther and Leonard Meiselman
Anita and Arthur Merims
Anne Paktor
Doris and Robert Pletman
Phyllis and Arnold Ritterband

Carl Rosner
Risé and Lawrence Routenberg
Barbara and William Rowen
Alice and Lester Rubenfield
Eve and Sy Scharf
Polly and Alvin Schwartz
Susan and Donald Sommer
Roberta and Don Steiner
Lisa and Beno Sternlicht
Este and Samuel Sylvetsky
Ann and Paul Zonderman

Master Chef

Arleen and Mike Brilliant
Naomi Bristol
Celia and Joshua Diamond
Edna Doigan
Lynell and Eric Engelmyer
Laurey and Steven Goldberg

Sandra and Harold Haber
Jane and Edwin Kintz
Cara and Carl Korn
Arlene and Harvey Mendelson
Ann and Alan Posner
Sadie Schneider

Marcia and Marvin Snyder
Cynthia and Clifford Tepper
Alice and Richard Toll
Anita Wigler
Monika and Robert Woll

Executive Chef

Joan and Gary Adelson
Susan and Howard Axelrod
Jerome and Norman Cohen
Randy and Robert Fox
Deb and Art Friedson

Sharon and Rabbi Robert Kasman
Ellie and Ed Kiss
Josie and Stanley Kivort
Robin and Ron Scharf
Martin Siegel

Martin Storm
Alice and Jason Tepper
Barbara and Stephen Wasser
Debbie and Jay Yablon

Sous Chef

Anonymous
Helen Aberbach
Shelley and Gene Altman
Janet Altschuller
Fran and Mark Aronowitz
Nancy Bell and Eli Taub
Jill and Ron Bucinell
Sophie and Albert Carlick
Chao Family
Pearl and Sam Clevenson
Kim and Steve Cohen
Elissa and Michael Freedman
Phyllis and Sidney Friedson
Janie and Richard Garnett
Sara and Andrew Gavens
Marilyn and Arnold Glass
Sally Goldstein

Mery and Dan Gross
Nancy and Eugene Haber
Betty and Alex Hallenstein
Adriane and Ben Hertzendorf
Natalie and Bruce Hyman
Iris and Jimmy Israel
Ruth Kaplan
Edith Kliman
JoAnn and Walter Krefetz
Ava and Richard Lubert
Elaine and Marvin Lubert
Rosalind and Werner Marx
Lois and M. Richard Mendelson
Barbara and Alan Miller
Natalie and Robert Oshins
Gert Prager
Elaine Rotman

Judith and Bradford Ruthberg
Harriet and Alan Sandler
Charlotte Saunders
Sciaky-Corderman Family
Schultz Family
Muriel and Walter Shapiro
Ricki D. Shapiro and Michael Consolo
Susan Sharfstein and Joe Shiang
Esta and Henry Skoburn
Marilyn and Harry Soffer
Lori Stark and David Shapiro
Valerie Stark
Ruth and Harry Talmon
Rose and Paul Westheimer
Sylvia and Herbert Winer
Ellen and Robert Zirin

Apprentice

Fran and Malcolm Abrams
Judith and Edwin Brown
Barby and Stanley Harris
Clara and Kevin Mednick

Lorraine and Richard Mont
Lillian Ornston
Karen and Allan Pearlman

Ellie and Lawrence Schantz
Pat and Leroy Seftel
Betty and Murray Weissman

Other Contributors

Hilary and Richard Anapolsky
Susan and Matthew Behar
Susan and Alan Bell
Lyudmila and Mikhail Borodulin
Valerie and Richard Brooks
Lillian (Toots) Cohen
Janet and Miles Deixler

Lin Eisner
Hillary Fink
Lynn and Al Finkel
Irene Goldberg
Maya and Boris Goldgof
Laurie and Sam Jaffe
Ellen and Eric Kerness

Fran Madison
Sally and Samoil Moise
Beth and Robert Nevins
Joanne and Stanley Seltzer
Nina and Adrian Swierczewski
Estelle Weinstein
Sharon Astyk and Eric Woods

Index

Bold face recipe name indicates an accompanying photograph.
Bold face recipe number indicates an accompanying diagram.

C

E

ℋ
Hints and Tips

$\mathcal{K}$

$\mathcal{N}$

O

P

Q

Quiches
Quick-Prep Recipes for all Occasions 322

R

Rice

S

Salad Dressings and Marinades

W

What to Do in a Pinch

Divine Kosher Cuisine Order Form

Individual DKC Books: _____   @ $ 32.95 each $ _____

Six-packs of DKC Books: _____   @ $180.00 each $ _____

Companion CD Discs: _____   @ $ 9.95 each $ _____
    (Only one companion disc per book purchased.)

                                                   SUBTOTAL $ _____

Sales Tax: (Shipments to NY State only — Add appropriate tax) $ _____
Shipping Cost: **$5.00** for 1st book and **$3.00** for each additional book
to each address, **$15.00** for each six-pack, no postage for discs. $ _____

                                             FINAL TOTAL $ _____

NOTE: Individual books will be packed in separate boxes. Six-packs are in one case.
Method of Payment: Check _____ (Make payable to: Agudat Achim-Cookbook)

       Credit Card (Specify) MC_____ VISA _____

Check: _____ Credit Card Account: _____ Exp. Date: _____

Customer Signature: _____ **Date:** _____

MAIL TO: Divine Kosher Cuisine
               2117 Union Street
               Niskayuna, NY 12309

Contact us: Phone: (518) 344-1190 — Fax: (518) 346-6807
E-mail: divinekosher@nycap.rr.com — Website: www.divinekosher.com
PLEASE COMPLETE REVERSE SIDE OF FORM

===

Divine Kosher Cuisine Order Form

Individual DKC Books: _____   @ $ 32.95 each $ _____

Six-packs of DKC Books: _____   @ $180.00 each $ _____

Companion CD Discs: _____   @ $ 9.95 each $ _____
    (Only one companion disc per book purchased.)

                                                   SUBTOTAL $ _____

Sales Tax: (Shipments to NY State only — Add appropriate tax) $ _____
Shipping Cost: **$5.00** for 1st book and **$3.00** for each additional book
to each address, **$15.00** for each six-pack, no postage for discs. $ _____

                                             FINAL TOTAL $ _____

NOTE: Individual books will be packed in separate boxes. Six-packs are in one case.
Method of Payment: Check _____ (Make payable to: Agudat Achim-Cookbook)

       Credit Card (Specify) MC_____ VISA _____

Check: _____ Credit Card Account: _____ Exp. Date: _____

Customer Signature: _____ **Date:** _____

MAIL TO: Divine Kosher Cuisine
               2117 Union Street
               Niskayuna, NY 12309

Contact us: Phone: (518) 344-1190 — Fax: (518) 346-6807
E-mail: divinekosher@nycap.rr.com — Website: www.divinekosher.com
PLEASE COMPLETE REVERSE SIDE OF FORM

Customer Identification:

Phone Number: (|__|__|__|) |__|__|__| - |__|__|__|__| Purchase Date: _____

Name: _____   _____
                First   Last

Address: _____

City/Town: _____ State: _____ Zip: |__|__|__|__|__| - |__|__|__|__|

Fax Number: (|__|__|__|) |__|__|__| - |__|__|__|__| E-mail Address: _____

If books are to be shipped to a different address, please provide information below.
We are happy to enclose gift cards. Please include message.

Books: _____ Discs: _____ Name: _____

Address: _____

City/Town: _____ State: _____ Zip: |__|__|__|__|__| - |__|__|__|__|

Books: _____ Discs: _____ Name: _____

Address: _____

City/Town: _____ State: _____ Zip: |__|__|__|__|__| - |__|__|__|__|

===

Customer Identification:

Phone Number: (|__|__|__|) |__|__|__| - |__|__|__|__| Purchase Date: _____

Name: _____
                First   Last

Address: _____

City/Town: _____ State: _____ Zip: |__|__|__|__|__| - |__|__|__|__|

Fax Number: (|__|__|__|) |__|__|__| - |__|__|__|__| E-mail Address: _____

If books are to be shipped to a different address, please provide information below.
We are happy to enclose gift cards. Please include message.

Books: _____ Discs: _____ Name: _____

Address: _____

City/Town: _____ State: _____ Zip: |__|__|__|__|__| - |__|__|__|__|

Books: _____ Discs: _____ Name: _____

Address: _____

City/Town: _____ State: _____ Zip: |__|__|__|__|__| - |__|__|__|__|